# WHERE IS TURKEY HEADED?

## CULTURE BATTLES IN TURKEY

Boston, Febr. 5, 2015

# WHERE IS TURKEY HEADED?

## CULTURE BATTLES IN TURKEY

Rainer Hermann

BLUE DOME

Originally published in German as *Wohin geht die Türkische Gesellschaft? Kulturkampf in der Türkei* in 2008

17 16 15 14      2 3 4 5

*Published by* Blue Dome Press
535 Fifth Avenue, Ste.601
New York, NY 10017-8019

www.bluedomepress.com

Library of Congress Cataloging-in-Publication Data Available

ISBN: 978-1-935295-21-1

Cover photos by Cihan News Agency. Top photo: Turkish Olypiads finale at Istanbul Atatürk Olimpiyat Stadium in front of 250,000 spectators on June 15, 2013. Bottom photo: 2013 Gezi Protests against the government's urban development plan for Istanbul's Taksim Gezi park which developed into mass protests all over Turkey.

*Translated by* Betsy Mayer

*Printed by*
Imak Ofset, Istanbul - Turkey

# Contents

# Acknowledgments

I would like to thank the staff editors of the Blue Dome Press for their astute editing of the English text. I also would like to sincerely thank three friends who proofread the German manuscript and saved it from mistakes: Felix Körner, Siegfried Nauhaus, and Christoph Neumann. I would never have understood Turkey without having discussed it in detail with Şahin Alpay, İshak Alaton, and Aydın Engin. They showed me the way, and I would like to thank them especially. I would also like to thank Ruth, my daughter, who was the first critical reader of the manuscript. The remaining mistakes and shortcomings are my very own.

Mostly, I would like to thank Ursula Hermann. I would never have left for the banks of the Bosporus without her and without her patience, understanding, and love, this book would never have been written.

# Preface

After seventeen years of living in Turkey, the author decided to take stock. Of course, many books have already been written about Turkey. Most of them are either chronological histories of events that orient themselves along dates or colorful reports describing what it is like to live in this fascinating country. This book wants to achieve something quite different. Turkey has changed a great deal in the last two decades; the country is in flux. The impulse for this flux always originates with a society that has discovered its diversity and is pushing back omnipotent government control. The book describes the transition Turkish society has undergone, and it ponders how this transition has changed the politics, economy, and culture.

The author is an economist and scholar of Islamic studies. This has had an impact on his point of view. As an economist, he learned to think systematically and to have an interest in the processes within these systems. He set off to Turkey in 1991, as an Islamic scholar with a good working knowledge of the country's history, culture, and religion, and also with affection for its people. The author was very lucky, as he could not have completed his interdisciplinary studies at four universities, in four countries, if he followed the way today's academic system operates.

The book is divided into three main chapters. Chapter One describes the basic order of the Republic of Turkey, the urban elite of the state, and its dogmas. Chapter Two describes how Anatolian underdogs became Turkey's counter-elite, the path that led them into government, and their conflicts with the old elite. Chapter Three describes the darker aspects of Turkey today, including disadvantaged groups and violence, as well as the nicer aspects of Turkey's relations with Germany, and its lively cultural scene. All chapters of the book are newly introduced to the audience, except for the four reports at the end of the subchapters, which appeared in the *Frankfurter Allgemeine Zeitung* daily newspaper. The author was an eye-witness to most of what he described; sometimes he even participated in the encounters.

Istanbul, March, 2008

# Preface to the English Edition

## Wrong turn of the once-reform government – Quo vadis,[1] the AK Party?

Things change quickly in the sociopolitical sphere. Since the first publication of Rainer Hermann's *Where Is Turkey Headed? Culture Battles in Turkey*, the political landscape in Turkey has shifted significantly. In 2007, the AK Party government, led by Prime Minister Recep Tayyip Erdoğan, was viewed, both at home and abroad, as being a reform government, fighting the long entrenched "deep state" and democratizing Turkey.

The European-Union inspired democratic reforms that were introduced during the ruling AK Party's first term in office were welcomed by Turkish society as it hoped to cast off its anti-democratic straightjackets, one after another. In the spring of 2010, the Parliament, following the lead of Prime Minister Erdoğan, further accepted a series of sweeping constitutional reforms. These constitutional amendments did not, however, achieve the required two-thirds majority in the Parliament to immediately implement the changes at that time; therefore, it was put to a referendum on September 12, 2010. These reforms—which curbed the power of military courts, making the military more accountable to the civilian courts, abolished the immunity enjoyed by the generals of the 1980 coup, gave more rights to women and various segments of the society, made the judiciary more accountable, expanded personal freedoms, and limited state power over individuals—were hailed by the Enlargement Commissioner in the European Union as "...a step in the right direction as they address a number of long-standing priorities in Turkey's efforts towards fully complying with the EU accession criteria." In September, 2010, the reforms passed with 58% of the vote. Though

---

1 *Quo vadis* is a Latin phrase which means "Where are you going?", or more precisely "Whither goest thou?"

there was still work to be done on the democratization front, the reforms were seen as a good starting point.

Partly on the strength of these reforms and the government's promise of replacing the current 1980 coup constitution with a new "civic constitution" in its third term, the AK Party won its third term in power in the 2011 general elections, this time with an unprecedented 50% of the vote. Right after this landslide victory, Erdoğan declared that the first term of his government was their apprentice period, the second term, their journeyman period, and the third term would be their "mastership period" (*Ustalık Dönemi*).

In his reconciliatory balcony speech, Erdoğan promised to head a government of all people, not only the 50% who had supported his party. The vast majority of the public had, therefore, high expectations that the government would launch a new wave of reforms in its third term; however, for the Erdoğan government, "mastership" implied expanding its domination over the state. In its third term, the Erdoğan government has shifted its priorities significantly, thus proving the outstanding artfulness of its "mastership period." It has increasingly been taking on features that heavily contradict its conception of being a democratic reform party. Moving away from earlier reforms, the government has focused on a series of confrontations with opponents—both real and imagined. The Prime Minister himself is now taking the lead with his harsh and aggressive rhetoric of "othering," and even demonizing, some influential people and various segments of society. This aggressive rhetoric has been used to cover up the enormous corruption and graft scandal that erupted in December, 2013, and in many ways, is no different than the dirty rhetoric of "reactionaryism" (*İrtica*) employed once to disguise the siphoning of banks during the 1997 post-modern coup era (See also the Appendices).

There have been smaller positive steps, of course. The government finally repealed the ban on headscarves in public places. While proponents of freedom of expression celebrated this, it angered some from the secular elite that had long controlled the levers of power in Turkey. But many other important reforms languished: EU reforms, a new "civic" constitution, and the democratic initiatives on the concerns of the Alevi and Kurdish citizens have been pushed to the backburner, brought up at moments of need or convenience, when the government hopes to remind voters of its reform credentials.

After working for Turkey's bid to join the European Union for almost a decade, albeit half-heartedly, Erdoğan now has a strong liking for Putin's Russia, asking him to include Turkey into "the Shanghai Five" in January 2014. Indeed, his remarks shocked EU proponents both at home and abroad when he described the Shanghai Cooperation Organization (SCO) as an alternative to the European Union; he even went so far as to describe the EU as a burden. The same Erdoğan, who seeks to shift to presidency in August 2014, wanted to consolidate his position by creating a strong "executive presidency" within the framework of a new constitution that was to be drawn up during his third term in office. However, his government's unenthusiastic effort to draft the new "civic constitution" was abandoned after it became clear that the inclusion of a powerful office of presidency was unfeasible under the prevailing circumstances. Unfortunately, the faltering EU reforms and the long debate on the design of the civic constitution disappeared into political oblivion. Despite the AK Party government's democratic initiatives on improving the human rights of Kurdish citizens and its holding a series of Alevi workshops, it has not taken active steps to deal with the concerns of disadvantaged groups. Real progress has mostly slowed, and they have become wedge issues, mostly exploited as a strategic move to lure voters ahead of elections.

It was only two years after the 2011 general elections that a small and peaceful environmental protest in Gezi Park, a small alcove of trees and fountains located in the concrete heart of Taksim, was broken up by police using excessive violence—tear gas, rubber bullets, and water cannons on May 31, 2013. Afterwards, massive protests sprang up all over Istanbul—and the rest of the country. The three weeks of unrest that followed represented the most serious challenge yet to Erdoğan and the AK Party's supremacy. Though the protests, which began peacefully, eventually turned destructive, the security forces were widely viewed as being the instigators through their tactics of violent suppression. In all, six protestors died, hundreds more were injured, and thousands were arrested. Erdoğan called the protestors thugs, and praised the police for their actions. The same Erdoğan has now dismissed several thousand police officers and prevented prosecutors from carrying out their duties right after dozens of people were detained due to the recent bribery and corruption probe.

In the aftermath of the protests and all this corruption, discontent simmered. Erdoğan blamed various forces—Israel, America, Germany, and supporters of the Islamic scholar Fethullah Gülen—for stoking unrest within the country. He blamed foreign envoys for turmoil and even threatened to expel the US ambassador in a public rally in the Samsun province. Then, the US ambassador to Turkey, Francis Ricciardone, refuted Erdoğan's claims that the US was "behind Turkey's graft probe," and the US demanded the Erdoğan government condemn false news reports about the ambassador that were published in pro-government newspapers. The Prime Minister, however, kept picking up on the allegation; he seems not to have considered the possibility that his policies were exacerbating the schisms within the country and were rolling back many of the freedoms and democratic reforms he, himself, had overseen.

Unlike the confrontational stances of the Prime Minister, President Abdullah Gül has taken a more moderate approach. He stated then that he was proud of the initial motives for the Gezi Park protests, as they began due to environmental concerns similar to those seen in developed and democratic countries. He also called for common sense and "maturity" from both the government and protesters to end the days-long tension during the Gezi Park protests, emphasizing that "authorities should exert serious efforts to lend an ear to differing opinions and concerns" in a democratic society. Nevertheless, Gül has not been implicated in the recent corruption probe, and has remained mostly silent about the issue.

In the meantime, the government under Erdoğan has instituted many other policies that were seen as authoritarian and reactionary. A number of journalists who had been critical of the government's response to the Gezi Park protests were forced out of their jobs. The government has widely been viewed as attacking those who disagree with their belief that Turkey is a conservative society that should be governed by radically conservative policies. Instantaneous measures and restrictions on the sales of alcohol riled some within the secular elite. Indeed, Turkey's chronic problem with the freedom of press is swept back to the agenda once again after all those cases opened against media groups and journalists due to their reports about the ongoing corruption and bribery probes. There are also some indications that the Syrian opposition groups have received support from the Erdoğan government, in the hopes of overthrowing the Assad government and preventing the formation of an autonomous Kurdish region in Syria. As the situation in Egypt has worsened, the Erdoğan government has become increasingly isolated in their support for the deposed government of Morsi and his Muslim Brotherhood supporters. Erdoğan's power, both at home and abroad, has never been on shakier ground.

In November, 2013, Erdoğan announced his intention to close over 4,000 privately operated preparatory schools across Turkcy, instead of instituting pedagogical measures to elevate the underperforming public education system. These schools offer tutoring for students as they prepare for the highly competitive college entrance exams—and often fill the void left by a struggling public education system. This decision—which was widely denounced, including within the AK Party—was viewed not as a pedagogical measure but as an aggressive assault on the Hizmet movement, which is popularly known as the "Gülen movement" in the West and as "cemaat," or the community, in Turkey. Hizmet is a worldwide group of moderate believers, mostly Turkish Muslims, who are loosely united by a shared faith in the teachings of Gülen and Said Nursi. They believe in the importance of tolerance, interfaith dialogue, and education. The supporters inspired by the movement have opened schools in Turkey—and in about 150 countries worldwide.

Hizmet movement's apolitical, moderate beliefs have long been at odds with Erdoğan's more muscular, capitalist stances. There has been suspicion within the AK Party—unfounded—that those inspired by Gülen operated within the judiciary and the police, and were working to undermine Erdoğan's power. The movement's Journalists and Writers Foundation (GYV) responded the claim and other slanderous accusations made about the Hizmet movement, denying any involvement with the ongoing investigations. The foundation, of which Gülen is the honorary chairperson, reiterated that "the Hizmet movement nurtures a heartfelt desire for Turkey's being endowed with true democracy, transparency, full-fledged rule of law and shows due respect to the nation's democratic preferences and to Parliament." However, the AK Party has moved, without any legal basis, to purge the government ranks of many civil servants, mainly those who were claimed to be the supporters of the Hizmet movement since the election victory in 2011. On the other hand, the decision to close the preparatory schools was seen as the start of government's engaging openly in a lynching campaign against the movement.

A month later, on December 17, 2013, corruption charges were brought against over 40 people, including the sons of three important government ministers, prominent businessmen, and the general manager of state-run Halkbank. The suspects stand accused of rigging state tenders, obtaining construction permits for protected sites and accepting bribes for major urbanization projects, helping foreigners get Turkish citizenship with forged documents, and involvement in export fraud, forgery and gold smuggling, mainly to Iran. Instead of probing deeply into the claims and rooting out the corruption, Prime Minister Erdoğan had long turned a blind eye to the suspicious relationships between the ministers in his cabinet and some businessmen, especially the Iranian businessman Reza Zarrab, who is currently under arrest for bribing the ministers, rigging state tenders, money laundering and facilitating the transfer of 87 billion euros from Iran through his various firms in Turkey, thus helping Iran bypass international financial sanctions imposed due to its nuclear program.

While Erdoğan tried to sweep the dirt of the corruption under the carpet and blamed the scandal on what he called a "parallel state," a veiled reference to the Hizmet movement, his longtime friend and former Minister of Interior, İdris Naim Şahin, pointed the finger of blame directly on "a political and bureaucratic oligarchy at the helm of the AK Party" and reproached this corrupt oligarchy, in his resignation, for having "unclear intentions." Though Erdoğan first pretended that he knew Zarrab only as a "good guy" who made charitable donations, it was later leaked to the press that, eight months before the investigations, Erdoğan was informed in detail, by the National Intelligence Service (MIT), about all the corruption issues involving the Iranian businessman. Later, the US Ambassador to Turkey, Francis Ricciardone, also made public that the US had already asked Turkey to cut the state-run Halkbank's Iranian financial ties; Halkbank is now accused of suspicious money transfers and gold trading with Iran. The case has caused seismic shocks through Turkey, sharply dividing those who defend the increasingly authoritarian practices of the government and those who think that democratic reform process needs to accelerate while the depth of the massive corruption must be uncovered.

While the government prevents the public officials from fulfilling their duties and emphasizes the principle of the "presumption of innocence" for the suspects of the ongoing corruption investigation, it feigns ignorance about the same principle when it comes to those public officials. More than three thousand police officers, and hundreds of police chiefs and bureaucrats, and 115 judges and prosecutors have been dismissed without any legal basis. These removals were done without any court orders, legal investigations, or evidence of unlawful activity on behalf of the officials; they were carried out only on the basis of scandalous remarks and slanders hurled at these public officials, accusing them of being members of a "parallel state" or "gang." Such rhetoric violates the very same principle of presumption of innocence. In the absence of a hate crime law in Turkey, Erdoğan's use of such a harsh and discriminatory language about public officials and certain segments of society, comparing them even with the aberrant terrorist assassins (Hashashins) in history, amounts to a sort of hate speech, especially when this blatantly discriminatory language is used by someone in a position to influence public opinion and lead people to hatred and animosity against certain people.

The prosecutors who conduct the corruption probe are threatened, and the private and personal details of their lives, including their international flights and hotel stays, are disclosed in public rallies. Parliament Speaker Cemil Çicek launched an investigation into Chief Ombudsman Mehmet Nihat Ömeroğlu over allegations that Ömeroğlu intimidated the Chief Public Prosecutor Zekeriya Öz into dropping the corruption investigation. The chief ombudsman, however, denied the claim that he had been tasked by the Prime Minister to give up the probe while he accepted that he met with the prosecutor. Several weeks after this event, an official report was made public by the main opposition party leader, Kılıçdaroğlu, who stated that Justice Ministry Undersecretary Kenan İpek threatened the İzmir chief public prosecutor to stop a tender-rigging investigation in İzmir in January, 2014. Accordingly, İpek wanted the chief public prosecutor to remove the prosecutor conducting the probe from his post. An undersecretary—who is directly subordinate to a member of the cabinet—cannot make such a grave mistake without the support of political power behind him. The ministry of justice would normally resign when a scandal like this happens in democracies, and the undersecretary would at least be dismissed even in a malfunctioning democracy.

In the face of all the flagrant government pressure and interventions in the judiciary, Turkey's second-highest political figure, Cemil Çiçek, who is the Speaker of Parliament and a deputy from the ruling AK Party, warned that the independence of the judiciary is currently over and done with. "Article 138 of the Constitution (which deals with judicial independence) has become extinct in this country," Çiçek said, complaining that those in power do not act in line with Article 138 of the Constitution, which says: "Judges shall be independent in the discharge of their duties;… No organ, authority, office or individual may give orders or instructions to courts or judges regarding the exercise of judicial power, send them circulars, make recommendations or suggestions.…No questions shall be asked, debates held or statements made in the Legislative Assembly relating to the exercise of judicial power concerning a case under trial."

Recently, the Erdoğan government also drafted the Supreme Board of Judges and Prosecutors (HSYK) bill to further expand its power and create a judiciary mechanism that is dependent on itself, thus rolling back the Venice Commission and European Union-endorsed reforms in the 2010 referendum. If approved, the judicial board will be subordinated to the justice minister of the executive branch, and he will decide on investigations and the reassignment and removal of all judges and prosecutors, who will have to pay utmost attention to the very sensitivities of the government. Instead of allowing prosecutors and judges to independently pursue the investigations, the executive branch now "intervenes" in the process in an effort to cover up the corruption; it dominates the judiciary every way that it can and punishes those who publish scandalous government documents. Having a long list of the military interventions in its history, the government's "judicial intervention" is no less than a coup—now only with a difference that it is a civil one! Obviously, the separation of powers recently died in Turkey where the rule of law and accountability are totally disregarded, judges and prosecutors are purged, and courts abolished right in the middle of the ongoing corruption cases.

The police, which are subordinated to the executive branch, now refuse to obey orders from prosecutors and courts, which are normally their superiors in the judicial process. The newly appointed head of the Istanbul Police Department, for instance, openly defies the orders of prosecutors. While Justice Minister Bekir Bozdağ, who is also the head of the HSYK, permitted the investigation of those independent prosecutors who had launched the corruption probe, he did not allow prosecutors to start an investigation concerning this new head of the Istanbul

Police Department. In similar fashion, the Interior Minister Güler removed from office all police chiefs who collected evidence about corruption claims concerning his son, starting right after the corruption probe became public, until his resignation a week later. Minister Güler found the entire fault with the police he dismissed because of their finding about $1 million cash and six electronic steel vaults in the apartment of his son, instead of abiding by the law and following the example of well-functioning democracies such as the US, where a congressman was officially charged after wads of "cold cash" were found stuffed in his home freezer.

As he did with the Gezi protests, the Prime Minister denounced the investigation as politically motivated by forces hoping to bring him down—the US, foreign powers, and those who hope to form "a parallel state." But despite his best efforts, the investigation has picked up steam. Though Erdoğan fired the chief of police in Istanbul—and over 40 other cities—and deposed the prosecutor in charge of the investigation, the three ministers whose sons were implicated resigned. On the way out, one of them—Erdoğan Bayraktar, the former Minister of Environment and Urban Planning—implied Prime Minister Erdoğan was directly involved in some deals that were under investigation. He said, "A big part of the zoning plans that are in the investigation file and were confirmed were made with approval from Mr. Prime Minister," and called on the Prime Minister to resign in order to ease the turmoil over the continuing corruption investigation.

It is a case that seems to encapsulate all of the current problems facing Erdoğan and his government. A government that was very recently known for its expansions of freedoms and democracy has fallen prey to the same traps of power that the former elite were corrupted by—the very structures that Erdoğan spent his early political career, as Istanbul's mayor, railing against. As Turkey, and especially Istanbul, has rapidly modernized, the AK Party has increasingly been accused of corruption, of awarding projects to companies friendly to the government and then rushing to complete them. These projects have been pushed forward, oftentimes against the will of Turkey's citizens.

Groups that oppose the will of the oligarchy around the Erdoğan government have increasingly been silenced and marginalized, oftentimes through the accusation of "treason," oppression, and hate speech. The accusation of treason, for instance, has been made often against anyone with an opposing stance. Prime Minister Erdoğan himself pointed the finger at the President of the Turkish Industrialists and Business-men's Association (TÜSİAD), Muharrem Yılmaz, who stated that Turkish businessmen were uneasy about the controversial Supreme Board of Judges and Prosecutors bill which would subordinate the judiciary to strict government control, and that foreign investors and entrepreneurs would be wary of investing in a country where there is no respect for the supremacy and rule of law and where public procurement laws have been changed more than 160 times by the ruling AK Party according to the emerging public procurement tenders. For instance, in 2013, the penalty for tender corruption in public procurements has been reduced from seven years down to three years, letting offenders off even without any claims for compensation. Instead of increasing the government's accountability and transparency and bringing public procurement legis-lation in line with international standards, Erdoğan openly accused Yılmaz of "treason" at an AK Party rally in Ankara, without offering any evidence or legal grounds for such a claim. The companies of the "trai-tors" are frequently pressured through frequent government inspec-tions, red tape, threats, and various fines.

This small oligarchy at the helm of the AK Party resorts to all kinds of dirty "perception management"—all in an attempt to control the per-ceptions of the public, and thus cover up the massive corruption, which is often referred to as the biggest in the history of Turkey. In a column from January 26, 2014, titled *The Biggest Media Mogul of Turkey*, Bülent Keneş, of *Today's Zaman*, wrote about this, saying:

> [T]he prime minister controls numerous pro-government and par-tisan media outlets either directly or through indirect repressive methods and has emerged as Turkey's biggest media mogul. The prime minister's every speech is broadcast live either voluntarily or reluctantly by at least 17 national TV channels and he enjoys more power and authorities than a media boss on the management of at least half of these channels.

> Moreover, it is the prime minister who directly decides who should work as editors in at least seven national newspapers. People are then supposed to believe in these media outlets which have become the most functional component of this mafia system. It is sad to observe that this media order has been successful in per-suading some segments of society.

On the other hand, in order to prevent the media from reporting the details of the corruption investigations, the ruling party uses all the means at its disposal, especially exploiting regulatory agencies to come down on certain media outlets, people, firms and even banks, which it labels as "traitors." In this lynching campaign, many leading Turkish businessmen and corporations, including the İstikbal furniture company, the Koza İpek holding, whose media assets include *Bugün* daily and *Bugün* TV, and the Koza mining company, were targeted with various forms of frequent government inspections, fines and permit cancellations—only because of their sympathies, affinities and worldviews. The order for the closure of the goldfield of the Koza mining company, for instance, had come due to so-called allegations of the absence of "environmental permits and licenses document." Koza mining company—one of the latest victims of government silencing—first declared that the decision to halt production in the goldfield was illegal, and then restarted its activities within two weeks after a court ordered a stay of execution for the halting of its operations.

In this aggressive government-led assault, the Erdoğan government exploits all of the regulatory agencies for the sake of influencing public opinion and inducing their behavior favorable to its interests. Perhaps its most egregious and shocking move has been its efforts to close down Bank Asya, whose founders include people close to the Hizmet movement. It's a unique, and sad, situation—a government deliberately attempting to bankrupt a national bank in its own country.

Working towards this goal, the spin doctors in pro-government media outlets first started churning out fabricated stories about Bank Asya, which the bank tried to refute. The bank also waited for the Banking Regulation and Supervision Agency (BDDK) to step up and put an end to the whisper campaigns which aimed to create a panic among its depositors. Although it is the mission of the BDDK to take immediate steps and initiate legal procedures against any individuals or publications which systematically organize attacks against banks, the agency did not take any steps to protect Bank Asya, but let the aggressors off with a simple warning of the possible repercussions they may face. Similarly, the Capital Markets Board (SPK) opted to remain silent, allowing government-backed aggressors to discredit the bank. This all happened despite the current Banking Law, which clearly states that any action or words that may harm banks' reputation are strictly forbidden and that felonies are punishable with fines and imprisonment. The small oligarchy even forced the owners and administrators of quite a few companies, including the chairman of Turkish Airlines, to withdraw all the money from their accounts in the bank.

The Radio and Television Supreme Council (RTÜK), another regulatory agency, imposed fines on those TV channels that broadcasted visuals of shoeboxes and bankrolls in news related to the corruption and bribery investigations. This move was taken because, for instance, the police officers' carrying out a raid in the house of the state-run Halkbank General Manager Süleyman Aslan, found TL 4.5 million in shoeboxes! There are also video images, telephone conversations and records of payments, implicating some ministers of Erdoğan's cabinet in accepting multi-million dollar bribes from the Iranian businessman Reza Zarrab. In one particular surveillance video, Zarrab is seen as entering the office of the Minister for EU affairs, Egemen Bağış, with a suitcase and leaving without it.

Still another state regulatory agency, the Savings Deposit Insurance Fund (TMSF) seized the assets of Mustafa Sarıgül, the Istanbul mayoral candidate of the main opposition party, after he and his business partners failed to repay a loan dating back to 1998. So, the agency is now after the loan 16 years later, thus disrupting Sarıgül's bid for the Istanbul mayoral post just three months before the general local elections. At the end of the day, all these regulatory agencies, whose sole raison d'être is to be independent of government influence—and, of course, to enforce regulations in the public interest—have turned out to be institutions at the mere service of the ruling party.

Simultaneously, the government is also working on limiting the freedom of communication on the Internet through an "emergency" Internet (censorship) law that will give power to the transport and communications minister to erase or ban any disagreeable content, which is part of the government's effort to cover up the corruption. The government has also banned police reporters from entering police departments and precincts in order to prevent them from obtaining and covering news in police departments. With all the recent fait accompli bills, bans and news blackouts, the Erdoğan government aims to take Turkey back to the direction of the old one-party rule, even to the former censorship-savvy iron curtain countries.

In the past several decades, the relationship of the center to the periphery has already changed, and outsiders in the Anatolian periphery have now become the insiders, but the means of power—its authoritarian reach—have not changed. In 2007, Erdoğan was the reformer fighting the structures of the "deep state." With that battle won, Erdoğan and the new small oligarchic elite around him now represent the status quo, the new power. Their unlawfulness and authoritarian tendencies cannot be reconciled with the democratic values of the rule of law and accountability.

Turkey is at a crossroads. In March, 2014, the municipal elections will take place. In August, 2014, the country will vote in its first direct Presidential elections; Erdoğan is widely expected to run. In March, 2015, the next general elections will be held and a new prime minister will be chosen. The results of these three elections will determine the country's trajectory—towards authoritarianism or towards democracy.

The direction of the new Turkey should, and will be, towards a fully democratic, social constitutional state—which complies with the EU standards, and is governed by the supremacy and rule of law—and a government accountable to both the Parliament and the public.

Istanbul, January, 2014

# Introduction

## Turkey conflicted with itself –
## When citizens can no longer go swimming

T empers in Turkey have flared every ten years. In 1960, 1971, and 1980, the military intervened directly and deposed elected governments. After 1980, the generals stopped their "conventional" intervention of sending tanks into the streets. In a "postmodern" coup in 1997, they overthrew the government of Necmettin Erbakan, an Islamist; this time, their aims were achieved indirectly, by government institutions applying pressure.

Ten years later, however, the military failed in its attempt to make use of mass protests in order to weaken the government of Recep Tayyip Erdoğan, and to undermine the election of Foreign Minister Abdullah Gül as president. The government applied three consecutive measures to retain the control that was slipping away. First, the military's warning on April 27, 2007, that Gül not be elected president fell flat, and then the state party—the Republican People's Party (Cumhuriyet Halk Partisi, CHP), founded by Atatürk, disgraced itself during the parliamentary elections of July 22, 2007. Finally, on March 14, 2008, the judiciary, the third lever of the Kemalistic elite, sprang into action by initiating proceedings to ban the ruling Justice and Development Party (AK Party), which survived the proceedings, when the country's top court ruled against the AK Party's closure on July 30, 2008.

All three attempts at disempowering the AK Party were linked to the assertion that the secular order of Turkey was at risk. Indeed, Erdoğan and Gül were rooted in political Islam. However, it was not a case where secularism was at risk, or where some version of Islamism threated Turkey. The overwhelming majority of Turkish people want the separation of state and religion. Secularism has been firmly embedded in the Turks' attitude and everyday life for decades. The majority of Turks are devout Muslims; they are religious but not orthodox.

The lines of conflict are not between secularism and political Islam. The breaking point is somewhere else completely. At first glance, the two camps differ as to their life styles. One camp would like to keep all religiousness out of the public view; the other faction professes publically to be Muslim as a part of its cultural identity. Yet even this first impression is not comprehensive, because there were changes in Turkey between 1997 and 2007. Society grew stronger at the expense of the state, diversity reclaimed part of the monopolistic state policy, and during those years, the most important branch of political Islam turned into a democratic reform party.

There are not many countries where state and government are as diverse as in Turkey. Ever since the founding of the Republic, the state has wanted to modernize society from the top-down. To this day, the military, the judiciary, and the central bureaucracy represent this state. During the one party rule from 1923 to 1950—and during the years of the direct military dictatorship—state and government were one. However, as soon as there were elections, the state machinery would suspiciously observe the elected parliaments and governments to detect whether they deviated from the state policy drafted after the founding of the Republic. A liberal government does not require an ideology. Turkey, however, used to have an ideology—and it still does—i.e. Kemalism, named after the founder of the Republic of Turkey, Mustafa Kemal Atatürk. The driving force of Kemalism has, however, waned during the last 20 years.

For decades, the state and the machinery it appointed was more powerful than the elected government and society. This changed from 1997 to 2007. Turkey became more liberal and more democratic, and its society was freeing itself from the shackles of government ideology. An alternative to this ideology of state power began in Anatolia, the "heartland" of Turkey. This ideology had prevented Turks from displaying their pluralist diversity for too long. A pent-up disappointment over an ideologically indurated government was the catalyst for the reform process that was gearing up. The prospect of becoming an EU member was the second catalyst for this reform process, including the Copenhagen Accession Criteria. They gave the reform process a direction, and became the guidelines for change in the parliament and government. There was resistance against the reforms, however, and there were many setbacks.

The old urban elite have still not fully admitted that the situation has reversed. During recent years, the urban elite has had to recognize that it is a minority and can no longer bully the country into doing what it wants it to do. It no longer has the monopoly to shape society, or the right to define culture. Anatolia has produced its own elite and now demands its place in the government, and increasingly, in the state. The culture of the state's wealthy, western-oriented urban elite contrasts with Turkey's own culture, which accomodates both local and modern global values, deriving its identity from its thousand-year-long tradition of Islam in Turkey.

In the past ten years, the relationship of the state and the government has changed. The old elite are on the defensive; Turkey has become pluralist. The movement of political Islam has also changed during this process. Erbakan, the Prime Minister deposed in 1997, had founded and embodied a political Islam that positioned itself along Sharia, the Islamic laws. Erbakan sought political Islam that resembled the Muslim Brotherhood, and spoke deprecatingly of the West as being decadent. Erdoğan and Gül, on the other hand, separated themselves from Erbakan, and governed Turkey after 2002 looking towards Europe. They head a self-confident, dynamic new middle class whose women wear headscarves. They no longer see Islam as being the guiding principle of political action, and rather see it as a part of their cultural identity. Prime Minister Erdoğan and President Gül accepted the separation of state and religion, which the founders of the state had assigned the country as an avant-garde. Less than ten percent of Turks question their commitment to the state-religion separation. This was in direct contrast with the old elite, who interpret even privately-observed religiousness as a signal of an impending coup. The basic question, therefore, is not whether religion is allowed to be evident in politics, but rather if it can be evident in society. Should religious practice be free, or should the government impose regulations on it, as it has done in the past? To what extent should a state have an impact on religion? Is a devout citizen who practices religion in private also a loyal citizen?

In Germany, the culture war answered these questions in the last quarter of the 19th century. What happened in Germany under Bismarck cannot really be applied to Turkey. But there are unmistakable parallels.

Bismarck closed monasteries and banned the Jesuit order; half a century later, Atatürk abolished the dervish lodges (*tekkes*) and outlawed their order (*tarikat*). Bismarck introduced civil marriage and, in the "Pulpit Paragraph," sent ministers to prison that "referred to affairs of the state during a proclamation in a way that endangered the public peace." Atatürk similarly curtailed the power of the Islamist clergy in Turkey. Bismarck and Atatürk wanted to separate state and religion because they both saw clergymen as endangering the state. They each wanted to impose their rules on religious institutions—one of them on the Catholic Church, and the other one on Islam. In doing so, they both achieved measures of success and failure.

Bismarck and Atatürk set the pace for the separation of state and religion in their countries. This radical step became the crucial aspect of modernization—both in Germany and in Turkey. But politically, the laws that were passed during the Prussian culture war strengthened the party that represented the institution that Bismarck wanted to deprive of power. In the Reichstag election of 1874, the Zentrum party doubled its number of votes. The elections represented a rebellion against Bismarck's restrictive laws. In the Turkey of today, the Justice and Development Party (Adalet ve Kalkınma Partisi, AK Party) was the beneficiary of increasing criticism of the restrictive practice of secularism, exerted by the government elite who invoked Atatürk. Bismarck's Pulpit Paragraph was not rescinded until 1953, after it had been in force for more than eighty years. More than eighty years after the founding of the Republic of Turkey, the reforms of the AK Party not only democratized politics, they also removed outgrowths of the Turkish version of rigid secularism.

The AK Party profitted from the division of the country into an urban state elite and a demographic majority that no longer wanted to be governed by this elite, perhaps even more than it benefitted from the criticism of restrictive secularism. This majority has fled the Anatolian outskirts and has arrived at the centers of large cities. Behind its growing strength, the AK Party became the mainstream political party.

The two factions face each other distrustfully; fear keeps them at a distance. During mass protests against Erdoğan's government in the spring of 2007, the women of the government elite credibly stated that they were afraid of losing their rights. They expected that if Erdoğan's government gained even more power, they could be forced to wear a headscarf, or would have to first ask their husbands before getting a job. This is because many women of the Kemalist elite insinuated that "other" women only wear headscarves because they are forced to do so. They cannot imagine that most of the "other" women wear it because they want to—for religious reasons or maybe even as a form of protest. This has two consequences. On the one hand, they like to see themselves as the liberators of Muslim women from bondage and stupidity. On the other hand, they believe that, after the assumption of power by the new counter-elite, they would also be forced to wear a headscarf.

This conflict was not the first time that the educated and Western-oriented middle and upper classes in the large cities were nervous that people who were different from them were assuming public roles. At the beginning of the fifties, right after the one-party rule ended, when the migration of poor and uneducated rural people from Anatolia into the large cities had started, a representative of the elite, which was the only elite at the time, described the deep division that divides Turkish society, even to this day, with an apt phrase: "The people are overpopulating the beaches, citizens can no longer go swimming." (In Turkish: *Halk plajlara akın etti, vatandaş denize giremiyor.*) The man who said this, Fahrettin Kerim Gökay, was Governor of Istanbul from 1949 to 1957, and was one of the leading representatives of the Republican People's Party (CHP).

The "citizen" referred to in the quote was—like the Governor Gökay himself, who was a professor of medicine—educated and culturally versed in the West, potentially spoke several languages, was not particularly interested in religion, and was a member of the urban middle and upper class. The "people," however, were not educated, lived in Anatolia, were not interested much in Western culture, and practiced Islam. In Turkey, the very words "citizen" and "people" had long been used to refer to what was the top and what was the bottom. As long as women who wore a headscarf did not go to the university, they were not a threat to the old secular elite. But as soon as they reached the universities, they were no longer servants, but at eye-level, and thus a challenge. Today, "citizens" and "the people" are educated; both have acquired wealth, and live in the same cities, but they have different life styles. For the first time, "others" are invading the public space of the old urban elite.

These elite are still unwilling to share this public space with the new "citizens" of their republic—those who used to be, "the people."

What has divided the two groups has always been their background, and thus the religiousness of Anatolia. Right before the Republic was proclaimed, Mahmud Esad Bey (1892–1943), one of Atatürk's closest allies, had described Islam in a public discussion in the Ankara train station in 1923: "Islamism is an obstacle to progress... With this religion, people are stagnant, we perish and no one takes us seriously," he complained. It is also to be noted that quite a few founding fathers of the Republic had favored Protestant Christianity. The diplomat and writer of short stories, Ahmed Hikmet Müftüoğlu (1870–1927), for instance, admired Martin Luther. By translating the New Testament into German, Martin Luther created a new confession (*mezhep*), a new language, and a new nation. The early republican reformers of his ilk in Turkey liked how Protestantism had nationalized religion, how religion was interpreted in a modern way, and how it conceded only a small amount of influence to the church leaders compared to the influence of Islamic religious scholars. If there was to be a religion, then it had to be along these lines. Traditional Islam, however, was to be reserved for the impoverished and uneducated Anatolians.

The founders of the Republic imposed their vision of modern civilization on a society that was underdeveloped and backward. To do this, they employed all the means that the state machinery had at its disposal, including its monopoly on force. They demanded obedience from the people, not individuality. Due to its all-encompassing modernization project, the state was above society. Society was supposed to follow the state unanimously.

In order to reach this unanimity, the state elite created "fake images" of those who supposedly endangered this new order. They insinuated it was mainly the religious people and the Kurds who had been rising against the new Republic. The Ottoman Empire had already suppressed the riots of the Kurds, who had been demanding more local self-determination. From the onset, elites of the new Republic fought all the possible elements of resistance, mainly the religious people and the rebellious Kurds, using prohibitions and violence. The state viewed these groups as questioning the postulated unanimity of society. In order not to endanger their project, the founders of the Republic had foregone democracy and the maintenance of liberties. And this is why the unsolved problems continued to become virulent, again and again. The Kurdish question was not solved during all these decades; neither was the relationship of the state with Islam, or the Armenian problem.

While the auditorium of the first parliament of the Republic was still adorned with this quote in Arabic letters, "Hakimiyet milletindir" (Sovereignty rests unconditionally with the people), that power actually came from above. The people were to keep quiet and serve the state. The civil politicians enforced politics from above and from the center of the capital. If things became unmanageable, the army forced the country back on track. It was predictable, and kept returning the power back to politics. Since the coup of 1960, the army primarily sees itself as a protagonist in politics, and it may take a stand on a regular basis—and intervene—even without democratic legitimacy, with the judiciary at its side. Between coups, it completed the work that it viewed as necessary for the protection of the Republic and the unity of state and nation. The most important tool it employed against dissident intellectuals was prohibiting political parties and procedures. There is no other country in Europe, where as many parties have been banned since the Second World War as in Turkey. The opponents of Turkey's EU membership have used the judiciary as their preferred leverage to effectively discredit Turkey and its reform process abroad.

Aspects of the conflict in Turkey include determining the leeway of religion in secular states, as well as the relationship of the center to the periphery. Both aspects underlay the ever present leitmotif for the country: What is the Turkish nation and who has the right to define it? The old state elite had wanted to create a homogenized Turkish nation according to its own image. But it met resistance from those who insisted on the right to be different, and who did not want to assimilate themselves. Nation building takes time. Usually, nations are devised, and nationalism creates its own identity. It constructs the myth of cultural homogeneity and differentiates itself via the culture it has defined. This is also how the founders of the Republic tried to shape a unanimous Turkish nation.

The initial process was started by young Turkish reformers who had been demanding the transformation of the Ottoman multinational empire into a Turkish national state since the late 19th century. This process was continued by the founders of the Republic, with the proclamation of the Turkish national state. From the outset, their historians propagated the existence of an old and glorious Turkish nation, having its roots with the Sumerians and the Hittites. In reality, however, the homogenous Turkish nation of the twentieth century had come about in their hands. The Turkish flag, which derived the same symbols and design from the late Ottoman flag, the national anthem, which was adapted as a result of a country-wide competition in 1920, and the map, with a geographic depiction of Turkey, became the factual instruments to create this nation. Everyone was to speak Turkish, independent of what their mother tongue was. Atatürk's omnipresent busts and pictures became part of the Turkish national iconography. The photographs of the first decades of the Republic depicted individuals without individuality, all of whom were interchangeable. Women wearing headscarves were not part of the picture. Instead, men wore tail-coats, and women wore skirts, like in the West, during festive occasions.

The transition from a multinational empire to a Turkish national state was painful. When compared to the Habsburg Empire, which had concentrated national communities in one place, the Ottoman Empire had many ethnicities, spread over a large territory. Although most people who lived in the Republic were now Muslims, ethnically, the country was a patchwork quilt. In addition, the culture of Sunni Muslims was what was represented most often, while Alevis were a strong Muslim group.

Although the majority of the Anatolian population was of Turkish ethnicity in the new Republic, there were many others, living all over the entire county, who were not Turkish, and who did not consider themselves to be ethnic Turks like the Sunni or Alevi Turks who lived alongside them. As the Ottoman Empire began to decline, and gradually shrank in size, the Turkish speaking Muslims from Bulgaria, as well as other Balkan Muslims, including Bosnians, Albanians and Pomaks, had migrated to the Empire's heartland in Anatolia. Azerbaijanis, Georgians, Circassians and Chechens, arrived from the Caucasus, while Uzbeks and Kyrgyzes came from Central Asia. Cossacks and Tartars came from southern Russia. Caucasian Lazs live on the Eastern coast of the Black Sea; Hemshinli Armenians, some of whom still speak Armenian today though most have become Sunni Muslims, are their neighbors along the far northeastern part of the country. Most Kurds, who predominate the Southeast and who have also migrated to Turkey's major cities, Ankara, Izmir, and, of course, Istanbul, are Sunni Muslims, though a small minority of Kurds is Alevis or Yezidis. Some Kurds speak Kurmanji, others Zaza.

The Süryani Christians of Tur Abdin are Syrian orthodox Monophysites, who speak Aramaic Turoyo, which Jesus would have understood. The Arabic speaking Chaldeans also speak an Aramaic dialect and, like the Süryani—but unlike the Western church—believe that Christ had only one divine nature. With these exceptions, the majority of the Arabs who live in Turkey are Sunni Muslims while Arab Nusayris are the small Shiite minority.

Until recently, Türkmen Yörük tribes, who are Sunni Muslims, moved about with their nomadic tents. Sephardic Jews from Spain and North Africa had settled in large cities, and Ashkenazi Jews later came from Eastern Europe. Roma continue to live in Istanbul and Edirne, as they did in the past. There were also Greek Orthodox Christians in Istanbul, who had been living there since the Byzantine Empire. Further masses had emigrated from the Peloponnese in the 18th century, including Armenian Christians, whose homeland has been Anatolia for thousands of years.

This is what a homogenized nation state was supposed to be created from. The state elite used two tricks to achieve this. On the one hand, they turned all Muslims into Turks, and declared Christians "foreigners." On the other hand, they proclaimed the culture of urban Sunni Turks to be ideal. Minorities who did not want to follow suit were ridiculed or persecuted. Campaigns were launched to speak Turkish and to hire people of only Turkish origin. The people who became part of the declared majority culture felt safe while those who did not want to assimilate, and who did not become part of the dominant Turkish culture, were discriminated against. Aside from the Kurds, mainly non-Muslim minorities were affected. Many of them were dispossessed by the "asset tax" in 1942. Oppressions such as the one in 1934 against the Jews, and in 1955 against Greek Christians, drove away those people who were no longer welcome. As such, more and more of them preferred to not attract attention. On the outside, many of them acted like Muslims and gave their children Muslim first names.

However, the pressure to assimilate also grew for Muslims who were not Turkish. Starting in 1949, every village and field name was "Turkified." The new Turkish names had nothing to do with the history of these places. The state installed a commission in 1957 to speed up the renaming of places and to coordinate it. Not only were all citizens to be incorporated by a homogenized Turkish nation, but the village and town names were incorporated, too—in other words, the memory of the people. Recently, however, there have been initiatives to restore the former geographical names, and a recent legislation passed in the Parliament that restores the names of villages, towns and provinces, primarily Kurdish, to their former native names. So, the province of Tunceli would be called Dersim again while the districts that were renamed Güroymak and Aydınlar would be called by their old names of Norşin and Tillo, respectively.

People did not become aware of all the different identities until the nineties. The coup of 1980, the constitution that was written by the military in 1982, and the fight against the Kurdish PKK—which is listed internationally as a terrorist organization by states and organizations, including the United Nations, NATO, the US, and the European Union—had once again militarized the political discourse and curtailed freedoms. However, beginning in the nineties, more and more civil liberty groups were challenging this discourse. Human rights and peace groups were founded; secular and Islamist feminists spoke up. The arrest of the PKK-leader Öcalan in February of 1999 ended the most intense phase of the conflict between the state and the PKK. The beginning of EU reforms introduced a political liberalization. It is no coincidence that the recognition of cultural rights played a role in the discussion about human rights and the EU process. This was due to the fact that a lot of Turkish citizens define their identity via their culture, which is outside of the Turkish one that the state prescribes. But even if they are not ethnic Turks, their self-concept is that of citizens of the Republic of Turkey.

An expert commission had prepared a report about the situation of human rights on behalf of the first Erdoğan government. The research group, affiliated with İbrahim Kaboğlu and Baskın Oran, presented their report on October 1, 2004, and they suggested softening the previously restrictive concept of citizenship. Instead of the sole Turkish identity ("Türk") there were to be two identities: the primary Turkish citizenship ("Türkiyeli") and the secondary one of the cultural identity in question. Kaboğlu and Oran were immediately accused of "inciting hate."

The deconstruction of the official state ideology had started a long time ago and could no longer be stopped. But it did not question Turkishness in itself, nor the laicist order of the Republic. In fact, the attack was aimed at the alleged homogeneity of the republic and the lack of differences between the citizens. Turkey is in the process of recognizing the diversity of its society.

"The moment I was able to completely cast off the straightjacket, I recognized that I was becoming free myself and that I had started living naturally, that I was free," said Fethiye Çetin, the lawyer. She had grown up believing, as a matter of course, that she was Turkish. Then her grandmother, shortly before she died, told her that she had grown up an Armenian who had survived the persecution in 1915 as a ten-year-old, and had been saved by a Turkish officer, who had adopted her. "I am a crossbreed and that makes me happy," Çetin admits gaily.

To this day, Turkey's history revolves around the question: Who is Turkish? Of course everyone who travels with a Turkish passport is Turkish. But is everyone who has this passport—and only these people—Turkish? Is it possible to be a Turkish citizen and to be a Kurd at the same time? Or an Armenian?

The current debate in Turkey provides two answers. One of them is: Turkey is a Turkish national state. Citizenship is coupled with belonging to the Turkish nation. State and nation are therefore married, in a Catholic way. This is the modern Turkish-Kemalist tradition. The second answer is: the voluntary pledge binds a citizen to the Turkish constitution. If someone binds the nation itself to the state, violates the human rights of those people who want to be different than what the postulation of a homogeneous Turkish nation alleges, it violates those who insist on an additional identity to that of the Turkish one. In order to guarantee pluralism, state and nation must be divorced from one another. This is the Ottoman postmodern tradition. The EU process contributed decisively in enforcing this way of thinking.

Turkey is discovering its diversity and is utilizing it creatively. In the nineties, the pioneer music publisher, Hasan Saltık, started collecting the diverse music of Anatolia and publishing it on CDs. He called his collection, "Kalan Müzik" (literally, "Music that has remained"). The folklorists of the early republic had also collected music out in the countryside. But they were only interested in this music if it could be used in favor of the Turkish national culture.

Anatolia has never been an American melting pot or a Habsburgian multi-ethnic mosaic. Ethnicities and religions live together closely in Anatolia, and they mix. The transitions were always in flux. The young Turkish photographer Attila Durak's exhibition, in 2007, with 173 portraits from all over Turkey, was called "Ebru," a painting technique that dates back to the Ottomans, where the artist adds a different color to a dark fluid foundation. The colors do not mix, and do not dissolve. They touch each other, but they are not separate from one another.

This is how Turkey repeatedly created many peoples with new cultures for thousands of years. They never remained the same; they were always in flux. Many nations of people have always lived together, with their different religions, in Anatolia and Thracia. They brought along their languages and their traditions, their music and their food. They have influenced one another, they have learned from each other, and they have lived together. Today, their freedom to be different is greater than ever, but it is not sufficient to maintain this diversity. A Turkey which generates vitality based on diversity will be strong, and will take leave of the cycle of authoritarian tempests. This book is dedicated to those who have crashed monotony and who promote the return of Turkey's inimitable diversity.

# Chapter I

## The Founding Axioms of the Republic of Turkey and How They Are Challenged

# The Basic Order of
# the Turkish Republic

## The state creates its own citizens

The First World War had been lost, and most of the territory that forms today's Turkey was occupied. The Ottoman Empire, consisting of many nations and religions, would soon perish. The Republic of Turkey would take its place.

The war for liberation, headed by Mustafa Kemal, who later became Atatürk, lasted four years. On May 19, 1919, Mustafa Kemal Pasha left Istanbul aboard the old Bandırma postal ship bound for Samsun, an Anatolian province on the Black Sea. He assembled like-minded people, and organized the resistance against the European occupiers.

This resistance had actually begun at the very onset of the Ottoman Empire's defeat in the First World War. Anatolian people struggled to thwart the occupation forces, through active and passive means of resistence, and many members of the Ottoman military as well as officials and scholars formed secret organizations, including the Sentinel Association (*Karakol Cemiyeti*), to start an independence movement. The freedom fighters liberated one region after the other from within Anatolia–Samsun and Sivas, Erzurum and Ankara. They drove away the allies and launched their new country from Ankara. On October 29, 1923, Atatürk celebrated his victory in Ankara by proclaiming the "Republic of Turkey"—*Türkiye Cumhuriyeti*.

The new state was created thanks to the military's vigor. Atatürk's soldiers saved Turkey's borders in their battle against the European superpowers. On July 24, 1923, the Peace Treaty of Lausanne revised the constrictive treaty of Sèvres. In Lausanne, the Allies recognized the "Republicans" as negotiating partners who added another diplomatic victory to their victories in Anatolia; they managed to have the treaty of Sèvres revised. Save for a small area around Ankara, the victorious European powers had divided Anatolia among themselves in the treaty of Sèvres on August 10, 1920. The treaty of Sèvres had also envisioned a Kurdish and Armenian state. This treaty continues to play an important role in the collective memory of Turks. Many nationalists still believe that the superpowers in Europe were intent on dividing and weakening Turkey.

In 1923, Atatürk's soldiers had won the War of Independence. In the same year, they founded the new state, a republic, which the allies acknowledged soon thereafter. However, this new state did not have the alleged homogenous Turkish nation yet. 75% of the Ottoman territory had been lost, along with 85% of its population. What had been lost were the old identities; new ones had still to be created. The Ottomans were history, but the Turkish citizen was not yet created. And there were a lot of minorities living in Anatolia that were neither ethnic Turks nor Muslims.

The situation in France, more than a century before, had been similar. In the year of the French Revolution, every second citizen of the Republic had spoken a mother tongue other than French. The central state did not enforce French as the language of all people until later. In Germany, the German-speaking nation was first. They created their state and its institutions. But who was the population of the newly established state of Turkey? The founders of the Republic were faced with a unique situation in 1923.

The Ottoman Empire that had collapsed was a multinational state with Islamic legitimacy. The Sultan, the worldly leader, was also Caliph— the head of all Muslims. The founding elites, mostly the soldiers of the War of Independence, however, wanted a republic that was different. They wanted to transform it into a secular and homogenized national state—a modern state modeled after the European "nation states." The founders of the state surrounding Atatürk thought that the secular, nation state was an important instrument for the modernization of an exhausted, backward country. Atatürk's motto was that he was going to raise Turkey to, "the level of contemporary civilization." Europe was the opponent in the War of Independence, yet Europe was also the measuring stick for modernization. The state provided a complete instrumentarium for this modernization: centralized bureaucracy, enlightened intellectuals, the judiciary, and of course the founders of the state—mostly the military.

Now they required a "homogenized" nation state with a sharp focus on Turkishness. But who was Turkish? In the Ottoman Empire, the elite and the sultans of the Oğuz Turkish descent identified themselves as Ottomans, not as Turks. Along with the Turkish peasant majority living in Anatolia, the word "Turk" had long been used to refer to all Muslim peoples of the multi-national Ottoman Empire, and the expressions of "turning Turk" and "becoming Muslim" were interchangeably used, especially in European sources. It was also used as a contemptuous word for lower classes, well into the 19th century. The word "Turk" had a nice sound to it when Atatürk upgraded it considerably with what became a legendary saying: "Ne mutlu Türküm diyene" (How happy is the person who says 'I am a Turk'). The saying continues to be part of the credo of the Turkish national state, and it continues to play a central role in the cult of the state by being prominently displayed in public buildings and on large squares. Those who are unable to pronounce this saying, or do not want to, are stigmatized.

Undeniably, a pure Turkish race had long ceased to exist. The Turks had emigrated from Central Asia to Anatolia more than a thousand years ago. When they arrived, they merged with other people. First with the Byzantinians, whose empire they had taken over; then with the Armenians, who lived in Anatolia; then with the Bosnians and Albanians from the Balkans; with the Kurds and Arabs from upper Mesopotamia; with Circassians, Chechens, Ossetians and Georgians from the Caucasus; with the Laz from the coast of the Black Sea; and with the Tartars from beyond the Black Sea. The upper classes of the Ottoman Empire had merged with Christian Balkan people by "devşirme," which entailed young boys being brought to the capital and converting to Islam. They rose to become the bastions of the Ottoman state, including illustrious names such as Grand Vizier Ibrahim Pasha (d. 1536) and Sokullu Mehmed Pasha (d. 1579); the Great Admiral Barbaros Hayrettin (d. 1546), son of a Turkish feudal lord on Lesbos and a Greek woman, as well as the great architect Mimar Sinan (d. 1588), son of Greek or Armenian Christians. Many of the favorite women of the great Ottoman Sultans were also Christian women from the Balkans. The most powerful one among them was the Ukrainian Roxelane (1506–1558), the woman married to Sultan Suleyman (1495–1566), who is referred to as the "Magnificent" in Western history.

The new Republic wanted to define itself as separate from the Ottoman Empire. It was going to be a nation-state, Turkish and secular. The task
was not a simple one. France could have been a role model. Atatürk had
read French philosophers in their original texts when he was a student.
Atatürk took over the idea of secularism and a central state from France,
but not the concept of the citizen. Intially, he did not have the courage to
declare everyone who lived within the boundaries of the republic as a
nation of "Turks."

The founders of the state struck a new path and defined their new
Turkish nation on the basis of Islam, of all things, thus remaining loyal to
their Ottoman heritage. As a consequence of the turmoil of war, large
migrations commenced. In 1922, Turkey and Greece agreed to exchange
people; on January 30, 1923, they signed the treaty in Lausanne. Turkey
suggested it; Greece and the victorious powers agreed. By signing the
treaty, the contractual parties agreed to exchange their minorities. Whoever professed to be Greek Orthodox had to leave Turkey and settle in
Greece while Muslims in Greece had to leave their homeland and move
to Turkey. 1.2 million Christians emigrated from the area that makes up
Turkey today, while 400,000 Muslims moved from Greece and other parts
of the southern Balkans to Turkey. The Gagauz people, who live in Mol-
davia, are ethnic Turks who speak Turkish. But since the majority was
Christian—and still are today, they were not welcome in the new Turkish state that was being created.

Turkey had rid itself of almost all people who were Greek Orthodox,
even those whose ancestors had lived in Anatolia for thousands of years.
Istanbul and the Western part of Greek Thrace remained the exception;
the Greek Orthodox Christians were allowed to stay in Istanbul, and
Muslims who lived in Western Thrace did not have to emigrate. After the
exchange of people, the supposedly secular Republic of Turkey lagged
behind the Ottoman Empire, whose reforms in the 19th century had given
equal rights to Muslims and Christians. It was the first ethnic purge of
the 20th century, even if it was not violent. It had been preceded by the
first specific policy of destroying a people of the 20th century. The "Committee for Unity and Progress" of the Young Turk rulers, who had taken
over the Ottoman Empire during a coup in 1913, commanded the displacement of the Armenian people to the Der Zor Province of the Empire
in 1915. According to Turkish historians, 400,000 Armenians died or

were killed; international historiography estimates the number of victims to be 1.5 million.

Even years after the Republic had been founded, non-Muslim citizens with a Turkish passport were still considered to be an annoyance. First, Jews were attacked in the area around Edirne in Thrace in 1934. Then, the Asset Tax (*Varlık Vergisi*), ordered in 1942 by President İsmet İnönü, the closest companion of Atatürk during the War of Independence, led to the expropriation of the majority of non-Muslim business people and to the "Turkeyfication" of the economy. The provoked rabble demolished the properties of the Greek minority on the night of September 6–7, 1955, during the Turkish "Reichskristallnacht"—a term originally used for the Nazi attack on Jewish people and their property in Germany and German-controlled lands on the night of November 9–10, 1938. Now the Greeks understood that they were not welcome, and most of them fled the country.

Turkey did not see itself as a nation created of its own will, to which anyone could become a member and feel as if they belonged. In that respect, France had not become the role model. During the Ottoman Empire, the religious communities had been called "Millets," whereby the religious head was also the political head in non-Muslim *Millets*. In other words, the patriarch was also an ethnarch.. Not until the second half of the 19th century was this personal union dissolved. The Ottomans were the last one to recognize non-Muslims as equal Ottoman citizens. The Ottoman Empire, which had not differentiated between ethnic groups, but between religions, remained the role model, to some degree.

In fact, there was confusion between the application of a nationalistic exclusion to non-Muslims and an anti-religious secularism to Muslims, which went much beyond the French laicism. Therefore, everyone who demanded rights represented a danger to them, and the person who left the ruling Turkish nation was a double traitor: a traitor to Turkishness and to Islam. This attitude was the backdrop to the murder of the Turkish-Armenian intellectual Hrant Dink in Istanbul, in 2007, and in May 2007 murder of Necati Aydın and Uğur Yüksel in Malatya, who had converted to Christianity and who worked with the German missionary Tilman Geske, who was tortured to death with them.

For a long time, the Sunni Muslims had been the "ruling nation" (*millet-i hakime*) of the "ruled nations" (*millet-i mahkûme*) during the Ottoman

Empire. In the Republic, the majority Sunni Turks continue to consider themselves to be the "ruling nation."

Just like the multi-national Ottoman Empire was always regarded by its contemporaries as the "Turkish Empire," after the principal ruling ethnic group, the founding fathers of Turkey considered all Muslims who lived in the Republic to be "Turks." Deriving from European ideas of nationalism, the widespread Western thoughts of nationalism and nation state were adopted. The ruling "millet," or nation, included even the Kurds, because the Peace Treaty of Lausanne did not mention them as a minority. It only granted that status to the non-Muslim minorities. The dominant interpretation of the Peace Treaty also included the Armenian Apostolian Christians, who had survived the Young Turks' policy of annihilation in 1915, the Greek-Orthodox Christians, who had not been among the people exchanged in 1923, and the Jews as minorities. The Kurds were added to the Turkish majority population as Sunni Muslims. Even the heterodox Alevites, of which the majority were ethnic Turks and the minority were ethnic Kurds, did not count as a minority.

The people of the state had finally been defined. The Cultural Revolution could start as the next step. The six principles of Atatürk, which were formulated in 1931, were to give it a shape and a direction: Turkish "Secularism" (*Laiklik*), "Republicanism" (*Cumhuriyetçilik*), "Nationalism" (*Milliyetçilik*), "Statism" (*Devletçilik*), "Revolutionism"—referring to the process of constant revolutionary transformation (*Devrimcilik*), and "Populism"—referring to the vision of a homogeneous classless society (*Halkçılık*).

The state and its institutions had planned to lead the uneducated masses into the modern era along these principles. Right after the Republic was proclaimed, the Kemalist Cultural Revolution was launched from above. On March 3, 1924, the Caliphate was dissolved—in other words, all Muslims being governed in the Muslim community, and Abdülmecid, the last Ottoman Caliph, left the country. On November 25, 1925, the "Hat Law" defined clothing to be worn in public: the red fez disappeared, and men had to wear the Western style peaked cap. On December 13, 1925, the religious orders (*tarikat*s) were banned. In 1926, after all Islamist courts of law had been dissolved, Swiss civil law was introduced, then the Italian penal code, and in 1929, the German code of criminal procedure. In 1928, Atatürk replaced the Arabic alphabet with the Latin alphabet. Women received the right to vote in 1930 and became eligible [to be voted for] in 1934. Family names were introduced in 1934, and in 1935, Sundays were instituted as a weekly day of rest.

In 1928, Article 2, which states that "Islam was the religion of the Turkish State," was struck from the constitution, and in 1937, "Laicism," the Turkish version of secularism, obtained constitutional status. The office of religion, "Diyanet İşleri Başkanlığı" (initially it was called "Diyanet İşleri Reisliği"), was already an important instrument of the state used to control Muslims and create a homogeneous Turkish nation. Atatürk was able to start the Cultural Revolution because people revered him as the leader of the War of Independence, and because he was in control of all instruments of the state, primarily the bureaucracy, the military, and the justice system.

The late Ottoman intellectual and statesman, Ahmet Cevdet (1823–1895), had similarly brought the actions of the state into focus, and was of the opinion that society was not capable of developing a positive dynamic of its own, that the state would then have to cater to. Several decades after Ahmet Cevdet, the Turkish state was made of steel. It remains strong to this day: its institutions see themselves as political actors who guide. Today, these "state" institutions are firmly convinced that they represent the true will of the people as an enlightened avant-garde, even if they never have to face the voters. The Kemalist understanding is that the sole task of government and parliament is to transmit the will of the state to society in a kind of "transmission." Governments come and go; parliaments are elected and dissolved again. However, the institutions of the higher-ranking state may not be changed: not the office of the president of state, who is the successor to Atatürk as the head of state and commander-in-chief of the armed forces, not the coup constitution of 1982, which codifies the primacy of the state, and not the National Security Council (MGK), which had long been controlled by the General Staff after 1961 (but has finally been civilized by appointing a civilian statesman as MGK secretary-general, which was passed—along with further limitations on the role of the military—by the Turkish Parliament in a 2003 reform package). These controls were initially put in place because the controlling state, which acted far beyond mere administration, did not want to lose its modernization project, and risk losing one of its institutions or having the "homogeneity" of the nation revealed to be a fiction.

The birth defect of the Republic has thus not been corrected yet: that the state came before the nation, and that it wants to shape "its" Turkish nation with its instruments and without democratic legitimacy.

## The center "civilizes" the province

The state is the center and it resembles a fort, protected against uncivilized people who live in the provinces. The aim is to remove the lack of civilization, and so the state elite's rule stretches from the center to the far removed corners of the country. Center and periphery are at odds, and the trench between them is deep. In a ground-breaking essay, which appeared in 1973 in the magazine, *Daedalus,* Şerif Mardin, a leading Turkish social scientist, called it "the most important trench in society," to explain the politics of the time.

The representatives of the state's elite include the Republican People's Party (CHP), which Atatürk founded in 1924. In 1946, Turkey allowed elections and a multiparty democracy. For the first time, the Democratic Party (DP) became a serious challenger to the CHP. But at the time, the CHP had nothing better to do than warn their followers: "Don't go to the towns and villages in the provinces to gain the support of the people; that would only undermine national unity!"

Fahrettin Kerim Gökay, the governor of Istanbul from 1949 to 1957, was even more direct. "People are crowding the beaches; citizens can no longer go swimming," he said. The *Cumhuriyet* daily published the accusation as a headline. The division that Şerif Mardin described could not be expressed better: the name of the daily is the Turkish word for "Republic"; Atatürk founded it, and to this day, it is the mouthpiece of the Kemalists. The "citizens" are the educated, westernized state elite of the center. The "people" consists of non-educated people from the periphery, who are only waiting to be elevated to the level of modern day civilization by the state elite.

The state elite had always cocooned in the center. They watched and controlled the periphery, but did not get involved with it. Despite its name, the "Republican People's Party" (CHP) never managed to gain access to the rural population. During the War of Independence, Atatürk had his eye on Anatolian peasants, who were classic Turks. His successors thought these peasants were uneducated, backward, and not civilized. The bureaucracy of the central state did not develop an idea of how they could mobilize this rural population from within. Moreover, they were like engineers at the drawing board in trying to devise a strategy of how to deal with the people at the periphery. The attempt of a mobilization from above failed. Nobody trusted anyone else: the center did not trust the periphery; the periphery did not trust the center.

No bureaucrat of the center ever volunteered to step foot into the underdeveloped periphery because they believed that the project of elevating Anatolia to the level of contemporary civilization could be conducted from the capital. There was only one attempt by the elite intellectuals who published the magazine of *Kadro* (cadre) from 1931 to 1935 that tried to mobilize the people who lived in the Anatolian periphery from within. They saw themselves as a revolutionary cadre, and wanted to carry their socialist and social revolutionary ideas to the underdeveloped provinces in order to link the economic and social development to the War of Independence.

Aside from this group, all other state elitist modernizers turned their nose up at everything they assumed to be in faraway Anatolia: the Islamic religious orders, whom they considered to be deeply medieval, and the ethnic groups whom they always suspected of separatism. If the new secular state was to prosper, both would have to be eliminated. However, the provinces in Anatolia were bothered by the fact that their taxes would be financing the wealth of the cities of the elites, and that this same elite was curtailing their rights.

The state elite also did not change their attitude when the Democratic Party (DP) was founded in 1946. They won the first free elections in 1950 so triumphantly because they spoke for the "people" whom the "citizens" did not want to see on their beaches. The Republican People's Party (CHP) was for a state economy that was planned and regulated by the bureaucracy; the Democratic Party was in favor of a free market economy. The Republican People's Party defended the tutelage of the central bureaucracy of all parts of the country; the Democratic Party promised a reduction of bureaucracy. The Democratic Party did not want to hinder the religious practice of the people by prohibition, as opposed to the practices of the 27-year long one-party rule of the Republican People's Party. It did not want to put much limitation on the freedoms of thought and worship—lifting, for instance, the Republican People's Party's ban on calling to Prayer in Arabic, viewing the freedom of worship as part of the inalienable human rights.

The Republican People's Party stood for Secularism (*Laiklik*) and Statism (*Devletçilik*) as represented by the dominance of the state elite and the bureaucratic center. As the representative of the democratic periphery, the Democratic Party attempted, for the first time, to reduce the distance between the Anatolian provinces and the Kemalist center. For the first time, the periphery had a political voice; economically it was slowly developing as a free market economy. Railroad systems had been built during the governments of the Republican People's Party; the governments of the Democratic Party built roads. The Democratic Party was more interested in private enterprise, thus the periphery now had access to the cities where the Anatolian people sold their handicrafts, and the agricultural and other products of their small businesses. The state elite continued to vote for the Republican People's Party; the demographic majority of the periphery helped the Democratic Party obtain an impressive victory. The rural-conservative party made use of this by granting more liberties in the economy and in the region. However, they increasingly took on features that contradicted liberty.

Following its ten year rule, the Democratic Party Goverment was overthrown by the military, the strongest instrument of the state, on the pretext that the founding principles of the Republic were being eroded. The military dissolved all political parties, arrested the President, the Prime Minister, and other members of the Democratic Party cabinet, deputies and officials, finally executing Prime Minister Menderes and two members of his cabinet in their first coup on May 27, 1960. In the aftermath of this coup, the military dominated most aspects of society and re-established the status quo.

A lot of the present-day crises can be explained by the conflict between the center and periphery. Take, for example, the arrest of Yücel Aşkın, the rector of the University of Van, on October 14, 2005. Van is situated in the far east of Turkey, where powerful clans like the Kurdish Buruki determine everyday life, and where the religious community of the prominent Islamic scholar, Said Nursi, is especially powerful. Nursi was the most important contemporary scholar who hiked clear across Anatolia.

In 1999, the powerful university council, "Yüksek Öğretim Kurulu" (YÖK), a bastion of the Kemalist central state, had sent pro-secular Aşkın as a reformer. He was to liberate Van from Kurdish separatism and Islamic obscurity, because with its rebellious stand against the central power, Van had made a name for itself over the years. When he was there, Aşkın elevated the level of the university. As rector, he managed to collect prominent scientists, and as a hobby pianist, he gave classical concerts. As a Kemalist, he tried to limit the influence of the Kurdish clans and the community of Nursi. He had a blacklist of employees who were not reliable—who, for example, rejected the ban on students' wearing headscarves at the university. He initiated disciplinary procedures against quite a number of people; a lot of them lost their jobs. The office of public prosecutors launched investigations in April 2005; his house was searched on July 14, and he was arrested on October 14. Three days before he was arrested, Hüseyin Çelik, the former minister of education from the ruling AK Party and a prominent member of the Kurdish Buruki clan, arrived in Van. Two days after the arrest, he left again.

The government of Erdoğan sided with the regional will to self-assertion; the state apparatus, however, sided with the rector who had been arrested. The chairman of the Higher Education Board (YÖK) at the time, the stalwart Kemalist Erdoğan Teziç, visited his colleague in prison, together with all rectors in Turkey. After their return, the then-President Sezer welcomed the group demonstrably in Ankara. Aşkın was released soon after; the conflict between center and periphery, however, continued.

This conflict has existed since Atatürk. The fraction that had capitulated to Atatürk in the first parliament had the majority in the Grand National Parliament (TBMM) in Ankara. They formed the nucleus of the later state elite. They were opposed by a heterogeneous fraction which historians today refer to as, the "second group," and which would have preceded the later Democratic Party, if they had not been dispelled so quickly. They were demanding something Atatürk did not want: a greater focus on Islam in the public space and a decentralization of the state; and furthermore, liberal economic and social politics.

The conflict between the center and the periphery also characterized the Ottoman Empire, mainly during the 19th century. But it panned out differently there than in the rest of central Europe. Mardin argues that there had also been collisions of the dominant center with the powers of the periphery, between nobility and the cities, the citizens and the industrial workers. But every collision led to a further integration of the periphery with the center.

Unfortunately, these two sides never fully reconciled. During the Ottoman Empire, the sultan himself controlled bureaucracy and the army; no part of the bureaucracy was in the hands of independent regional lords. A bureaucrat was even a "kul," a servant of the sultan, at least until the reign of Sultan Mahmud II (1785–1839). He did not pay taxes and only served his lord, who also owned all of the land in the empire. The army, the backbone of the Ottoman Empire, even gave the whole state apparatus its military nature; it played a primary role in state affairs. This apparatus was referred to as *pars pro toto*, until the 17th century, when it became "askeriye," or the "soldiers' caste."

Two cultures opposed each other: the civilization of the Ottoman city, and the Anatolian province, with its peasants. The city represented order; the province, with its confusing diversity of ethnicities and religious practices, suggested impending chaos and rebellion. A refined urban culture evolved in the city, influenced by the municipal and courtly culture of the Seljuks and Persia. The modernization of the education system gave the urban elite new options, which remained mostly inaccessible to the Anatolian province. Thus, a bureaucratic elite emerged. The elegant Efendi, who put himself at the service of his state and let himself be led by it, became its prototype. While these options remained inaccessible for the people who lived in the periphery, the Islamic scholars were their most important source of knowledge. The Ottoman urbanites, therefore, increasingly attributed these religious scholars—who played a minor role in the city—as part of the dangerous periphery. The people who lived in the cities and their isolated elites developed more of a man-centered, secular life style, especially in the last two centuries of the empire; the people who lived in the Anatolian province, however, increasingly searched for their salvation in Islam. Thus, before the Republic was even founded, the provinces had the reputation of being a "refuge of religious action." Their kind of Islam was considered to be as backward as the people who lived there.

The cultural alienation between the rulers and the ruled increased from one century to the next. It comes as no surprise that the periphery repeatedly rebelled against the arrogance of the Empire's urban center. They also defended themselves against the domination of the Young

Turks, from 1908 to 1918, whose efforts towards uniformity and centralization were increasingly robbing the provinces of their independence. These defenses were without avail.

When Atatürk ascended to power, he made use of the powerful central state which had been developed by the Ottomans and then given a further boost by the Young Turks during his cultural revolution. The center of political power had shifted from Istanbul to Ankara. And there, Atatürk was confronted with the "uncivilized" and "unruly" periphery. He had access to the most powerful instruments the state had at its disposal to control them: the military, the judiciary and the bureaucracy, as well as the Republican People's Party, which served as the arm of the state in politics.

## Not all Turks acquiesce

Initially Kemalism, which represented the totality of Atatürk's principles, was liberating. Rarely has there been a comparable modernization episode in all of history. That is why the Grand National Assembly of November 24, 1934, bestowed upon President Mustafa Kemal the family name Atatürk, "Father of the Turks." His speeches and sayings became part of Kemalism, which is "Atatürkçülük" in Turkish. This served as the state's foundation for modernization, without compromise. But soon, Kemalism became an authoritarian ideology which prescribed the state from above, enforcing it against all resistance—a straightjacket that constricted a society that was growing from below, giving it no room to unfold.

And so the history of Turkey became a history of conflicts with the groups which felt rejected. New groups kept rising up against the Kemalist state ideology. Every conflict questioned a taboo of the Republic; everyone challenged the Kemalist Project. The conservative Muslims no longer wanted to come to terms with the fact that the state and its monopoly on religious affairs was pushing them out of the public space, and that trying to impinge upon the diversity of religious beliefs would curtail religious practices; the Kurds rose—to this day—against Turkish nationalism, which excludes them and does not give them the right to be an ethnic group; the left asked whether there would not be any strife in Turkish society and whether everything must be directed at what the state prescribed; the liberals opposed the fiction of a closed homogeneous society.

This modernization was met with resistance early on. Already, in November, 1924, former officers from the War of Independence had gathered around Ali Fuad Cebesoy and Rauf Orbay, and established the "Progressive Republican Party," with the approval of Atatürk. They wanted to subjugate the state to the sovereignty of the people, and would have become a liberal alternative to the state-supporting Republican People's Party (CHP). But the party was already outlawed by June, 1925. After the rebellion of the Kurdish Sheikh Said, in February, 1925, the state relentlessly attacked all opposition. From 1925 to 1938, there were a total of 17 rebellions started by Kurds, conservative Muslims, or both groups.

After multiple-party democracy had been introduced following the Second World War, the supporters of the Kemalist state were faced with new dangers. The conservative rural population represented the demographic majority, and for the first time, the government. The military's mission was repeatedly in danger of not being able to maintain its modernization, which had been ordered from above, and they toppled three governments with coups d'etats: a "correctional revolution" on May 27, 1960, in order to reestablish the Kemalist principles, which the conservative government of Adnan Menderes, with its free market economy and allowance Islam in the public space, had infringed upon; then, on March 12, 1971, the "Memorandum," which toppled the conservative Demirel government that had also gained support from the rural population; and finally, on September 12, 1980, to break the political blockade in parliament and to end the street-fights between the nationalist "right wingers" and the communist "left wingers."

After the military coup d'etat of 1980, the traumas of the first decade of the Republic returned: "separatism" (*bölücülük*) and the "religious reactionaryism or backwardness" (*irtica*). Until 1999, ethnic strife kept the country on tenterhooks, and from 1984 on, it forced the separatist Kurdistan Workers' Party (PKK) into conflict with the state.

In the late nineties, the focus shifted to the victories of the Islamist Welfare Party, and the danger of a religious reaction. With its "soft, postmodern" coup of February 28, 1997, the military initiated the resignation of the Erbakan government.

Ten years later, the army stepped in again. First, it wanted to prevent the election of Foreign Minister Gül as president of state, issuing a memorandum on April 27, 2007, and then launching its largest cross-border operation since 1999 by bombing the PKK targets in Northern Iraq.

The founders of the Republic had tried to formulate a systematic state policy. They summarized the principles of Kemalism, which had been named after Mustafa Kemal Atatürk, in the aforementioned "six principles" (a.k.a. "six arrows"; see also the section, titled *The Dogma of the Elite* in Chapter One). After the reforms of Turgut Özal in the eighties, these principles largely disappeared from the public discussion. The state elites were never able to hide that, despite state policy—which conjured up the unity of state and society, and the homogeneity of that society— the society had been deeply divided for decades.

The prospect of an EU membership created the opportunity for one of the widest-reaching consensuses: the vast majority of people saw it as a means for the democratization of the state apparatus. The Kurds were hoping for cultural autonomy in the course of the EU process, and Muslims for more religious freedom. At the same time, the secularists saw the secular character of the republic as the "common legal vested rights" of the member states (acquis communautaire) that would exclude the introduction of the Islamic law, and the Turkish nationalists saw the territorial integrity of the country being guaranteed with an EU membership. The EU process presented an opportunity to terminate the traumas of the republic democratically, and to correct its birth defects. The further the goal of an EU membership moved into the distance, the more support the PKK, which was ready to resort to more violence, and the more the military interfered with day-to-day politics.

Once more, the Kemalist national state perceived certain groups as "the enemy from within": practicing Muslims, the Kurds, the Leftists and the Liberals, supplemented by the non-Muslim minorities. At the same time, the state was threatened by globalization from the outside. While the European Union promotes and rewards globalization, prying open state-oriented structures and enforcing civil society, Turkey's inclusion into the global economy pushes the state back and strengthens private companies. The "inner" and "outer" enemies both question the Kemalist modernization project in which all actions emanate from the state, and which places all actions at the service of this state.

The state knew how to defend itself from the "inner dangers." The military took over directly three times. In 1997, it toppled a government in a postmodern coup without staging a military intervention; most recently, in April, 2007, it threatened the Erdoğan government. The judiciary at the army's side outlawed all parties that deviated from the Kemalist modernization project. There is not a single country in Europe where more parties have been outlawed than in Turkey. Furthermore, retired officers and policemen often establish shady, semi-legal paramilitary units, without any transparency whatsoever, under the illusion that they are "protecting" the state their way by eliminating "inner enemies."

This practice is not new, either. "Teşkilât-ı Mahsûsa" was an infamous special unit during the Ottoman Empire, established by the War Ministry in 1903 to combat Arabic separatism and Western imperialism, and, after 1913, the separatists in the Balkans. Naturally, it was also used against the Armenians, the implication being that they were collaborating with the Empire's arch enemy, Russia. "Teşkilât-ı Mahsûsa" took all those to task whom they suspected of opposing their state. They tortured and killed them. Everything remained secret, including the financing of the special unit, which supposedly included 3,000 armed men, and which even fought enemies abroad. During the Ottoman Empire, "Hamidiye Regimenter," which was also paramilitary, had suppressed rebellions in Diyarbakır and Erzurum, in 1905 and 1907, respectively. The regiments were similar to those special units that the Republic employed in the late 20th century to fight against the PKK. The founders and upholders of the state believed they were threatened, a belief which persists today. The immunity of civil servants was not revoked from criminal prosecution until 1999, in the context of EU reforms—a decision that has partially been rolled-back recently. Today, the representatives of the state fear that their state could be weakened, and they protect it fiercely, with all the means that the state has at its disposal.

# The State and Its Elite

## The military as founder and guarantor

The military sees itself as the father and guardian of modern Turkey, and not without reason: Atatürk and his generals won the War of Independence against the European occupiers. They founded the republic, and with the help of an authoritarian education dictatorship, Atatürk oriented it along what he thought was the civilization of the West. The six principles that were to shape his republic included, for instance, "Republicanism," "Laicism," "Nationalism" and "Statism"; but not democracy and human rights. Hitler, Stalin, Mussolini, and Franco were Atatürk's contemporaries. Atatürk distinguished himself from them because he had a civilizing goal for his republic. In many aspects his republic was more advanced than European democracies, for example, in terms of women's equality. But a real democracy is not what the successful General Kemal Atatürk had in mind, like his successors. Democratically elected politicians have the will of their voters in mind. The generals, however, do not trust the people, and thus politicians. They claim that if they gave them free reign, the result would be "Kurdish separatism" and "religious reactionaryism," the first endangering the central state, the latter, Laicism.

The generals, therefore, have added a new level to democratic politics: state policy. Axiomatically and indivisibly, they summarize what democratic politics cannot touch and where it has no leeway. This includes maintaining the central state and the rejection of any kind of decentralization, hanging on to rigid, authoritarian laicism, and rejecting the freedom of religious exercise, keeping religiousness out of the public space.

The issue of Cyprus is also part of the state policy in which the generals do not want to move even one step towards a compromise with the Greek-Cypriots. That is why 3,000 soldiers remain stationed on the island. On the one hand, the army does not want to give up Cyprus to be able to protect the Turkish motherland. On the other hand, it sees itself as a protective power of Turkish-Cypriots who were repeatedly subjected to massacres by the nationalist Greek-Cypriots before the island gained independence in 1963, and until the intervention of the Turkish army in 1974.

The parliament and the government embody democratically legitimized politics. However, the central state comprises those institutions which defend the foundations of the state on behalf of the state's policies. Until the contested election of Abdullah Gül as president on August 28, 2007, state politics claimed the office of the president for itself. In addition, it created authoritarian institutions such as the National Security Council (MGK), which eventually turned out to be a consultative body with a civilian majority in 2003, the powerful Higher Education Council (YÖK), and the State Security Courts (DGM), which were finally abolished in 2004.

Whoever has created the state and sees it as his property is not likely to hand it over lightly. Whoever serves within its institutions is convinced that he alone represents the true will of the Turkish nation, with the order of being allowed to educate and guide them from above, as well as watching over the elected representatives. The range of democracy can only be as great as the generals, the guards of state politics, allow. And yet, the majority of Turks are proud of their army. They are usually proud of supposedly being a nation of horseback riders and soldiers. A thousand years ago, they had advanced from Central Asia to Anatolia in equestrian groups that resembled cavalries more than a federal association. For a long time, Europe had been afraid of the Ottoman Army. Arabian rulers employed Turkish mercenaries for their safety, and as bodyguards. The Ottomans later changed and became infantry units created from devshirme soldiers.

The army is still an important symbol of national unity. Within the state protocol, their representatives are higher than in any other country in Europe. Holding the fifth highest rank, the Chief of the General Staff immediately follows that of the Prime Minister and comes right before the Minister of Defense. When the elected Mayor of Ankara has a reception in Ankara, in terms of protocol, he is outranked by the appointed Governor of the Province (who is elected not by the direct popular vote but by the cabinet decision, based on a proposal from the Ministry of the Interior, with the final approval of the President of the Republic).

The Turkish Army is the second largest army in NATO, and in Turkey it is the guarantor of continuity. This is ensured by the cadet schools where young recruits are raised with the awareness of belonging to elite which, unlike the civil institutions of the country, stand for efficiency and integrity. This elite leads and defends the Republic against enemies from without and within, and the concept of oneself as being better than civilians is more than just conceit. During the late Ottoman Empire, the education standard that military academies offered was already higher and more progressive than any other school. Prussian generals, particularly Colmar Freiherr von der Goltz (1843–1916), were largely responsible for their reorganization. These German generals made sure that the military academies provided the most up-to-date technological and scientific expertise available. Even today, when compared, it is the military academies that train their students to think more than any other Turkish school, albeit within a strict positivistic ratio.

On March 13 of every year you can hear the name "Mustafa Kemal" during the morning roll call, to which all cadets reply, "Here!" in unison. This is the moment when every single person physically becomes Atatürk; the commitment to Atatürk unites everyone. His battle is theirs: against religious reactionaryism and against Kurdish separatism. March 13 is the anniversary of the inclusion of Atatürk into the military academy. He came from humble origins, but the Ottoman army was open to the intelligent and ambitious young man.

Not much has changed about that. Most prospective officers are from the cities in the provinces, and from the lower middle class. A military caste that recruits its new cadre from within itself did not exist during the Ottoman Empire, or during the Republic. These cadets, mainly from the middle class families in the provinces, acquire an esprit de corps in the military academies; they are oriented along the axioms of Atatürk, which forms an officer corps that has become the guarantor for the continuity of the Turkish army. No other institution in Turkey is as closed and homogeneous. The children of city dwellers become entrepreneurs and professors, doctors and lawyers. The young cadets make less money than they do, but instead, they have officers' clubs in the most beautiful places in Turkey. And above all, they are certain that they embody the highest Turkish virtues, including efficiency and integrity, discipline and obedience, achievement and patriotism.

This self-concept becomes the mandate to intervene when what was entrusted is in danger. When there is an acute crisis or the threat that Atatürk's heritage could be revised, then the military has a whole range of instruments at its disposal. They can step in directly and depose a government, as they did in 1960, 1971, and 1980. They can provide civil politicians with "recommendations," which no government would dare ignore. The government of the Islamist Necmettin Erbakan toppled over the "recommendations" of February 28, 1997. They can mobilize public opinion by merely stating opinions, and they can trigger an impulse to achieve their goal.

The generals do not want to govern. They only want to make sure that politics remain on the "right path." When there is an emergency, they pull the emergency brake with a coup d'etat, as on September 12, 1980. Thirty people had been killed in the months before that, during daily street fights between left wing and right wing extremists. The Chief of the General Staff, Kenan Evren, later said that they had waited eleven months for the right moment to step in. In retrospect the deposed Prime Minister Demirel wondered how the street terror could have stopped overnight, suggesting that the left and the right could have been master-minded from one and the same source. At any rate, it is a fact that psychologically, the army had prepared the coup of 1960 along those lines: launching rumors in advance, which piqued emotions—including stories that the police had supposedly put body parts of teenagers through a meat grinder.

With every coup, the military invoked its legal obligations. What they meant was the "Law pertaining to actions of the Internal Services" (İç Hizmet Kanunu), which was enacted in the 1961 constitution written after the coup. It had then become the license to intervene. Article 2 stated the following: "The military is obligated to teach the art of war and to apply it to protect the Turkish homeland, its independence, and the Republic." Article 35 was even more concrete in serving as the basis for future coups; it stated: "It is the duty of the military to protect and observe the Turkish homeland which is defined by the constitution." It has recently been amended as follows: "Turkish Military Forces is responsible for protecting the Turkish homeland against external dangers and threats, ensuring the protection and strengthening of the army forces in a deterring way, performing the duties abroad as assigned by Turkish Parliament, and helping to provide international peace."

Obviously, none of the coups solved even one of the core problems of the Republic. Quite the contrary, they kept pushing back the country's development in the country's attempt to solve its inner contradictions. Ultimately coups taught politicians to be irresponsible, because they knew that the army would step in as a corrective. The last direct coup, in 1980, was also a throwback for the country. New anti-terror laws focused on intellectuals in particular, who would not acquiesce in the face of state power; thus, they were brought to trial in the State Security Courts that were established under the 1982 coup constitution. Special units, dominated by the right wing "Grey Wolves," were set up to fight against the Kurdish PKK; Kurdish nationalism was further incited by the continued renaming of old Kurdish villages and towns. The ban on worker's strikes was expanded, and the new university commission (YÖK) removed all autonomy from the universities.

The new constitution of 1982 defined these and many other restrictions. Like the constitutions of 1924 and 1961, it had not been drawn up by elected parliaments, but commissioned by the military. The national referendum, during which the constitution of 1982 had been accepted, was preceded by a campaign in which criticizing the design was put under penalty. Before they returned to their barracks, the generals wanted to create an order that would not force them to intervene every ten years. The new constitution therefore converted the National Security Council (MGK) into an institution with a direct impact on politics, via the military, equally represented by politicians and generals. The preamble of the new constitution stated that the "Operation of September 12, 1980," had served to save the "existence of the holy Turkish state." In 1995, the word "holy" (*kutsal*) was replaced by "sublime" (*yüce*). What remained unchanged was the spirit of the constitution. The state continues to remain at the center and is based on the assumption that citizens must serve the state. A large number of the representatives of the state continue to act in this spirit.

Meanwhile, the first "free elections" after the coup did not develop according to the likes of the generals. After every coup, the Sovereign had elected the party which he considered to be the antipode of the military. This happened in 1983, too. The military had expressly warned of electing Turgut Özal's "Motherland Party" (ANAP). However, Özal was victorious. By opening the country, liberalizing the economy, and removing taboos from politics, he brought forth the second turning point since the founding of the Republic. He answered the two great challenges of the Republic—the Kurds and Islam—not with repression, but with more democracy.

The pragmatic Özal, who was from Malatya, in central east Anatolia, challenged the military like no other politician before or after him. He attended military parades in shorts and a baseball cap, and he prevailed in a power struggle with the military over the participation of Turkey in the war to liberate Kuwait, in November, 1990. It was not Özal who resigned, but the chief of the general staff, Necip Torumtay. Özal died in 1993. The former Prime Minister Süleyman Demirel was his successor as president. He had been toppled as Prime Minister in 1971 and 1980, and had learned his lesson. Under his leadership, Turkish politics became streamlined again, and no one had the courage to show the military the necessary limits which are present in a democracy.

Mesut Yılmaz, who had been Prime Minister several times for a few months, tried it once, without success. In the spring of 1998, he headed a coalition government once again. In March, 1998, he sharply attacked the leaders of the army in a rant, saying that he had not given them the order to proceed against the religious reactionaries and that he had installed a department in his presidential office that was investigating suspicious actions. Therefore, there would be no further need for "The West Study Group" (BÇG), a clandestine group formed within the military to contribute to the staging of a well-planned coup.

This secret organization within the Turkish general staff had initially been commissioned to gather incriminating material, which could be used in a criminal investigation against Turkey's "enemies from within." After the government of Erbakan had been ousted, the focus was primarily on the "religious reactionaries."

"The West Study Group" was furtive; it was probably dissolved in late 2002. The "Republican Study Group" (CÇG) replaced it within the Secret Service of the Gendarmerie. The National Security Council had also met once a month, in secret, for a long time. One of the great reforms of Erdoğan's government, in 2003, was to diminish the generals' leverage to be active in politics by truncating the Council and turning it into an advisory board. This was accomplished by placing a civilian at the head of the National Security Council, in August, 2004. The position was given to career diplomat, Mehmet Yiğit Alpogan, who had been the Ambassador in Athens before; Alpogan replaced General Şükrü Sarıışık.

The reform of the National Security Council took a lot of Turks by surprise. They would have never imagined their glorious army capable of doing the things that were uncovered. First, there was the "Red Book"—the "Political Document pertaining to National Security." The chief of the general staff handed it to the new Prime Minster during the first meeting of the National Security Council. A retired general and earlier General Secretary of the National Security Council once said that when an elected official read the "Red Book" for the first time, they would revise their policies. On 27 narrow pages and 42 paragraphs, the "Red Book" spelled out the most important concepts of the military. They provided the General Secretary of the National Security Council with competencies which turned it into an inner power center of the Republic. The "Red Book" became the "secret constitution" of Turkey, and everyone involved had to remain silent about it. Its existence was further proof of the distrust of the state elite and the military towards the workings of society and democracy.

The Turkish public was shocked to realize that they had been subdued for decades with the help of psychological warfare. This had been the task of one of the four departments of the National Security Council, which were dissolved in 2004. All secret service information was collected and evaluated in a second department. The "Public Relations" department, in turn, was supposed to launch disinformation campaigns in order to "remove danger from within and without," and to protect the "territorial integrity of the state, its independence and the principles of the revolution of Atatürk."

The incident that took place in the small Kurdish town of Şemdinli, in November, 2005, also falls under the category of "psychological warfare." The number of assassinations in the Kurdish majority Southeastern region that were never solved is not known. But on November 9, a passerby caught an assassin after he had hurled a grenade into the bookstore of a well-known Kurdish intellectual. He was not killed, though a bystander was. The assassin, Veysel Ateş, a former member of the PKK who now was working for the Turkish State, had hoped to flee in a car waiting in the wings, in which Ali Kaya and Özcan İldeniz were sitting, two members of the gendarmerie, which is part of the army.

In the trunk of the car were more weapons and lists of people and plans specifying where they were to be assassinated. The intention of the assassins was obviously to use targeted murders to once again set into motion the spiral of violence between the Turkish military and the Kurdish PKK, in order for clandestine interest groups to benefit from the growing instability in the region.

The public prosecutor, Ferhat Sarıkaya, wanted to expose the connections of the assassins to high-ranking officers and was put in charge of the task. Sarıkaya also wanted to prosecute Chief of the General Staff, Yaşar Büyükanıt, who had referred to one of the arrested members of the gendarmerie—who is equipped by the army and active in those places where the police do not have outposts—as a "good chap," with whom he had spent time as commander of the army in the region. Sarıkaya received a dishonourable discharge for allegedly misusing his office with the intention of destabilizing the army in their war against terror. The accused were referred to a military court, which acquitted them in December, 2007.

According to Mithat Sancar, Professor for Public Law in Ankara, the army kept creating a sense of crisis, and in so doing, kept suggesting that they were indispensable. And indeed, the army was doing everything to step in front of the public with their immaculate olive green uniforms. And therefore, in public opinion polls, it is the institution that the public continues to trust the most. It ranks far ahead of parliament, parties, and politicians. However, for the first time, high-ranking officers were sentenced to prison terms for corruption and misconduct, regarding suspect bids, in 2005 and 2007: first the retired marine commander, İlhami Erdil, then the army general, Ethem Erdağı. In a representative survey conducted in May, 2007, 79% of Turkish journalists said that they trusted the Turkish army. It was by far the best approval rating any institution had. On the other hand, in November, 2006, another survey had determined that 58% of Turks rejected the notion that the army should involve itself in politics. Only 14.5% were in favor of it.

The military will only be able to keep a clean slate if it suppresses critics. In April, 2007, the news magazine, *Nokta,* which specialized in critical reporting about the army, was forced to close. The generals accused it of undermining the reputation of the institution. Yet *Nokta* had unearthed unheard of practices of the military: three cover stories, in the spring of

2007, kept the public mesmerized for weeks. First, *Nokta* reported that the army kept precise lists of journalists who were for and against them. The general staff did not issue a denial, but instead stated that the list was only a draft.

Then *Nokta* published excerpts from the electronic diary of the former Admiral, Özden Örnek. It was written in 2004, and in print, it comprised 2,000 pages. In it, Örnek describes how he had planned a coup against the government of Erdoğan that year. Şener Eruygur, the commander of the gendarmerie at the time, had organized coups—sometimes in parallel and sometimes separately—which no one had ever joined, because the chief of staff at the time, Hilmi Özkök, had opposed them. During the debate that accompanied the publication of the journals, Özkök said that it would probably be best if the matter was investigated. Örnek conceded that there had been a journal, but that he had deleted it—though obviously not all of it. Örnek was of the opinion that his honor had been violated, and he sued the magazine. However, no one sued this coup-crazy admiral for planning a coup against the elected government! Instead, soldiers who were part of the anti-terror unit stormed the publishing house of *Nokta* with a search warrant issued by the military court and confiscated everything in sight. One more edition was published. It reported on how the army intended to use the alleged civil society associations to corner the government, and maybe even topple it. Somewhat later, in late April, 2007, there were mass protests. Many of the civic associations which staged them were not even known to the civil servants who were responsible for them in the Ministry of the Interior, maybe because they had been founded spontaneously, or were fictitious. One of the organizers, however, was well-known: the "Kemalist Thought Association" (ADD). One of its two leaders was one of the generals behind the unrealized 2004 coup, Şener Eruygur.

The coup did not take place for a few reasons—because the United States had refused its support, because the Turkish press had not joined the generals, and because there had not been a call for help from the public, according to Alper Görmüş, the editor in chief of *Nokta*. Earlier coups had obviously been better prepared psychologically; now, the Turks no longer wanted to be "educated" and led by the army. Görmüş resigned after his newsroom was turned upside down. An investigation against him could result in a prison term of up to six years and eight months.

The editor, Ayhan Durgun, capitulated. He could no longer withstand the psychological warfare, and he stopped the magazine. The army received a few bruises, but was victorious over yet another "enemy from within."

The generals did not always have their focus on "the enemy from within" instead of the "enemy from without." From 2002 to 2006, the general staff had a chief whose nickname could have been, Citizen in Uniform. The four years during which Hilmi Özkök was in charge of the general staff almost completely overlapped with the first four years of the first AK Party government. It wasn't that Özkök liked Prime Minister Erdoğan and his party—in fact, he repeatedly criticized the government—but his critiques were more moderate than his predecessor, Büyükanıt.

This moderate criticism was hardly sufficient to satisfy the restless lower ranking officers. There had been a kind of unwritten agreement between Özkök and Erdoğan: neither of them fuelled the mood and the army retreated to shadows. Özkök respected the demarcation line that a democracy draws for the non-elected actors. He had kept a reign on the two coup-crazy generals in 2004, and publically, he promoted a new interpretation of Atatürk's philosophy and revised the curriculums of the military academies accordingly.

A few months before he left office, in March, 2006, Özkök asked the cadets of the Istanbul War Academy not to be biased and oppose others' opinions. He also told them that people whose opinions differed were not automatically a traitor to the homeland, but that everyone could benefit from a different opinion. No wonder there were people in the AK Party who saw Özkök as the successor to President Sezer, who was to leave office in May, 2007.

Özkök retired in August, 2006, and his successor, Yaşar Büyükanıt, restored the old order, but not without wanted, and unwanted, protection from the critics against Turkey joining the EU. The more remote the prospects of EU membership seemed, the less restraint Büyükanıt had to be subjected to. With him in charge, the army re-emerged on the political stage. When he assumed office in August, 2006, he let the people who wanted a different and more democratic republic know, without doubt, that their dream would never become reality as long as there was a military. Moreover, he announced additional measures in the battle against Kurdish "separatism" and against religious "reactionaries." "Neither the republic that the most sublime leader Atatürk founded will be reversed nor the country divided," said Büyükanıt.

In October 2006, he launched a well-orchestrated scenario for the coming elections of 2007. Initially, his service chiefs had conjured up various dangers facing the Republic. Then Sezer expressed that he witnessed religious reactionaries like he never had before. On October 2, Büyükanıt crowned this crescendo with a speech before the War Academy, in which he warned the electorate not to deviate from the path of laicism. Ultimately, he said, there were forces in the country who wanted to change course and give the term "laicism" a new definition. When Erdoğan met with the American president in the White House a few hours later, it was this cold fall wind from the Bosporus that he had at his back. The speeches of the generals and the President strongly resembled the memorandum of the generals on February 28, 1997, against Prime Minister Erbakan—a memorandum that ultimately forced him to resign. This time, however, the generals' announcement did not result in the same desired effect.

Büyükanıt issued another warning during his visit to Washington in February, 2007: that since its founding, the Republic had not faced a greater threat. If that is how it really was, then this meant that the military would have violated its obligatory duty of supervision. In order to correct this omission, "Anonymous" placed an explanation on the website of the general staff on April 27, 2007, shortly before midnight. The Parliament had met that afternoon for the first round of voting to elect a successor for President Sezer. The candidate of the ruling AK Party was Foreign Minister Abdullah Gül, whose wife wears a headscarf. The generals saw this as a threat to the Republic.

The army followed the situation with "care," the anonymous warning stated darkly. It further stated, "The military is firmly determined to fulfil the clear tasks defined by law." And then, Anonymous gave a reference to the "Internal Service Law," which was drafted after the 1960 coup in the 1961 Constitution, thus providing the basis for interventions in politics. That is how officers had reasoned after coups in the past.

The new memorandum only raised questions. Its style was bumpy, and Büyükanıt was thought of as a man of integrity who would not hide behind the anonymity of the internet. The memorandum was followed by mass protests against the government of Erdoğan, which was coordinated by the military's "Republican Work Force," as reported by the *Taraf* daily newspaper on June 7, 2008. To do this, it had established contact with 225 "civic" associations. What followed was a judgment of the Constitutional Court that prevented the election of Gül as president and new elections of the Parliament.Gül was, therefore, elected president only after the following election.

There were also other things one could read on the website of the general staff. The speeches of Russian President Vladimir Putin appeared on the website around the same time Büyükanıt visited Washington, in February, 2007. These speeches were viewed as signal that the general staff saw an alternative to the Western model, and also as an indication that there were sympathies in the officers' corps for an anti-democratic and authoritarian order patterned after Putin's Russia.

For outsiders the army continues to be a "black box," and its inside light can hardly be assessed. It is also difficult to determine the ideological leanings within the homogeneous officers' corps. Officially, the head of the army supports Turkey's EU membership. But the military is decidedly against preconditions that result from the Copenhagen Accession Criteria, for example granting the Kurds more rights.

During the term of the General Staff Hilmi Özkök (2002–2006), the criticism voiced by the army had been less strident. The Iraq War had significantly worsened the relations of Turkey, especially that of the military, with the United States. Washington did not forgive the Turkish military for not being forcibly in favor of transiting American soldiers through Turkey. The government of the AK Party had proposed granting the transit, but the majority of the Parliament turned it down. 71 members of the AK Party and all members of the CHP, which is affiliated with the army, voted against it. However, they did open the Turkish airspace for American fighter planes. The presence of American soldiers in Iraq, however, prevented the Turkish Army from engaging with the Kurdish PKK across the border. In the eyes of the military, the United States lost its charm as an alternative to the EU. This downturn in the relationship with Washington made it easier for Erdoğan's government to implement important reforms, such as limiting the authority of the National Security Council and disclosing the military's expenditures.

Yet the transatlantic American faction continues to be strong. Most high-ranking officers continue to fulfill an important part of their training in the United States. They do not, however, project their sympathy for America to Europe. The "Sèvres Complex" continues to be present in the minds of these officers, according to which the West continues to pursue the division of Turkey, as stated in the 1920 Treaty of Sèvres. There is a third faction of officers beside them seing Turkey as an independent regional power. They sympathize with Putin's Russia, they work together with Israel for arms, and they view Iran as a potential partner, in the long-term, once it has gotten rid of the mullahs. The pro-European fraction has had a hard time since Özkök has left. They see an EU membership as completing Atatürk's vision, because Atatürk had said that there is only one civilization: the European one. A political role for the military, however, is incompatible with European democracy. The generals are therefore faced with the decision to either give up their political privileges, or the dream of Europe. Nothing indicates that they will voluntarily renounce the custodianship of modern Turkey and hand it over to democratic institutions.

## Justice as legal protection

The armed forces create security by keeping enemies of the state—both within and without—in check. The judiciary at its side sees itself as an unarmed power. It also wants national security—or in other words, to defend the State. When in doubt, it will make pronouncements in State's favor. Constitutions and laws facilitate the work for judges, lawyers, and prosecutors. For a long time, they did not protect the basic rights of the individual of the state, but the state of the individuals. Independent constitutional judges criticized Turkey as being a "juristocracy," in which the sovereignty of the appointed judges was above that of the people and the parliament.

During the EU accession process, which began in 2001, legal understanding took a turn towards reform. The new penal code, which went into effect on April 1, 2005, places the protection of the individual above that of the state. People who torture in order to make the alleged enemies of the state talk can now be punished severely. The new Civil Code, which went into effect on November 22, 2001, puts men and women on an equal footing. The derogatory term "karı" for woman is no longer in official use, but simply woman (*kadın*). Women's rights are now above those that claim to protect the "honor of the family."

The legal paragraphs have changed; the mentality has remained the same. Therefore, the first civil general secretary of the National Security Council, the career diplomat Alpogan, who was in office from 2004 to 2007, urgently demanded further training for judges and prosecutors. A lot of Turks see the judiciary as an obstacle to the implementation of the reforms that were decided on by Parliament. New laws are not applied, and quite a few representatives have tried to stall the reform process. It will take time to change this mentality, which is fixated on the state. Until now the recruiting mechanism of the judiciary made sure that there was esprit de corps, and that those who felt obligated to defend the state and guarantee its safety were the ones who advanced.

Whoever broke this unwritten rule was banned. This is what happened to the public prosecutor, Ferhat Sarıkaya, who also mentioned the name of the chief of the general staff, Büyükanıt, in his investigations into the assassination attempt in the Kurdish village of Şemdinli. Before that, he had initiated the arrest of the strictly Kemalist university rector Aşkın. The reason Nuri Ok, who was the Senior Prosecutor of the Republic and the chairman of the High Council of Judges and Prosecutors (HSYK), gave for the dishonorable discharge of Sarikaya was that he had misused his position for politicization. The chairman of the Attorney's Association of Ankara, Vedat Ahsen Coşar, admitted that the decision had been made following the suggestion of the military. Sacit Kayasu was another prosecutor who received a dishonorable discharge. In 2000, he had prepared a court case against the generals who participated in the coup of 1980. The prosecution wanted to make the generals accountable because, among other things, they had ordered the arrest of 650,000 people and the surveillance of 1.6 million people.

Sarıkaya, Kayasu, and others were fired because they dared to question the inviolability of the state, seeing that they were the defenders of the state who, for a long time, were on equal footing with the judges in Turkish courts. As opposed to the prosecutors, the defense was not on equal footing, but lower—which is where Sarıkaya and Kayasu were relegated. This was one, among many things, that an EU commission, under the leadership of the Swedish judge, Kjell Brörjnberg, criticized in a February, 2006, report on the Turkish justice system. The report suggested 48 changes, including that the public prosecutors were no longer to have their offices in the building where the court was; that they should use a different door than the judge to enter the courtroom; that they should sit at the same level as the defense attorneys, across from the judges; and that they remain in the courtroom when the judges sojourn to reach a verdict.

The Turkish justice system is not independent; it is political. The constitutional court gave a taste of that when it annulled the first ballot of the parliament's attempt to elect a new president in 2007. The opposition parties in parliament, especially the Republican People's Party (CHP) and a number of small factions, had boycotted the ballot, on April 27, in order to prevent the election of Abdullah Gül as the President of the Republic. The same day, the CHP filed suit at the Constitutional Court (AYM). The idea for the complaint of unconstitutionality was provided by the senior prosecutor, Sabih Kanadoğlu, at the Cassation Court (Yargıtay). He was the first one to have said that the last means to prevent the election of a member of the AK Party to the presidency would be to boycott the election, and that the Constitutional Court would declare that two thirds of all parliamentarians would have to be present for the first round of elections.

That personal view is exactly what the court declared on May 1. This last minute necessity for a quorum of 367 parliamentarians, however, had not been achieved in 1989, when Turgut Özal had been elected, and not in 1993, during the election of Süleyman Demirel, and also not in 2000, when Ahmet Necdet Sezer was elected. But it was supposed to apply for Gül, because the state did not want Gül. The military, however, backed the application of the CHP, and Sezer demanded that all judges come to see him to explain that it was their responsibility to vote for the petition. It should be noted here that Sezer already knew most of the constitutional judges well, either from when he himself had been the head of the Constitutional Court (AYM), or because he had appointed them. This is mainly because of the fact that the appointment of the leading lawyers and judges was one of the responsibilities of the president. It was not until the victory of the AK Party, on July 22, 2007, that Sezer admitted that it had been a mistake to prevent Gül's being elected.

Tülay Tuğcu, the then head of the Constitutional Court (AYM), had visited Sezer at the time. In 2001, her vote had contributed to banning the Islamist Virtue Party (FP), and two years later, the Kurdish Party (DEHAP). She had supported constitutional cases against the abolishment of the death penalty. She was of the opinion that the law that gave the Kurds a minimal right to learn their language was as unconstitutional as the one that would have permitted non-Muslim minorities to purchase real estate. In August, 2001, she had warned the politician Erdoğan that, as a result of his conviction for a "thought crime," he would not be allowed to found a party. Tuğcu, who came from a classic civil service family in Ankara, referred to herself as an "enlightened democrat capable of action."

Defending democracy is not the focus of the judiciary; rather, it is the protection of the state. To this purpose, judges and prosecutors outlaw parties, they forbid political activities, and limit the freedom of expression. Since 1968, the Constitutional Court (AYM) has banned more than two dozen parties. They were exclusively parties of the Islamists, the Kurds, and the extreme leftists, and the decisions were exclusively due to the expression of opinions of individual politicians. During the nineties, a large number of parties were banned. Most of them returned quickly, under a new name. In June, 2001, during a visit to Ankara, the (then) German Federal Minister of Justice, Herta Däubler-Gmelin, criticized the prerequisite to ban a party and the associated restrictions on the freedom of expression. A change in the constitution, in 2002, made the requirements for a ban considerably more restrictive. Since that time, expressing an opinion does not suffice for a ban.

From 1991 to 1994, the Constitutional Court (AYM) banned several Kurdish parties: the Labor Party of the People (HEP), the Freedom and Equality Party (ÖZEP), the Freedom and Democracy Party (ÖZDEP) and, on June 16, 1994, the Democracy Party (DEP). HEP was banned because its representative, Leyla Zana, repeated part of her oath in Kurdish at the Grand National Assembly of Turkey in 1991; the DEP was suspected of having relations with the PKK, for which the DEP issued a denial. In 1994, the Kurdish politician, Murat Bozlak, founded People's Democracy Party (HADEP). It won 37 offices for mayor, in April, 1999, in regional elections, including in Diyarbakır. At the time, court proceedings to ban the party had already been continuing for three months. There had been several investigations against HADEP after party congresses, either because the Turkish flag had not been raised or because the Turkish national anthem had not been sung during the congresses. They were also alleged to have been in contact with the PKK. The party cadre, however, declared that they had merely demanded more rights for the Kurds living in Turkey.

HADEP was banned, and its gap was filled by the Democratic People's Party (DEHAP) that was founded in October, 1997, and which had been on hold. Sabih Kanadoğlu, the Senior Prosecutor at the Court of Cassation (Yargıtay), had already introduced the proceedings against HADEP and later against DEHAP. Before the Constitutional Court proclaimed its decision, on May 17, 2005, DEHAP merged with the newly founded Democratic Society Party (DTP). In November, 2007, Kanadoğlu's successor, Abdurrahman Yalçınkaya, initiated the proceedings to ban DTP and combined it with a political ban against 221 members of the party for the duration of five years. The reason the senior prosecutor gave was that DTP was the "center of activities against the indivisible unity of the state with its country and its nation." Following the 2007 elections, 20 DTP delegates were in the Parliament.

Necmettin Erbakan's Islamists did not fare much better than the Kurdish parties. First, the National Order Party (MNP) was banned in 1971, then the National Salvation Party (MSP) in 1980; in 1998, it was the Welfare Party's (RP) turn, and in 2001, the Virtue Party (FP) was banned. The Felicity Party (SP), which was founded in 2001, had so little impact that it did not have to be banned.

The Constitutional Court (AYM) had banned the Virtue Party, by a count of eight votes to three, because of violations against the laicistic order of Turkey. Furthermore, the court stripped two of its deputies from their seats: Bekir Sobacı, because he had referred to the generals—who had initiated the postmodern coup against Prime Minister Erbakan on February 28, 1997—as being of bad stock (*sütü bozuk*); and also the valiant publicist, Nazlı Ilıcak, because she had defended her colleague, Merve Kavakçı, who had appeared in the Parliament in 1999 wearing a headscarf.

The constitutional judges also imposed a five-year political ban on Sobacı, Ilıcak, Kavakçı and two other members of the Parliament. Banning someone from politics is combined with the ban of their political party. But justice cannot always assert itself. They were not successful in banning Erdoğan from politics, to keep him at a distance. It started in 1997, when Erdoğan, who was still the Mayor of Istanbul, held a speech in Siirt, where his wife had been born. He quoted from a poem by the ideological father of Turkish nationalism, Ziya Gökalp: "The minarettes are our bayonets, the mosques are our barracks." In most countries, reciting poems is part of the freedom of expression, but in Turkey, this incident landed on the table of the court for state security. The State Security Court (DGM) in Diyarbakır sentenced Erdoğan, on April 12, 1998, to ten months in prison without probation for quoting this passage from a poem by Gökalp. It was based on section 312 of the Penal Code, which prosecutes "transgressions of opinion," i.e., "the incitement of the population point-ing to class, race, religion, confession or region." Erdoğan lost his office and another part of his sentence was a life-long ban on participating in poli-tics. In March 1999, Erdoğan started his prison sentence; four months later, he was released again.

During the EU reform process, the Turkish Parliament struck sec-tion 312 from the criminal code, but Erdoğan's criminal record remained untouched. The judiciary tried everything to stop the unstoppable rise of Erdoğan, who understood that he would only be able to be a politician in Turkey if the country adhered to European norms. As such, he turned to the European Court for Human Rights. He founded the AK Party in August, 2001, together with others—most of whom belonged to the mod-ernization faction of the banned Virtue Party, which had risen up against the party patriarch, Erbakan. Kanadoğlu, who was still the Senior Defense at the Court of Cassation (Yargıtay), presented his opinion to the Consti-tutional Court (AYM), which stated that Erdoğan should neither be allowed to found a party, or be in charge of one. On January 10, 2002, the court demanded that the AK Party strike Erdoğan from the list of their found-ing members. His lawyer, Hayati Yazıcı, commented sharply that other parties were the political rivals of the AK Party, and not Kanadoğlu and the Court of Cassation. On September 22, the High Election Council (YSK) denied Erdoğan the permission to be a candidate in any constituency refer-ring to the time he had spent in prison, and on October 19, the Constitu-tional Court (AYM) decided in favour of Kanadoğlu.

This is the burden with which Erdoğan entered the parliamentary elections of November 3, 2002. Proceedings to ban the party had also hov-ered above the AK Party, in case Erdoğan should not resign, but those proceedings were stopped. Erdoğan also turned the elections into a pleb-iscite on the ban on politics, and won triumphantly. On January 22, 2003, the court decided once more that Erdoğan did not fulfill the legal require-ments to be the head of a party. The next day, the AK Party stubbornly confirmed him as their head. There was yet another opportunity for

Erdoğan to be elected into the Parliament as the High Election Council annulled the election in the district of Siirt because of irregularities.

Before that decision, the new Parliament had already annulled the prison terms, which had been declared on the basis of paragraph 312, which had itself been rescinded. President Sezer vetoed the change, but that did not have any consequences. Senior Prosecutor Kanadoğlu, however, reasoned that people who did not fulfil the legal prerequisites for candidacy on November 3, could not be a candidate this time around, either. Other legal experts reasoned that 30 months after the general parliamentary elections, a retrospective election would be legal. But the tide seemed to have turned. For this one time, Kanadoğlu and his friends did not succeed. Erdoğan was a candidate in Siirt, won the seat, became a deputy, and in the Parliament, was elected Prime Minister of Turkey.

Erdoğan was already Prime Minister when another senior prosecutor, Nuh Mete Yüksel, had Erdoğan arrested because of the "attempted change of the laicist constitutional order." The State Security Court in Ankara, which Yüksel worked for, denied the application. The year before that, Yüksel had caused a sensation when he initiated proceedings against the offices of the German political foundation in Turkey. The charges were based on a book by the dubious publicist, Hablemitoğlu, who was Professor of History for the Revolution of Atatürk in Ankara. His book insinuated that the German foundation spied for Germany, and that they had been commissioned to undermine the unity of the Republic of Turkey. They were unable to prove the insinuations, and the lawsuit was stopped. When Hablemitoğlu was murdered on December 18, Kanadoğlu, one of the senior prosecutors, grieved that Turkey had lost a selfless son, and Yüksel, another senior prosecutor, cried: "Laicist and democratic Turkey, bound to the principles and the revolution of Atatürk, will live to eternity!"

What Nuh Mete Yüksel was unable to finish was accomplished by Abdurrahman Yalçınkaya. In one of his last official acts, lame duck Sezer, who was already in the process of leaving, had appointed Yalçınkaya senior prosecutor at the Court of Cassation (Yargıtay), against the recommendation of the senior judges. On March 14, 2008, he initiated the proceedings to ban the AK Party by handing over 17 binders. The application, which was referred to by critics as a coup de justice, also demanded a political ban against 71 politicians of the AK Party, among them President Gül and Prime Minister Erdoğan. Yalçınkaya declared that he had decided to take this step because the AK Party was preparing an Islamist state, and he wanted to stop them before it happened. The pinnacle of the 61 charges against Erdoğan was his statement issued after the verdict, on June 29, 2004, of the European Court for Human Rights, pertaining to the wearing of headscarves, in which he stated that a secular court did not have the permission to pass judgments on religion. The accusation was that when Gül was Foreign Minster, he tolerated that Turkish diplomats abroad supported the building of schools which were financed by people who were inspired by the ideas of the Turkish preacher, Fethullah Gülen. The respected, liberal constitutional legal expert, Ergun Özbudun, commented that it would not be possible to ban a party based on either of the reasons, and he instead recommended banning the population and getting a new one from the universe.

Two weapons that the judiciary applies—banning parties and politicians—hurt parties and politicians. They use their third weapon to take aim at intellectuals who deviate from Kemalist state politics. Recent reforms have made that harder, but there is still sufficient latitude. On June 20, 2003, the Parliament removed Article 8 of the Anti-Terror Law, and Paragraphs 159 and 312 of the Criminal Code, which were the paragraphs that restricted freedom of thought. However, the delegates replaced the latter one with the new Paragraph 301. It penalized the "Denigration of Turkishness" and the institutions of the Turkish state. One addition was to ensure that criticism in government bodies, which were not intended as insults, would not be penalized. After further abuse by Turkish lawyers and judges, pressure to strike or modify the paragraph grew from governments in the EU and thinkers in Turkey. Due to the resistance of the nationalist wing in the government, the Government Spokesman, Cemil Çiçek, had to explain that there was no concensus in the cabinet for the reformation of the paragraph, in January, 2008.

A section like the one numbered 301 is also quite common in Western democracies. However, in Turkey, the interpretation of this section by judiciaries follows a different mentality, one that is restrictive. Radical-nationalist lawyers, such as Kemal Kerinçsiz, have since initiated several dozen proceedings against intellectuals on the basis of this section. The first victim of the plaintiff Kerinçsiz was the Armenian-Turkish intellectual, Hrant Dink. On October 6, 2005, he was sentenced to six month long suspended prison term because of denigration of Turkishness.

Dink's offense—he was known for his linguistic humour—was an article in February, 2004, in the Armenian-Turkish bilingual weekly, *Agos,* where he criticized the Armenian Diaspora because it demanded exchanging, and "poisoned Turkish blood with pure Armenian blood" from Armenians in Turkey. While even the public prosecutor thought this wordplay had to do with the Armenian Diaspora, the judges did not. Second proceedings against Dink started on February 9, 2005, because he had said in a talk show, "Instead of saying: 'I am a Turk, honest and hard-working,' I prefer to say: 'I am a citizen of Turkey [Türkiyeli], honest and hard-working.'" At that point, the picture of Dink was already circulating on the web pages of radical-nationalist circles. On January 19, 2007, he was shot to death by one of these fanatics out in the street.

The murder alarmed the intellectuals who had accompanied Dink to his court appointments and against whom proceedings were also being conducted on the basis of paragraph 301. The Nobel Prize laureate, Orhan Pamuk, had also been charged, first because of his statement that one million Armenians were killed in Turkey during the First World War, and then for saying that the Turkish Army was a greater danger to democracy than the AK Party of Erdoğan. The first statement was to have demeaned Turkishness; the second one was supposedly an insult against the institutions of the Turkish state. On January 23, 2006, the district court in Istanbul halted the proceedings against Pamuk.

But there were still more than two dozen proceedings based on the same paragraph against other prominent liberal journalists, including İsmet Berkan, Murat Belge, Haluk Şahin, Hasan Cemal, and Erol Katırcıoğlu. They had criticized a court's decision preventing a university to hold a scientific conference on the Armenian issue. Furthermore, a publisher is being prosecuted because he had published the bestseller, *The Fairies of Izmir,* by the Greek poet Mara Meimardi, which describes the life of minorities in the formerly multi-ethnic city. The writer, Zülfü Kışanak, was also sentenced because of a book about the villages which the Turkish army had evacuated and destroyed during the fight against the PKK. Before that, in October, 2005, the Istanbul publisher, Fatih Taş, had been sentenced to six months in prison because of a book about a journalist who had disappeared; the crime: vilification of the Turkish state.

The Turkish state has a hard time dealing with freedom of thought. The trauma of the collapse of the Ottoman Empire is part of the reflex behind protecting the Turkish state. Such a trauma should never again be inflicted upon the Republic. A second part is based on the inherent error of the Republic's founding, i.e. it is up to the state to form the nation. The fear is deep that the state could lose control of the power. During the Cold War, a student who wanted to cut a hammer and sickle from the peelings of an orange was convicted. It was the reformer, Turgut Özal, who died in 1993, who laid the foundation for an understanding of the freedom of thought. Many laws have changed since, but the thinking of many judges and prosecutors has remained the same.

## The state party CHP as political arm

The judges and public prosecutors of the juristocracy see themselves as the party and the protagonists of politics. They are members of the party who refer to the authoritarian modernization order from the twenties; the weaker the political party that they are affiliated with—the CHP, founded by Atatürk—becomes, the more involved they get. Since the introduction of multiparty democracy, after the Second World War, they have only won two elections, in 1973 and 1977. At the time, their charismatic leader Bülent Ecevit was at the zenith of his career. As the state party, which governed alone, from 1923 to 1950, it did not have to solicit voters. During its long one-party rule, CHP considered its mission as representing the state and the bureaucracy on the political stage and as securing their interests. The CHP is, therefore, the party of the status quo from when the center dominated the periphery without restrictions. When the Turkish voters had a choice, the outskirts always voted for the big parties to the right of center from which the reforms originated: during the fifties, it was Adnan Menderes' Democratic Party (DP), during the eighties, Turgut Özal's Motherland Party (ANAP), and now the AK Party.

During the parliamentary elections of July 22, 2007, the CHP and the AK Party faced each other as the most important rivals. The CHP represented the party of the old center and the status quo, and the AK Party represented the party of the periphery and reform. The AK Party won in all provinces in Turkey, including amongst all professions, all age groups, and—with the exception of the richest 20%—all income groups. CHP is virtually not represented east of the capital city of Ankara, and it only achieved a majority with the richest 20% of Turks. As judged by their own standards, however, it did not lose among the voters, because it does not represent the interests of the voters, but the interests of the state, as was the case during the elections of July 22, 2007, when it received 20.8% of the vote. Two days after the elections, Deniz Baykal, the head of the party, declared that the party was not a party like all the others. And he was right.

His deputy, Onur Öymen, however, bewailed the fact that the elections were illogical. He must have read Bertolt Brecht and thought that "the government should elect a different people." The old logic of the CHP was becoming evident, i.e. the electorate was not educated and thus had to be guided by the avant-garde machinery of the state, because in the end, it was only the military-civil apparatus in Ankara that knew what was best for the people. That was why the CHP called itself the "Republican People's Party" and not something on the order of the Republican State Party. However, it was at the election booths that it was becoming increasingly apparent to the state elite that they were a minority. Yet, they insisted on continuing to own the state and resisting change that came from below, according to the Armenian Turkish intellectual Etyen Mahcupyan.

Atatürk was a revolutionary; he turned Turkey into a new state. His party was accepted into the Socialist International after the Second World War. But it was only the label of the CHP that was leftist; in reality they did not want to encroach upon the status quo. The CHP started moving away from leftist politics under its leader Deniz Baykal, who became the spokesperson for devout nationalists. But when the CHP was in the opposition, it started becoming weaker, and the military and the judiciary increasingly filled the political gap.

The CHP supports the military getting involved in politics. In closing ranks with the generals, they do not want to compromise to solve the Cyprus conflict; they are also quite reserved when it comes to Turkey's EU membership. They demand a cross border operation in Iraq's Northern Kurdish region, and in their own country, they reject a political solution to the Kurdish conflict, just as they reject giving non-Muslim minorities equal rights. They are blocking the democratic reform processes and do not have a social issues agenda. They have not established a program to solve the problems in the areas of health and education. They also do not explain what they want to do to reduce the economic imbalances and how to aid rural development.

The number of members of the Socialist International who would like to exclude the CHP is on the rise. In April, 2007, Jan Marinus Wiersma, the speaker of the socialist faction in the European Parliament, and Vice-President of the Social Democratic Party in Europe, was very vocal in his criticism of Baykal, the then head of the CHP. In April, 2007, Wiersma accused Baykal of striving for a Tunisian type of democracy. At the time, Tunisia was certainly not a democracy, but a dictatorship which, like Baykal, justified its actions by maintaining secularity. Wiersma was relentless, adding that Baykal was being influenced by the national socialist leaders of the Middle East and maintaining that he did not have a social democratic agenda.

Wiersma was merciless when it came to the CHP, but he praised AK Party's reforms introduced during the early years of 2000. Baykal has put off many social democrats, including his former general secretary, the intellectual Ertuğrul Günay, who was elected into the Parliament for the AK Party by the constituents of Istanbul, on July 22, 2007, and ranking second behind Erdoğan. Günay complains bitterly about the disintegration of the CHP and sees the AK Party as being the party of social justice. After the elections, Erdoğan made him his Minister of Culture and Tourism.

Since 1935, the white-colored "six arrows" (referring to Atatürk's "six principles") on a red surface have been part of the Republican People's Party logo. But Baykal only made use of one of them—Laicism, while continuously holding Nationalism on reserve. However, before the elections of July 22, 2007, the liberal *Radikal* newspaper had warned that Baykal was playing Russian roulette if he really believed that the elections could be won with his battle cry "Save Laicism." Instead of developing solutions for Turkey's burning problems, the CHP was staring exclusively at the interior and exterior enemies of Turkey. This was an observation made by Fuat Keyman, a leading political scientist in Turkey. CHP was no longer a leftist, social democratic party, but merely enamored of the state and its machinery. *Cumhuriyet* (the Republic), the newspaper founded by Atatürk, continued to act as its organ, but not its party newspaper. The then editor in chief, İlhan Selçuk, was one of the major policy makers of the Kemalist discourse, and he was one of the founders of the "Kızılelma" coalition. The term combines the loose alliance of the leftist and rightist nationalists. And so it was no coincidence that in the summer of 2007, Baykal joined the election campaign, stating he was willing to enter into a coalition with the right-wing Nationalist Movement Party (MHP).

Ziya Gökalp (1876—1924), who had made Turkish nationalism socially acceptable on an intellectual level, and whose poem had led to Erdoğan's
prison sentence, had referred to the ideal country of the Turks, which
reached from Anatolia to Central Asia, as "Kızılelma." Everyone who is
joined under this roof is fixated on the notion that they have been given
the historical task of saving Turkey from the "threat from abroad." They
see the Turkish War of Independence as on-going. The bandwidth of the
Kızılelma coalition ranges from the Grey Wolves of the MHP to Baykal's
CHP to the Maoist Doğu Perinçek, the spearhead of those denying the
Armenian "genocide" and who has excellent relations with the Turkish
Secret Service, MİT.

Despite the fact that the CHP is a member of the Socialist International, there is one thing that it is not: a social democratic party. At any rate,
the terms left and right do not apply in Turkey. In 2007, the ones who
voted left were the secular state elite and rich people who did not want to
change anything, or at most, very little; the devout Anatolians, who live
along the periphery and who have been excluded from the state, were the
ones who voted right. Left meant an authoritarian state and an equally
authoritarian laicism; right stood for a democratic society. Left often meant
defending the state in a defensive nationalism; right mostly entailed opening the country with reforms and democratizing it.

It was a lesson for the CHP, during the elections of July, 2007, that
they lost liberal and leftist intellectuals. They no longer voted for the
CHP, but for independent candidates or the AK Party. The CHP has, however, no need for a lively discourse, because their party logo consists of
the "six arrows" and the political axioms to that direction. The stronger
institutions of the state make sure that they are not lost.

## Bülent Ecevit, the Anatolian leftist

No other politician in the second half of the 20th century inspired and
divided the Turks like Bülent Ecevit (1925–2006). The man with the
dark cap was the hero of the Turkish military landing in Cyprus, in 1974,
and the embodiment of hope for the International Socialist Movement. He
was a politician and a poet, an intellectual and an ideologist. His life reflected the two sides of the republic: the legendary chairman of the CHP
came from the urban state elite, and in the eighties he was significantly
involved in distancing the CHP from a European kind of social democrat-

ic politics. As he once said, the tree of social democracy would not be able to bloom in the Anatolian plain.

Ecevit was born in Istanbul, on May 28, 1925. His father was a professor of medicine. When his father was elected to the Parliament for the CHP, by the request of Atatürk, the family moved to the capital, Ankara. However, the son returned to Istanbul to attend university; he studied English literature at the elitist Robert College. At Robert, starting when he was 13, Ecevit always carried a German Erika typewriter with him; with this typewriter, he wrote his first poems. When he was 16, he started translating Indian poetry. He inherited his love of the arts from his mother, who was a well-known painter.

He inherited his love of politics from his father. His career began in the Press Office of the Turkish Government, in Ankara. In 1946, Ecevit was sent to the Press Office of the Turkish Embassy, in London, where he studied Sanskrit at the School of Oriental and African Studies (SOAS), and where he learned more about India. The pacifist, philosophical religions and philosophies of India captivated him.

Back in Ankara, he became an art critic for the media organ of the CHP, *Ulus* (The Nation). He successfully completed his military duty and studied at Harvard for a year, with a scholarship from the Rockefeller Foundation. In 1957, he was elected as a delegate to the Parliament of Ankara. At *Ulus*, he first rose to become a head of a department for politics, and later editor-in-chief. In 1961, after the 1960 military coup, when they had commissioned Atatürk's close friend İsmet İnönü to form the new government, Ecevit was appointed again, this time as Labor Minister. The state party CHP, which had governed alone until 1950, had become decrepit; the Communist Turkish Workers' Party (TİP) was elected into parliament and stole the show from the CHP.

Then Ecevit revived the party again. From 1966 to 1971, including the year of the second military coup, he was general secretary under Chairman İnönü, against whose objection, he introduced the term "to the left of the center" (*ortanın solu*) and translated the slogan of the Bulgarian Peasants' Party into Turkish: "The earth belongs to people who cultivate it and water belongs to those who use it," which in Turkish reads, "Toprak işleyenin, su kullananın." Ultimately, the 1971 military coup made İnönü and Ecevit part ways. İnönü defended the coup, Ecevit rejected it. The break was accomplished during the historical party convention in 1973, in which Ecevit took the place of İnönü as the head of the party. İnönü retreated from politics and died the same year; his followers founded the Party of Trust (Güven Partisi). Late in 1974, they helped the arch rival of Ecevit, Demirel, who was the conservative tribune of the people, in a coalition that made up the government majority.

But the 1970s was Ecevit's decade. He won the elections twice for the CHP, in 1973 and in 1977, something that the CHP never managed to accomplish again. He was supported by a wave of popularity on account of his being a critic of military coups and a defender of social justice. Turkey was unexpectedly in a spirit of optimism. But Ecevit needed the Islamist Erbakan in order to form a government. His decisive action in sending Turkish troops to Cyprus, on July 20, 1974, strengthened Ecevit's popularity even more. Five days before that, the Cypriot National Guard had ousted President Archbishop Makarios, and introduced a kind of "union" (Enosis) of Cyprus with Greece. Ecevit was now Karaoğlan, the Turkish mythical hero, a popular hero with a dark cap and a blue shirt. A poster depicted him with a helmet, a Kalaschnikov over his shoulder, and a dove on the other shoulder. Until his death, Ecevit rejected any compromises to resolve the Cyprus conflict as being treason.

Unfortunately, the insurmountable animosity between the rivals Ecevit and Demirel fostered the expansion of terror in the streets of many large cities. The weapons and economic embargo that the United States had imposed after the Turkish military landing in Cyprus left its traces. The short-lived governments under Ecevit's leadership, enabled by his poaching parliamentarians, plunged the country into a cycle of instability. The terror between left and right escalated; it even divided the police into a right wing (Polis Birliği) and a left wing (Pol Der). On September 12, 1980, the army staged a coup for the third time. Ecevit was arrested in a military base near Çanakkale, Demirel in Antalya. On October 11, both were released but placed under house arrest and banned from politics.

The affable Demirel did not follow orders and immediately started pulling strings again. Ecevit however stuck to the ban and isolated himself. He turned away from his party leaders, especially from Baykal, who prior to politics, had been teaching at the University of Ankara, and who kept scheming against Ecevit. While in isolation, Ecevit contemplated the situation and founded the *Arayış* (The Search) magazine. Seven issues were published, and in Ecevit's thinking, they represented a turning point. He turned away from European social democracy and founded his concept of "the Democratic Left" (Demokratik Sol).

Before 1980, Ecevit had occasionally insinuated that Turkey lacked the prerequisites for a real social democracy, as it did not have a working class. He had already been skeptical about class struggle due to the fact that Atatürk's principle of Populism (*Halkçılık*) emphasized the uniform will of the people. India became a role model again. Ecevit had already translated the Indian poet, Rabindranath Tagore, into Turkish, and now he was beginning to take pleasure in the work of Indian politician, Jawaharlal Nehru. In the future, he no longer wanted to align the CHP along European social democracy, but rather along Nehru's Congress Party. The aim was to develop a Turkish Anatolian leftist party on the basis of national features.

When he was no longer banned from politics, he did not want to have anything to do with the CHP. He inspired the founding of the Democratic Left Party (DSP). His wife, Rahşan, who was also his political companion, to whom he had been married since 1946, took over the leadership of the party in 1985, when it was founded. She continued pulling the strings in the background when Ecevit became the head of the party himself, in September 1985. The wealthy building contractor Hüsamettin Özkan had helped the Ecevits financially during the hard times. The Ecevits, who did not have children themselves, treated him like an adopted son, and Ecevit made him his Deputy Prime Minister, from 1999 to 2002. Yet Özkan was reputed to have contacts with the underworld. Ecevit also established contact with the influential preacher Fethullah Gülen, after which the two poets exchanged poems. Ecevit believed that he had detected a facet in Gülen's Islam that he had encountered among India's religions.

In the eighties, Ecevit, who had been leftist and always had nationalist tendencies, became a nationalist. It was more important for him to retain the special features of Turkey than joining the EU. Already, in 1974, he had rejected applying for membership in the EU, which the EU had offered simultaneously to Greece and Turkey. After a number of scandals, the voters rewarded him for his integrity in the parliamentary elections of 1999, which was unique among Turkish politicians, and made the DSP the strongest party. After his transformation, it was no coincidence that he entered into a coalition with the nationalist MHP, and became the Prime Minister for the fifth time. It was a sad punch line in the Republic's history that the wrong developments, that were the responsibility of his predecessors, almost ended in state bankruptcy at the end of his last term in office. Ecevit, who had become old and sick, turned to the International Monetary Fund for help and found the strength to carry out a painful redevelopment program. The voters were not grateful. They punished him and his party during the election of 2002 with a humiliating result of 2%. Ecevit resigned. On November 6, 2006, the only representative of the state elite who was ever able to inspire a majority of Turkish society, died.

# The Dogma of the Elite

## Kemalism as straightjacket

T he Republic founded upon the unity of state and party would be unimaginable in a western democracy. In 1930, the representatives of the state party realized that their cultural revolution was not taking root. Islam continued to play a much larger role in the everyday life of the people than the teachings of Atatürk. Rebellions and revolutions in rural areas kept challenging the new rulers. A new approach was necessary to create the new Turkey "from above." The result was a new ideology which summarized Atatürk's revolution in six principles and which pushed the military out of the limelight until the first coup of 1960. In 1931, the Republican People's Party (CHP) started referring to itself as "republican, nationalist, close to the people, statist, laicistic, and revolutionary." The six principles were already called the six arrows (*altı ok*) back then. Since that time, they have adorned the red party flag of the CHP. In 1935, the six arrows received constitutional rank. Turkey was then a one-party state, and so the program of the party could become part of the constitution.

For long centuries, the elites of the state had mostly been from among the military and the central bureaucracy. The Ottoman Empire and the Republic were, indeed, no exception in terms of boring and maintaining the system. During the one-party rule in the Republic, the military officers received a more regular, formal education, and the religious scholars were replaced by secular intellectuals, while the elites of the non-Muslim minorities disappeared. The traditional elites remained; the basis for legitimacy, however, changed. It was no longer Islam and respect of ethnic-religious diversity that formed the state, but a new ideology that could be characterized by the six arrows: Turkish "Nationalism" (Milliyetçilik), "Secularism" (Laiklik), "Republicanism" (Cumhuriyetçilik), "Statism" (Devletçilik), the "process of constant revolutionary change," referred to as

Revolutionism (Devrimcilik), and the vision of a homogeneous society without classes, referred to as Populism (Halkçılık).

The reformers of the Ottoman Empire had failed to bring western modernity and Islamic culture into balance. Theoretically, the women were to be modern while retaining their traditional virtues. The great novels of the 19th century revolve around the subject of taking on modernity from the West, but not the western lifestyle. In his novel, *Eflatun Bey ve Rakim Efendi,* written in 1876, the reformer Ahmed Midhat contrasts the Westernized master Eflatun, a gambler and womanizer, with the hard working, modest and French-speaking mighty Ottoman gentleman, Rakim.

The Kemalist reformers no longer had a high opinion of this duality. They admired the West, assumed its positivistic sciences, and introduced New Year's Eve balls. A new lifestyle was created in the urban state elite which had already started to take hold among the officers trained in modern war academies. The Kemalist reformers recognized that the prerequisites for this kind of modernization were not present in the periphery, because the periphery was "oriented backwards," and was situated beyond the access of the state. Thus, state and party had to use an educational dictatorship to convey their *"weltanschauung"* (comprehensive worldview) from Ankara to the most distant corners of the Republic.

Democracy is not one of the six arrows and neither is freedom. That is how the bureaucracy of the central state was able to attempt to enforce their modernization project against all resistance. The CHP was merely the connecting link between the state and the people. The bureaucrats in Ankara dominated society by planning the economy, and with their intellectual discourse, and also by developing a state of national security which incessantly saw its existence as endangered. Society did not have any leeway; the state always had the last word. More and more, the six arrows were becoming an authoritarian and repressive version of modernity which left no room for pluralism.

From 1923 to 1950, the CHP was the only party representing state and society in politics. Kemalism had set itself the goal of reaching the level of contemporary (western) civilization during this quarter century. In Europe, the era of Fascism had begun, and in Turkey the government was also enforcing its agenda in an authoritarian manner. This did not change until after the Second World War, when multiple-party democracy was introduced. However, the Cold War made it possible to settle for a formal election democracy, which still did not recognize pluralism.

This did not start to change until globalization also swept up Turkey, and Turkey started undertaking the first steps in the direction of the EU. To do this, Turkey had to become more liberal and more pluralistic, which subjected Kemalism to a very crucial test: on the one hand, Turkey wanted to be a part of "contemporary civilization," and on the other hand, it had to relinquish the government's self-concept as symbolized by the "six arrows." Yet, time had already changed the content of the arrows. Only the CHP and the bodies of government refused to believe it.

Bülent Ecevit undertook a remarkable step in this direction in November, 2005, one year before he died. What Ecevit demanded was that the "six arrows" of today be different than those of 1931. In other words, they had to be redefined, because their reality had changed. He was of the opinion that Atatürk had been neither a right nor a left winger, but someone who brought about change with a high degree of flexibility. And it was this flexibility that the arrows had to reflect. Ecevit had intended to write a book about this, but this project was overtaken by his death.

The history of the Republic is a history of limited success. In only three generations, Turkey experienced changes for which other countries needed two centuries: Turkey accomplished the transition from a dynastic monarchy to a functional democracy, from an agrarian nation to an industrial emerging nation. By moving much closer to Europe, they clearly set themselves apart from their neighbors in the Middle East. They regarded it necessary as the economic policies had failed. After the Second World War, Turkey and Japan had the same per capita income level, and Turkey's was three times higher than that of Korea's. Then, Turkey fell behind in the second half of the 20th century.

The constitution still contains a reference to irrevocable "principles and the revolution of Atatürk." The institutions of the state still do not concede that the pledge of a democratic, secular, and social constitutional state is the only thing to hold the Republic together. A large number of groups within society do not identify with the "principles and the revolution of Atatürk." Moreover, the six arrows are the emblem of the CHP, and only every fifth Turk voted for the CHP in the parliamentary elections of 2007.

Turkey did not always develop linearly, and the six arrows mark the places where the development repeatedly came to a halt, because these places are the straightjackets that stifle and exclude parts of the society. Those who have been excluded are now challenging the established order, and the more blunted the arrows became, the more they lose their function as the only legitimate role model; and the more what had been excluded is appreciated. The fiction can no longer be maintained that a strong state can shape a homogenized nation and must lead it. Diversity replaced homogeneity.

The principle of Nationalism (Milliyetçilik) had excluded the Kurds if they were not willing to be assimilated. Since the founding of the Republic, they have rebelled against it and demanded that ethnic diversity be honored on Turkish ground.

The principle of Laicism (Laiklik) had not separated state and religion, but had entrusted the state with the sovereignty of organizing religion and of interpreting religious sources. When democracy returned, so did Islam, and Muslims demanded freedom of religion from the government elite and that the state keep out of religion.

During the seventies, when the leftists no longer wanted to acknowledge that there should be no classes but only a homogeneous nation, the principle of Populism (Halkçılık) had been macerated.

Liberal Turks criticized that the principle of Republicanism (Cumhuriyetçilik) alone was what defined the form of government. No one wanted to return to the Caliphate, or beyond that, to a theocracy. But without human rights and pluralism, the Republic could not guarantee democratic development. In the eighties, the reformer, Turgut Özal, tossed the principle of Statism (Devletçilik) out the window by liberalizing and opening the Turkish economy.

The last principle, that of "constant revolutionary transformation" (Devrimcilik), had been betrayed by the Kemalist ideology itself by failing to understand the dynamics of Atatürk's thinking, transforming them to a stagnant dogma.

Repeatedly, Turkish intellectuals have suggested overcoming this standstill by striking Article 174 from the constitution; it states that, "Atatürk's principles and the revolution" should be protected. The first time this was demanded was in 1997, in the legal report for the TÜSİAD

Industrialist Association, which was titled, "Democratization Perspectives in Turkey." It was delivered by the liberal legal expert, Bülent Tanör.

Ten years later, in June 2007, Erdoğan commissioned the leading liberal constitutional expert of the country, Ergun Özbudun, to draw up a new constitution for Turkey, which if approved, would be the first civic constitution approved by a democratically elected parliament. The driving force behind the attempt on the design of a new constitution has unfortunately disappeared into political oblivion. If the Erdoğan government did not abandon its attempt on the design of a civic constitution, it would protect the constitutional rights of the citizens, instead of the constitutional rights of the state. It could finally have loosened the straightjacket obstructing the path of Turkey to an open and pluralist society evolving as a liberal democracy.

## Laicism as ersatz religion

Laicism and nationalism rank the highest among the six arrows. They legitimized the Turkish national state and the new Republic more than the other arrows; they gave it a new identity. The Ottoman Empire was a multi-ethnic state and Caliphate. The Turks were only one of many ethnicities of the Empire, and the Ottoman sultan as caliph claimed to be the head of all Muslims.

The Turkish version of laicism did not introduce the separation of state and religion, and also not the neutrality of the state towards religion. Rather, Turkish laicism empowered the state to always keep the religion under control. On the one hand, laicism justifies banning Islam from the public space, but on the other hand the state only recognizes and promotes the Sunni majority's interpretation of Islam, namely the Hanafi legal school, in order to pave the way for constructing a homogenized, uniform nation. It is one of the four legal schools (*madhabs*) of Sunni Islam. Banning Islam from the public space has not been accomplished, and conservative Muslims and Islamists have re-conquered the public space. Recognizing only one form of Islam in order to create a "uniform" nation is also about to fail. Heterodox Alevites and the non-Muslim minorities continue to demand freedom of religion.

Turkey has had religious freedom; everyone can practice their beliefs in their private lives. But the state controls, restricts, and even excludes, the organization of religion from public life. According to Başkın Oran, a well-known political scientist and critic of the Kemalist state doctrine, the institutions of the state have raised laicism to *become* religion. Anitkabir, the grave of Atatürk, is the Kemalists' Ka'ba; Oran refers to Atatürk's speech, "Nutuk," before the second congress of the CHP, from October 15 to 20, 1927, that lasted several days, as their Qur'an. In it, he described the War of Independence and the victory over the opposition against him. Hadith renders the words and deeds of the Prophet Muhammad within Islam; in Kemalism, the words of Atatürk take their place.

During the War of Independence, Atatürk was still hoping to mobilize the power of religion. He had people refer to him as Gazi, which means Holy Warrior. The way Greece and Serbia used religion as a means to unify their nations and to found their national states made quite an impression on him. Not much later, however, he enforced the authoritarian version of laicism, and the state took a stranglehold on Islam. *İrtica*, religious reactionaryism, is the verbal bludgeon that was lobbed at everyone who obstructed the path of the new rulers. *İrtica* is Arabic, and means to return to the old. The earlier Muslims had referred to those who wanted to return to Jahiliyyah, the pre-Islamic period of ignorance, with that term. At the beginning of the 20th century, the term was the curse of the authoritarian Young Turks against all those who wanted to re-establish the despotism of Sultan Abdülhamid II, who had been overthrown.

In the Republic, the new rulers used the expression against their opponents who rejected Atatürk's Cultural Revolution and who deviated from his principles, whether for religious, ethnic, or political reasons. When they used the expression *irtica*, they deprived their opponents of all legitimacy. They chose a religious term, and thus made clear to what extent they themselves followed an ersatz religion. The more the one-party rule and the educational dictatorship weakened, the more often the Kemalists used the term. They assumed that their opponents were working under the protection of democracy as a long-term agenda to undermine the principles of Atatürk. Then, as now, they felt challenged.

And yet they themselves had introduced an authoritarian practice with their version of rigid laicism. Atatürk founded a commission, in 1927, that was to create an "enlightened contemporary Islam" (*çağdaş İslam*). It was headed by the historian and religious scholar, Mehmed Fuad Köprülü (1890–1966). The commission translated the Qur'an into Turkish and suggested that the *muezzin*, or caller to the Prayer, should no longer perform the call to the Prayer in the original Arabic, but in Turkish. This was forcibly imposed upon all *muezzins* throughout the country. Martin Luther and his Bible translation had an important impact on German national sentiment, and it became the role model for the reformers in Turkey. Despite these enforcements by force of state authority, the further suggestions of the commission to adapt the prayer times to work times, and to no longer kneel or prostrate in mosques, but to sit as if in church, did not stand a chance.

The goal of the Kemalists was not a secular state that does not interfere with religious practice of the people. Their goal was to disempower the Islamic clergy from the inheritance of Islamic civilization. An authoritarian laicism, as practiced by Turkey, is not required for a secular society. Due to the fact that Islam does not recognize an institution such as the church, the state had an easy time subjugating Islamic way of life, to the point of excluding religious organizations from public life. While recognizing the primacy of the Sunni Islam of the majority, only as a unifying power, it did not accept religious diversity. Thus, non-Muslim minorities and the Alevites do not have their own legal status as denominations. They can organize themselves as associations and foundations. During the mass protests against the Erdoğan government, in April and May, 2007, the speakers who said that they were worried about the continued existence of the Laicist order were indignant that Christian missionaries were endangering the Republic by distributing Bibles.

In the secular societies of Europe, the states and the churches coexist in peace. Both respect each other, but the state defines the limits of the autonomy of religion. In democratic countries, democracy ranks higher than laicism, because even in functional democracies that do not have a complete separation of state and religion such as in Germany, democracy prevents a downward slide into an authoritarian church-state. In France, in 1905, on the other hand, where Catholics and secularists had battled each other fiercely for a long time, the law that granted the freedom of religion and determined that the state would not recognize denominations, and would not finance churches, brought peace to society.

Whereas the EU only accepts secular orders that legitimize and organize themselves in a purely secular way, it does not prescribe a binding model while providing a lot of wiggle room. Turkey is a secular state with a Muslim population. But that does not make them an Islamic state, even if staunch Kemalists don't acknowledge that a devout Muslim can have a strong preference for a democratic, secular state. If the state elevated Islam constitutionally as its religion, and derived some of its laws from Sharia, then it would create an Islamic state.

Officially, Turkey is a laicist Republic; unofficially, Sunni Islam is the state religion of this laicist Republic. Since 1923, it has provided the cohesion to solidify the identity of the nation-in-progress. The state turned the office of the "Şeyhülislam," which was a member of the cabinet during the Ottoman times, into the religious office, called "Diyanet İşleri Başkanlığı"—Directorate of Religious Affairs, during the Republic. And then there were the Sunni-Islamic based "Religious culture and moral knowledge" classes as an obligatory class for all pupils, no matter what their religion. Society, however, was already largely secularized; believing in God was a private affair, and the laws that regulated everyday life were not derived from Islam, but from common law. The Turkish sociologist, Nilüfer Göle, reasons that the early Islamists in Turkey had already been shaped by Turkish laicism, especially by the public-secular education system. They had also adapted themselves to the laicist Republic in their public behaviour. TESEV, an independent research institute, had determined the share of those who thought that the laicist character of the Republic was in danger was the highest among the wealthiest Turks, with 40% concerned. Elsewhere, the percentage was much lower.

A large majority of the population has accepted secularization because it has grown steadily for the lasted two centuries. The prospective of an EU membership is the current incentive to continue on this path. Islam is part of the Turkish spiritual and cultural identity, but not part of the way they see themselves politically. While devout religiousness reveals itself more in the public space, it does not mean that Islam is turning into Islamism and becoming politicized. In August, 2003, *Hürriyet* daily newspaper published a survey conducted by the political scientist, Yalçın Akdoğan, among the functionaries of the AK Party and the Islamist SP—Party of Blessedness. According to that survey, 68% of the functionaries of the AK Party rejected involving Islam in politics, while only 24% of the SP, the father of political Islam and affiliated with Erbakan, did so.

Islam had been politicized under Erbakan, who had showed the depth of how far his Islamist parties could go. The Kemalist establishment set the boundaries quickly. Reformers such as Adnan Menderes (1899–1961),

Turgut Özal (1927–1993), and Recep Tayyip Erdoğan (born 1954) used Islam only as a part of their cultural identity, and they only questioned the monopoly of the state over religion. Thus, when the institutions of the Kemalist state ideology call out "İrtica" (religious reactionaryism or backwardness) today, it has more to do with defending their power than with the impact that Islam has on politics.

Turkey will only be a liberal democracy when the principle of laicism has been subordinated to that of democracy. That is what Sezer, President from 2000 to 2007, warned repeatedly. Trust is necessary for democracy to be strong enough to exclude the transformation into a theocracy. Democracy does not supplement the Kemalist-arrow Republicanism. The way the principle of laicism is interpreted can change, which is what Osman Arslan, the President of the Cassation Court (Yargıtay), demanded on October 6, 2006. During the traditional speech that was held to open the court that year, Arslan said that the constitution did not provide an unequivocal content for laicism. By saying that, he brought down the wrath of Büyükanıt, the Chief of Staff, who insinuated that Arslan was attempting to provide a new interpretation of the term laicism. But that is precisely what Turkey needs.

## Turkish nationalism as a source of strength

The white crescent and star on the red surface glows on a hill in Sarıkamış, in Eastern Anatolia, where more than 75,000 Turkish soldiers were killed by a Russian army that was better equipped in the freezing cold of minus 30 degrees in the winter of 1914. They had sacrificed themselves for the homeland and the flag carries their heroicism into the present. After the establishment of the Republic, they put an exaggeratingly huge flag—a flag which occupies a surface area of more than 150 square meters—which is visible even from a distance of fifty kilometers.

Nothing is too big for the Turkish flag. The Turks celebrated the 75th anniversary of the Republic with an entry into the Guinness Book of records; solemnly, they carried the largest flag that had ever been made through the city of Istanbul. Flags flap in the wind everywhere, on every corner of the Bosporus, on every hill, in public squares. If only the hearts of the state elites, who hoist the flag, were as large as their beloved red cloth.

But they are not. For the Kemalist establishment, the Turkish nation is to be homogeneous and everyone who insists on being different becomes an enemy from within. Official "Sunni Islam," which is packaged within laicism, and Turkish nationalism are to guarantee this homogeneity. The state and its institutions use Islam as an instrument to create a nation. Nationalism is therefore, first and foremost, an affair of the state. And thus, "insulting" the Turkish nation becomes an insult of the Turkish state, and therefore is prosecuted in accordance with Paragraph 301 of the Criminal Code. The early ideologist of Turkish nationalism, Ziya Gökalp (1876–1924), had not trusted individuals and their reasoning. That is why he recommended the awakening of the national collective consciousness as the best way to open up contemporary civilization.

Usually, nationalism tries to maintain the goal of the national state by which it finds legitimacy. This is true in Turkey, too. As all power emanated from the state in Kemalist Turkey, this state still sees itself as one with the nation, and this nation is to be homogeneous, Turkish nationalism wants to remove all deviations from this ideal. Unlike France, various peoples who live in Turkey and profess their loyalty to this state do not become Turkish citizens.

Instead of focusing directly on the people possessing the citizenship of Turkey, article 66 of the 1982 Constitution has a different emphasis in its definition for Turkish citizens: "Everyone bound to the Turkish State through the bond of citizenship is Turkish." The affiliation of the individual is thus to the Turkish state and not to Turkey. Yet Atatürk had not saved a nation, but a country that reaches from Kars, in the East, to Edirne, in the West. He found the Republic of Turkey, not a "Turkish state." There is no other Turkey than that of the Republic. In addition, Turks live outside of the borders of Turkey. The Constitution therefore exceeds the borders of the Republic, taking on Pan-Turkish features; so, it is not surprising that the infamous paragraph 301 is still considered to be the best weapon against freedom of expression, punishing all "insults and denigrations" against Turkishness.

Atatürk had had other plans. During the first years of the Republic, he had considered Islam to be the common denominator of the population. He recognized that Turks and Kurds were different, and Arabs and Albanians, the Laz and the Circassians, too. It was not until the thirties that he attached importance to ethnic Turkishness on the basis of the "Turkish history thesis." Ayşe Afet İnan (1908–1985), one of the adopted daughters of Atatürk, helped him develop it. She was a historian, and used daring constructions to "prove" that Turks had always settled in Anatolia, and that the Hittites and Sumerians were the successors of Turkish populations who had immigrated. Moreover, the sun language theory, which was abandoned again in 1938, claimed that all languages had developed from Turkish.

This kind of ultra nationalism has two different cloaks. Leftist ultra secular nationalists, such as the Kemalists, refer to it as "ulusalcılık," in accordance with a term that they coined from the ancient word of "ulus" (nation) that started to be recycled again by language revolutionaries in 1932. The ultraconservative nationalists, however, prefer "milliyetçilik," a term that originated in the Persian-Arabian tradition. Leftist nationalism is in the tradition of the non-religious and racist Young Turks, and has completely parted ways with the religious traditions of the past. Conservative nationalism on the extreme right, however, continues to affiliate itself with Islam. Thus the Turkish-Islamic synthesis that states that it was Islam that perfected Turkishness originated in this conservative nationalist environment. In the end they both mean the same thing: both endeavors to create the unity of a "homogenized" nation state with Turkish identity at its core, and neither of them see room for pluralism, the basic rights of the individual, and a modern democracy.

Until the nineties, the leftist *ulusalcılar* and the conservative *milliyetçiler* avoided each other. Then, they became better acquainted under the roof of an ideologically colorful alliance that refers to itself as "Kızılelma" (literally "red apple"), named after the original homeland of the Turks. They moved closer in their agendas in the weekly magazine, *Türk Solu* (The Turkish Left). Articles are written by the Grey Wolves, the constitutional judge Yekta Güngör Özden, and the painter, Bedri Baykam, a staunch leftist Kemalist. What their spokesmen have in common is to protect the Turkish community from the outside and to re-establish their own kind of ideal world of the past. They see themselves as victims of history and fierce outside powers; they rage against the EU reforms, and their nationalism becomes a third world ideology along with their retreat from the globalized world. The outer enemies are identified quickly: they are the neighbours and superpowers that allegedly are afraid of a strong Turkey—a Turkey that they, therefore, allegedly want to weaken and ultimately distribute among themselves.

This entails very wild conspiracy theories circulating within these circles. Jews are supposedly buying up Eastern Anatolia to integrate the upper reaches of the Euphrates and Tigris into Eretz Israel. And it was the United States that triggered the terrible earthquake, in 1999, to destabilize Turkey. Germany was afraid that it would lose its supremacy in the Balkans, and was also weakening Turkey. These are some of the allegations these circles spread. A bestseller that was published before the parliamentary elections of 2007 insinuated that Prime Minister Erdoğan was a Jew and an agent of America who had the assignment of selling Turkey to the United States, giving the Kurds their own state, and re-establishing the Greek Pontus Empire. These are all from the book titled, *Musa'nın Çocukları: Tayyip ve Emine* (*The children of Moses: Tayyip and Emine* [Erdoğan]), by the nationalist author, Ergün Poyraz.

Nationalist ideologues cannot manage without enemies from outside the state. One of the specialties of Turkish nationalism is that it also requires enemies from within. The greatest fear of these nationalists is the indivisible unity of state and nation, where minorities who are neither Turkish nor Muslim are a bother. The enemies are everywhere, including the non-Muslim minorities that are degraded and become native foreigners (*yerli yabancılar*) as well as those Kurds who do not want to be Turks.

The nationalists have three battle cries: "Turks only befriend Turks" (Türkün Türkten başka dostu yoktur), "Turkey to the Turks" (Türkiye Türklerindir) and "Love it or leave it" (Ya sev ya terk et). A Turk is good and the "other" is bad. These slogans are particularly appealing to uneducated and unemployed young men in the cities. Violence against this fictional enemy from within is the next logical step. This violence is fed by an educational system whose indoctrination includes sensitive political and historical subjects instead of enlightening people prudently.

The renowned Turkish political scientist, Levent Köker, therefore warns of parallels to the beginnings of National Socialism in Germany, that there was a trend towards violence in the Turkey of today, and that these nationalists do not think that democracy is capable of solving national problems. He adds that they see the world as a stage for constant conflict and war, and that an urban proletariat in rags had infiltrated the lower middle classes, also alleging that paramilitaristic groups who wanted to save the state and fight those they deem to be enemies of the state had formed within the more nebulous circles of government. Köker warned that with the help of these components, nationalism would easily be able to become fascist. This was the danger that was imminent if the EU reform process was interrupted. Köker feared that if reforms were abandoned, foreign investors would retreat and plunge the country into a deep economic crisis with an authoritarian regime taking hold.

The result would be a racist and xenophobic nationalism. Certainly, not every Turkish nationalist is of that opinion, but its excesses are disturbing. They are expressed in books that have become bestsellers. Thus, Hitler's *Mein Kampf* and the thriller *Metal Storm* (*Metal Fırtına*) hit record sales, in 2005. *Metal Storm* describes an atomic war between Turkey and the United States which ignites in Northern Iraq. The books of the right, by the Pan-Turkist, Nihal Atsız (1905–1975), continue to sell well. One of them is, *The Death of the Gray Wolves* (*Bozkurtların Ölümü*, 1946), another one, *Revival of the Gray Wolves* (*Bozkurtlar Diriliyor*, 1949).

Together with them, Atsız, who of all Pan-Turkist activists had the greatest sympathy for the national socialists, laid the intellectual foundation for a Turkish ideology of race. The violence-prone nationalist youth organization later named itself after his books, the "Grey Wolves" (Bozkurtlar). In 1944, Atsız denounced the left-liberal Turkish intellectual, Sabahattin Ali, as a traitor to his country, and when Ali reported him to the police, the young activists burned the novelist's books. Later, Atsız unfortunately declared that the Armenians had deserved what happened to them in 1915 and that the Kurds should watch out that the same did not happen to them.

The last time xenophobic nationalism reared its ugly head was after the Armenian-Turkish intellectual Hrant Dink was murdered on January 19, 2007. Four days later, more than 100,000 Turks marched the eight kilometers from the publishing house of Dink's newspaper, *Agos*, to the church for his funeral. They carried posters with banners that read "We are all Hrant, we are all Armenians." In doing so, they were following a tradition. In Berlin, Kennedy had emphatically said "Ich bin ein Berliner"; in Solingen, on May 29, 1993, when four Turks were killed, a German newspaper had used the headline, "We are all Turks"; and the Greek newspaper, *Ta Nea*, chose the same banner headline after the severe earthquake on August 17, 1999.

But some radical Turkish nationalists did not let the empathy and sympathy for the renowned Dink count. In football stadiums, they rolled open placards that read "We are all Ogün," the murderer of Hrant Dink, and a variety of politicians who were part of the opposition screeched: "We are not Hrant and not Armenians, but Mehmet and Muslims." Prime Minister Erdoğan did not join this chorus, and instead swam against the current. "Nationalism means serving the homeland and the nation," he said. If someone was racist and discriminatory they were not a nationalist. "We embrace everyone who is a citizen of the Republic," he added. The chairman of the opposition party, Party of the Nationalist Movement (MHP), Devlet Bahçeli, accused Erdoğan of having an "allergy against the value of Turkishness."

Erdoğan's pragmatic government was confronted by an increasing wave of nationalism between 2005 and 2007. The EU process was faltering, government compromises concerning the Cyprus issue had remained without a concrete result due to the politics of obstruction on the Greek part of the island, the outside pressure to recognize the "genocide" of the Armenians was on the rise, to the point that some Western countries have threaten to arrest the deniers if they happen to enter their customs, and the terror of the Kurdish separatist organization, PKK, had returned. These factors gave the nationalists an ideological backwind, with which the government had nothing to counteract.

The flag mania started with the wind, and generally speaking, symbols have become the greatest force of nationalism: the flag, with a crescent and star—which was also used during the Ottoman period and then became a part of the War of Independence; the omnipresent image of Atatürk, the leader of all times (*ebedî şef*); and the Turkish map as a cartographic silhouette symbolizing the state and its indivisibility. Visions for the future do not contain these symbols, but whoever does not use them excludes himself from the community and becomes labelled as an enemy from within. Based on this fear, flags in red and white exert a magical attraction. The education system and schoolbooks make sure that many do not question the symbols and axioms.

## The indoctrination in Turkish school books

The History Foundation (Tarih Vakfı) has a special place among Turkish NGOs. It was founded by social scientists that had taught and done research at universities until the military coup in 1980. Then, the military government removed them from their teaching positions. Since that time, the researchers have published more than one hundred monographs about the past and recent history of Turkey, and they have founded scientific magazines and organized international conferences.

They entered new territory in 2003. That is when the History Foundation started investigating 190 Turkish schoolbooks. They had all been approved by the Ministry of Education and were all in use in elementary and primary schools. The books' statements on respecting human rights, the individual's attitude towards the state, and respecting others were investigated. "The result exceeded our expectations," said the general secretary of the History Foundation, Orhan Silier, who summarized the individual studies, in the preface for the anthology.

The Turkish scientists concluded that the books presented difference as a danger, thus abetting discrimination; that they contained an ethnically racist nationalism that culminated in the glorification of the state that was to be obeyed blindly; that the obligatory class of National Safety taught, until very recently, at all high schools demanded the subjugation of the individual to the state, whose existence was threatened from all sides; that democracy was reduced to the formal staging of elections without discussing processes of participation and forming opinions; and that the schoolbooks for literature gave Turkish authors who lived outside of Turkey much more space than world literature. The schoolbooks for other classes also tended to treat the world marginally.

Thus, education is one of the areas where the transformation to democratic thinking is very backward. That was no surprise. The nationalists, both right-wing and left-wing, want their position in public service to be within the ministerial bureaucracy in order to protect the state. The palladium of the nationalists was always the Ministry of Education; there they made sure that the textbooks that indoctrinate the priority of the state and the meaning of national security were circulated.

The "National Security" class set the pace—which was an obligatory ninth grade class, taught at all schools until it was recently lifted. Generally, it was taught by retired officers whom the commander of the nearest barrack suggested. The textbook was written by a commission within the general staff. The objective of the class, according to the History Foundation, was to educate pupils to become proud and obedient citizens of a militaristic nation. Until 1998, the structure of the Turkish military was the focus. Then, it focused on the principles of Atatürk, as well as the "tricks that are done to the Republic of Turkey," which was the heading of one of the chapters in the textbook.

The pupils were to "think, live, and act" like Atatürk and learn how to think strategically. The textbook taught that all neighbouring countries wanted to expand at the expense of Turkey, and that the large states of the world wanted to prevent a strong Turkey. A homogenous Turkish nation was invoked that perceived these games of the enemies from without.

But it also detected the dangers from within posed by non-Muslim minorities and the separatist elements. Nowhere did the textbook mention the Kurdish issue as a political conflict. All otherness was ascribed to external origins. Politics were reduced to handling external and inner enemies of Turkey. The stereotypes that the National Security class provided returned again, in all other textbooks, as axioms that were inviolable and hovered above everything else. The textbook on National Security stated the following: "No opinion can be protected that is directed against the Turkish national interests." And also: "The states of those Turks who had not assembled around their national interests will collapse within themselves very soon."

An elementary schoolbook proclaims the following for social studies: "The principle of nationalism serves the unity of our nation against the threats from outside." Later: "Some neighbouring states place themselves in the path of the striving of Turkish society to develop rapidly and modernize." In secondary school, pupils are confronted with the following recognition: "The fact that we learn about other cultures from the mass media can also be damaging because it could have a negative effect on our national culture." Even the elementary level science textbook states: "If we buy goods from other countries, we are giving them our money." And a textbook for the History of the Revolution of Atatürk states: "If nationalism is suppressed, Turkish existence will come to an end."

World history is symbolized by the battle between the cultures, and geography also teaches lines of attack and defense from a military viewpoint. The state takes center stage again. The textbook for sociology in secondary school teaches the following: "When observing personal liberties, the survival of the state must always be considered. One of the basic duties of the state is to limit these freedoms." This textbook is *pars pro toto* and the attitude of curtailing basic rights also pervades other textbooks.

The state ranks above all else. A textbook for philosophy in secondary schools states: "An institution is required to obstruct the forces that create chaos for society. The state is the institution that has a monopoly on the use of force." The fact that these developments are not in favor of the individual is what the elementary social studies textbook teaches: "Individuals are free as long as they do not break through the unity of the state and the nation." The author Mehmet Semih Gemalmaz concludes that the textbooks honor authority and demand a culture of obedience. Individuals' rights are not recognized by the state but bestowed by it.

Naturally, this state also determines the axioms of politics. From the textbook on, "The history of the revolution of Atatürk" for secondary school: "Above all, politics must be understood as the politics of the state." Democracy goes into decline and becomes a formal mechanism and the subject of democracy is no longer the citizen but the nation.

The music textbook encourages students to sing the national anthem with passion, and the textbook for Turkish literature at the secondary level praises the love of the Turkish language as the central element of national unity. Languages such as Italian and Greek are devalued as being phonetically ugly, and the Turkish language elevated as being superior. Even the textbook for sciences of elementary school sees the blood of our martyrs in the red of the national flag. Generally speaking, dying as a sacrifice for the Turkish state is a recurring theme for all levels and subjects. The textbook for social studies at secondary school reads: "Our predecessors gave their blood to protect our country and are buried. They sacrificed their life to make this country the homeland of the Turks. We also must make all sacrifices possible in order to protect this beautiful country."

In some other old textbooks, minorities only interfered with this idyllic setting. A book on Turkish literature for secondary schools described minorities as being Christian herds. The sociology book of the secondary level further defined minorities as follows: "It is a category of people without the same social rights as Turks." The Armenians were, for instance, described in the book on the Turkish history of revolution as follows: "They were neither innocent nor loyal towards the state; they were traitors and enemies in every respect."

Such language reveals that the schoolbooks served, and many ways continue to serve, indoctrination, writes Tanıl Bora in his contribution for the anthology. Bora quotes Altan Ateş, the vice president of the Curricula Commission of the Ministry of Education. "The goal is to raise pupils to become people who share the same opinion. In the era of modern information technology this is not always as easy as in the past," Ateş said regretfully. Turkish schoolbooks continue to indoctrinate a nationalism that blanks out the world, that spreads a xenophobic fear of others, and that subjugates all actions to the Turkish state which continues to be sacred, at least in the textbooks.

# From Outsiders to
# Counter-elite

## Departure into the cities

odernity conquered Turkey via the cities, mainly via Istanbul. The Ottoman cities had separated the living and working places. The living space at the time was largely separated from the public space and the working world; each room could have several functions. In the 19th century Ottoman Empire, a new European lifestyle expanded in the metropolis along the Bosporus. Modern houses were reserved as living space; they were made of stone and richly decorated, and every room had only one function. Either they were a salon or a bedroom, a dining room or living room or foyer. Whether the Doğan Apartmanı near the Galata Tower, the elegant street of Meşrutiyet Caddesi in Tepebaşı, or the modern apartment buildings in Akaratler—for the first time, the residences became part of the public space: There were cafés around the corner, people strolled in the streets, the opera house opened in the evening. Modern Istanbul did not want to be any different than the large cities in Europe, and Istanbul was continuously involved in exchanging trade, commerce, and visitors.

The turning-point came in 1923. Ankara became the capital, while Istanbul withered away and turned into a wallflower at the border of the new Republic. The Ottoman Empire, whose capital had been Istanbul, was open to the world. The Republic of Turkey cloistered itself away from the world and wanted to create the new national state. From then on, Turkey looked inward. The center of gravity had shifted to the inside of Anatolia. From there, the founders of the Republic wanted to end the unresolved conflict between the urban center and the rural outskirts. The big cities were not the only ones who wanted to appreciate modernity. The center no longer wanted to merely control the outskirts; it wanted to change it, too.

The Turkish state has a hard time dealing with freedom of opinion. Part of the reflex to protect the Turkish state is explained by the fall of the Ottoman Empire. Such a trauma cannot happen again. A second factor in the restriction of speech and opinion are the errors made when forming the nation. There is a deep-seated fear that the state could lose control of power. During the cold war, a student who wanted to shape a hammer and sickle from an orange peel was sentenced to prison. The reformer Turgut Özal, who died in 1993, laid the foundation for an understanding of the freedom of thought. A lot of laws have changed in the meantime; judges and prosecutors, however, remain unchanged.

Naturally, the state took modernity into its hands. The centralized bureaucracy in Anatolia wanted to trigger industrialization with the new state ventures. The attempt failed utterly: the state proved to be a miserable entrepreneur in Turkey, too. There was a lack of capital in Turkey; protectionism prevailed in the global economy. For the first time, there were modern apartment buildings in the provincial cities, high and not beautiful in an aesthetic sense, but a new way to live. However, the founders of the Republic did not trigger an independent modernization in Anatolia, or try to connect Anatolia to modernity. Anatolia mostly remained a poor house.

Change did not occur until Turkey's transition to a multiple-party state after the Second World War. And then, modernity did not come to Anatolia, but rather Anatolia proceeded to move to the modern cities in Western Turkey. That is when modernity started to germinate in the provinces. In 1950, the conservative government of the Democratic Party (DP) replaced the state party CHP, and new highways began to make the country accessible. For the first time, Anatolian farmers and the owners of small-sized enterprises could market their products themselves in the cities—and more, they found employment there.

The new Menderes government broadened the scope of private companies, and Istanbul started to breathe again. Entrepreneurs built new factories around the borders of Istanbul, as well as in the nearby cities of Izmit and Bursa. A rural exodus commenced, totally transforming Turkey. In 1960, one third of the population of 32 million inhabitants lived

in cities. In 2007, 70% of the 73 million people lived in cities. The countryside was vacated and the rural exodus has been largely completed.

At the time, the exodus had taken place because people hoped they
would find work in the cities. They found work in the factories, but they
did not find apartments. If they had enough money saved, they bought a
small condominium. Building contractors specialized in handling small
amounts of money and the needs of immigrants. They purchased land
from the owners and built tenements with cheap low-quality materials
and sold the apartments to Anatolian immigrants.

But these Anatolians generally arrived without any savings, and when
they did, they usually settled on foreign land near the factories that
belonged to the state and overnight (*gece*) they built (*kondu*) little houses from the most basic materials—without building engineers, without
architects, without building approvals. Old Turkish common law states
that houses that are built overnight cannot be torn down. And so soon,
two-thirds of the inhabitants of Istanbul lived in *gecekondu*s which
stretched over hills, stuck to steep slopes, and spread in every free direction—this soon happen in all other large cities such as Ankara, Antalya,
Izmir and Izmit.

The red color of their unplastered brick buildings spread deeper and
deeper into the green lungs around Istanbul. A patchwork rug of Anatolian villages grew around Istanbul and the city became a mosaic of Anatolia. Approximately one million Istanbulians who owned the city half a
century ago still live in the center of the cities and selected gated communities. The other 14 million or maybe even 16 million people are immigrants and their children—like Erdoğan, the former Mayor of Istanbul, who
is now the Prime Minster of Turkey. His parents had arrived in Istanbul
from the impoverished city of Rize, along the Black Sea; Erdoğan was
born in the dock area of Kasımpaşa, in 1954.

The *gecekondu* houses initially had two or three little rooms, but no
plumbing and no electricity as they were built overnight without permits,
and their quarters were not marked in the tourist maps. Tourists would
not have gone to see these quarters anyway; they would not have gone
to Sultanbeyli and not to Dudullu. It took decades for them to develop
into normal city districts. It generally started with an election or a district. The candidates courted the new population majority in Istanbul to
gain their votes. They promised that they would connect these new quar-

ters to electricity and water, and even promised to enter them in land registers to transfer owners' rights to them.

If the people who lived in the *gecekondu*s found a real job, they improved their houses. If there was an entry in the land registry, they made arrangements with building companies to build houses for several families on the piece of land. For example, the arrangement might be that the building company would build twelve apartments, with the building company owning six—which they would sell, and the remaining six would belong to the emigrant who now was suddenly not poor, and maybe even wealthier than old Istanbulians.

Today, there are almost no *gecekondu* quarters left. Most of them have been legalized and integrated into the cities. The *gecekondu* homes were small, and the flat buildings symbolized the social rise that their inhabitants had been denied. The trench that had divided the center and the outskirts of both the Ottoman Empire and the Republic of Turkey continued, but now within the city. The Anatolians who arrived remained provincial. They did not take on the lifestyle of the urbanites but increasingly had an impact on the city. Istanbul no longer had a center that everyone revolved around. However, the structures of Anatolian villages continued to exist in microcosm of the *gecekondu*s.

The *gecekondu*s were never slums. The slums were occupied by members of the lowest urban class, and they remained urban. Villagers who found work in the city and who wanted to rise settled in *gecekondu*s. They did not take along the whole social structure from their villages. They no longer had an *ağa* in the city—large landowners who had exploited them but who represented them to the outside world and protected them. They were on their own now, and initially without the opportunity to rise. They did not profit from the liberty that the cities had to offer. The leftist parties did not embrace them because they saw themselves as the urban avant-garde from the elegant parts of the city, and they were (and are) above climbing down into the depths of Anatolia, even if Anatolia has become part of their metropolis.

There was another outcast who embraced the outcasts in the *gecekondu*s: Erbakan's Islamist Welfare Party (Refah Partisi). It organized efficient neighbourhood groups, recruited microcredit organizations, and procured jobs. If someone settled into a *gecekondu*, a functionary or a sympathizer came along and offered him a small microcredit loan to start up a general store (*bakkal*). A few years later the man would return and say that thanks to his help and the grace of Allah, he had made it and that he would give another new immigrant the amount of money that he himself had received a few years before. And so the network of functionaries and sympathizers grew dense.

During elections, people who lived in *gecekondu*s voted for the party that had helped them in their everyday life. In November 1992, communal elections had to be held in six municipal districts outside of the election cycle, because they had become so large due to the exorbitant number of people who had moved to Istanbul. Five mayors who had not been born in Istanbul were elected of whom four belonged to the Welfare Party (RP).

Despite the success, the tensions within the party increased because it was becoming evident that the Islamist movement was divided into two sections. The rural conservative wing around the Party Chairman Erbakan preached the same sermons in the cities as in the rural areas. These traditionalists wanted to apply the leverage of a strong state to implement Islamist order. On the other hand, the "leftist" and youthful wing, surrounding Erdoğan, was close to these new city people and intended to solve the immigrants' problems in a pragmatic way. The call for Sharia had become irrelevant for this faction of the party. These modernizers were engaged in society. They did not want to give the almighty state more power, but wanted to wrest more tolerance and deference towards human rights.

In order to better understand all the changes, one should go back to early 1980's. What had been built up over decades was discharged after 1983. Though the generals around Kenan Evren who were involved in the coup restored the old central state regime, they governed only for only a brief period of time. From 1983 on, the year that the generals had returned to the barracks and Turgut Özal had been elected, Turkey underwent great change. The centralist state was in a crisis from which it did not recover. Within the state, the collective movement of the Homeland Party (ANAP) was questioning the basic axioms of the Republic. Then, there was the rise of the Islamist Welfare Party (RP) and after 1992, the new self-confidence of the Kurds. All over the world, globalization was triggering a vacuum that ended the isolation of the country.

Özal made use of these factors and prevailed in liberalizing the economy and parts of society and politics. The first civic society groups were established that went beyond the reach of the state. From below, the demand to democratize the authoritarian guardian state could be heard, and it did not stop. A new civil society freed itself from the state and the institutions of this state lost their sovereignty to define what was to remain irrevocable. Secular intellectuals, such as Mehmet Altan, Cengiz Çandar and Hikmet Özdemir, all advisers of Özal, kicked off a discussion on how to create an open and pluralist order. They called their project "the Second Republic." One does not need a large amount of imagination to realize how the Kemalist state elite demonized these intellectuals and their project.

But city air is liberating. And this particularly held true for the new Islamist intellectuals. Previously, their thinkers had been the sheikhs who had presided over religious orders (*tarikats*) in Anatolia. Not until they arrived in the city were independent and creative intellectuals, such as Ali Bulaç and Fehmi Koru able to prevail. Unlike the sheikhs, they were not close to the traditionalists surrounding Erbakan, but rather they were the renewers around Erdoğan. Their new urban discourse flanked Erdoğan's political rise intellectually. And Erdoğan was moving even further away from Erbakan's bombastic rhetoric and from the oppressive ideology of the state's elite.

The new Muslim thinkers started as Islamists. The dialogue began with a few secular, reform-oriented intellectuals. They got to know each other and exchanged views with one another. The leftist-liberal sociologist, Nilüfer Göle, tells about how the others initially seemed very strange to her. "How can you live so close together and be so different," she thought to herself. By talking to the "untouchables," she became "impure" herself in the eyes of the Kemalists, she said laughingly during an interview. The more she talked to intellectuals, such as Ali Bulaç, the more she realized that they were closer to her than many secular Kemalists she spoke with. They talked about whether one could be modern and Muslim at the same time, and that triggered a creative tension in Bulaç. The discussion was lively, and Bulaç initially did not want to admit that modernity and life as a Muslim could be harmonized, is how Göle remembered it. But then she came to see that one did not have to be westernized to be modern, and that globalization had opened several doors to modernity.

But for someone like Bulaç, for whom modernity meant Westernization, he was not integrated into the Republic, no matter whether he lived in the city or continued to live in Anatolia. Those who had settled along the boundaries of Istanbul and other cities were the ones who felt the modernization arrogance of the urban state elite. Those "down there" did not want to become like those "up there," with their white lace gloves. They did not want it, and they were incapable of doing it. The urban elites were of the opinion that those "down there" did not have any of the requirements needed for modernization, and that is why the Anatolians searched for an alternative to the elitist self-concept of the laicist Kemalists. They found it within the Islamic values of the Anatolian outskirts from which they had arrived.

The conditions were positive: compared to the earlier generations of the Kemalist state elite, the coup generals of 1980 had less animosity towards Islam because the generals back then used the Turkish-Islamic synthesis as an antidote for Communism. Intellectuals who had conservative values developed the synthesis that stated that Turkishness would become complete with Islam. That is why Islam could maintain its presence in the public space to some extent. The economic liberalization under Turgut Özal was another contributing factor. For the first time, entrepreneurs who were not part of the state elite could be economically successful and amass wealth.

Urban air makes you free and money creates independence. For the first time, the city was bringing forth independent Muslim intellectuals; for the first time, the economy was producing successful entrepreneurs who considered themselves devout Muslims and still felt well in the globalized economy. Now Muslims were also climbing up the career ladder; vertical mobility had been made possible. A new Muslim middle class was being created. Muslims were no longer the people out in the country, uneducated and poor. They were also in the cities, increasingly educated, had university diplomas and money, and they were able to consume. In a society that, for a long time, had identified Islam with the past, a level of modern Muslims was coming up. The Anatolians had arrived in the city, they rejected the European *alafranga* (from "à la française") lifestyle of the modern elite, and they were developing their own Muslim modernity.

They wanted to be a part of the modern world, too, with what they brought from Anatolia and with what made them different from the elitist urban class, who continued to look down on them. Their Islam was not a political Islam; their goal was not an Islamist state or the introduction of the Islamic law of Sharia. But Islam was part of their cultural identity, and this identity had a stronger individualistic identity than the Kemalist State doctrine, which relied on the collective and which left little room for the individual.

Muslim modernity has many faces that took hold in cities, via migration and liberalization. One of the faces is that of a veiled woman. Visibility of the body of women is at the center of the debate between the old elite and the new middle class. The Kemalists interpret the headscarf "problem" as the duty of equality of the sexes, which had been Atatürk's goal. They regard the headscarf as a symbol of protest against the laicist state establishment that qualifies women who cover their hair as being backward. Young Muslim women, however, interpret it as the sign of their freedom. By covering their hair, the conservative classes can leave their houses and can become part of the men's world. They can go to school and to university, can have a job, and lead their own life.

Particularly, the development of the headscarf illustrates the history of these women. Their mothers wore the traditional light colored, loose-fitting coat, the "pardösü," and a light-colored, loosely tied headscarf. Many of the daughters are well educated, successful in their jobs. They consciously choose the headscarf (*başörtüsü* in Turkish), turning it into a fashion article, bright and expensive. It has also started to be referred to as *türban* since 1984. Clothing manufacturers have adjusted to the new Muslim middle class, and specialized in the new Islamic fashion, in "tesettür." They conduct fashion shows displaying their colorful, Islamic products on large billboards.

The women cover their hair and their arms. But they are also self-confident, and their clothing is a work of aesthetic appeal. Some women prefer suits and pants that are tight, and frequently they wear jeans. They have their own Islamic cafés, which do not serve alcohol but which are integrated into bookstores. Young men and women are involved in discussions in these stores. Like the urban elite, they take their vacations in beach towns along the Mediterranean, but in hotels that show sensitivity to Islamic values and have separate pools for men and women. The women go swimming in the ocean with the new type of bathing suit that is called *haşema*, covering the entire body and hair.

They want to be modern, but not like the European "à la française" style. They do not want to assimilate and exaggerate, especially with the object of dispute, the headscarf—the otherness of their identity.

This emphasis on difference does not facilitate communication. Many people from both sides accept confrontation. The fact that the new middle class can have this confrontation with the old elite is a sign that they have become powerful. Parents and grandparents were stranded along the boundaries of the cities when they arrived. The lifestyle of their children has changed radically without them copying the old elite. The young Muslim women are professional and successful. With their clothing, they have changed the way they consume. They want to consume high-quality products. If a person can consume, they have arrived in modernity and in the middle class. By consuming, the middle class is present in the public space, and by consuming they show the old elite that they have caught up and are worthy.

## Industrializing the province

There is a stubborn myth that Anatolia will always remain poor. Actually it is poverty that drove people away from Anatolia and into the cities of the West, whether Istanbul or Frankfurt, Ankara or Munich. The large exodus has come to an end. Vast regions are empty. During the past decades, Turkey has urbanized more than any other country. And those who remained find work in the Anatolian province.

Turgut Özal, the short heavy-set man from the Eastern Anatolian city of Malatya, he of an unorthodox pragmatism, had given the starting signal and caused an uproar in Turkish politics. His mother had been an active member in the order of the Naqshbandiyyah, as was his brother, Korkut Özal. Turgut Özal had good relations with the itinerant preachers of Anatolia. He was the first leading politician who undertook the pilgrimage to Mecca, stating casually that the state was secular but that he, as an individual, was not. Özal thus aptly expressed those honest, artless terms that European social scientists had coined, such as objective and subjective secularism. Objective secularism divides religion and the state, and thus creates the basic condition for modernity and autonomy of the individual. Subjective secularism, on the other hand, allows the religion of the individual and his being embedded in that tradition.

Asked what his favorite book was, Özal once answered, "Lucky Luke, what else?"—the comic hero of the Belgian artist Maurice de Bévère. A cowboy brings order to the Wild West; Özal brought order to Turkey. There has not been a politician since Atatürk who has had a clearer vision for his country. The unorthodox and straightforward Özal, a practicing Muslim who embraced people from all walks of life with love, moved the ossified Republic further along, first as Prime Minister, from 1983 to 1989, then as President, from 1989 to 1993.

The year 1983 marks the first important turning point in the history of the Republic. Özal found an answer for the two most important challenges Turkey was facing: Islam and the Kurdish question. He said that he was a Muslim and that his mother was Kurdish. Özal answered both challenges with more democracy, and a "de-dramatization." When Özal died, on April 17, 1993, Cengiz Çandar, one of his closest advisors, wrote: "His early death throws us back ten years." The nineties actually became a lost decade for Turkey. After Özal, the state elite managed once more to have the West on their side. Although the West had changed their mind about how they thought the Turkish state treated the Kurds, it still continued to think that the more Turks committed to the Kemalist version of laicism, the more secular Turkey would be. And so the West supported the way the authoritarian state treated Islam. It was not until AK Party won in November, 2002, that Özal's incomplete reform work was continued.

Özal did not shy away from taboos. When he learned that the historical office of the Ecumenical Patriarch of the Orthodox Church was still in ruins because no one had had the courage to agree to it being rebuilt after it had burned down in 1941, he immediately signed the approval for a new construction. During a visit to the United States, he heard that Turkey's determination not to recognize the Armenian "genocide" was an obstacle for Turkey; therefore, he said, "What happens if we compromise with the Armenians and end this issue?" When his words were heard in Ankara, it sparked fury among the state elites and the military. There were harsh reactions against him even from the deputies of the ruling ANAP, which Özal himself founded. This time, state politics was victorious over Özal.

Yet he was able to maintain his course in economic policies. He broke with Turkish state capitalism, opened the isolated country, and unleashed the powers of the market. He is quoted as saying once, "We are happy

that we do not have oil, and so we have to work hard to make money."
Özal's reforms were the basis for the boom of the eighties, and for something that the Republic had never known: the industrialization of Anatolia. It brought with it a new class of entrepreneurs and self-employed
people who defined themselves by their Islamic values. Proudly, they
referred to themselves as Anatolian tigers (*Anadolu kaplanları*). One of
Özal's greatest achievements was to trigger the formation of a Muslim-
Anatolian middle class.

Kayseri is situated in the geographic center of Anatolia and became
the prototype of the young tigers. The sociologist, Şükrü Karatepe, was
mayor there from, 1994 to 1998. The state elite removed both him and
Erdoğan from their offices. When the former university professor was a
private citizen again, he wrote a book. In it, he wrote, "The people in
Kayseri build their lives on plans and calculations; they refrain from politics because they do not like the risks. Instead, they want to advance
their businesses." Today, 50 of the 500 richest Turks live in Kayseri. Kayseri is an economic success story. Kayseri is also a place where Islam
and modernity live in harmony.

Before Özal started his reforms, there had been no industrial operations in the part of town called Hacılar (literally Hajjis), named after the
pilgrims to Mecca. Today, nine of the 500 largest industrial operations
are headquartered in this part of Kayseri, at the foot of an extinct volca-
no. Most of them were started because devout Muslims had pooled their
modest funds. Some of the entrepreneurs expanded their factories and
grew of their own devices, like Mustafa Boydak. Today, he is one of the
largest manufacturers of furniture in Turkey, and the sales of his holding
have surpassed one billion dollars.

Boydak's product range illustrates the leap which the Anatolian
tigers are still in the process of accomplishing. He devised the *kanepe*—a
flat wooden structure which one could sit and sleep on. Today, he produces a complete range of modern furniture and sells them under the
brand labels İstikbal and Bellona, conquering export markets. He says of
himself: "We in Kayseri share the opinion of Calvinism that work is a
form of worship." Saffet Arslan's furniture company, İpek, is smaller and
younger, but it already supplies all the big export markets. His father
supported the company by weaving rugs. The son is a devout Muslim,
too: "Islam demands that people live modestly, do not do anything that

is unfair, and be honest and productive." That is why Arslan has not only created jobs, but has built two schools and has further provided more than 200 pupils with scholarships.

Entrepreneurs such as Mustafa Boydak and Saffet Arslan can be regarded in a sense as the practitioners of Muslim Calvinism in Anatolia. The former mayor, Şükrü Karatepe, is their theoretician. He was the one who invented the term Islamist Calvinists.

"In order to understand what is happening in Kayseri you have to have read Max Weber," says the former university professor. When he was a student, he had read, "Protestant Ethics," and saw it applied in the city of his birth. People worked hard in Kayseri; they did not waste money, but invested it. In Kayseri, a profit was seen as God's approval. In Kayseri, religion is the motor of development, and it has strengthened people's own self-concept.

The Turkish sociologist, Hakan Yavuz, speaks of a quiet Muslim Reformation that started in Kayseri, Gaziantep, and many other industrial towns of Anatolia. He reminds people of the impact that Sufi orders and the itinerant preacher, Said Nursi, had on developing this work ethic. The job of acquainting the West with this Anatolian version of Calvinist work ethic goes to The Berlin Research Institute European Stability Initiative. "Islamic Calvinists" was a study they published in English, in 2005. The various entrepreneurs, and the phenomenon of the Anatolian Tiger, arose out of the blue. They grew on their own, generally without using any bank credit and without intervention from Ankara. Quite a few companies continue to finance their investments in cash. Nothing indicates that they have stopped growing or have reached their limits.

In 1997, the army drew up a list of companies that were established by "Yeşil sermaye" (Islamic capital), and therefore dangerous. They also forbade their relatives to buy products that were manufactured by these companies. This blacklist included Anatolian tigers and, of course, Ülker—the leading manufacturer of cookies, chocolate, and Cola Turca. The founder of the company, Sabri Ülker, was a close friend of Turgut Özal. One of Erdoğan's sons was one of Ülkers' independent distributors. The Holding is a sponsor of a successful basketball team and a festival for classical music. In December, 2007, Ülker bought the Belgian chocolate label, Godiva.

There is another thing that such companies of the Anatolian tigers have in common: they are members of the Industrial Association MÜSİAD, which was originally founded by devout and successful Muslim entrepreneurs in Istanbul, in 1990. Officially, they referred to themselves as the Association of Independent Industrialists and Businessmen (Müstakil Sanayici ve İşadamları Derneği). A lot of people, however, see "Mü" in MÜSİAD as "Müslüman" (Muslim). While TÜSİAD, the Association of Industrialists and Businessmen in Turkey, represents the cream of the crop of the Turkish economy in Istanbul, MÜSİAD sees itself as a stakeholder of small and medium-sized businesses whose owners have a stake in Islamic values, aside from just capital and work. During its first years, MÜSİAD published the magazine, *Homo Islamicus*, to show entrepreneurs how to use Islam as a source of ethics in a competitive economy.

MÜSİAD and the businessmen associated with it want to prove that Islam is compatible with the globalized world. They do not see the West as a source to imitate, but as a competitive partner. Locally, their values have been defined, but they see their place in the globalized world. MÜSİAD offers their 4,000 members workshops for them to learn how to survive. They meet to exchange ideas on a regular basis, and the association makes it possible for the smaller companies to meet government ministers and conquer the inevitable ministerial bureaucracy.

The Anatolian tigers are successful businesswise; they are harvesting the fruits of globalization. This new middle class is the backbone of Erdoğan's AK Party. This new class would never vote for the party that represents the old state elite and embodies their arrogance. The Muslim-Anatolian citizens want a stable and prosperous Turkey, which takes its place in a globalized world. Therefore, they support the austerity course which the International Monetary Fund (IMF) imposed on the country in 2001, and they support EU reforms more than the old elite and its supporters.

The Anatolian Tigers have a lot of names: Kayseri and Konya, Kütahya and Kahramanmaraş, Çorum, Denizli and Eskişehir, Gaziantep and Hatay, Sivas and Tokat. Their push did not start until the eighties in Denizli, an old textile town. Today this town has certain German-Swabian characteristics, despite its streets that are lined with palm trees. Industry consisting mainly of medium-sized businesses and unemployment is a term from the past. Denizli does not attribute its success story to a small number of large companies, but the many medium-sized companies and their entrepreneurial spirit. During the daytime, you only see elderly pensioners in the cafés. If people look for work, they find it. Nobody emigrates from Denizli, but many immigrate there. Profit is invested in state-of-the-art machines so that industry remains competitive. "Even if we are twice as expensive as China, we will remain competitive with our flexibility and quality," says one of the entrepreneurs.

Denizli's success is being felt elsewhere, too. Industrialization is taking effect in neighboring cities. Nihat Zeybekçi, the mayor of Denizli, has reached an interim goal. "In the past, our economic system was close to communism," was the succinct statement the mayor, who was born in 1961, made. But the Anatolian tigers, as in Denizli, swept away the state capitalistic communism. Zeybekçi was elected to participate in overturning state capitalism because one cannot dismantle bureaucracy, but only remove it. It goes without saying that Zeybekçi is a member of the AK Party.

## Turning one's back on political Islam

The AK Party was founded in August, 2001. Many of the founding members had grown up during political Islam. But their new party was not to be a conservative people's fringe party, but rather a conservative people's party that derived its cultural identity and values from Islam. Unlike the earlier Islamist parties, the AK Party saw itself as a democratic party and part of a secular order that does not question this order, even if they— like other parties—had weaknesses regarding inner party governance being democratic.

The process that began in the middle of the 20th century was a long one. During these last decades, Turkey has not returned to Islam. Instead, it was Islam that returned; the reason being that Atatürk had put a thick layer of ice over religious life after the founding of the Republic. Religion continued to exist beneath that ice. When the layer of ice melted, Islam returned, with religious orders and groups, such as the Naqshbandiyyah and the Nur movements. The Democratic Party (DP) entered into close relations with them, and managed to convert the religious frustration of Anatolia into votes. In 1950, they were elected. But the power continued to be with the state, and it toppled the government of Adnan Menderes in 1960.

In 1969, Necmettin Erbakan founded his first Islamist party, the National Order Party (MNP). From that point on, a new political Islam began to challenge the Kemalist establishment. Erbakan had named his movement "Milli Görüş" (National Vision), suggesting that he alone represented the interests of the Muslim nation. Before that he had represented the out-skirts in Ankara as President of the Union of Chambers and Commodity Exchanges of Turkey (TOBB)—in other words, small and medium-sized operations in Anatolia. The MNP leader Erbakan demanded the reintro-duction of Friday as a weekly holiday, and he took Sharia into account when laws were passed. In 1971, the MNP was banned, and Erbakan found-ed the National Salvation Party (MSP). Until the MSP was closed down after the coup of 1980, Erbakan was a junior partner member of three coalition governments from 1973, when the party received 11.8% of the votes.

Erbakan achieved his greatest successes with the Welfare Party (RP), which he founded after the coup of 1980. But he had to wait for Özal's death, because Özal had integrated the conservatives as one of the four factions in his Homeland Party (ANAP), thus neutralizing the National Salvation Party. In his student years, Özal was a member of Milli Görüş; later, he was a candidate for Erbakan's National Salvation Party (MSP). Then, he ignored Erbakan's politics. Özal did not want to elevate Islam as the constitutive characteristic of a party; he also did not want to give the state priority within the economy. It was not until after Özal's death that Erbakan could enter the limelight again.

In the regional elections in April, 1994, the Welfare Party (FP) was the strongest party for the first time. In the parliamentary elections in Decem-ber, 1995, 21.3% of voters voted for them, more than for any other party. In June, 1996, Erbakan was elected Prime Minister of a coalition govern-ment that the Right Path Party (DYP) also belonged to. On February 28, 1997, the military sent the government a memorandum via the National Security Council. The generals demanded curtailing the scope of the Islam-ic İmam-Hatip schools and the Qur'anic summer schools, as well as clos-ing the religious orders and restricting the wearing of Islamic clothing, especially the headscarf, in public. On June 28, 1997, the government of Erbakan/Çiller gave into the pressure that the generals (and the public) were exerting, and he resigned.

Erbakan failed because, as the head of government, he was not look-ing for compromises, but was holding on to his confrontational style. His targets included the consumption of alcohol, the decadence of the West and the veneration of statues in public squares, which were in contrast with the strict interpretation of Islamist values. The rhetoric of the party continued to be directed against Europe and towards the Muslim Third

World. The economic politics were focused on state interventions and suggested the utopia of a just order (*adil düzen*) that would remove all injustices and imbalances in the distribution of income. In politics, he could not dispel the doubts that he was misusing democracy as an instrument to establish an Islamist state.

When Erbakan was toppled by the postmodern coup of February 28, 1997, only a few people missed him, among other things because the voters had recognized that Erbakan was not waving a magic wand and that people's every day life had not improved. Erbakan was forced to acknowledge that while the majority of the people were religious, they did not want an Islamist regime. February 28, 1997, showed the Islamists just how far they could go; the era of the generation of political Islam had come to an end. During the first phase in the sixties and seventies, they had opposed modernization with the central state with their challenging, blatant Islamism. The second phase marked the rise and fall of Erbakan in the nineties. Step-by-step, Erbakan was edged out of politics. After the first political ban that was imposed in 1982, and lasted until 1987, he received another political ban in 1997. When it ended, Erbakan was elected as head of the Felicity Party (SP), in 2003. The following year he left office as a result of being convicted of embezzling money from the Welfare Party (RP), and left the party.

After the overthrow of Erbakan and the ban of the Welfare Party (RP), the third phase commenced during the nineties. The follow-up party, the Virtue Party (Fazilet Partisi, FP), acted considerably more modest. Expressly, it was in favor of the secular order in Turkey, for a pluralist order, and for a free market economy. On May 14, 2000, the Founding Party Congress of the Virtue Party (FP) took place in Ankara. Because of the political bans that had been imposed on them, Erbakan and Erdoğan were not present. Then something outrageous happened. In a country whose political culture was based on not questioning the decisions made by the leadership, but following them blindly, Gül challenged Recai Kutan, who was the candidate of Erbakan at the congress, to become the head of the party, and Gül received more than 40% of the vote. In June, 2001, the Virtue Party was banned.

The ban of the Virtue Party (FP) had already deepened the chasm between the Traditionalists (*Gelenekçiler*) around Erbakan and the Renewers (*Yenilikçiler*), whose leaders, Recep Tayyip Erdoğan and Abdullah Gül, distinguished themselves. The renewers around Erdoğan now took the ban of the Virtue Party as a welcome occasion to break with Erbakan's Milli Görüş Movement.

## Erdoğan versus Erbakan

In 1969, Erdoğan (born 1954) joined the youth organization of Erbakan's National Order Party (MNP), and he rose on account of his rhetorical talent, even though members of his party who were also his friends were irritated that he wore un-Islamic shorts when he was in public and did not undertake any political propaganda in his sports club.

In 1975, he became the chairman of the Youth Association of Erbakan's National Salvation Party (MSP) in Istanbul's Beyoğlu district, to which the old residential quarter of Kasımpaşa belongs. In 1976, he became the chairman of the Youth Association for all of Istanbul. The gifted orator and organizer gradually established a base in Istanbul, and so Erbakan's Welfare Party (RP) selected him as their mayoral candidate for Istanbul in 1994. Due to the fact that four candidates who had good prospects shared the votes among each other, 26% was sufficient for him. Erdoğan had just turned 40. From then, on he became an inherent part of Turkish politics.

Despite misgivings, Erdoğan's politics were not Islamist, but very soon became pragmatic city politics. The city became cleaner and greener, and public transportation was diversified to help ease the heavy traffic of the metropolis. The water supply was secure once again. He borrowed money abroad and implemented billboards on municipal busses and in public squares, which became a new way to make money. For the first time, the inner city shipping lines did not end the year with a deficit. Erdoğan opened the first subway, and after the heating systems switched from brown coal to gas, it was possible to breathe again in the smoggy winter weather. The notorious corruption in the city's administration declined considerably. Under Erdoğan, the worst case scenario for companies that received an order from the municipal administration was that they had to supply a payment-in-kind, such as an ambulance or some kind of equipment for a school to individual districts. In 1995, he renovated the "Darülaceze" elderly care centers (literally, "Home for the Needy") and consulted with the Greek Patriarchy and Istanbul's Chief Rabbinate when there were questions that pertained to Christians' and

Jews' places of worship. To the extent that he desired respect for his religion, he met other religions with respect, Erdoğan said.

The old elite's dislike of the upstart from the have-nothings has, unfortunately, continued. Mesut Yılmaz, the hapless successor of Özal at the head of the Homeland Party, summarized it once by saying that a mayor had to be intelligent, have culture, and a university education. That infuriated Erdoğan. His reply had a threatening undercurrent when he said that he was an Istanbulian from the Kasımpaşa district, which is famous for its manly, rough fellows. And if necessary, he was going to act like a real Kasımpaşalıan. The Turkish saying "like a Kasımpaşalıan" means: beware, don't play around with the tough guy from Kasımpaşa.

Erdoğan's success is also due to the fact that he never quite rid himself of this street-reflex from his childhood and youth. Sometimes, the temper of a boy from the street becomes apparent in his behavior as a leader. In Kasımpaşa, people did not treat each other as delicately as people did in high-class Pera. Once, he was asked what kind of music he liked to listen to and he replied: "Orhan Gencebay and, of course, Müslüm Gürses." It was a clear acknowledgment that he was a fan of what the Turks refer to as "Varoş Culture." That is the lifestyle of those who have moved away from Anatolia, live in poverty in suburbs (*varoş*) of the big cities, and develop a kind of counter culture, i.e, "Varoş Culture."

Its canon includes neither the classical Turkish literature nor foreign literature. But they listen to the sentimental songs of Orhan Gencebay, Müslüm Gürses, and Ibrahim Tatlıses. These songs are about unrequitted love, a city yearning for the idyll one left behind. *Arabesque* is what this art form is known as. Its hybrid kitsch questions all hierarchies of bourgeouis taste. *Arabesque* creates a joy of living all its own in the low income groups that live on the outskirts of the cities. This is the kind of music Erdoğan listens to and when he was mayor, he once rejected ballet as being "pornography."

When Erdoğan reached the top, it was an Anatolian have-nothing who succeeded: one who is from the periphery, who has finally arrived in the center, and who wants to finally be treated humanely. The establishment came up with all kinds of hurdles to obstruct his getting there, but it was in vain.

On December 6, 1997, he visited Siirt, the capital of a province in the far Southeastern part of Anatolia. His young wife, Emine, was from there, from the rural district of Aydınlar. When her parents were still young, it was called Tillo, in Kurdish. This was one of the early retreats of the great preacher and renewer of Turkish Islam, Bediuzzaman Said Nursi, whom the apparatchiks of the early Republic had persecuted for 35 long years. It was in the Siirt province that Erdoğan gave a speech in which he quoted a poem.

Indeed, Erdoğan loved quoting poems frequently in his speeches. Going back to 1973, the young Erdoğan had won a competition reading poetry in Istanbul. Later, he became an admirer of Islamic mysticism, Sufism. His thoughts and feelings were reflected more by poems than in prose. The poem Erdoğan recited during his visit in Siirt was a poem by Ziya Gökalp, the ideologue of Turkish nationalism, written between the defeats of the Ottoman Empire and the Balkan Wars, and the War of Independence of the Republic. For decades it has been part of every textbook; every pupil knows it. The poem has the following verse: "The minarets are our bayonets, the domes our helmets, the mosques our barracks and the faithful our army." Erdoğan's final words were greeted by huge applause: "Let us come together under one roof to be citizens of Turkey."

That did not impress the Kemalist establishment, and the judiciary lunged back: "Inciting hate on the basis of religion," is what was stated in the indictment, and on April 12, 1998, the Court for State Security, Diyarbakır, sentenced him to ten months in prison for reciting that poem and a lifelong ban from politics. The Final Court of Appeals confirmed the sentence. In other countries, the sentence would have been categorized as an injustice, but in Turkey, it was pronounced in the name of national security. Erdoğan was demoted as mayor and started his prison term in March, 1999. Initially, he seemed to have given up hope completely: "In the future they will punish me when I read license plates instead of a poem." Then, his spirit flared up again. Poets, Erdoğan said, landed in jail when they read their poems out loud and that he could only hope that those who just listened to the poems did not also land in jail.

This center forward was not intimidated by the red card. He wanted back on the playing field, and he wanted to score goals again. He spent four months in prison, but was released early. He started his long march through Anatolia. He did not leave out a single province, no municipality. On August 14, 2001, he founded the Justice and Development Party (Adalet ve Kalkınma Partisi, AK Party) together with like-minded people.

The paragraph that caused Erdoğan to be sentenced had already been amended by Ecevit's government. Another politician who had suffered the same fate had returned back into politics. But they stopped Erdoğan from doing this. The game became grotesque; the establishment kept coming up with new hurdles. Erdoğan was not allowed to be a founding member of a party, could not be elected as a head of a party, was not allowed to be a candidate in the parliamentary elections, and was not allowed to enter a by-election—a special election held between general elections to fill the vacant parliamentary seats.

However, the last sentence was somehow reversed, and Erdoğan was elected as a delegate in the by-election of the Siirt province. On March 15, 2003, he had finally reached his goal: the Parliament elected him as Prime Minister. His self-concept was such that a head of government did not represent one of the metropolises, but a province that had been completely neglected in the past. Erdoğan quickly started a rapid fire series of reforms. During his first term in office, Turkey changed more than in all the decades before that. The economy finally started to boom, and Turkey was closer to Europe than ever. In prison, Erdoğan had realized that he could only be a politician if Turkey followed European norms.

Erdoğan had changed, mainly during the nineties and in prison. The Nobel Prize laureate Orhan Pamuk was also convinced that Erdoğan had changed. As someone who made up characters and played with them, he was sure that he was right, Pamuk once said. Erdoğan traversed the long way from being an Islamist to becoming a Muslim democrat. In 1996, he referred to democracy not as a purpose but as a means. His political career began at a time when Zia ul-Haq took over in Pakistan and Islamisized the country, during which Khomeini lead the revolution in Iran. He gave one of his sons the name of the Islamist leader, Necmettin Erbakan, and once he visited the Afghan Islamist leader, Hekmatyar. In 1992, he said it was impossible to be secular and a Muslim at the same time. Close friends, such as Özal's brother, Korkut Özal, and the entrepreneur, Cüneyd Zapsu, familiarized him with Western values.

When he founded the AK Party in August, 2001, he said: "Islam is my personal frame of reference; my political frames of reference are the constitution and the democratic principles." When Angela Merkel visited Turkey in February, 2004, she said that the German Christian Democratic Party and the AK Party based their values on religion, but that they separated religion and politics.

Islam is essential for Erdoğan's personal morals, but not for politics in a practical sense. After founding his party, he declared: "I do not agree with you, but I will do everything I can to make sure that you can freely express your opinions." And after his triumphant victory on July 22, 2007, he called out to his jubilant followers: "Now I would like to ask you to be quiet, really quiet." Then he added: "I do not want your joy to make the others suffer!" He wanted to reach Atatürk's goal with everyone—to raise Turkey to the level of "contemporary civilization."

Early on, during his years as mayor of Istanbul, a very influential Turkish journalist had recognized that Erdoğan was the only Turkish politician who had the makeup of a real leader. The process of letting go of his political mentor, Erbakan, was already completed at that point. Erbakan remained the same Islamist fundamentalist that he had always been. Erdoğan, however, became a political realist. Erbakan continued to dream of an Islamist state; Erdoğan respected democracy and justice, even the Turkish version. Erbakan continued with a strict Islamist discourse, spoke of Sharia, and an Islamist state. Erdoğan, however, recognized that practical problems could only be solved with pragmatic policies, not religious phrases. The traditionalist Erbakan kept women away from politics; the young modernizer Erdoğan promoted them within the party and relied on them during campaigns. Erbakan thundered against the EU as a "Club of Christians"; for Erdoğan it was, "an association with common values that Turkey could also join." Erbakan wanted a strong state; Erdoğan was familiar with the everyday problems of every day people from his time in Kasımpaşa.

While Erbakan failed as prime minister, Erdoğan was successful in his work as the mayor of Istanbul. Erbakan had tried, time and again, to stop Erdoğan's rise. In 1991, Erdoğan wanted to be a candidate for the parliament in Ankara, but Erbakan managed to push through one of his minions. It was against Erbakan's will that his Welfare Party (RP) selected Erdoğan as their candidate for mayor in Istanbul, in 1994. Erdoğan would no longer let himself be used by Erbakan to collect money from Turks in Germany for the party.

Erdoğan distanced himself from Erbakan and rallied modern Muslim thinkers, such as Ali Bulaç around himself. When Erdoğan was in prison, socialist human rights people visited him. Since that time, they have been close friends with him. Neither Erbakan nor one of his confidantes visited Erdoğan while he was in prison. They did not even extend a word of comfort. The break was made.

This break became more evident when the Virtue Party (FP) was founded in 1998, after the Welfare Party (RP) was banned. The fundamentalist Erbakan and the realistic politican Erdoğan, who were both banned from politics, sent their respective confidents into the running when a new chairman was elected. It was a close call when Erbakan's candidate, Recai Kutan, celebrated his victory over his challenger, Abdullah Gül.

The Virtue Party (FP) was banned soon thereafter. Erbakan and Kutan founded their follow-up party, the Felicity Party (Saadet Partisi, SP) in 2001. Its name was to be reminiscent of the Golden Era (Asrı Saadet) of the first four caliphs who were guided by law. During the parliamentary elections of 2002, it achieved a mere 2.5% of the vote and disappeared into oblivion while 34.3% of the electorate voted for Erdoğan's Justice and Development Party (AK Party). Erdoğan's party has been in power since 2002. Erbakan never forgave his renegade protegé. As recently as July, 2007, he demanded Erdoğan to show "remorse" and his return to the Millî Görüş movement.

Erbakan is forgotten, but during the election, one in two Turks voted for Erdoğan's AK Party. He turned out to be a star in Turkey, and he felt at home on the international stage of politics. He does not speak a foreign language, but it is astonishing how confident the boy from Kasımpaşa has become in his dealings with the big shots of the world. His body language is self-confident, and he looks athletic. During the Football Championship in 2004, in Portugal, he was always the first one to congratulate his Greek colleague Kostas Karamanlis every time the Greeks won. In concert with the European government leaders, he has learned not to continuously bash his dialogue partners with words—as he did in the beginning—but instead to listen and to be involved in a dialogue. What a difference compared to the know-it-all attitude of earlier generations of politicians.

Erdoğan's greatest political dream is to fulfill Atatürk's dream of leading Turkey to Europe. He has already fulfilled one dream: in December, 2002, only one month after he won the elections, the son of a simple sailor from Kasımpaşa walked up the steps of the White House in Washington although he was only the head of the ruling AK Party but not elected to the Parliament yet, put aside holding the prime minister's office. But it was not the last time that the most powerful man in Turkey was welcomed in the Oval Office by the most powerful man in the world.

## Transformation of Islamists

The Turkish political scientist, Ziya Öniş, describes five factors that had an impact on the transformation of Turkish Islamists. First of all, the authoritarian secularism, as expressed on February 28, 1997, showed the Islamists their limits within which they could operate. The Islamists understood that they could not question the secular order. Secondly, the Islamists had learned to maintain themselves in a representative democracy and could say that it contributed significantly to their moderation. Since they reacted positively to the democratization process, they became a power that demanded even more democracy.

Thirdly, the liberalization of the economy produced a class of Muslim entrepreneurs and academics who saw themselves as the winners of globalization. The rising Muslim middle class wanted more freedom and greater political involvement, but was not interested in a conflict with the secular establishment that would only endanger their achievements.

Fourthly, almost all political participants, in Turkey and in the EU, had recognized the EU as the external anchor with which they would be able to enforce their goals. Devout Muslims would see the EU as a guarantee to be able to maintain their Muslim identity, vis-a-vis the secular establishment. According to Öniş, the EU was a life-line and would cushion the confrontation between Islam and secularism.

Finally, intellectuals and civic groups always promote the democratization of a country, whether they are from the leftist liberal group or the Islamic group, because both denounce the deficits of Turkish democracy. The urban intellectuals in Turkey were formed by a secular environment, and this was more pronounced than in any other country of the Islamic world. The traditional Islamic institutions were too weak to produce creative thinkers. Intellectuals, such as Ali Bulaç and Fehmi Koru, and associations, such as MÜSİAD, were largely responsible for the pendulum in the Islamist movement swinging in favor of the modernizers. Several favorable inside and outside processes also came together. All together, these developments enabled the transformation from a movement of political Islam to a party that was obligated to the principle of a free democracy, according to Öniş' study.

The modernizers said good-bye to Erbakan's political Islam, which was anti-Western and, just like Kemalism, authoritarian. The movement of political Islam was in the midst of a transformation, shedding its skin. Erdoğan and Gül were no longer interested in confrontation with the secular establishment, but in social and political agreement. They were interested in the individual, their position towards the state, and strengthening society, vis-a-vis the state. In their belief, Islam must provide a frame for values and ethics that the individual practices privately. That kind of Islam is no longer political but cultural.

Erdoğan's and Gül's AK Party became the political representative of the rising middle class which had a history of inner Turkish migration. The AK Party marks the transformation of Post-Islamism to a neoliberal, globalization-friendly party. During the long process of separating from Erbakan, Erdoğan recognized that it was impossible to solve problems and win elections with Islamist slogans. While serving a sentence in prison for reciting a poem from a schoolbook, he recognized that Turkey did not need Islamism, but freedom.

Thinkers, such as Ali Bulaç, have established a democratic discourse within Islam. And it is separating itself from the political Islam of Erbakan. He said that the new generation of Muslims were defending human rights and basic rights, and were being political on the basis of democracy; they were promoting civic society, but did not want to gain access to the state as a means to power. He found a plausible comparison for this transformation. There was a time when people lived in homogeneous villages. Everything was the same. Then the inhabitants of the villages came to the cities, and various lifestyles were crowded into one space.

This theory could be to a world where there were over two hundred states for 3,000 ethnicities who spoke 8,000 languages. The world had become pluralist, and everyone was different than the next person. And the conclusion that Bulaç drew was: "Democracy is maintaining these differences."

## The Anatolian Tigers of Kahramanmaraş

It is nine in the evening. The day is not over yet for Mehmet Kanbur. The boss of the largest ice cream manufacturer in Turkey enters his cafe. While entering, he puts on a white apron and steps behind the sales counter. He does this every evening when he is in his hometown of Kahramanmaraş in Turkey's Southeast, where foreigners assume everyone is poor, but where one of the most amazing success stories in Turkish history happened. Twenty years ago there was no industry along the slopes in the foothills of the Taurus Mountains. Since then, Kahramanmaraş has grown and become one of the 15 largest industrial producers of the 81 provinces in Turkey.

That morning, like every morning, Mehmet Kanbur had arrived at his factory at 6 a.m., and that afternoon he was picking up Prime Minister Erdoğan, with whom he has been friends, at the airport to bring him downtown, where 70,000 people were waiting for the head of government. Along the way, they had Mado ice cream, from Kanbur's production; and now, a few hours later, the ice cream manufacturer is standing behind the sales counter, calling a boy in from the street, giving him an ice cream. Mehmet Kanbur is a happy person, and it is obvious every minute of the day.

"Working is like worshipping God," he adds during a quiet minute. "The highest form of worshipping God." He adds that God does not want people to only pray and fast; that God wants people to produce and create things, and help their neighbours. "Anatolians do not tire, they are hard workers and tolerant," Kanbur says about the characteristics of his compatriots, and lastly what he implies are his own as well. It was from this work ethic that the term Muslim Calvinist was derived.

If Anatolians work hard, success is inevitable; like with Mehmet Kanbur. For four generations, his family has been selling ice cream. It is made from the milk of the goats that graze the hills of the Taurus Mountains and from the snow of the mountains. The cafe has been here since 1850. In 1985, Mehmet Kanbur crossed the borders of his hometown. He called his patisserie's ice cream, "Mado," a composition from "Maraş Dondurması," which means ice cream from Kahramanmaraş.

By then, he was producing it industrially, and the label Mado started its success story—first in Turkey, and then beyond the borders. The Anatolian from Maraş, which is what the town was called until 1972, introduced franchising to the Turkish food industry. Mado is being sold in more than 200 cafés of the same name, and also in 22 countries, all the way to Australia. A fourth of his sales are generated by export. He laughs again. "Didn't you Europeans mistrust new labels from Japan and the Far East 20 years ago?"

Despite their friendship, Erdoğan should be grating on the disciplinarian Kanbur's nerves. The politician is never on time. And he is two hours late in Kahramanmaraş, too. Yet none of the 70,000 who had been waiting along the wide promenade left, and at the end of it was the platform upon which Erdoğan would start pacing with a microphone.

Yakub, a textile worker, has come because, on July 22, 2007, he is going to be voting for Erdoğan's AK Party. He is waving the blue flag of the AK Party with the emblem of the light bulb, and he is embarrassed to say that, in 2002, he voted for the Homeland Party (ANAP).

The pharmacist, Emrullah, will also be voting for the AK Party and Erdoğan, and also for the first time. Like Yakub, he says that he does not trust any other politician. Mustafa, a loan specialist with an agricultural cooperative, should actually be turning his back on the AK Party, because Turkish agriculture is not doing very well on account of the subsidies that have been slashed. "But the country is doing better than ever," he adds.

Like many others, Cuma and Ömer have travelled quite a distance, from a village near Elbistan. "If you ask me, three things have improved compared to 2002: the health system, price stability, and the infrastructure," the retired Ömer says enthusiastically. Cuma, who works as a bus driver, nods. Both leave early and do not hear the second part of Erdoğan's speech. They want to be home before it gets dark. They hear how Erdoğan names all the districts of Kahramanmaraş that his opponent Baykal, who is the head of the CHP, is avoiding. After he has named all the obstacles that the state elite are placing in his government's path, the Prime Minister calls out to the crowd: "You are the will of the people!"

This election would "test whether there is democracy in Turkey and whether the will of the people is being accepted," İsmail Alkış' predicts. He is standing in front of Kahramanmaraş branch of the Industrial Association, MÜSİAD. It is his duty to support the economic development in Anatolia. Alkış points out that he is not a member of the AK Party. Yet he likes Erdoğan. "There were three Prime Ministers in Turkey who did something for the people: in the fifties, Adnan Menderes; in the eighties, Turgut Özal; and now, Tayyip Erdoğan," he stresses. But, "material incentives did not suffice for success," he explains. In Anatolia, it was proven that work is a form of worship, and that a lot of small enterprises can become big if they unite.

One of the cities that accomplished industrialization on their own and without state aid was Kahramanmaraş. It is one of the more than one dozen Anatolian industrial cities. In the city itself, the average income per person is above the average in Turkey. Mehmet Balduk, the President of the regional Chamber of Industry and Commerce, says proudly: "You cannot spend any money on luxury here." All income is reinvested in new machines for the textile industry, which halved their price per piece, and was thus able to conquer the cheap Chinese competition; in the food industry; and in new cement works. "99% of all investments are done by people from the area," says Balduk; not very many of the young industrialists are from the families of the old land owners.

Most of them made their modest starting capital by trading agricultural products in the region—or like Mehmet Kanbur, with his family-owned Yaşar Patisserie and the ice cream.

It is after midnight. Customers keep arriving at the patisserie on Trabzon Street. "Yes, we also brought a new coffee house culture to Turkey," Kanbur says enthusiastically. People sitting at the tables are politicizing more than usual. A convoy of cars that are part of the Nationalist Movement Party (MHP) drives by noisily. As the music gets quieter in the distance, Kanbur says that the people are very aware of what the chairmen of the CHP and MHP, Baykal and Bahçeli, have accomplished during their time in office—or not accomplished.

Ali Çiçekçi and his brothers also took over their enterprise from their father who, in 1970, had founded a factory that produced copper pots and pans. But after a while, copper was no longer fashionable; steel was en vogue, and Ali Çiçekçi switched over to stainless steel, in 1989. In the beginning, he sold his goods in Ankara and Istanbul. Then, in October, 2003, the German Technical Cooperation (GTZ) expanded their project of "Supporting the economy in Anatolia," to Kahramanmaraş. Since that time, six experts have been consulting with the small textile and stainless steel processing operations and hot chili marketers about quality management, strategic planning, and marketing. For the first time, the owners of small enterprises are visiting trade fairs, adjusting their products to demand, and entering new markets.

Çiçekçi replaced the manual production with modern machines. His operation now produces 1,500 stainless steel pots and pans, and 1,500 aluminum ones. He sells them under the "Saflon" trademark; 85% of the production goes into export. Çiçekçi mainly sells his products in Germany, Italy, Dubai, and Iran. In 2008, he took part in a trade fair in China. Çiçekçi is one of the ten, out of 55, manufacturers of cooking ware who managed to achieve a breakthrough in Kahramanmaraş, the center of this industry, not including Istanbul. In June, 2007, the first trade fair for local manufacturers took place in Kahramanmaraş. The large buyers from Germany and Turkey arrived, and the trade fair was a huge success, and will be repeated annually.

Hanefi Öksüz did not need the GTZ project. In 1985, when he had just received his degree as a mechanical engineer in Istanbul, he returned to Kahramanmaraş. Instead of taking over his father's small cotton plantation, the son started a small factory to process this cotton. Almost every year, he added one new enterprise. Today, Öksüz employs 5,000 people in the 16 companies that belong to Kipaş Holding, and is thus the largest employer in the province. His holding was ranked number 30 in the list of the largest industrial enterprises in Turkey. The core of this list is made up of integrated textile operations, which includes everything from producing the thread to garment construction.

Öksüz lists his sales as being approximately 400 million dollars. He exports 15% of that directly. If one adds his pre-production for other exporters, the share of his direct and indirect exports in the holding rises to 95%. Every year, the consolidated sales of the holding have increased by 20%. In 2007 alone, Öksüz invested 125 million dollars in the classic operations of his holding and 60 million in a cement plant. He has no problems getting foreign-currency credits from international banks, and because he is solvent, he finances a significant part himself. His first foreign investments were in Egypt, and he donated two hospitals and five schools to his hometown of Kahramanmaraş. So, Hanefi Öksüz's Kipaş Holding is another success story of the Anatolian Tigers, which have developed into little industrial centers without government subsidies, and which have become the foundation of the sustained Turkish upswing. Öksüz likes the term tiger. Like a tiger, with its fantastic eyes, he is able to see the opportunities that arise. Öksüz is optimistic: "Turkey has commenced a great development." He thinks that while Istanbul, the gateway to the world, is the suitable location for commerce, Anatolia is the right location for production.

"In Kahramanmaraş industrialization did not start until the middle of the nineties," Mehmet Balduk, president of the local industrial chamber of commerce, explains. In the beginning, there was the recognition that the city was not a transit point, like Adana, and not a tourist attraction like Antalya; that agriculture produced products that only had little value-creation potential, and that commerce alone would not suffice. The large landholders were not the ones who had become industrialists, but the small business people. The first three industrial operations were established, in 1984, during the era of the reformer Turgut Özal; one year later, there were already a dozen. From 1995 on, the customs union of the EU, and new ideas, like leasing equipment, buoyed the development. Ultimately, it was the economic stability of recent years that helped.

In 2007, the industrial production reached 1.5 billion dollars; a fourth of it was exported. After the large investments were finalized, the production value in 2008 was projected to rise to 2.5 billion dollars; this is what Balduk expected. The only limitation that growth has is the inadequate education system that does not prepare young people for jobs, Balduk laments. That is why the chamber and entrepreneurs were investing more in new and modern schools.

After midnight, Mehmet continues to stand behind the sales counter. He does not emphasize that he is the boss of his 5,000 employees, but does what all his employees do. "It is not the chair that makes the boss, it is the person who sits on that chair," he says. He wants to set an example. "Nobody is supposed to believe that he has gotten rich and no longer has to work," he explains, capturing the Muslim variation of the Calvinist work ethic. This is the kind of Anatolian people that the AK Party values. During the elections of 2002, the city sent eight delegates to Ankara; seven belonged to the AK Party. Five years later, things were no different.

# Chapter II

---

## The Counter-Elite
## on Its Way to Power

# Conquering Government Power

## The near bankruptcy of the old elite in 2001

February 19, 2001, was the beginning of the end for the old Republic. The monthly meeting of the National Security Council had only lasted 15 minutes. It ended in an uproar, with Prime Minister Bülent Ecevit storming from the assembly hall, lamenting that something unusual had happened. President Necdet Sezer, who was chairing the meeting, had leveled a severe and unreasonable accusation at Ecevit, and adressed him in a way that was inconsistent with, "our state traditions and habits." Sezer, who was known for his bad temper, flung a copy of the constitution at Ecevit in the presence of the five most important military representatives, and accused him of obstructing justice during an investigation of corruption. Sezer supposedly also demanded that several ministers resign.

The value of the Turkish Lira plunged immediately, and the stock exchange collapsed. At this moment, no one was suspecting that the dams were breaking and that Turkey would be faced with one of the worst recessions since the founding of the Republic. Ecevit, the elder statesman of Turkish politics, mustered all of the energy he had to counter speculations that he would be resigning. He was a sick and old man, ravaged by disease. In a counter attack, he accused Sezer, whom he had suggested for the office of President in April 2000, of unnecessarily triggering a state crisis in economically difficult times.

Sezer saw things differently. The former chairman of the Constitutional Court had advanced and become the new "good guy" of Turkish politics. As president, he was committed to enforcing a constitutional state and fighting corruption. He was of the opinion that Ecevit, who had never been particularly interested in money and who had absolute integrity, did not support him enough. Sezer still did not see himself as president, but as the supreme constitutional judge. He was the first head of state to make use of Article 108 of the constitution, which gave him the power to secure "the legality of administration." He reactivated the old State Inspection Council (DDK), which is under direct authority of the President, and ordered it to bring to light irregularities at the state banks and private business banks that the government had been forced to take over because of their impending illiquidity.

The nineties were a lost decade for Turkey. Politically, the old dangers in the form of Kurdish nationalism and political Islam were more present than in any era since 1923, and the state elite made it perfectly clear that the Kemalist modernization doctrine did not offer enough room for both. The big parties in the political middle lost votes that went to the extreme nationalist parties and the Islamist Welfare Party. Economically, Turkey lost momentum internationally while the rich became richer and the poor remained poor within the country.

In a study in early 2001, the governing body of the Turkish Industrial Chamber of Commerce (TOBB) stated that politicians had wasted 195 billion dollars. That was the equivalent of the gross national product at the time. Without this waste, the Turkish economy would have grown by 9.2% every year. Instead, they needed a whole decade for the income of every citizen to increase that much. Everyone was aware of the fact that the state, which formerly had been revered as being "holy," had become a free-for-all. Politicians had emptied the vaults of the state, without restraint, to keep their clientele happy.

The Turkish parties had long ago ceased trying to attract voters with programs and ideas. They weren't people's parties, but clientele's parties. The heads of the parties misused their presence in the state by securing influential people who were able to mobilize voters with presents from the state's coffers. They made the state banks provide credits that were never paid back, or that had an interest rate that was far lower than the galloping inflation. They pumped large agricultural subsidies into areas where their voters lived; they privatized state-run operations and passed them on to their minions. Delegates provided masses of voters they were close to with jobs in the local enterprises, while these salary lists were generally much longer than the list of people who were actually employed there.

The state degenerated to such an extent that it became an object of prey, and was plundered. In 2001, the three largest state banks had a depreciation requirement for "loss of function," which was what credits of more than 30 billion euros that could not be collected were called. That was the equivalent of a fifth of the gross national product. Furthermore, these banks were increasingly undermining the role of the Central Bank by creating random liquidity, and thus driving inflation up. The state had to take on the losses of the 13 private banks that had dried out their owners; at the end of the plundering process, these deficits had shifted to the state in order to secure private savings. Altogether, this made up more than 10% of the gross national product.

What these modern bank robbers had in common was that they were protected by politics. A prime example was Cavit Çağlar, prodigy of Süleyman Demirel, political veteran. With protection of the state, he had taken over the flourishing internet bank, had plundered it to the last cent to benefit his textile empire, and before the private depositors had a chance to storm the bank, the cunning Çağlar had sold it to the Savings Deposit Insurance Fund (TMSF).

First, the Turkish judiciary acquitted him of all guilt. In December, 2004, he was then sentenced to three years and 10 months in prison, plus a penalty of 100 million euro. Avni Balkaner, the former owner of Yurtbank, also had to start a prison sentence in 2004, but for 34 years.

The Uzan family, whose members had grown up in the shadow of Özal, and had become even richer under Süleyman Demirel, were particularly greedy. At the zenith of their power, the Uzans belonged to an economic empire, including construction and chemicals, plus several cement works and two newspapers that, along with six television stations, spread their fame. In 1993, the Uzans bought the first privatized power supplier, Çukurova Elektrik. The company was one of the favorites of the Istanbul stock exchange. They were even joined by Mark Mobius, who at the time was managing an investment fund of 7 billion dollars at Franklin Templeton Investments. Then the family patriarch, Kemal Uzan, pulled all liquidity out of the company to finance the growth of his Rumeli Holding, and to uphold his legendary lifestyle of luxury, that included planes, yachts, and luxury apartments in London and New York.

Mobius lost only once with Uzan; the Turkish state lost several times. The deposit insurance fund had to pump 5 billion dollars into the finance institutions, İmarbankası and Adabank, several times after the Uzans had helped themselves to its coffers. İmarbankası had enticed them with the highest interest rates that any Turkish bank paid.

Most investors, however, lost everything, because the Uzans had transferred the money to offshore accounts that were not covered by the deposit insurance fund. The two telecommunication companies, Motorola and Nokia, were also victims of the Uzans' criminal activities. They paid credits worth billions to the Uzans to finance the technological development of Telsim, the mobile telecommunication services provider they both owned. Billions flowed to other accounts, and in the summer of 2003, a court in New York demanded that the Uzans pay back 4.2 billion dollars to Motorola and Nokia. The Uzans had also cheated Motorola and Nokia by excluding them from participating in annual general meetings that had been called on a short-term basis. In these meetings, they enforced a capital increase, which is why Motorola and Nokia kept losing shares in Telsim.

The names Çağlar and Uzan stand for white collar crime, which was wide-spread in Turkey, but are now mostly a thing of the past. The state footed the bill. The deficit in the national budget grew continuously; in the critical year, it reached 17% of the gross national product. The state had stopped being a welfare state oriented towards spreading the wealth to those in need. Instead, the state of the Republic of Turkey was distributing free loans (totally unethical sinecures): it was paying a wide range of all kinds of subsidies; it was filling the holes within state banks and state-operated companies; and it financed exports that only existed on paper. The result was not a free market economy, but a political stage that positioned everyone to have easy access to money.

It resulted in a distribution, Turkish-style, and it was to the detriment of the poor. The state financed its deficit by increasing the money supply. The consequence was an inflation rate around 70%, under which the poor suffered the most. The rich had it easier, because they bought high yield bonds with which the state financed its deficit. The returns on the loans were frequently around 25%, and they increased the wealth of the already rich, urban state elite. Even standard companies could not resist the pull. Almost every year during the nineties, the interest derived from the income of the 500 largest companies in Turkey was higher than the profit from their core business.

But the interest load was financed from taxes that everyone had to pay. The poor had their revenge by increasingly cheating on their taxes and continuing to build their *gecekondus* on government ground. This kind of economic mechanism killed all economic dynamics. The only way out was named by the economist Eser Karakaş—to fulfill the Copenhagen Criteria, and to establish a modern transparent state in Turkey that respects the law, acts with reason economically, and that is accountable.

But for this to happen, Turkey needed a new generation of politicians. The old ones had not learned a craft, except for expensive clientele populism. Increasingly, the parties were spent; their leaders were getting old. For almost half a century, only one political quartet had determined what was happening in the state of politics: the conservative, Süleyman Demirel (born 1924); the left-wing nationalist, Bülent Ecevit (1925–2006); the Islamist, Necmettin Erbakan (1926–2011); and the ultra nationalist Alparslan Türkeş (1917–1997). The mechanism of justice had been suspended.

It would take a few years until entrepreneurs, politicians, and even generals had to take responsibility in court. The first politician whose wealth was confiscated was Koray Aydın, the Minister of Public Works from 1999 to 2002. In 2004, the retired Admiral, İlhami Erdil, was the first high officer to be in a civil court since 1976. Among other things, he was to have provided jobs to his daughter's letter-box company. The Chief of the General Staff at the time was believed to have launched the case against Erdil.

A coalition had been in power from 1999 to 2002: the Democratic Left Party (DSP) of Bülent Ecevit, the Nationalist Movement Party (MHP) of Devlet Bahçeli, and the Homeland Party (ANAP) of Mesut Yılmaz. The Republican People's Party (CHP) was no longer even a member of parliament; instead, there were two nationalist parties, the DSP and the MHP, and the liberal ANAP. These groups were fully blamed for the economic crisis. The straw that had broken the camel's back was the uproar that swept through the National Security Council meeting on February 19, 2001.

Despite the fact that there had been a number of mutual assistance agreements with the International Monetary Fund (IMF), the last one dated December, 1999, the government could not maintain a consolidation course. The deficits grew; the inflation increased. In order to maintain at least a shaky balance and avoid a collapse, the government was offering incentives that triggered further inflows of money necessary for survival. But in doing so, they were perpetuating a system of waste. As long as the political system was stable, the markets expected Turkey to pay its debts.

This evaluation changed within hours on February 19. Both Turkish and foreign investors pulled their money out of Turkey, and an unprecedented capital flight commenced. The Turkish Lira lost 40% of its value in a very short time. The Turkish economy shrunk by 9% that year.

The two nationalist parties were the support of the government. Instead of isolating Turkey, they had to watch Turkey increasingly being included in the global economy and the international system. In December, 1999, a new treaty with the IMF was enforced; it was not even half-heartedly implemented by the government coalition, and the EU bestowed the status of candidate upon Turkey at the Summit of 1999, which Ecevit had tried to avoid attending until the last minute. Two years later, after the attacks of September 11, 2001, because of its geopolitical location, Turkey became a part of the war against terror.

As a consequence of the severe crisis, in May, 2001 the government had to enter into a new accession treaty with the IMF. The IMF had become an important "anchor" for Turkey, because it provided a certain amount of accountability in politics. Since 1963, Turkey had had an association treaty with the EU, and since 1996, it had the customs union with the EU that had had no impact on its political and economic development. In the nineties, the weight of the "coalition" that was in favor of an EU process grew, but it was essentially born by civic society. The crisis of 2001 changed this. It was a severe blow for all parts of Turkish society. From then on, a large majority of the population wanted an EU process to stabilize the unreliable politics and the volatile economy.

Initially, however, the mutual assistance agreement with the IMF remained the only anchor. The agreement made Turkey the largest debtor of the IMF, and it ensured that for the first time, Turkey kept its promise. The prerequisites were favorable, because this time the IMF saved Turkey directly from state bankruptcy. Turkey turned to the economist Kemal Derviş, who was internationally renowned, to implement the program. Derviş was the Vice-President of the World Bank since 1996; his parents were close friends of the Ecevits. Derviş, a young and talented economist, had always seen himself as a social democrat and had consulted with his political mentor, Ecevit, in the seventies, had studied in London, and at Princeton, from 1973 to 1976, and had tried to direct Ecevit away from the path of statism and towards a free market economy. Derviş threw in the towel, had a career at the World Bank, and returned as a super Secretary of Commerce to save the nation.

In 1994, Derviş had stated: "The system is not capable of cleansing itself." Among other things, he had already pleaded to get rid of the state banks. Now was the time. The CHP, which was in the opposition, demonized him as an "agent of the IMF." However, Derviş was unperturbed in implementing the reform program. He put the Turkish economy on new and healthy feet, and the reforms became the basis of the economic upswing, from which another party was also able to profit: Erdoğan's Justice and Development Party (AK Party), which had not been founded yet.

At first glance, the 15 reforms of Derviş were not all that spectacular. They were called the Law to Reform the Tobacco and Sugar Markets; they created the autonomy of the central bank, and created efficient bank supervision; and they prepared the privatization of the state banks. But as a whole, they revolutionized economic politics because they placed a fire wall between politics and the economy, and prevented politicians from grabbing the resources of the state to spread among the people to mobilize voters. Politics had to be done differently: with programs and with ideas. That is where the traditional parties failed, and so they were punished in the parliamentary elections of November 3, 2002, and disappeared politically.

## The triumph of the new elite in the elections of 2002 and 2007

A landslide victory is generally the political term for what happened in Turkey on November 3, 2002. But as a fact it was more: it was a turning point that can only be compared with the elections of 1950, when the voters had ended the one-party reign of the Republican People's Party (CHP). This time, they were exchanging almost every politician in Turkey. During the elections of 1999, the three coalition parties—the DSP, MHP, and ANAP—had received 55% of the vote. Three years later, their vote was only 15%. All three government parties did not achieve the restrictive 10% clause; none of the ministers were reelected. Ecevit's DSP party was the party that was punished the most severely: with 1% of the vote, they suffered an ignominious defeat. The time of politicians such as Ecevit had come; the time of politicians like Recep Tayyip Erdoğan had begun.

The new AK Party replaced the CHP/DSP. The result was not like manna from heaven. In April, 2001, when the crisis was climaxing, and four months before the AK Party was founded, 38% of Turks said they would not give their vote to any party. Three years before that, it had been only 5%. But now, as a result of the deep recession, the population was rejecting the political caste and the political system. The authority of the government had been crumbling for years.

It started during the nineties. On November 3, 1996, Abdullah Çatlı, the most well-known "godfather" of the Turkish underworld had been killed, along with a beauty queen, in an accident near Susurluk. Sedat Bucak, a conservative member of parliament, survived the accident, which brought to light the corrupt networkings of parts of the government, the security apparatus, and the underworld.

The devastating earthquake of August 17, 1999, fuelled people's anger with politics that proved to be incapable of helping quickly and efficiently. Ultimately, the eruption of the economic crisis on February 19, 2001 was the straw that broke the camel's back. Now, everyone knew that the state did not exist for its own sake, but that it had degenerated and become the object of prey of the greedy. The state was no longer credible. The constitution still listed it as a "holy state." Turkey was about to experience a complete overhaul of its political system.

The tribunal on November 3, 2002, initiated it. Only two parties were represented in the new parliament: with 34.4% of the vote, the AK Party had 363 of the 550 delegates, while the CHP had achieved 19.4%. Once again, the result revealed the fronts of the culture battle, in which the AK Party represented the periphery that hitherto had been excluded from political and economic power, while the CHP embodied the Kemalist state elite of the center. The chasm was the same as in 1950, when the Democratic Party (DP) triumphed over the CHP, relegating them to the opposition. Since then, the state elite had applied its options to make sure that the opposition parties did not nullify the axioms of their state; this meant that the basic issues of the Republic had not been solved for half a century.

The electoral mandate for the AK Party was clear: they were to produce more wealth through better economic policies and more democracy by embedding Turkey in the EU. For decades, Turkey had suffered through a lot of rhetoric for all, and generous sinecures, or unethical "gifts," for a few. Now, the electorate wanted a real market economy and social justice; they wanted a democratic state that served the individual and society, not itself. The traditional parties had failed. The vacuum that they had left was conquered by the AK Party; both to the right and the left of center. The CHP was virtually no longer a social democratic party. The "third path," for which Tony Blair and Gerhard Schröder had provided a blueprint, had never really interested them.

The new AK Party was the beneficiary of the ideological ossification of the CHP. On November 3, 2002, they benefited from the electorate being completely fed up with ideologies. Ideological slogans had had an impact on the election in 1999.

Only a short time before, the PKK head Öcalan was arrested and the country had been in the grip of nationalistic euphoria. The state and its security were at the center once again. But in 2002, the economy determined the elections. None of the parties that represented in the Parliament returned back to the Parliament.

Ziya Öniş, a Turkish political scientist, ascribes the triumphant victory of the AK Party to three acts: firstly, the AK Party had profited from the failure of traditional parties, which included the fact that the CHP no longer felt responsible for social justice. Secondly, the AK Party had managed to attract both the winners and the losers of globalization, and thus established contact with electoral alliances across all levels of society. Thirdly, they had been able to utilize the success of the pragmatic mayors of the Islamist RP and FP, which many of the AK Party candidates had belonged to.

Their voters were also rewarding the fact that the AK Party had been sufficiently credible in distancing itself from their Islamist predecessor party and no longer demanded an Islamist state, but merely freedom of religion in a liberal democracy. It was the only party that represented society and the rights of the individual, with the intention of protecting these rights against an authoritarian state. Even if their founders grew up as members of the Islamist movement in Turkey, the AK Party was closer to the liberal basic tenets of Europe.

The AK Party continued their economic reforms in their practical government policies that had been negotiated with the IMF, including the restructuring of public finances. It put the relationship with the EU on a new basis. Earlier governments had rejected parts of the Copenhagen Criteria, on account of "Turkey's distinctive features," as being unacceptable; the new government processed each and every one of them. For the first time, they sent their foreign policy advisers to the European Parliament and the EU Commission to find out where there was a concrete need for action and to promote Turkey on a very personal level.

As a result of the Iraq War, Turkey moved closer to the German-French axis in the EU. They were more flexible than all other Turkish governments when it came to Cyprus politics, and they supported the plans of the UN to overcome the division of the island; this failed due to the Greek-Cypriotic South. Meanwhile, the CHP, that was the only opposition party, was increasingly pursuing ossified nationalistic policies. Waiting for a weak phase of the government, or a confrontation between the government and the military, was a futile strategy.

The AK Party, which had a majority in parliament, passed one reform after the other, especially during its first two years in office. Abdullah Gül, who had been Prime Minister Erdoğan's deputy from November, 2002, to March, 2003, conceded that new laws alone would not suffice; that they would have to be implemented, too, and that there was hidden resistance at work that his party must overcome. With the help of the reforms from 2002 to 2004, Turkey was taking a big step in the direction of a liberal and pluralistic democracy.

Capital punishment was abolished; so, too, was the State Security Court (DGM), which had imprisoned members of the opposition for reasons of "national security." What was expanded significantly was the scope of freedom of expression, even if there were still restrictions. The penal system was modernized, juvenile courts were introduced, torture was abolished from prisons, and investigations against those who tortured were given priority. The right of assembly was improved, and it became more difficult to ban a party.

A new penal law was developed that protected individuals from the state. Also, a new penal code and a new civil code abolished the "honor" of the family and instead awarded women rights. Additional reforms allowed Kurdish language courses to be given, and gave non-Muslim minorities rights. However, these have already been curtailed by the bureaucrats in the ministries.

At the center of the "Seventh Reform Package" of July, 2003, was restricting the scope of the military's influence. The National Security Council and its General Secretariat were deprived of power in that their function was reduced to mere consultation. For the first time, the Parliament debated the defense budget that, previously, the General Staff had allotted itself.

Despite these impressive reforms, the fear in parts of the population did not abate that the AK Party had a "secret agenda"; the party was supposedly endeavoring to erect an Islamist state. The proof allegedly was that the Ministry of the Interior was allocating liquor licenses to the local authorities and that there were mayors who wanted to restrict serving alcohol to certain parts of the cities. However, these cases were also met with resistance within the AK Party. Abdüllatif Şener, who was deputy prime minister from 2002 to 2007, rejected prohibitions like this as not being modern, and demanded that different lifestyles be respected.

The question as to whether adultery was an offense that should be included in the new penal code started a heated debate. What triggered it was that the wives of leading politicians in the AK Party saw this section of the code as a means to proceed against women whose husbands married second wives before imams. Mainly, they were enraged about a second wife of a prominent minister from Eastern Anatolia. After that, traditional party circles began wanting to prosecute adultery; even the CHP was in favor of prosecuting it. Due to pressure exerted by the EU, the initiative was dropped.

The fact that the government did not extend the term of office of Süreyya Serdengeçti, the successful Governor of the Central Bank, caused a sense of nervousness in the financial markets. Like other governments before, the AK Party wanted to fill important positions with loyal followers. First, the government wanted to replace Serdengeçti with a banker who was managing a bank that operated according to Islamic prohibitions of interest. After there were protests from the financial circles, it decided on an expert who had had a career in the Central Bank, and who was close to the AK Party. After the victory of Hamas in Palestine, in 2006, there were also irritations on account of the fact that the AK Party—not the government—welcomed Khaled Meshal, Hamas' radical head, to Ankara. The party had hoped to persuade him to pursue a more moderate course. But in doing so, it stepped out of line of the European consensus. The irritation remained. The AK Party did not insist on its standpoint regarding two topics that are important for the Islamic section of their voters: the issue of headscarves and the Islamic Imam-Hatip schools.

The secret agenda of erecting an Islamic state invoked by the Kemalists, however, remained a chimera that only they believed in. That is what the parliamentary elections of July 22, 2007, showed. The AK Party was elected more triumphantly than any other party in the history of Turkey. In the last forty years, no other party has received such a clear vote to govern. The AK Party increased its share of votes from 34% to 47%. It was not the laicist campaign that the government elite had conducted for weeks that decided the elections, but the economic situation, which was better than ever, after four years of an AK Party government. The election refuted the assertion that the dispute in Turkey was about secularism and Islamism. This formula proved to be yet another attempt of the old elite to save parts of their power.

The AK Party emerged from the elections as the first widely rooted people's party in Turkey. The people who vote for the AK Party are Muslims, but the politics of the AK Party is not Islamist. The voters do not see a contradiction between the secular character of the Republic and its private practice of the Muslim religion. During the 2002 elections, the young AK Party had attracted voters from all classes, but most of their leading politicians were rooted in political Islam. This changed in the 2007 elections. Well known liberals and leftists were voted into the Parliament instead of former Islamists.

These were politicians like Ertuğrul Günay, the earlier general secretary of the CHP, when it was still pretending to be a social democratic party, and Mehmet Şimşek, one of the most well-known liberal economists in Turkey. Both became ministers in the new government. Others included Haluk Özdalga, the former crown prince of Ecevit; Zafer Üskül, a famous constitutional legal expert; Reha Çamuroğlu, a well-known Alevi thinker; and the popular filmmaker, Osman Yağmurdereli. All of them joined the Parliament for the AK Party. The reason Özdalga gave for joining the AK Party was that he thought it symbolized the best opportunity for the democratization of Turkey, and that it was the only people's party that represented all parts of the country.

The AK Party arrived at the right time. It offered voters an alternative when voters had turned their backs on traditional parties—their politicians and the old order—and wanted to settle accounts with them. After the triumphant victory of July, 2007, the chances of correcting the early mistakes of the Republic and installing a modern democracy in

Turkey were better than ever. A first important step was a new constitution—the first constitution in the history of the Republic to be written by civilians and not by the military. In June, 2007, before the elections, Erdoğan commissioned the leading constitutional expert of the country, Ergun Özbudun, to begin writing it. He assembled a group of six constitutional experts. They referred to the spirit of their draft as liberal and democratic. He placed great emphasis on strengthening the civil rights and constitutional liberties of the individual, vis-à-vis state power. The six authors fashioned the section on civil rights and constitutional liberties on the European Human Rights Convention and decisions by the European Court for human righs. The authors followed the Anglo-Saxon interpretation of secularism, which allows public and social expression of religion as long as it does not infringe upon the affairs of the state. Özbudun commented that the design thus moved away from the radical model of laicism, that was patterned after the French version, and that it strengthened secularism. It's regrettable that the attempts for a civic constitution have unfortunately been left out altogether.

## The party of the counter-elite:
## On their way to a democratic people's party

The July 22, 2007, election turned the AK Party into the voice of the Turks. In 69 of the 81 provinces, it was the strongest party. The AK Party was the clear winner, even in the strongholds of the CHP, such as the Marmara region around Istanbul and along the Aegean coast. They received more votes in every age group than any other party; 51% of women voted for them. Except for the richest 20% of Turks, the AK Party led among all income classes. But the result was not a coincidental byproduct of Election Day. In September, 2006, Konda, the leading polling institute in Turkey, predicted results that were very close to the actual election results.

The AK Party has been successful because its politics were pragmatic, and they benefitted large parts of the population. Because of their emphasis on social justice, their neoliberal economic politics binded prosperous small and medium-sized entrepreneurs with the poor. With its approach of recognizing the rights of Kurds within the scope that government politics has to offer, the AK Party is significantly more popular with the Kurds than the Kurdish "Democratic Society Party" (DTP). With its EU reform process, it won secular liberals that had become disenchanted with the secular state elite. The AK Party was, and in some ways still is, a remarkable example of how Islamists can become Muslim democrats.

This transformation has not been completed yet. The AK Party has been unable to attract a large group in the population: the majority of the heterodox Alevis does not practice the pillars of Sunni Islam that includes the daily ritual of prayer and the pilgrimage to Mecca. Even though they revere Ali, the son-in-law of Mohammed, they are also indifferent to the theology of orthodox Shiism. At least every fifth Turk belongs to this demonination that was persecuted during the Ottoman Empire. Until Deniz Baykal rose within the CHP, they were devoted followers of Atatürk's party. After Baykal, some of them rejected the CHP, but they do not trust the AK Party yet. In 2003, Erdoğan declared that Alevism was not a separate religion. The liberal approach in other areas of politics had not entered religious politics yet, but change was about to happen. The well-known Alevi intellectual, Reha Çamuroğlu, was elected to parliament for the AK Party. On behalf of Çamuroğlu, on July 15, 2007, one week before the elections, Erdoğan visited the most important Alevi lodges in Istanbul, where he spoke with the spiritual heads of the Alevis—the Dedes, and promised to put 2,000 Dedes on the salary lists of the Diyanet, the Turkish Directorate of Religious Affairs; this was a first step towards recognition. Up until then, the Diyanet had not recognized the Alevis as an independent form of Islam.

The AK Party was not glued to ideologies. It was a pragmatic party with several wings. It covered politics to the right of center, where Muslim values are important to conservative voters and the gains from globalization are important for freelancers. It also covered social democratic politics to the left of center, where the concerns are social justice, the state as a regulator (but not as a participant) of the economy, and the acceptance of various lifestyles. As the political scientist Öniş put it, the AK Party had become a "new kind of hybrid formation."

Yet it initially sought membership with the conservative European People's Party (EPP). While it hovered before the gates, the Socialist International Coalition, which wanted to rid itself of the CHP, got in touch with the AK Party. The German CDU and CSU keep the AK Party at bay in the EPP. But the German CDU and the AK Party have since institutionalized their relationship. The general secretary and parliamentary groups meet on a regular basis to single out various things they have in common in their programs: CDU and AK Party are people's parties based on values and market economy; family, self reliance, and the principle of subsidiarity rank high in both parties.

Originally, the AK Party was established around politicians who were part of the Islamist "Millî Görüş" movement of Erbakan, but today, it houses several factions. The first and most important of these factions consists of the "post Islamists" around Prime Minister Erdoğan, President Gül, Minister of Justice Mehmet Ali Şahin, and Abdüllatif Şener, who used to be the Deputy Prime Minister and who returned to work at university in 2007. Their circle also includes Foreign Affairs Minister Ali Babacan, even if he did not enter politics until 2001. They relinquished the Islamist discourse in favor of politics that emphasized the rights of the individuals and the meaning of Islamic values for a person's identity. The second election of 2007 weakened the second faction, "the Islamist wing." This included the former Speaker of the Parliament Bülent Arınç, from 2002 to 2007. In 2007, the cabinet did not include a number of Erdoğan's companions, including Ali Coşkun, Abdülkadir Aksu, Osman Pepe, and Mehmet Elkatmış.

The third faction comprises conservatives and liberals who left the traditional central parties of the Homeland Party (ANAP) and the Right Path Party (DYP) and joined the AK Party. They include the Deputy Prime Minister Cemil Çiçek, the Minister of Education Hüseyin Çelik, and the former Minister of the Interior Abdülkadir Aksu. The State Minister responsible for foreign trade, Kürşat Tüzmen, who used to be a member of the Nationalist Movement Party (MHP), is considered the leader of the fourth nationalist faction. These factions also include individual persons who do not make up a wing of their own. Erdoğan brought them along as technocrats from the Municipal Government of Istanbul, like the Minister of Transport Binali Yıldırım and the Minister of Environment and Forestry Veysel Eroğlu; or he found them among the bureaucrats, such as the foreign policy expert and former ambassador, Yaşar Yakış, who had been the Minister of Foreign Affairs during the short Gül government.

The youngest faction is made up of liberals and leftists, such as Güney, Özdalga, and Üskül. And then there are influential personal advisors of

Erdoğan, such as the successful entrepreneur, Cüneyd Zapsu, and the American expert, Egemen Bağış, an economist who was trained in New York.

Erdoğan won independence because they recognized that the AK Party had become the most important political formation that wanted to bring democracy to Turkey. The policies of the AK Party were pragmatic, but they approached the EU reforms in a more radical and decisive way than any other party. There was no reference to Islam in their party's program. This was because it saw itself as a conservative, Muslim-democratic party of the people that combined modernity and Islamic values and reforms by maintaining Turkey's own culture.

Unlike their Islamist predecessors, the AK Party did not look down on the EU as a "Christian Club." It recognized that with the help of the EU reforms, Turkey could develop into a secular and pluralist democracy in which it would maintain its Muslim identity. Furthermore, it was beneficial that the majority of the population supported the EU course, because no other party was pursuing credible EU politics. The EU thus became an important instrument during the early phase of the party: it implemented its political goals via EU-reforms, and its progress in moving closer to the EU secured the support of the electorate, while pulling earlier critics to its side. The EU had become a model for democracy for leading politicians, and a "life-line" for democratization and economic stability. Politicians and voters of the AK Party also recognized that Muslims live better in democracies than in authoritarian states.

In doing so, the EU is provided support for the transformational dynamic from the outside that Turkey lacked inside due to the lack of historical precedent. It is also an instrument to curtail the major influence the military and the bureaucrats have in the country. Euro-sceptics, who prefer the model the United States has, are also raising their voice within the AK Party among other things because religion plays a greater role in the US (at least on private TV channels) than in Europe. The judgment for the case of a university student, named Leyla Şahin, on June 29, 2004, of the European Human Rights Court gave the Euro-sceptics within the AK Party ammunition. The court had decided that the state had not violated the human rights convention when it suspended Leyla Şahin from university for wearing a headscarf.

Since the middle of the decade, Euro-scepticism within the AK Party was on the rise—for other reasons, too. People had become disillusioned with the EU because Brussels had not rescinded the embargo against Northern Cyprus, contrary to what they had promised. Increasingly, members of the AK Party were critical, saying that the EU was rewarding Greek-Cypriots, even though the Greek-Cypriots rejected the EU's plan to reunify the island—while at the same time, the EU was discriminating against Turkish-Cypriots, even though they had agreed to the plan. Like most representatives of the secular state, elite members of the AK Party claimed that the EU was setting different standards for Turkey's EU accession process than for any other candidate county. One subject these circles discussed was that while the EU demanded more rights for minorities in Turkey, it was not making any statements as to the Turkish-Muslim minority in the EU member Greece.

After the triumphant victory in the July 22, 2007 elections, the AK Party did not require the EU course as much as before to provide legitimacy to their politics. After 2002, however, they had started with the EU course more convincingly than any of the earlier governments for three reasons: in order to gain national and international legitimacy and to prove to doubters that their fears were unfounded; in order to give a new balance to the relationship between military and government; and to enable more freedom of religion in Turkey. Since the proceedings that were initiated to ban the AK Party on March 14, 2008, the party has been more focused on its EU and reform politics once again.

Despite emerging criticism of the EU, the AK Party is continuing to pursue an active and pragmatic EU policy. Their foreign policy is also not ideological. It dropped the hard nationalist line of their predecessors, and except for Armenia, it has good relationships with neighbor states. They accept Turkey as a beneficent regional power, and it has become a stabilizer in a turbulent region. It's possible, however, that recent events—especially in Egypt and Syria—could change this regional balance, as some of the government's decisions have isolated it from traditional allies.

The AK Party continued the policy of Turgut Özal from the eighties. There are other aspects by which Erdoğan's AK Party and Özal's Motherland Party (ANAP) can be compared. Both had taken over the government with an absolute majority soon after they were founded. Both relied on private business. Both were composed of a large number of comparable factions, and both refrained from the polarizing style of their predecessors. The Motherland Party, however, found itself in the midst of a crisis when the political ban that the generals had placed on politicians was rescinded early in 1987. With the return of conservative Demirel, the nationalist Türkeş and the Islamist Erbakan, the corresponding groups turned their backs on the Motherland Party and joined their old leaders again. Seeing that the old political caste has been fully discredited by the voters, this danger does not seem to exist for the AK Party.

The greatest danger that the AK Party faces is that it is still an "Erdoğan Party" tailored to its charismatic leader. There are hundred thousands of grass roots volunteers who work in cities and districts that the political rivals have never heard of. The continuous grass roots level work in the years between the elections is one of the greatest strengths of the party. On Election Day, there are several experts who are already preparing the next election campaign. And they conduct it in the places where the voters live. Other parties send their speakers through the country in convoys. In the cities, they switch over to busses and thunder down to their audience from above. Then they leave the city without having spoken with the voters themselves.

If the AK Party wants to become a lasting force in Turkish politics, the party will have to institutionalize more in the coming years. The history of Turkey has taught them that there are hardly any loyal voters who continuously commit themselves to one party. Therefore, how long the AK Party will remain in government depends on how the economy develops. If the economy continues to grow, the self-employed people who are part of the new Muslim-Anatolian middle class will be content; so, too, will those who demand social justice. Social politics demand growth, but growth presupposes that there is an inflow of foreign capital and that will only flow as long as the country is stable and is spared confrontations. However, after a decade of being mostly conciliatory, the Erdoğan government has grown increasingly confrontational both within and without the country, and it has even gone so far as to roll back some of the democratic measures they instituted after their last landslide victory.

# The Dispute between the Old and the New Elite

## "White Turks" against "Black Turks"

Erdoğan was still the Mayor of Istanbul and he was about to start his prison sentence. That is when he turned to his followers in October, 1998, and said: "In this country there is a division between White Turks and Black Turks; your brother Tayyip is a Black Turk." Later, when he was Prime Minister, he continued to refer to himself as a "Black Turk" for some time, as for example in his interview in the New York Times, on May 11, 2003.

It was not Erdoğan who had invented this catchy saying. It goes back to the Turkish sociologist, Nilüfer Göle. She was the first scientist of the old elite to investigate the changes in political Islam in Turkey and the Muslim women's movement. She was one of the first who had no fear of interacting with Islamists, and she nourished intense contact with their intellectuals. She divided her academic career between the Bosporus University in Istanbul and the Sorbonne in Paris.

During the mid-nineties, she coined the phrase about the "White Turks" (*beyaz Türkler*) and the "Black Turks" (*siyah Türkler* and also *zenci Türkler*). She defined "White Turks" as being the secular urban upper class that held the political power for centuries and also the power to determine what was to be considered culture. Black Turks, on the other hand, were all those who looked down on the state elite. They were considered to be uneducated and provincial; they lived out in the country, were poor, and were devout Muslims.

The White Turks listened to Bach's Well-Tempered Clavichord, went to see Mozart's opera, Cosí fan tutte, and attended New Year's Eve balls. Most Europeans felt close to them, especially since the White Turks had a command of foreign languages. Meanwhile, the White Turks pay homage to an authoritarian and undemocratic understanding of politics. They are close to Europeans culturally, but not politically.

The opposite holds true for the Black Turks. They mostly listen to sentimental Arabesque tear jerkers by Orhan Gencebay and Müslüm Gürses, they celebrate their weddings in the austere halls of municipal "Düğün Salonu," where alcohol is not served, and there is no western-type of dancing. Culturally, they are not close to the Europeans; few speak a foreign language. But they are the ones who want the reforms and a modern democracy. They want to free themselves from the authoritarian yoke of the supposedly "enlightened" elite and give simple people the right of self-determination.

The self-appointed elite of the Republic is well-educated, and frequently has studied abroad. Their careers take place in government positions or the private business sector of the metropolises; their lifestyle is western and does not leave any room for other life designs. They worship the military as the reincarnation of their state, and they look down on all religiousness in public—including Islam just as much as any other religion. Consensus is not the focus, but power.

The party of the "White Turks" is the Republican People's Party (CHP). Half of the voters from the richest 20% of Turks voted for the CHP in the July, 2007, elections; only 23% of the richest voted for the AK Party. This trend was repeated for university graduates. The last representative of the political hierarchy of the "White Turks" was Necdet Sezer, the President from 2000 to 2007. On account of his office, he was not allowed to belong to a party. But it was no secret that he was affiliated with the CHP.

During Sezer's term of office, the chasm between the White and Black Turks grew. However, the will of the people catapulted the AK Party into the government. Most wives of the leading politicians wear a headscarf, and Sezer did not simply want to see this piece of cloth in his presidential palace in Çankaya, where Atatürk once resided. And so he always sent two kinds of invitations for official receptions. The first one went to politicians whose wives did not cover their heads; they were invited with their wives. The other invitation was sent to politicians whose wives, like Erdoğan's wife, wore a headscarf; this invitation was addressed only to the men.

Politicians of the CHP pointed out that they did not see the lifestyle of politicians of the AK Party as being "contemporary." The "Hat Law" that forbid wearing the Ottoman Fes and prescribed wearing Western hats had been passed 80 years before. In an interview with the *Vatan* newspaper, on October 10, 2005, Onur Öymen, the deputy chairman of the CHP, demanded that Erdoğan should follow Atatürk's example during the public holiday on October 29, the Day of the Republic, and organize a ball, put on a tuxedo, and dance with every woman who appeared at the ball. Then Erdoğan would thus have proved to the world that he had arrived at the height of "contemporary civilization." Yet neither Demirel nor Ecevit had danced with their wives in public. For days, the Turkish press mocked the "Öymen's dance criterion" and whether tuxedo and a waltz were enough to be a European.

These elite had long lost their credibility for the Black Turks. The wealth was distributed very unevenly, the government institutions were working more and more inefficiently, and an all-encompassing agreement within society was not in sight. During the 2002 and 2007 elections, the Black Turks showed who had a majority, and what the will of the people was. A competition had commenced, in terms of political, economic, and social supremacy. In the long term, the Black Turks were in a better position. Demographically, they were a majority, and politically they were better organized, via the AK Party. If Erdoğan had not been their leader, they would have had another one.

Thus, the White Turks fall back on laicism as their last weapon of defense. It is authoritarian, and if necessary, it is enforced by the military. But the "White Turks" are only using laicism to distract from the actual conflict: the law between the traditional state elite and the new Muslim-Anatolian middle class. However, the latter does not question the separation of state and religion. It only wants freedom of religion the way it is practiced in other secular states in Europe, too. The White Turks claim that the "Black" majority has a "secret agenda" to gradually Islamisize Turkey. But its agenda is not all that secret, but visible for all to see: democratize Turkey, implement human rights, and respect minorities. Maybe the White Turks are the ones who have a secret agenda, with their battle cry "Save Laicism": they want to use the means of the state to prevent losing their privileges and sinecures. They are the ones who are obstructing globalization and Turkey becoming a member of the EU—and also privatization and foreign capital. According to the Turkish motto:

"Küçük olsun, benim olsun," even if it is small, the main thing is that it belongs to me.

The biographies and lifestyles of Erdoğan and Gül are different than those of Ecevit, Baykal, Sezer, and the generals. Anatolia's rural population has blazed a trail to the top, and Turkish society has become more pluralist on account of Turkey's urbanization, its transition to a market economy, and its Muslim-Calvinist ethics. They started by immigrating to the cities. That is where mobility towards the top started, and this led to those who had been excluded politically and culturally now being present.

Nothing is like it used to be. Today, the Black Turks have an elite that is educated and economically successful, that has a modern consumer lifestyle, and that has fun in their leisure time, even if that is in accordance with their Islamic values. Politically and socially, they have become self-confident. They no longer hide in their ghettos, but have become a part of the public, even with their wives and their headscarves. To the shock of the old elite, they even appear in their elegant Istanbul districts such as Nişantaşı and Bebek. For many of the old elite, their world is about to come tumbling down, and their wish is "to return to the way things were." The state remains as secular as ever and no one wants to change that. A new lifestyle that is Islamic and modern has become a visible alternative to the Western modern lifestyle. A counter-elite has emerged, and it is challenging the traditional elite. There are two areas where these two groups are irreconcilable: headscarves and the Islamic İmam-Hatip schools.

## A black sheep in the public space: the headscarf

No other country in Europe has a stricter ban on wearing headscarves than Turkey, and there is no other country where wearing a headscarf or not is as conflicted. A majority of Turkish women wear a headscarf, and they have three standard options to do so: the traditional "başörtüsü" worn by peasants, the citified and modern "turban," and the strict black "çarşaf." Independent research institutes have determined that the majority of Turkish women are in favor of loosening the strict ban on wearing headscarves. The secular state elite—the White Turks, however, consider the headscarf to be a symbol of a lifestyle that is incompatible with laicism; they interpret the headscarf as a symbol of political Islam, and therefore they reject it. The Black Turks reply that it is a religious obligation and a civil right; the headscarf has become a symbol for them as to what extent they are ostracized by the White Turks.

The frontlines were firmly drawn and there was no solution in sight. Quite the contrary: the culture battle around a piece of cloth became more vehement and more grotesque. In April, 2007, the military and the state elite were bothered by the fact that Hayrünnisa Gül had decided to wear a headscarf, and thus blocked the election of the President. But it was not she who was to be elected President, but her husband, Abdullah Gül.

The headscarf is more than a bone of contention in Turkish politics. It keeps occupying the courts. In 1999, the 47-year-old widow, Hüda Kaya, and her daughters went to prison for seven months. A court had convicted them of "violently pursuing the overthrow of the Turkish Republic." The three of them participated in a demonstration at a university against the ban of wearing a headscarf. After they were released from prison, Hüda Kaya founded an NGO and continued her campaign.

Both sides represent their position in an aggressive way that excludes any approximation. It is a collision of two mutually exclusive lifestyles and opposite principles. By placing herself out of gaze, a woman who wears a headscarf is less visible in the public space because she is excluding a part of herself by becoming less visible than a man who does not need to conceal himself. Democracy, however, takes place in public and demands a public space. So, one can easily feel emphaty with a woman with headscarf who demands more public space while observing her religious obligations and privacy, all at the same time. On the other hand, those who want to strictly ban wearing a headscarf are excluding women even more from society. The government excludes women who wear a headscarf, but not the men who are in favor of abolishing the ban on wearing headscarves.

The Turkish judiciary has never clearly determined locations where it is prohibited to wear headscarves. The general practice is that neither students nor teachers are allowed to wear headscarves at schools and universities. It dates back to an administrative ruling on dress code that the military junta passed in 1980, and that the Ministry of Education rendered more precisely in 1982. The Higher Education Council (YÖK) was to implement the regulation at the universities and there were several other persistent attempts to extend this ban to other areas, especially after the post-modern coup of February 28.

In 2003, the head of the Turkish Council of State (Danıştay), which is the highest administrative court, kicked the witness, Hatice Hasdemir Şahin, out of the court because she was wearing a headscarf. Indeed, the court knew her. She was a lawyer and did not wear a headscarf when she appeared in court as such because women in official functions are not allowed to cover their hair when entering sovereign space of the state, including parliament. It therefore caused an uproar when the newly elected Merve Kavakçı dared to appear in the Parliament with a headscarf, in 1999, as a delegate of the Islamist Virtue Party (FP), but was banned from swearing her oath in the Parliament. Both Kavakçı and Ilıcak—the non-scarfed delegate who defended Kavakçı entering the Parliament wearing a headscarf during the oath-taking session—lost their mandate.

In 2005, President Sezer expanded the public space where headscarves were not to be worn by including the Çankaya Presidential Palace. Before that, he had started inviting delegates whose wives wore headscarves to official receptions. This was discontinued in 2005. From then on, every officeholder was forced to pass a ban on wearing headscarves for "their" public space.

There is still no Turkish law that expressly bans wearing a headscarf. The defenders of the ban on wearing headscarves invoke Section 174 of the Constitution. This section has the provision that eight reform laws that have the goal of "elevating Turkish society to the level of contemporary civilization and protecting the laicist character of the Republic" cannot be abolished. One of these laws is number 2596, which was passed on December 3, 1934. It prohibits wearing "specific" (i.e. religious) clothing. In 1934, the majority of the Turkish women wore the traditional headscarf worn by the rural population, referred to as "başörtüsü" (literally, "head covering"). The founders of the Republic obviously did not have this headscarf in mind for their ban.

After the Iranian Islamist Revolution of 1979 the black "çarşaf," which the wives of radical Islamists wear to this day, appeared in Turkish streets. The traditional robes that cover the entire body had existed in devout Eastern Anatolian provincial cities, such as Erzurum and Bayburt, since the Ottoman Empire.

But it was the "türban" that became really popular with the new Muslim Anatolian middle class. This "türban" is complicated to wrap. It covers the hair and ears, and its bright shades have caused it to increasingly become a fashion object. It was this "türban" that became an unpopular symbol that challenged the White Turks' understanding of ultra-secularism. The goal was to ban this modern headcovering from public places. The traditional, uneducated mothers had worn a "başörtüsü" without thinking much about it. Daughters who were educated and emancipated consciously chose this modern headcovering.

The judiciary had the task of preventing a spread of the "türban." And they could be relied upon to do this. On December 13, 1984, the government council rejected the court action of a student against the new dress code of the Higher Education Council (YÖK), from 1982. On March 2, 1989, the Constitutional Court (AYM) rejected a law initiated by Turgut Özal allowing students to wear a headscarf for religious reasons. In 1991, the Constitutional Court affirmed its earlier verdict. Despite the formal ban, the students could continue to enter the university grounds and take exams wearing a headscarf. Even during the annual university entrance exams (ÖSS), there were students who were resolute to apply wearing headscarves.

This changed after the generals' ultimatum on February 28, 1997, which led to the Islamist Prime Minster Erbakan being ousted. During the ÖSS exams, students wearing headscarves were now immediately turned away. From the winter semester on, most universities only accepted passport pictures of women who were not wearing headscarves. In January, 1998, one of the first official acts of the newly appointed rector of the Istanbul University, Kemal Alemdaroğlu, a staunch Kemalist, was to print a brochure that contained all verdicts of the Constitutional Court (AYM) and the Council of State (Danıştay) that had to do with the headscarf ban. From the winter semester of 1998/1999, he made sure that no student entered the campus wearing a headscarf. This regulation triggered huge demonstrations in the quarters around the university, in which Hüda Kaya and her daughters also had participated. The students devised a strategy and wore wigs over their headscarves. Until a sign appeared on the doors of the university that stated, "It is against the law to enter the university wearing a headscarf or wig."

On November 25, 2002, the Cassation Court (Yargıtay) confirmed the validity of the law. It interpreted the headscarf in public spaces as a "symbol of rebellion against the principle of laicism." Those who wore headscarves were regarded as implicitly declaring others as their "adversaries," thus endangering the public order. Among the White Turks, the fear actually is widespread that women wearing headscarves could exert pressure on those students who do not wear a headscarf. A loosening of the headscarf ban would open Pandora's Box, is their reasoning.

Shortly before the Ecevit government was deposed in 2002, the delegates of the three parties of his coalition government had asked for a loosening of the ban, upon which Sezer read them the riot act, saying that it was unconstitutional, and thus a non-issue for all times. Furthermore, he did not understand why students of the theological faculty covered their heads during the Qur'an classes, and the same ban should also be valid for them just like the ban applied for the students of any other majors.

The hardliners were supported by the European Court of Human Rights which, on March 5, 1993, had rejected the case of two Turkish students who did not want to accept that the new student IDs only accepted photos without headscarves. The judges determined that this regulation did not impinge upon freedom of conscience and the freedom of religion.

On November 10, 2005, the same court decided on the case of Leyla Şahin versus Turkey, and declared that the plaintiff had not been injured in her right to practice religion after the state had excluded her from studying at the university because of its ban on wearing headscarves. Their reasoning was that in democratic states, there were considerable deviations when determining the relationship between state and religion, and that each state, therefore, had the right to perform restrictions in the way the freedom of religion is practiced.

The fact that Turkey proceeded very restrictively was proven by the verdict of the Council of State (Danıştay), which on February 8, 2006, annulled the appointment of Aytaç Kılınç as the principal of an elementary school because she wore a headscarf when she was not at the school, stating that it was incompatible with a "contemporary laicistic education system." This once again expanded the public space in which the ban on wearing headscarves applied.

Nowhere was the trench between White Turks and Black Turks as deep as with the headscarf issue, and it has not been fully bridged during the past years. Prime Minister Erdoğan therefore sent his two daughters, Esma and Sümeyya, to study in the United States. At home, he promised that he would be loosening the ban on headscarves in every election campaign. The prerequisites for that are difficult because of the verdicts of the Constitutional Court (AYM) and the European Court for Human Rights. Article 174 also prescribes the principles of the headscarf ban for eternity—the principles that the opponents of the headscarf base their reasoning on. It would also not be advisable to put basic rights up to a vote in a referendum.

In one of his most important personnel decisions, President Gül named the professor of sociology, Yusuf Ziya Özcan, from the renowned English-medium Middle East Technical University, in Ankara, as the new chairman of the Higher Education Council (YÖK). His predecessors, Kemal Gürüz (1995–2003), and Erdoğan Teziç (2003–2007), were very rigid in their implementation of the headscarf ban at universities. In February, 2008, Özcan let the universities decide themselves whether they were going to permit women to wear headscarves, whereupon the rectors' conference, whose members had been named by the previous YÖK, immediately lodged a complaint about their new chairman.

What had preceded this decision was that on February 9, 2008, a majority of three quarters of the delegates had voted in favor of changing two articles of the constitution. The 10th article of the constitution, pertaining to the principle of equality, now included the formulation that this principle also applied to using public services. Article 42, which pertained to the right to education, was amended in that it was stated that no one could be robbed of their right to higher education. The rectors' conference classified this constitutional amendment as a counter-revolution, and the CHP entered a constitutional complaint. On June 5, 2008, the Constitutional Court (AYM) revoked the constitutional change, thus ignoring the intention of the Parliament.

The official dress codes did not only apply to universities, city halls, and hospitals. They also applied to public and private schools. Girls who attended the Islamic İmam-Hatip schools were allowed to wear long coats, but not headscarves. In 2003, students had protested against the ban by chaining themselves to their schools. The İmam-Hatip schools are the second ideological battle field between White and Black Turks.

# A repressed alternative to state schools:
# İmam-Hatip high schools

The founders of the Republic did not want to abolish religion. They only wanted to exert control over it and keep it on a short leash. Therefore, they established the first vocational schools, in 1924. Through these newly established schools, they wanted to train the prayer leaders and preachers in mosques—in other words, the *imam*s and the *hatip*s. Little by little, they opened 29 İmam Hatip *mektep*s, or middle schools. Because there were not enough students, they had to be closed again, in 1930. No wonder: the job prospects were not clear, and after switching to the Latin alphabet, in 1928, people could no longer read the old religious sources.

The schools for prayer leaders and preachers remained closed for almost two decades. During this time, there was no religious education in Turkey, except for the state-controlled Qur'an courses, mostly offered in summers when the school semesters ended. After the transition to multiple-party democracy the number of these schools mushroomed, this time as vocational high schools with a focus on religious education. Most of these new İmam Hatip high schools were opened under Suleyman Demirel, who was Prime Minister for several terms. During his terms, 327 vocational high schools were opened, not only religious ones. Tansu Çiller, Prime Minister from 1993 to 1995, managed to open 167 new İmam Hatip high schools. The Islamist, Necmettin Erbakan, who followed in 1996, only managed to open a modest number of 22 schools. And it was Erbakan who said that the schools were the "back yard" of political Islam in Turkey.

Erbakan's utterance of seeing İmam Hatip schools as their "back yard" was like a curse for the schools. It is a big part of why they are controversial. Since then, those who oppose the schools think they have been proven right and that only continuing theological universities should be open for the graduates of these schools. The proponents want to keep all disciplines at the universities open for these graduates. The conflict is carried out as irreconcilably as the one surrounding the headscarf. It also illustrates that the relationship of the government, society, and religion are the Republic's issues that have not been solved. The White Turks want to make the İmam Hatip high schools seem as unattractive as possible and criticize the fact that girls are also admitted, even if they cannot become an imam; the Black Turks insist that the discrimination should end, and that the schools should have the same rights as other secondary schools.

During an election event on March 2, 2004, Erdoğan called out: "I am a graduate of an İmam Hatip school, and my father did not send me to this school to become an imam." Erdoğan once again promised to cancel the penalty for the graduates of İmam Hatip high schools that the Higher Education Council (YÖK) had introduced in 1997, as recommended by the military. Technically, the penalty is a coefficient that the grade average of graduates of İmam Hatip schools are multiplied by along with the university entrance exam (ÖSS), resulting in a lower score that effectively only allows them to study theology at universities.

Erdoğan's government undertook two attempts to improve the situation of the schools. The intention of the first draft of the law of May 4, 2004, was to weaken the penalty. It failed after the protests by the general staff, YÖK, the rectors' conference, and ultimately President Sezer's veto. The second initiative, on December 15, 2005, wanted to pave the way for graduates of the İmam Hatip schools to obtain a second high school diploma from a regular secondary school or a correspondence school. This initiative failed on February 8, 2006, when the Council of State (Danıştay)— the highest administrative court—raised an objection. Afterwards the plans to upgrade the İmam Hatip schools vanished again. A willingness to come to an agreement was nowhere on the horizon.

Yet parts of the state elite had at one time promoted the İmam Hatip schools. In 1946, the delegates of the Republican People's Party (CHP) suggested in parliament to use "religious affiliation" as an instrument against the impending danger of communism. In their opinion, communism was now the only danger. They also realized that they would have to react to the new Democratic Party (DP) immediately. Yet Prime Minister Recep Peker rejected the suggestion of his delegates by saying that he did not want to replace one poison with another poison!

And that is why it remained up to the DP government of Adnan Menderes, which governed from 1950 on, to institute 19 İmam Hatip schools. The schools were to take seven years to produce "enlightened men of religion." From then on, the İmam Hatip schools reported to the Ministry of Education. The generals who had staged the coup in 1960 tried to close the schools twice. But they did not succeed. Rather, the conservative Prime Minister Süleyman Demirel, who governed from 1960 on, promised to open universities to the graduates of the schools. But that did not come about either. Because the generals who staged the coup in

1971 closed the middle school branch of the schools (it was reintroduced in 1974) and determined that the graduates were only allowed to study within the boundaries of their courses—in other words, religion.

In doing so, the generals had opened the doors to study for the first time. In 1971, there were only 72 İmam Hatip schools, with 5,200 students in attendance. Until the coup of 1980, the number of schools rose to 374, and the number of their students to more than 200,000. The quantity changed, as did the quality. A law that was passed in 1973 recognized the İmam Hatip schools as high schools and guaranteed that their graduates could study theology or any other major they could choose, according to their score on the university enterance exam. This also held true for the other specialized high schools for technology, commerce, and pedagogy. From then on, more graduates of the İmam Hatip schools decided to study Law, Political Science, and Pedagogy than Theology. Recep Tayyip Erdoğan did not only study theology, but economics. In 1976, actions brought forward by parents to the Council of State (Danıştay) made it possible that schools that were to train prayer leaders and preachers should also accept girls.

The generals who staged the coup in 1980 did not add any new İmam Hatip schools, but they made it possible for the graduates to study majors or specialties that had been chosen by them. Unlike Recep Peker, in 1946, they recognized that religion was a useful means in the battle against communism, and thus they promoted the Turkish-Islamic synthesis. Conservative Istanbulian intellectuals, associated with the historian İbrahim Kafesoğlu, had developed this synthesis during the seventies. It propagated that Turks had started to flourish culturally when they accepted Islam. The Turkish-Islamic synthesis became part of the official ideology; Islamic religion classes became obligatory courses at all schools for the first time and, like during the founding years of the Republic, Islam returned as a constitutive element of Turkishness.

Up until the memorandum of the National Security Council on February 28, 1997, which led to the overthrow of Erbakan's government, nothing changed about the statute on İmam-Hatip schools. Their numbers increased to 601, with 511,500 pupils, both boys and girls. This was the equivalent of 9% of all pupils at the middle school and high school level.

On February 28, 1997, the generals demanded that lawmakers introduce eight-year compulsory education for all within an obligatory training, the aim of which was to destroy the "İmam Hatip middle schools" completely. This law became binding on August 16, 1997. In a second step, the Higher Education Council (YÖK) introduced a penalty for the graduates of the İmam-Hatip high schools, thus denying them any access to universities, except the theology faculties.

The proponents of this suppression upon the İmam Hatip schools reasoned that the rise in numbers of pupils was a danger for the laicist order of Turkey, and furthermore, that the "uniformity of laicist education" had to be reestablished. The parents of İmam Hatip students replied that they sent their children to these schools because they could learn more about religion; other parents decided in favor of them because it was the private donors who had introduced a generous scholarship system for the children from homes with lower incomes; still others because they thought that their daughters were taken care of better at İmam Hatip schools than at other schools. Moreover, parents and children thought that, compared to other schools, the İmam Hatip schools were "morally pure."

Private donors also built the school buildings, the boarding schools, and the cafeterias. Many of them are vacated today. More and more schools are being closed. The measures of the "February 28, 1997 post-modern coup" have made the charm of İmam-Hatip pale. The numbers of pupils have shrunk enormously. Two-thirds of the places that are available are empty today. In a study conducted by the social science institute, TESEV, on İmam Hatip schools, İrfan Bozan comes to the conclusion that the penalty for the graduates reduced the number of pupils, and also the quality of the pupils, as a result of the dwindling motivation. Increasingly, private schools are the alternative that parents are turning to.

The representatives of the state elite are content with the condition that was achieved. Some of them even want to reduce the number of teachers of religion classes at these schools, which would make the schools inaccessible to girls again. Not all secular intellectuals agree. İsmet Berkan, the editor-in-chief of the liberal *Radikal* newspaper is worried about the development at the İmam Hatip schools, commenting: "If devoutly religious people and the graduates of İmam Hatip schools feel as if they are black and as if they are second class citizens, then it is an important subject that is of interest to all of us."

Meanwhile, there is a bonus that the graduates of theology receive, only if they choose to go to the theology faculty. In 1999, there were, at most, 1,200 places at universities to study theology, whereas there were 79,500 graduates of the İmam Hatip schools. By 2003, however, the number of İmam Hatip graduates had shrunk to 9,380. At the same time the religious authority, Diyanet, was complaining that there were 15,000 positions that they could not fill because there were not enough applicants who were qualified. Moreover, today, both the work of the Diyanet as well as theology studies have become more intellectually demanding as compared to a few years ago. The on-going development of Turkish Islam would not be possible without the Diyanet and theology studies.

# The New Elite and Islam

## The religious authority, Diyanet

The new Republic wanted to be secular, but the desire to shape a homogeneous Turkish nation was even stronger, and that could only succeed with the constitutive element of Islam. Therefore, the founding fathers of the Republic established a religious authority. It immediately followed the Ottoman Institution of Şeyhülislam, which had been abolished. It had examined the Ottoman Sultan-Caliphate's decrees as to whether they were compatible with Islam or not, had administrated the mosques and their prayer leaders, and had an influence on schools and on the judiciary. The Sultan-Caliphate had also based its legitimacy on Islam.

Some of the competence and responsibilities of Şeyhülislam had been distributed to new ministries. Its succeeding office was also ranked as a ministry. The Ministry of Religious Affairs and Pious Foundations (Şeriye ve Evkaf Vekaleti) was, indeed, one of the first specialized departments that had been founded right after Atatürk had set the date for the first meeting of The Grand National Assembly of Turkey (TBMM) as April 23, 1920. In the protocol, its minister's rank came directly after that of the Prime Minister. The reason for this was that Islam had been an important instrument during the War of Independence, and a means to create the Turkish nation. On March 3, 1924, the ministry was divided up into two authorities—the Directorate-General for Pious Foundations (Evkaf Umum Müdürlüğü) and the Presidency of Religious Affairs (Diyanet İşleri Reisliği); the latter one reported directly to the Prime Minister.

The Turkish-nationalistic reflex can still be felt in Diyanet's direct offshoot in Germany, the DİTİB (Diyanet İşleri Türk İslam Birliği, the Turkish-Islamic Union for Religious Affairs). But the institution has changed at home, in Ankara. Under its President Ali Bardakoğlu, whom Prime Minister Erdoğan appointed on May 28, 2003, Diyanet has become more theological and more intellectual. During Erdoğan's first governing period, it was directly subordinate to the Minister of State Mehmet Aydın, an internationally respected religious philosopher and an important Muslim thinker. The Diyanet sees itself less as an arm of the secular state, but increasingly as an institution that wants to revive theological discourse, including more spirituality and less state policy.

During the first years after the founding of the Republic, Diyanet was still very active. It commissioned the poet of the national anthem, Mehmet Akif Ersoy, to translate the Qur'an into Turkish, and it commissioned the theologian, Elmalılı Hamdi Yazır, to draw up a commentary of the Qur'an in Turkish. However, the politics then gradually continued to curtail the religious authority of the institution. It was not until the introduction of multiple-party democracy that the pendulum started to swing in a different direction. But then, Atatürk's followers, who were affiliated with İsmet İnönü, and who were considerably less flexible than Atatürk in terms of religious issues, made their peace with Islam. In one of his last official acts before the transition of the government to the Democratic Party (DP), İnönü's CHP-government reinstalled the old authority of the Diyanet, on March 29, 1950, and modernized the name. It became "Diyanet İşleri Başkanlığı" (Directorate of Religious Affairs) and new people were hired. The new DP government went even further. After the call to prayer had been called in Turkish for almost a decade—unique in the entire history of Islam—the call to prayer was done in Arabic again, the Qur'an began to be recited on state-run radio broadcasting stations, and new İmam Hatip schools were opened.

One year after the 1960 coup, the Diyanet received constitutional rank for the first time. A law from 1965 determined its tasks in detail: the religious authority was to answer questions of religion, draw up religious writings and translate them, distribute sermons, and work out programs to educate Turkish society and those Turks who live abroad. The constitution from 1982 also lists the Diyanet, this time among the executive bodies. It commissioned it to "cause the nation to act with solidarity and to establish national unity." The same constitution, which gives the state the order to form a religious authority, names secularism as one of the Republic's highest principles.

The Diyanet is one of the largest institutions in Turkey; it is the fourth largest expense item of the national budget. It is responsible for 78,000 mosques and 5,000 state-appointed Qur'an schools, and it employs 9,000 people, mainly imams and preachers, who are among the worst paid employees of the Turkish state. The Diyanet is the only state institution in which women are allowed to wear headscarves. The authority coordinates the Turkish pilgrimages to Mecca, provides religious legal opinions (*fatwas*), researches religious issues as the need arises, and is responsible for taking care of Turkish Muslims who live abroad.

The state has thus nationalized Islam, to a large extent. The Diyanet has been financed from taxes since its inception, and it has exclusively occupied itself with Sunni Islam and its Hanafi school of thought, one of the four schools of Sunni Islam. About 20% of Turks are Alevis, but the Diyanet only hires Sunni preachers, and it spreads Sunni Islam through the mosques. Sunni Islam is thus de facto the state religion of the secular Republic of Turkey. So far the Alevis have not succeeded in having their demand of being represented in the Diyanet fulfilled.

The AK Party has triggered initiatives to separate the Diyanet from politics and to transform it into an autonomous institution. It is being discussed if the government should cease appointing the President of the Diyanet, and instead give the deacons of the theological faculties at least a right of nomination. By creating a flat hierarchy, the prayer leaders are to have the incentive of career opportunities in the hierarchy. All of these approaches were blighted by President Sezer (2000–2007) and the opposition Republican People's Party (CHP). They feared the end of the control of religion by the government. On the other hand, Sezer also prevented new people from being employed in the almost 20,000 mosques, which were abandoned because of the Diyanet's lack of funds.

And yet, since Professor Bardakoğlu assumed office, there have been reforms. Bardakoğlu is considered to be one of the more moderate reform theologians in Turkey. He attended an İmam Hatip school, then he studied legal sciences in Istanbul, with a focus on Islamic law. The theological faculty of Istanbul's Marmara University appointed him as professor, and he spent time doing research in England and the United States. Two of his favorite expressions are "moderation" and "pluralism." He is the first president of the Diyanet who has been concerned about the problems of the non-Muslim minorities as well.

Bardakoğlu has initiated a lot of inconspicuous changes in Diyanet. Since 1999, a university degree in theology (further than graduation from an İmam Hatip high school) is the basis for the eligibility of employment. Bardakoğlu increased the theological charisma of the institution that, for a long time, had only administrated as an executive agency. And then there is the fact that since June 9, 2006, the Diyanet does not centrally prescribe the Friday mosque sermons. The generals had enforced a centrally prescribed sermon on February 28, 1997, but that led to a loss of prestige of the mosques. Bardakoğlu now wants the Muftis in the individual provinces to take up regional and local topics that they can focus on during the Friday sermons.

The Muftis, who are qualified to give legal opinions, do not report directly to the Diyanet; their function is like that of Christian bishops. Previously, the Muftis and their deputies had been men, but that changed under Bardakoğlu. He recognized that the Diyanet had hitherto not reached women. Muslim women prayed at home and were primarily active in the environment around Islamic orders. Bardakoğlu wants to get women back into mosques and provide them with religious positions. He is also convinced that women make mosques friendlier. In a first step, since 2006, he has named seven women as mufti deputies in cities such as Kayseri and Antalya. Though they preach to the women and can give *fatwas*, they are not allowed to give sermons to the congregations at mosques.

The next step of the Diyanet under Bardakoğlu was to employ women who had a degree in theology. The Diyanet now sends women abroad as religious official representatives, where they take care of Turkish Muslims. In 2006, there were already six of them. There are several hundred women teachers of the Qur'an and preachers (*vaize*); they teach the Qur'an and Islamic issues only to women and girls. But even this step is crucial because Qur'an courses are one of the major work places for women from conservative families. They can confide in other women in Qur'an courses.

There was a spectacle when Bardakoğlu criticized the Muslim men sharply, on January 27, 2006. It was a snowy winter day, and the men had fully occupied the Hacıbayram-Mosque in Ankara during the Friday prayer so that the women had to wait outside in the icy cold. But Bardakoğlu and the Diyanet rejected the circle of women around Beyza Zapsu, the wife of Cüneyd Zapsu, the advisor of Erdoğan, who appeared without a headscarf in the rows of men in the mosque and declared that this is the new normal.

However, female Turkish theologians are also pushing ahead. They want women to be able to attend funerals and stand around the casket. The renowned religious pedagogue, Beyza Bilgin, from Ankara demands that women should also be prayer leaders in mixed communities. She says that she is unable to find any such prohibition in the Qur'an. But so far, women have not been employed as prayer leaders or Muftis, but only as deputy Muftis, preachers, and as teachers in Qur'an schools. At least, religious women are now stepping out of their private sphere and are present in public.

In 2005, the Diyanet took up work on a new Qur'an commentary and a critical edition of the Hadith, which contains the quotations and actions of the Prophet Muhammad. The goal is to read the most important sources of Islam in a new way in the light of the twenty-first century. They are to be understood from the time when they originated and are to be interpreted in a contemporary way. Yet the people involved reject the terms reform and reformation. Rather, they want to distill the principles of Islamic belief and implement them in a contemporary way. They also want to provide the believers with the two most important sources of Islam in a historically sound way, by subjecting the tradition to the "immersion bath" of a critical review.

Bardakoğlu also brought a breath of fresh air into the Department for External Affairs (Dış İlişkiler Dairesi), one of the seven departments of the office. He appointed to its head the open-minded theologian, Ali Dere, a Hadith scientist who received his doctorate degree in Göttingen. The department has been commissioned to take care of Turkish Muslims abroad. To do this, it carefully selects the Imams who are sent to mosques in Germany, for example, and prepares them for their tasks together with institutions in Germany. They also send Turkish Islam consultants to Turkish consulates; presently there are thirteen of them who work in Germany. The Diyanet did not start attending to Turks who live abroad until 1985. That is when the office finally noticed that their co-patriots abroad were increasingly being influenced by Islamic orders and political Islam, such as the Milli Görüş movement of Erbakan.

Bardakoğlu and Dere have considerably improved the qualifications of Imams who are sent to Germany. The Imams are to stop treating Turks living abroad as the fifth pillar but encourage them to integrate themselves. For the first time, only graduates of theological faculties are sent abroad; these imams are no longer merely graduates of the İmam Hatip schools. They receive language training from the German Goethe Institute. Diplomats of the German Embassy and Felix Körner, the German Jesuit who works in Ankara, acquaint them with Germany and with the religious principles of Christian churches. For the first time the Diyanet also employed a Christian trainee from Germany who was writing a treatise on church-affiliated academies in Germany.

Despite the attempts of the Erdoğan government to reform the Diyanet, it continues to be an institution of the executive. Most of the ideas that it implements originated at the theological faculty at the University of Ankara, which is the place where the Turkish reform theologians are active.

## The Theology Faculty of Ankara

Its name makes one take notice. The faculty is not named after the Islamic law, Sharia. When the theological faculty of the University of Ankara was founded, in 1948, their founding fathers wanted a modern faculty like in the West. The new faculty was therefore placed under the charge of the Ministry of Education. Their professors were to think independently and not traditionally. Hence, they took on a Western tradition and named the first university for the research of religion, İlâhiyat Fakültesi, or Theology Faculty. The expectations were met.

The theological faculty of Ankara is the parent faculty of all theological universities in Turkey. The deacons of the other 23 faculties are, without exception, all graduates from Ankara, and their impact on the state's religious authority, Diyanet, is on the rise. A first generation of Islamic modernists, who were affiliated with Hüseyin Atay and Mehmed Said Hatiboğlu, virtually had gone unnoticed in the West. Thanks to the work of Felix Körner, a member of the Jesuit community in Ankara, the second group, affiliated with theologians such as Mehmet Paçacı, Ömer Özsöy, İlhami Güler and Adil Çiftçi, is already well-known.

It has become customary to refer to these reform theologians as the Ankara School. Hüseyin Atay, a Qur'an exegete and emeritus professor, was the one who launched it. As a modern Muslim, he said, you have to approach the Qur'an and not be suffocated by the dogmas. The scholars of Islamic law (fuqaha) placed themselves even in front of the Qur'an and only believed their own words, becoming prisoners of their views without giving answers to the questions of contemporary life. Atay gave one of his books the title, "İslam'ı Yeniden Anlama" (Understanding Islam Anew). This book says that the uncritical handing down of Islamic traditions over the centuries, and the negation of reason, is responsible for the "miserable condition" Muslims find themselves in today.

Atay questioned what a lot of Muslims—including critics of Islam—accept as being self-evident. According to Atay, the Qur'an grants not only the freedom to accept Islam, but also freedom of faith. He does not find proof, either in the Qur'an or in Muhammed's Charter of Medina, for the later practice of demanding that Christians and Jews subordinate themselves to Muslims as *dhimmi*s, who live under the protection of Muslim rule on payment of the *jizya*. Atay does not see "jizya," which is mentioned in Qur'an 9:29, as a tax for non-Muslims, but as a ransom from military duty. Men and women are equal before God, says Atay, and paradise is open to all just people, Muslims and non-Muslims. So, it is more important to be just than only saying one's prayers. Not everyone says "Allah" for "God" because Allah is an Arabic word. Courageously, he challenges the fundamentalists, stating that one cannot follow all parts of the Qur'an at every time and place. Every surah has its time and context, and the message of some surahs may be more appropriate for a given society.

Since the nineties, a second generation has been widening the scope of the Ankara School. It is to their merit that "the door to independent reaching of a verdict" (*bab al-ijtihad*) has been opened again—the door that the theologians of Islam's Middle Ages had closed in favor of "passing on tradition" (*taqlid*). They thus dared to tackle the most precarious question of Islam: how is a Muslim to treat the revelation of the Qur'an? For Muslims the Qur'an is the immediate and immutable word of God. In Christianity, however, God's word has become flesh, written down by humans. Christianity is based on the historical-critical exegesis of the Bible, due to the fact that the Bible itself expects historical shifts and human impact. Since the conclusion of the "independent judgment" in the early Middle Ages, Islam seems to be chained to traditions that have already been formulated, without the opportunity of developing further.

Most Muslim theologians, no matter what part of the Islamic world they are from, are focused on tradition, becoming scribes of the past instead of being creative thinkers, triggering new impetuses. Not in Ankara. Jesuit Felix Körner, who is an expert of Islamic theology, has determined, in two works about the Ankara School, what influence the Pakistanian intellectual Fazlur Rahman (1919–1988), who had been teaching in Chicago for years, and the German philosopher Hans-Georg Gadamer (1900–2002) have had on the second generation of the reformist Ankara theologians.

The liberal Muslim philosopher, Fazlur Rahman, laments that traditionalization had caused Qur'an theology to shrivel, and that the opportunity to find connecting factors to the modern era has been lost. Fazlur Rahman demands that ethical principals be distilled from the Qur'an and adapted to the times. Gadamer gave the Ankara theologians the hermeneutic tools to do so—to be able to read "old texts in the new context" of the present.

Körner considers the teachings of the Ankara theologians to be important not only for Turkey, but for the entire Islamic world, even if it is only the Balkans and Central Asia that seem interested. Körner's works show that Islamic theology can be intellectual and sophisticated, and that it does not just ruminate on what is already established. Körner is personally acquainted with most theologians who lecture at the Theology Faculty and the academics at the renowned English-medium "Middle East Technical University" (ODTÜ).

Ömer Özsoy is one of them, and he now holds the endowed chair for "Islamic Religion" in Frankfurt am Main, Germany, that is financed by the Diyanet. The chair of Islamic Religion is part of the Faculty for Protestant Theology. Özsoy's philosophy is based on his understanding that the Qur'an does not express itself in terms of the present, and that it does not deal with problems of the present—that there is no "one-on-one relationship" between the preaching of the Qur'an and the world of today. Özsoy thinks that the Qur'an is not a text that can simply be opened to answer today's questions. He characterizes the Qur'an as a historical form of the divine word and that every passage in the Qur'an is a spoken word. In order to understand that word, you have to understand the context that lies beyond the text.

Özsoy is married to the theologist, Nuriye Özsoy. She used to wear a headscarf, the strict "türban," which is tied in a knot at the back of the head. She considered herself a Muslim feminist; "when we wear a headscarf, we are removing ourselves from the grasp of men," she said. She stopped wearing the headscarf while she still lived in Turkey. In Germany, she was irked by the large number of women who wore headscarves without giving it any thought. She is trying to broaden the paths of her spiritual scope as a Muslim, with new things such as fasting cures.

Esra Gözeler is also a theologian. When she was still attending university in Ankara, she did not wear a wig over the headscarf, like other students, in hopes of repealing the ban on covering the hair, because she had never worn a headscarf. Yet like other women, she is very self-confident in the way she applies herself to Islamic theology. Like the religious educator, Mualla Selçuk, Deacon of the Theological Faculty in Ankara, she completed the first part of her post-graduate studies in Jordan. The men there did not want to accept her as a Muslim as she did not wear a headscarf. Afterwards, she went to Rome, of all places, to study at a Jesuit University, the papal University Gregoriana. Now she is concluding her studies in Ankara, but wants to stay in touch with the "White Fathers," the experts of Islam from the Catholic Church.

Esra Gözeler will possibly become one of the great Qur'an exegetes of Turkey. Her path as the master student of the Turkish Qur'an exegete, Mehmet Paçacı, has been sketched out. Her teacher, Dr. Paçacı, was born in the provincial town of Bolu, in 1959. First, his studies brought him from Ankara to Jeddah and Manchester. Later, he did research and taught in Kuala Lumpur, Rome, and Bamberg. Today, he teaches on the Theological Faculty of the University of Ankara. He was one of the first Islamic theologians to read the holy texts of the Jews and Christians in their original languages.

Paçacı is focused on the Bible, and post-biblical traditions, to understand the Qur'an, looking for and finding pre-Qur'an traces of Surah 112. Paçacı reasons that Prophet Muhammad was able to proceed on the assumption that his contemporaries knew these references. But he does not say that the Bible had an impact on the Qur'an. Rather, he believes that the Qur'an is part of a Semitic tradition. Elsewhere, Paçacı critically analyzes the historical-critical hermeneutics of the Protestant theologian Johann Salomo Semler (1725–1791). Semler differentiated between the word of God and the Holy Bible. The result, Paçacı sees, is that there were reasons for revelations in space and time for the Qur'an, and that today the goal should be to look behind the historical circumstances of the word for hidden ethical-religious principles, and to utilize them for the present. Paçacı thus equates hermeneutics and "Ijtihad" —in other words, the independent reasoning or personal interpretation of the Qur'an.

Paçacı's point of departure is the recognition that the principles of the Qur'an have a universal legitimacy, but that the revelation of the Qur'an took place in a historical context and referred to concrete historical situations. "Thus, understanding a text means understanding it anew each time," Paçacı wrote that the exegete is influenced by the times he lives in. Therefore, the implementation of the principles of the Qur'an would have to change to the extent that historical situations changed.

Like Paçacı, Körner develops a synthesis between the thoughts of Gadamer and Fazlur Rahman. Like Gadamer, he sees the exegete in a system of coordinates of space and time. Together with Fazlur Rahman, Paçacı focused on the general principles that the Qur'an is based on. Ultimately, the Qur'an does not only consist of direct instructions on how to act today, which is what the traditionalists like to say. Rather, the Qur'an is an ethical manual in which the norm for today is also to be derived from the individual instruction of the past. More recently, Paçacı was less involved in the Qur'an interpretations that were stimulated in the West, but rather, he propagated reestablishing the normative power of Islam from its own tradition.

The Qur'an was revealed in different occasions and in parts upon various concrete historical situations. Therefore, there is a distance between the text and its interpreter. Every reader has a different prior conception, has a different tradition of interpreting the Qur'an, and has a different present, which leads to diverse interpretations. The research done by the theologians in Ankara is not the only research that is diverse. Turkish Islam is diverse, too. TheTurkish Directorate of Religious Affairs (Diyanet), for instance, is more intellectual and at the same time more realistic. The theologians in Ankara think at a high level and work with the same means as their Christian colleagues in the West. However, this new theological discourse is not sufficient to reach the faithful. This will require an influential preacher, such as Fethullah Gülen.

## Fethullah Gülen, the preacher of the contemporary Islamic thinking

Gülen is a respected preacher with a huge impact on people from all walks of life—from the sophisticated intellectuals to students, from the rich businessmen to the ordinary men in the street. He has returned the concepts of religiousness and piety to the public space and become a major scholar and preacher of the contemporary Islamic thinking. When multiple-party democracy caused a revival of religious life, what followed were the influential people who emerged even after the dissolution of many Islamic institutions during the early Republic: preachers who—unlike theologians—were not affected by the destruction of the institutions. There were also the religious orders that valued mysticism that had survived underground. They held a strong allure for many Turks.

Fethullah Gülen is the most influential of these preachers who could address diverse people from various segments of society. He wants to lead people into prosperity with their belief and piety. To do this, he integrates religious belief and practice with the advancements of the modern age. Distinguishing himself clearly from the Islamists rebelling against the existing order, Gülen does not want to involve in politics but spiritually guide the people.

Preachers have greater importance in Turkish Islam than for any other Islamic peoples. Turkish Muslims follow mostly the canonized High Islam, which is represented by the Diyanet. But many Turks practice a populist Islam that is far removed from the orthodoxy of religious scholars. Before the advent of Islam, the ancestors of Turks in Central Asia followed the pre-Islamic religious practice of Shamanism in which preachers had powerful positions. During their migrations to Anatolia, the Turks were not converted by orthodox religious scholars, but by Sufi dervishes who had focused more on the practical and spiritual aspects of Islam than its purely legalistic aspects. Thanks to the preachers, Islam continued its dynamism during the first half of the 20th century.

Islam developed differently in each region—it developed differently in Afghanistan than in Africa, in Bosnia differently than in Bangladesh, in Pakistan differently than in Palestine. In the 20th century, Turkish Islam had its own development; it was the only country that had a Muslim population that went for secularization, introduced civil law, and based politics on secularism. They did not apply to Islam as the only means of struggle in the battle against the colonial powers like in other countries of the Islamic world, such as Egypt and Algeria.

This special path entailed the Ottomans, and then the Turks, generally having good relationships with the European countries of Latin Christianity, with Catholics and Protestants. They could therefore take on their progressive, scientific aspects unreservedly. The only group they had a conflicted relationship with was the orthodox Christian subjects who rebelled against the Ottoman Empire in the Balkans after the period of regression. The history of Muslim Arabs, on the other hand, was completely different: they lived in harmony with orthodox Christians whose intellectuals frequently introduced the cultural renewal of the Arabs. The Latin Christians, on the other hand, haunted the countries of Arabia as crusaders, and later as colonial powers.

Fethullah Gülen, who is a very influential scholar and preacher, has three goals. Firstly, he is endeavoring to present Islam to the modern age with a synthesis of Turkish Muslim culture and the advancements of the West. Gülen wants to use this kind of Islam to embed the Turks in Europe. Secondly, Gülen wants to empower the Muslimness of the Turks. Arabian Islam already produced the Sunnis, and Persian Islam produced Shias. Now, the contemporary Turkish Muslimness is to be compatible with modern Europe. Thirdly, Gülen is in favor of dialogue: among Muslim Turks and also with the followers of other religions. Gülen was the first religious leader who visited the ecumenical Patriarch Bartholomaios I, the head of Orthodox Christians, at his headquarters in the Fener (Phanar) neighboorhood of Istanbul. In Rome, he visited Pope John Paul II, and he met with the spiritual leader of the Sephardic Jews, the chief Rabbi, Eliyahu Bakshi Doron, in Istanbul.

Gülen searched for ways of presenting Islam to the understanding of the modern man. He preaches that people should practice Islam in their daily lives, rather than running after an Islamist government, because God judges people according to their actions and not according to the various forms of government they live in. Gülen does not focus on political aspects, but instead, aspects of morals and education. Education must convey modern knowledge; morals must provide the ethical basis for actions. If modern man is equipped with both, he can help shape the world and retain his identity as a Muslim. But this necessitates religion as a basis. Aside from all progress, religion remains the most influential energy to shape the lives of people, Gülen says. Religion shapes the values of people, and it keeps producing new civilizations. And Muslims must not leave this civilizational flow.

He tries to nourish the traditional spirituality with a spirituality that supplements all kinds of scholarship. Spiritual people require work, and

Gülen demands life-long learning and a work ethic that is focused on efficiency. In an example Gülen provides, pioneers do not despair, even if they are told to plant roses in the desert. The diligent Muslim work ethics of the new Anatolian middle class becomes apparent here. Gülen prepared the way for it, including the thinking of new Muslim intellectuals, such as Ali Bulaç, with broader perspectives.

In a long interview with the *Zaman* newspaper, published in March, 2004, in 10 installments, Gülen said, "15 or 20 years ago Muslims did not talk about democracy." The father of political Islam in Turkey, Erbakan, tended more towards looking for his place alongside the Egyptian Muslim Brotherhood than the democratic states in Europe. At the time, the intellectual Bulaç was more oriented towards the forms of government of early Islam and not the Copenhagen Criteria that have become the gauge for democracy within the EU. Today, Bulaç also recognizes them as a gauge.

In the interview, Gülen continued that there was no obstacle for democracy in Islam, and that a democracy also requires a metaphysical dimension, and that is what Islam could offer. Just as there are Christian, Jewish, and Buddhist democrats, there can be Muslim democrats. Islam suggests a kind of government that relies on a *social contract* for the will of the people to be expressed by free elections. Gülen demands that people should be able to discuss issues and elect governments freely. The same rights for all are indispensable, and these can only be protected by democracy. Rights such as the inviolability of life, freedom of expression and of religion, and private ownership cannot be questioned.

Gülen does not leave a trace of a doubt that Islam and democracy are compatible. When people live together in peace, the world would not drift into a civilizational conflict. But there can only be peace in the global village if everyone accepts other people as they are, respecting the differences between people as a valuable part of human existence.

It does not sound like a challenge for Western democracies. There is no need for Europe to be afraid of the Islam that is rediscovering its earlier dynamics and spirituality, that is returning creativity and tolerance to Muslims. During the March, 2004, interview, Gülen said that there is no such world as "the Islamic World," thereby avoiding the use of the concept of the "community" of Muslims throughout the world. He said that "there are places where Muslims live...There are some Muslims in different places around the world. Piece by piece, broken. I personally do not see the prosperous existence of Muslims. If Muslims, who will be in contact with the others and constitute a union, solve common problems, interpret the universe, read it really well, consider the universe carefully with the Qur'an, read the future very well, generate projects for the future, determine its place for the future, do not exist, I do not call it Islamic World." Muslims often live Islam as individuals.

Gülen does not want an abstract Islam. He wants an Islam that renews itself in every era and everywhere; an Islam that detaches itself from the terror of fanatics. Gülen detaches himself more decidedly and more frequently from terror than any other religious leader who invokes Islam. In the March, 2004 interview, he referred to Bin Laden as a "monster" that befouled the image of Islam, and that it will take a long time for this damage to be rectified. Strongly critical of those resorting violence and killing people in the name of religion, he said, "Those who kill people in the name of religion will not go to Paradise." Gülen blames the fanatics, stating that it was their responsibility that the majority of Muslims were subjected to false accusations: "We will not raise our fists against those who hit us, we will not vilify those who insult us." This is because Islamic mysticism teaches that compassion is the highest perfection of man; that mysticism teaches compassion, love and tolerance, and thus leads to knowing the All-Compassionate God.

Gülen says that it is the education system's fault that terrorists have come from among such "Muslims." Education should give people something to lean on and familiarize people with modern science. The Hizmet movement—which is popularly known in the West as the Gülen movement—is mainly an educational movement. Entrepreneurs who are inspired by him have founded schools in Turkey and more than 150 countries abroad. Their curriculums are modern; their focus is on modern sciences and foreign languages. They are among the best schools in Turkey. Their graduates rank very highly when it comes to the annual university entrance exams. Like all other schools, they report to the Ministry of Education, whose inspectors monitor the schools on a regular basis. They are founded by associations that were established by entrepreneurial Turks.

This is how schools are established: an entrepreneur who is inspired by Gülen visits him, addresses him as "Hocaefendi" (literally, "Respected

Teacher," or Master), thanks him, and tells him that he has given his life a new meaning and that now he would like to do something for the benefit of people. The master asks why he does not found and finance a school somewhere within or without Turkey. He gives him a few names of people who can help him. Inspired by the idea the entrepreneur immediately gets to work. In a couple of years he returns, telling Hocaefendi about the new school, and asks for another task. This time he may be sent to Turkmenistan or to Africa to build another educational institution.

Except for a modest library, Gülen has no property. His name does not appear in connection with any of the schools. But his name is spread with the help of this network. Independent Turkish entrepreneurs who are inspired by him also start factories and banks, such as Asya Finans, and media, like *Zaman* newspaper and the television station, *Samanyolu*. The Islamic scientist and scholar, Bekim Agai, from Bochum, was the first to investigate this network systematically.

With his emphasis on a conservative and compassionate Islam which also utilizes science to make people prosper, Gülen stepped into the footsteps of another great preacher, Said Nursi. Said Nursi died in Urfa, in 1960, after a life of imprisonment and long exiles, which had led him all over Anatolia as a preacher. He had preached that it was not only Islam that counted, but also the advancements and sciences of the contemporary age. He wanted Muslims to take part in progress. He never delved into the issue of the separation between state and religion. And yet the state elite made him the Muslim-Anatolian representative of evil, the anti-thesis of urban and secular Atatürk. The state elite, including the staunch Kemalists, also have a hard time with Gülen, whose birthday is listed as November 11, 1938, the day after Atatürk died. For this reason, and because of his poor health, Gülen has been living in a self-imposed exile in the United States since the late nineties.

Though they never met in person, Gülen refers to Nursi in his sermons frequently. One of Gülen's teachers was, indeed, a student of Nursi. Nursi preached to his followers face-to-face. Since then, technical means and possibilities have changed drastically, and Hizmet movement has become too large for personal meetings. Gülen's sermons were therefore spread on cassettes, CDs and DVDs, and later via television, radio, internet, periodicals, and newspapers.

After elementary school, Gülen, who grew up near Erzurum, did not attend any other kind of regular school. He acquired his knowledge as an autodidact. From 1958 to 1981, he was a preacher under contract for the Diyanet. After he retired as an official preacher, he continued to live and preach in Izmir. Frequently, Turgut Özal was part of the audience in the 80s, and he was the one who saved him from arrest after the coup. In the middle of the 90s, bourgeois politicians even tried to court Gülen, though he is always against the instrumentalization of religion in politics, as the traditional, moderate Muslim alternative to Erbakan's political Islamism. After Erbakan, Erdoğan became the politician of the "Black Turks" and asserted that his AK Party stripped of its "Milli Görüş" (National View) garb of the earlier period, acting for long as if they severed all their ties with political Islamism. While lenting support to the AK Party's democratic reforms, and especially the constitutional referendum, Gülen has always kept his distance from its political Islamism, which has become more apparent in its later years in the office. Though he was similarly regarded as the preacher of "Black Turks," Gülen proved himself reaching people from all walks of life in Turkey and abroad. His means consist of the word; his topic is Islam and the betterment of society in every way. The philanthropic services he inspired will help Europe and the global world to further prosper.

# The Politics of the New Elite

## Membership in the EU

The relations with Muslim societies will be crucial during the coming decades. The European continent's perimeter is surrounded by a region of crisis that stretches from the Caucasus over the Near East, to the Atlantic, and right through the Islamic world, where Europe gets its oil. This is also where the poor migrants live that Europe wants to keep at bay, and where the terrorist violence emanates from that is as much a threat for Europe as it is for the Islamic world. No group in Europe is growing as fast as Muslims. Islam reached Europe centuries ago, but it has not yet been accepted as a European religion, and it is still not accepted as compatible with the values and societies in Europe.

A modern interpretation of Islam is being established in North America for Muslims that live there. This is not happening in Europe. But Europe should be interested in developing an Islamic understanding that does not question the accomplishments of Western society. Pursuing membership in the EU is a great opportunity for Turkey, because Turkey is the first and leading country in the Muslim world that has a parliamentary democracy. Turkey is situated at the Southern outskirts of Europe and the Northern coast of the Mediterranean. This interface will be a decisive factor for Europe's security.

Its geographic location is beneficial for Europe. Turkey has the second largest army in NATO and provides reliable security; Turkish involvement in multilateral peace operations in Afghanistan, Bosnia, Kosovo, and Lebanon is proof of that. The West will not be able to win the war on terror on its own. The strategy must be for military and secret service actions to flank politics and squeeze dry the environment of terrorists. A war of civilizations is raging. But the trench is not between the Christian West and Muslim Orient. The war on terror can only be won if the West cooperates with moderate Muslims, and more Muslims recognize that Islam and democracy are compatible. They think Turkey is the shining example for what is possible for Muslims.

There will be a direct border for Europe with the conflicted region of the Near East. At any rate, the developments of the region will impact the stability and safety in Europe. The main question is where the border will be drawn: in Thrace or in Mesopotamia. If Europe should put the border between Greece and Turkey, the continent would not be solving the security problems right in front of its door. If Europe accepts Turkey as a member state, the EU would extend all the way to the oil fields in the Near East, and Turkey would have an impact on a region that is gaining importance for Europe. If they retreated from this region, Europe would merely be delegating responsibility to the United States again. Europe would still not have very much to say, if weapons do the speaking. Yet the consequences of weapons speaking would still be borne by Europe: because the people south of the Mediterranean would vote with their feet and leave their region.

The EU is not a state. That makes it possible for Turkey to be accepted by the EU. At some point, states stop developing, but the EU is changing rapidly and there is still no finalité européenne. The economic integration—the national market and the Euro—will change "Project Europe" from within. Political changes will trigger new rounds of expansion. In the past decades, every round of expansion brought change to Project Europe. In 1973, the EFTA-countries Great Britain, Denmark, and Ireland were accepted into the European Economic Community (EEC)—the ones that had recognized the superiority of the European region of the EEC. In the eighties, the EU expanded to include the young democracies Greece, Spain, and Portugal, which had originated from military dictatorships and whose economies were weak. The EU consolidated their democracies and modernized their economies. In 1995, the neutral Cold War countries were added. The two rounds of expansion, in 2004 and 2007, ended with the inclusion of twelve new members, some of which had deep scars from totalitarianism and the division of Europe. All these incentives for Europe's further development came from the outside. The next big challenge will be whether Europe will be able to find an answer to Islam.

European integration reinvented itself during every decade and every round of expansion. The common denominator remained: "Pax Europaea"—a space for peace, democracy, and wealth. The EU is growing. In times of globalization, the much implored overexpansion of Europe is losing its meaning. Everything is merging. The EU overstepped the border at which it could have been a super state with integrative depth long ago. The demand for the same speed for all members will significantly throttle the speed of development; varying speeds and concentric circles are already reality. Europe is moving away from the ideal of the past, of a national-state, and is moving towards a state of nations. The EU is moving towards a European empire: the return of large multi-nation states that are only held together loosely. The focus is a common foreign and security policy that incorporates peace and wealth, fights terror, and secures energy.

This kind of order for Europe has enough room for Turkey, reflecting the diversity of cultures in Europe. It acknowledges that Europe's "cultural heritage" is in flux and not written in stone; Europe's values are not exclusively European values. Dignity is an inalienable human right, not only in Europe. The continent is not made of one molding. One country produced the Inquisition, another country the Reformation, and another the Renaissance; the industrial revolution originated in one country, and the Communist revolution in another. All of that makes up Europe. Europe is not living off looking backward, and Christianity does not exclude others from love of mankind.

But does Turkey belong to Europe geographically? Anatolian Asia Minor was part of the Hellenist world. It was not until geographic borders created later assigned this cultural space to two continents. Culture or nature does not draw a distinct line between Europe and Asia. Europe's borders are random. Over the centuries, they were redrawn repeatedly in the East and the Southeast of the continent. While the author—who is writing these lines in his office in the European part of Istanbul—is gazing out of his office towards Asia, his gaze remains glued to the same city.

If Antiquity is a building block of Europe, it includes Asia Minor. Antiquity took place around the Mediterranean, including the west and south of Turkey. Herodot created history in Halicarnassos, Thales taught in Milet, Alexander the Great wanted to relocate the capital to Troy. Ionia, Aeolia, Pergamon and Ephesos, Paulus from Tarsus and Nicholas of Myra, the ecumenical councils of the early Christians: without Asia Minor, Western culture would be poorer.

The Peace Conference of Paris, in 1856, ended the Crimean War and was the beginning of the New Age; Article 7 of the Peace Treaty secured the Ottoman Empire's participation in public law in Europe. The Ottoman Empire entered the chorus of European powers that gave the Ottoman Reform Process impetus. From then on, Europe and the West became the point of orientation for the Turkish elite for whom modernization and Europe were one. They reformed their laws and the state, and they strove westward.

Following the Second World War, an Association Agreement was signed by the European Economic Community (EEC) and the Republic of Turkey, in 1963, promising the prospect of Turkey's membership. In 1974, the Turkish Prime Minister Ecevit turned down Brussels' offer to enter into accession negotiations. Greece had just gotten rid of its military dictatorship and accepted the offer and has been a member since 1981. European integration proceeded; Turkey remained outside. The constant domestic political conflicts kept the country on the brink, and from 1963 to 1999, its association with the community was not strong enough to trigger a reform impulse again. So the years passed during which Europe grew together and the distance to Turkey became even greater.

The Customs Union, which the EEC had held out for Turkey as a prospect—and that went into effect in 1996 after all of the technical requirements had been met—did not really change much. Trade increased many times over, but the Customs Union did not provide prospective membership. Therefore, it did not prove to be an anchor that prevented economic crises and ended political issues, such as the Kurdish conflict and the tensions associated with the rise of political Islam. The lesson learned—and the lesson learned during the expansion round in 2004—was that the EU could only trigger significant changes and reforms when it enables a country to join in the near future.

The 1999 summit of heads of states and governments of the EU, in Helsinki, provided Turkey with a formal membership perspective and also gave it a new impetus. It was the incentive to launch a reform process in the face of resistance, to democratize the political order, and to liberalize the economy. A government that had only been elected in 1999 drafted these reforms. Its two largest parties, the Democratic Leftist Party (DSP) of Prime Minister Ecevit and the Nationalist Movement Party (MHP) of his deputy Bahçeli, had been EU-skeptics up until that point.

The economic crises of November, 2000, and February, 2001, paved the way for those in favor of Turkey joining the EU—because increasingly, Turks saw that the country needed outside incentives and an anchor like the EU to remedy things.

But Ecevit's government coalition had a difficult time dealing with the new membership perspective. In March, 2001, it finally presented the "National Program," with which it answered the membership partnership of the EU. The EU had signalled to Turkey that it had a place in Europe, but not in its current state. The Turkish government avoided providing concrete reform agreements regarding the Kurdish question and the army's position in its "National Program." But Turkey became more predictable, including in terms of its foreign policies, and it was at work on the European profile that had been demanded of it.

Turkey brought the speed of its reforms up a notch when the AK Party took over the government, in 2002. A party whose leaders had grown up with political Islam brought Turkey closer to Europe than all the earlier parties, which had done lip service to modernization, according to a model Europe had provided. Two years later, the vigor with which the AK Party had pushed the reform processes slowed down, and resistance increased. There was a critical point where the reformers queried the traditional concept of government that the Kemalist elite were still not willing to relinquish.

The EU process democratized the former Islamists even more. Their Kemalist counterparts closed themselves off to this Europeanization, referring to Turkey's special issues, such as the Kurdish issue and the danger of a "religious reactionaryism." The AK Party continued to promote the reforms, and the former leftist parties, such as the CHP, increasingly turned out to be "defensive nationalists." The latter did not accept the package deal between reforms and an EU membership. That would reduce the political competition in Turkey to a battle between the "conservative globalizers" and "defensive nationalists," observed political scientist Ziya Öniş.

The EU awarded the reforms of the AK Party government by accepting membership negotiations, on October 3, 2005. The prerequisite for this was for Turkey to adequately meet the political Copenhagen Criteria—democracy and the rule of law, human rights and protection of minorities. The speed of the negotiations now depends on Turkey's fulfilling the accession criteria.

The word "negotiation for accession" is misleading, because nothing is being negotiated. What happens is that the EU has the 35 negotiation chapters that are opened, one by one, and the Turkish delegation travels to Brussels to prove that the requirements of each chapter have been met. Then the EU Commission closes the chapters, one by one. If Turkey gravely and permanently violated the principles of the EU, the Commission is entitled to suspend the negotiations. Every autumn, the EU's Progress Report states the status of the reforms and the deficits. The deficits that the Commission has mentioned are the Kurds' freedom of opinion and politics, women's rights, and non-Muslim minorities.

Turkey does not want to accept a "privileged partnership," as has been suggested as an alternative to full membership. On the one hand, Turkey is of the opinion that the status of the bilateral relations are already the equivalent of a privileged partnership, as Turkey does not have relations this close with another country. On the other hand, the term "privileged partnership" (*imtiyazlı ortaklık*) sounds negative to Turks. The "commerce privileges" granted to European superpowers were the most important reason for the fall of the Ottoman Empire.

There is incomprehension on the part of the Turks for the fact that the Greek South part of Cyprus has managed to repeatedly obstruct Turkey's path to Europe. In a region that is one of the Achilles heels of Europe, Turkey has managed to normalize all of its relationships with its neighbors—except for Cyprus and Armenia. Turkey has become more important than ever for the Near East. And still, the summit conference in 2006, in Europe, decided to freeze eight negotiation chapters for Turkey because it did not expand its customs agreement to include all of the new EU member states. In other words, they were frozen because Turkey refuses to open its sea ports to the ships of Greek-Cypriots and to open its airports to their planes.

In Turkey, government policies entail treating the Turkish part of northern Cyprus as the apple of the eye of the homeland, and to stubbornly reject all constructive suggestions that do not entail a de facto recognition of the division of the island. Erdoğan's government broke with these politics and supported a reunification of the island. Reunification failed in the spring of 2004—not, like in the earlier attempts, because of the Turkish-Cypriots, but because of the Greek-Cypriots and their rejection of the United Nations' plan to reunify the island. Thereafter, the EU promised the Turkish-Cypriots to lift the trade embargo—which has not happened to this day. As long as the trade embargo is not lifted, and Northern Cyprus remains isolated, no government in Ankara can open sea and air ports to the unrelenting Greek-Cypriots. This small island remains the largest stumbling block on Turkey's path to Europe. In the EU, opponents of Turkey can use this leverage at any time, with the help of the Greek-Cypriotic opponents of reunification, and can close the door for Turkey.

Turkey is, however, fighting for a full membership. As a regional power on its own, Turkey is too weak, and Russia would refuse to be included In a Black Sea association; an Islamic alliance of states is improbable, because Turkey sees itself as a European country. Parts of the military sympathize with the authoritarian Russia that was created by Putin. The Iraq War alienated Turkey from the United States, because it had denied transit into Iraq to American soldiers, thus moving Turkey closer to Europe. The autocratic actions of the Pentagon in this region irritated the Turkish military, which reluctantly accepted the fact that it would not be able to undertake any operations across the border for a number of years to follow Kurdish separatists. During the era of the Chief of General Staff, Hilmi Özkök (2002–2006), it resigned itself more than ever to the EU. It was not until late 2007, that the United States tolerated Turkish operations against the PKK in Northern Iraq. The military had a hundred thousand soldiers march towards the border and let Washington know that they no longer wanted to wait for American approval. Washington, which was afraid of another front in Iraq, resigned itself. The Turkish army wanted to prevent an autonomous region in Iraqi-Kurdistan that would lead to independence, and they were backed by a majority of politicians. More than ever, the army required a field to distinguish itself and that it could use to determine the public debate. Thus, they had once more bypassed the EU and reform discussion.

And yet, the prospect of joining the EU had created the largest consensus in Turkey since the founding of the Republic, in a way no other incentive had produced. Every group envisioned their goal being fulfilled under the roof of the EU. The devout Muslims see the EU as a guarantee to maintain the Muslim character of society in a secular order that prohibits the making of any law preventing the free exercise of religion. The Kemalists recognize that the "acquis communautaire," or the 35 chapters of the EU accession negotiations with Turkey, would exclude the much-feared introduction of Sharia and would anchor Turkey to the West. The Kurds, who as a group are the greatest supporters of EU membership, are hoping for cultural autonomy, and the Turkish nationalists think the territorial integrity of Turkey will no longer be questioned if an EU membership becomes reality. For the Kurds, an EU passport is more important than belonging to a state that will barely be able to survive.

Turkey's neighbors are closely monitoring events in Turkey. After the founding of the Republic, the Iranian Shah, Reza Pahlavi, and Tunisia's Bourghibas, followed Atatürk's Turkish model. But what is happening under Erdoğan is drawing wider concentric circles in the Near East. Turkey is in demand in the West, too. The September 11, 2001 terror attacks are giving new urgency to the necessity of a dialogue between Christians and Muslims.

## Foreign policy in the Near East

The two bridges that cross the Bosporus look as delicate as a silver ray of light. They span Europe and Anatolia. Turkey also sees itself as a bridge that wants to communicate via two cultures. But a bridge alone is not enough. Streets have to lead up to the bridges. But the road that accessed the Near East was closed for years. The Arabs were not interested in modern Turks, because they still saw the Turks as an Ottoman colonial power in the present. Why should they take, as a model, a country that Europe was showing the cold shoulder to on account of the human rights situation and the deficits in terms of democracy? What was graver was the fact that Atatürk had replaced the Arabic alphabet with the Latin alphabet overnight, thus cutting suddenly the relations between Turkey and Arabic-Islamic culture. Both sides were no longer interested in one another. Kemalist Turkey turned its back on the Arabian world, and the Egyptian intellectual, Khalid Muhammad Khalid, reflected the mood of the Arab nationalists under Nasser when he wrote that the terms "tyrant" and "Turan" (Persian word for homeland of the Turkic people) were virtually identical etymologically.

At the beginning of the new century, the bridge was reopened on both sides. On the one side, Turkey is pushing into the EU, and on the other side, it is entertaining the best relations with the Arabs since the founding of the Republic. Some things have changed in Turkish diplomacy; foreign policy no longer takes place under the premise of a zero-sum game—in other words, that good relations with one region must entail bad relations with another region. Quite the contrary: foreign policy has become an instrument that generates advantages for everyone involved, supposedly symbolizing a win-win situation.

Turkey's foreign policy makers have recognized that the regional importance of the country will only be realized if the bridge is widely used from both sides. Turkey's benefit to the EU increases as it increases its impact on the crisis region of the Near East. At the same time, the more successful Turkey is, the more it is looked up to by states and societies of this crisis region, and the more it is listened to by the big countries in Europe and the world. A Turkey that does not radiate towards the Near East is inconsequential for Europe, and a Turkey that is kept outside of the gates of Europe is not an example for Arab Muslims.

But that is what Turkey has become in the interim. All along the first two terms of Erdoğan government, the Arabs are suddenly interested in what is happening in Turkey. While he sits on stage next to the Muslim Prime Ministers of Egypt, Lebanon, and Malaysia, Erdoğan says that Turkey does not want to be a model. However, the star of the event of the annual World Economic Forum on May 22, 2006, in the Egyptian bathing resort, Sharm el-Sheikh, was Erdoğan. He repeated that Turkey is not a role model, but a model for what is possible for Muslims. The mixed audience that wanted replies from him was indirectly criticizing their leaders. They wanted to know what he recommended the Egyptian regime do to reduce the tensions with the Muslim Brotherhood and whether he saw the opportunity of a national dialogue in Syria, and what he had discussed with the Iranian President Ahmadinejad. Erdoğan continued to preach to his Arabic audience that dialogue is the only means to solve the present problems.

The Arab world regarded Erdoğan as a modern Muslim who integrates Islam and democracy, and they sought his advice. On the other hand, the leaders of the Western world, such as the American President and the German Chancellor, think that he should continue to talk to those who refuse to talk to the politicians of the West. They believed in Erdoğan because people listened to him and because they know that Turkey is practicing a foreign policy which is in harmony with that of the EU. Turkey also believes in negotiations and dialogue, and that military intervention is no longer a means to an end. Turkey has become a soft power, a regional power with good intentions. Like the EU, Turkey wants peace and stability in the region; they want to contribute to solving the Palestinian conflict, and prevent Iraq's falling apart and Iran's building an atomic bomb.

Turkey is undergoing change as much as the Near East is. The signposts of the past no longer function. For most Arabs, Turkey is no longer the successor of the Ottoman yoke that the Arab nationalists blame for the downfall of their culture. Turkey is no longer the Republic of Atatürk, which cut off all references to the Arabic world. Sunni Arabs need Sunni Turkey as a balance for Shiite Iran, which has gotten stronger. The perception in the Arabic world has also changed.

The Arabs flipped the switch on March 1, 2003, the day that the Turkish Parliament turned down the request that would have allowed American soldiers to transit into Northern Iraq. The American lament afterwards was that if they had opened a second front, they could have gotten a better handle on the insurgents—which was a way of indirectly saying that they could get more done with Turkey, than without. The Arabs, on the other hand, rubbed their eyes in disbelief: their authoritarian governments gave in to the Americans, but the democratic Turks had resisted. This was a lesson learned in democracy. What did the Turks do right, and what had they done wrong?

The Arab news channels, al-Jazeera and al-Arabiyya, reported extensively on the reforms of the Erdoğan government, the democratization of Turkey, and the economic boom. More recently, al-Jazeera has been reporting from two studios: from Ankara and from Istanbul. Authoritarian regimes see this development in Turkey as a threat to their existence.

The reason is that Turkey is managing what other Arabic states will be faced with in the future: to get rid of an authoritarian ideology from within and without, and to replace it with a functional democracy. The Turkish role model is an encouragement for those regimes that want to open themselves and for citizens who want to fight for more rights.

Secular, as well as Islamic, intellectuals are closely following what is happening in Turkey. The secular Egyptian intellectual, Abd al-Munim Said, noted in *al-Sharq al-Awsat*, the Arabic newspaper with the highest circulation, that the Turkish march was successful because it was not always done under the slogan, "Islam is the solution," which the Muslim Brotherhood propagates. The AK Party was not facing its political opponents by holding the Qur'an in their face, and thus, they were a "creative inspiration" for the Muslim Brotherhood. In turn, the Islamist Muslim Brothers were trying to understand what was so different in Turkey, and what they could learn from Turkey. Even secular intellectuals in the Gulf Region are hoping that the EU will not turn Turkey down. If that should happen, the radicals among them are afraid that it would be a boost for the Islamists. Then, they would be able to claim that moderation and change were not worth it, and they would place their bets on Sharia again.

It was the Turkish economy that was the reason for a reevaluation. Before Erdoğan's rise, Turkish companies had been exporting TVs and refrigerators, jeans and cookies into the Arab world. Since the late nineties, they could be found in the markets of Erbil, Aleppo, Cairo, Kuwait, Tripoli and Tunis. Gradually, they were getting rid of the prejudice of the "ugly" Turk. The products are reasonably priced, sophisticated, and "Made in Turkey."

Turkey will only be able to take on a regional leadership role if they have the trust of everyone. Erdoğan's Turkey won the trust of the Arabs and not lost that of the Israelis. Initially, the relationship between Ariel Sharon and Tayyip Erdoğan had been icy. Sharon had rejected Erdoğan's offer of negotiating. Then, he tested Erdoğan, who then supplied the goods. He established the first official contact of Israel to Pakistan, and a direct red telephone connection between the two heads of state was put in place.

After Simon Peres was elected as Israel's Prime Minister, in 2007, he praised Turkey and said that Israel profits from the Turkish negotiations with Syria, from the entrepreneurial initiatives in the Palestinian areas, and from the active role that Turkey plays in the Near East. When the Arab world was in uproar because of the archeological excavations on the Temple Mount where the Mosque of al-Aqsa is located, Turkey sent an expert commission, and the differences were smoothed. At the same time, Turkey maintained a good relationship with Israel and the Palestinian Authority.

Turkey was also successful when it initiated the neighborhood conferences for Iraq, and energetically moved them forward. It was during one of these conferences, in May, 2007, in Sharm el-Sheikh, that representatives of the United States and Iran sat at the same table for the first time. Consultations were a mechanism for Turkey to dampen the civil war in Iraq.

In Lebanon, Turkish Blue Helmets, who served the United Nations, were a contribution to bringing peace to the country. For the first time since the First World War, Turkish soldiers are back in the Near East (German soldiers are there for the first time, too), which is yet another sign that the relationship between Turks and Arabs is returning to normal.

In the nineties, Turkey had not managed to take on leadership responsibilities, vis-à-vis the new independent Turkic states of Central Asia. That would have disturbed the circles of Russia, and furthermore, the autocrats of these countries preferred the continued existence of their authoritarian regimes to the adventure of opening them to the outside. Turkey did not become attractive until years later, when it started its development process to join the EU with an eye on the Copenhagen Criteria.

## Economic politics

The Turkish economy is disproving its reputation that it is the predestined fate of Anatolia to be the poor house before the gates of Europe. But a lot of people continue to maintain that Turkey is a bottomless pit in which all EU subventions would disappear—a poor house from which millions of migrant workers would emigrate. That is what the media report, and it is what people want to hear.

However, the gaping hole between prejudice and reality is increasing. The boom along the Bosporus has not arrived in the heads of the critics of Turkey yet. The electorate and politicians are keeping their distance from Turkey. But not the economy and the foreign direct investors. When voters and politicians look towards Turkey, they see a glass that is half empty. The glass that investors see is half full. They invest billions of dollars and detect the transformation that is taking place in Turkey, evolving from an emerging country wracked by crises to a robustly growing economy.

Turkey embodies the growth market that many companies from the stagnating continent of Europe are looking for. They hope that Turkey will continue its adjustment to the EU and its body of regulations and provisions—the "acquis communautaire." For decades, the foreign direct investments (FDI) that had been pumped into the country never exceeded 1 billion. This changed with the EU perspective. In December, 2004, the European Council set the beginning of the negotiations for the following October, and in 2005, the FDI influx increased to 9 billion dollars. In 2006, it reached 20 billion dollars; in 2007, it was even more.

Already, 15,000 foreign companies have invested in Turkey; more than half of them from EU states: they are led by Germany, followed by Holland, Great Britain, France, and Italy. Half of the 2,700 German companies came after 2004. For a long time, it was only large companies, but then little and medium-sized companies discovered Turkey—even start-ups. Foreign investors are involved in a quarter of the 500 largest Turkish companies. More and more are following economic development and are settling outside the large cities, in Anatolia, where many Germans think that everyone who lives is poor and wants to emigrate to Germany. But that is the region where the Turkish economy is growing the fastest.

Indeed, Turkey was not an economic success story for a long time. When Atatürk founded the Republic, in 1923, Turkey had the same income per person as Japan. The Turkish economic policies had preferred the "wisdom" of the central bureaucracy to the powers of the market. From 1934 on, five-year plans drew a line every five years, the first plans outside of the Soviet Union. Unfortunately, the costs of Turkish democracy were high; until the semi-bankruptcy that occurred in February, 2001, the parties bought their votes with election bribes, and then plundered the government coffers. Turkey was often sick, and the disease discharged itself in feverish episodes and crises. The economy muddled through, from crisis to crisis. The years during which the Turks became poorer and poorer were 1991 to 1994, 2000, and, of course, 2001. The greatest obstacle on the way to the EU was not politics; it was the economy, which was a burden with millions of impoverished Anatolians and a government that siphoned off all credits and pushed interest rates up; and with an inefficient agriculture that soaked up one-third of working people like a sponge.

Then the movie went blank. Before the Turkish state hit the wall of not being able to pay, the International Monetary Fund (IMF) saved it and started a remarkable upswing with a program that consisted of 15 structural reforms. It did away with Turkey's irresponsible subventions, provided the Central Bank with independence and the financial industry with effective supervision by introducing the privatization and liberalization of various markets. The economy was now protected from the reach of politics and could finally unfold freely.

Success was inevitable. When looking at the most important overall economic data, the word "quantum leap" comes to mind. From 2002 to 2006, the Turkish economy grew every year by an average of 7%; from 2002 to 2007, the per capita income doubled to $5,350 USD; the national deficit went from 17%, in 2001, to only 0.7%, in 2006. In 2006, total national debt had shrunk from 91% of the GDP, in 2001, to less than 50%. Inflation remains the only facet where meeting the Maastricht Convergence Criteria is not in sight yet. It dropped from its long-term average value of 70% to 7.7%, in 2005. Then it climbed back up to 9.7%, in 2006. At 400 billion dollars, in 2006, the Turkish economy was greater than that of Belgium, Switzerland, and Sweden. By 2013, the Turkish government wants to make the Turkish economy move up to the sixth largest in Europe. In 1980, Turkey had exported 3% of its GNP; while in 2006, it was 22%, which is a clear signal that competitiveness has been achieved.

In 2005, the EU Commission attested in its *Progress Report 2005* that Turkey had an impressive economic performance, and that the economy was so robust, that it was no longer susceptible to the shocks of external origin. Turkey passed the tests in May, 2006, and 2007, when large investors pulled money from emerging markets. Unlike the large recession in 2001, the Central Bank was now independent, so it could quickly react with interest measures; the foreign exchange course was flexible and caught the market pressure; it was consolidated by the bank industry's speeding up of the downwards spiral, in 2001, with its high short-term foreign exchange liabilities. Every year, Turkey makes progress in fulfilling the economically relevant Copenhagen Criteria: the market economy functions better, and the Turkish economy is able to withstand the competitive pressure of the EU.

The International Monetary Fund had saved Turkey from collapsing in 2001. Now, the EU is to be the long-term catalyst for further convergence, for catching up compared to the richest industrial countries in Europe. This is not the first time the EU took on such a role; the EU and IMF helped Ireland, Greece, Spain, and Portugal to surmount their problems. Though these countries have now been going through a great economic crisis, they had indeed achieved a rapid change because they liberalized their economies fast, because targeted EU subventions reduced inequalities, and because foreign direct investments—which the EU process attracted—triggered a decisive modernization episode.

In Turkey, the customs union of 1996 was a first step in this direction. It opened Turkey and integrated the country into a globalized economy. The Turkish companies that hitherto had been protected by high customs barriers reacted with big investments to withstand the new competitive pressure. During the first ten years of the Customs Union, Turkish exports to the EU quadrupled to 48 billion dollars, and the exports of European states into Turkey tripled to 58 billion dollars. The EU is thus the most important trade partner of Turkey. The Customs Union only comprises industrial goods, while excluding services and agriculture.

In a second step, the economically relevant chapters of the accession negotiations will create the prerequisites for Turkey to become part of the EU domestic market. They will liberalize markets for energy, telecommunication, and traffic, and also adjust the public procurement sector, tax system, and environmental laws to EU norms. They will regulate food safety and consumer protection, the right of establishment, corporate law, and much more. "Acquis communautaire" changed the Turkish economy once again. Of the 35 negotiation chapters, two-thirds have an impact on the economy, either directly or indirectly. The Customs Union only covered three of the 35 chapters: the freedom of goods, competitive policies, and protection of intellectual property.

There was a huge influx of foreign direct investors in Turkey because the accession negotiations improved the basic conditions, and also because the market is attractive. The domestic market is growing fast, the production work continues to be reasonable, and the strategic situation at the interface between Europe, Asia, and the Near East enables access to interesting markets.

The population in Europe is aging, the markets are satiated. By 2045, the population of EU-27 will be around 460 million, and only 15% of them are 15 years old and younger. In Turkey, the population is young. Thirty percent are younger than 15 years old. By 2030, the population will grow from 72 million to 85 million, where it will stabilize. Their income per person and per year is only 29% of the EU average. They have started to catch up; the available income is rising.

Ultimately, the Turkish economy is growing because of investments from abroad that are impacting its structure. The time when Turkey exported hazelnuts and cheap t-shirts is a thing of the past. Ninety percent of exports fall to industrial goods, such as textiles, steel, major appliances, and cars. Automobiles and automotive parts are among the largest industries. They contribute one-fifth to the total exports, and the Turkish automobile industry has moved up to become the seventh largest production site in Europe. They manufacture one million cars and commercial vehicles a year, mainly for export to Germany, Italy, Spain, and Great Britain.

The clothing industry became the second largest export industry when the MFA agreement, which governs the world trade in textiles and garments, expired in early 2005. The treaty dated back to 1974, and contained quotas for the export of textiles and clothing to the United States and Europe. The contingents limited the export of developing countries to industrial states, but secured a certain sales volume for them. The Turkish clothing manufacturers did not go bust despite the cheap exports from China, with which they were forced to compete in the most important export markets. Early on, they had invested in high quality brands of their own, and also in fashion lines. Many leading fashion companies have their clothes made in Turkey or buy from Turkish manufacturers. Other Turkish industries have advanced, too. Forty percent of the televisions that are sold in Germany and the EU are labeled "Made in Turkey." Grundig, a symbol of the German economic recovery after the Second World War, no longer belongs to Germans but to the Turkish Koç-Group. Turkey is Europe's largest manufacturer of chemical fertilizers and the third largest producer of ceramics. In spring 2007, the Eczacıbaşı-Group purchased the traditional German company, Villeroy & Boch.

Turkey's network with the European and the global economy is becoming denser. Turkey borders a region that has more than 70% of the world's oil and is becoming one of the most important energy corridors in Europe. The oil pipeline that leads from Baku in Azerbaijan to the Turkish Mediterranean port of Ceyhan transports oil from the Caucasus and Central Asia to Europe, and thus prevents the oil from being diverted to the Far East. Turkey as a transit country could be recommended as an alternative to Russia. Two of the six gas pipelines (which ultimately will secure the gas supply in Europe) run through Turkey. Pipeline NG3 transports gas from Central Asia, Iran, and the Near East to Europe. It is currently in operation up to Greece, while the extension to Italy is under construction. From Greece, another pipeline will lead North through the former Yugoslavia; a second one goes via Bulgaria, Romania, Hungary, and Austria. Turkey is pushing for the inclusion of RWE—a German power company, into the pipeline project, the nickname of which is "Nabucco" while Russia is trying to get it under its control with the Hungarian gas company. NG6, another pipeline, is to form a ring around the Mediterranean connecting North Africa, Turkey, Greece, and Italy.

Foreign investors, especially banks, are also crowding into the service industry. Within only a few years, the share of foreign capital in Turkish banks grew from zero to 40%. Trend: rising because foreign large banks see great growth potential in the Turkish market. The assets of Turkish banks have only reached 80% of the GNP; that rate is 200% in the developed industrial states in Western Europe. Aside from companies from the United States (Citigroup and General Electric), financial institutes in Europe bought up Turkish banks—among them, the National Bank and the EFG Eurobank from Greece, BNP Paribas and Dexia from France, Fortis from Belgium, UniCredit SpA from Italy and HSBC from England.

The inflow of foreign capital may continue, but it could stop. What is important is the way the economic players react. It could be the beginning of a virtuous circle whereby continued reforms would have a beneficial effect on growth, jobs, and new optimism; that in turn would increase the acceptance for additional reforms. The opposite could happen, too— which would be a vicious circle: If the process of joining the EU stopped, the inflow of foreign direct investments would stop; growth would slow down, and reforms would be replaced by a new kind of protectionism.

Growth and new jobs make it easier for every Turkish government to continue the reform process. New jobs can only be created in the manufacturing industry and the services sector. When one takes stock of the past years, the result is positive. In 2005 and 2006, two million jobs were created outside of agriculture—more than ever before. This is mainly thanks to foreign investors. Here is the example of a German investor: In 1995, the subsidiary of Bosch GmbH employed 2,000 people in Turkey, today 7,000; in 2010, it will be 10,000. In 2007, Bosch intends to export goods worth one billion dollars from Turkey. Another example: Daimler AG employs 3,500 people in their two factories that manufacture buses and trucks in Turkey. That secures another 30,000 jobs in supplier industries.

Economically, the first decade of the 21st century was the most successful years in the history of the Republic. Turkey became a success story. Increasingly, the economy is not an obstacle on the path towards Europe, and actually, it is becoming a trump card. But Turkey cannot have a place in Europe until it has come to terms with itself. A Turkey that no longer blocks itself would be a real gain for Europe. As it is already the case with the economy.

## Truck tracks into Northern Iraq

The historical Silk Road has become the road of the trucks and the lifeline for the Iraqi economy. Every day 3,000 trucks push through the 850 km long stretch from the Turkish Mediterranean sea ports of Mersin and Iskenderun to Habur, the border post to Iraq. Their trips begin in modern industrial cities, lead along the border to Syria and past places in which Abraham settled—and they end in the poverty-stricken Kurdish communities which have been dried out by the sun. The trucks take at least two days for this trip because the two lane roads in the Kurdish Southeast of Turkey are not in a very good condition.

From his office, Kenan Uygur looks down on the port of Mersin which has become an important trading place for Iraq. This is where the oil tanks arrive from Lukoil. They are what Uygur is interested in, because he is a co-owner of the Turkish transport company Goltek that has entered into a partnership with two large companies for business in Iraq: with Litesco, the trading company of Lukoil headquartered in Geneva, and the American trading house "Refinery Associates of Texas" (RAOT). This is the company that won a bid from the Pentagon for the delivery of gas and diesel in Iraq; smaller bids went to three Turkish manufacturers of gasoline. The Texans get their gasoline from the refinery of the Russian oil company Lukoil in Burgas in Bulgaria. Goltek's fleet of trucks transports it into Iraq for RAOT.

Every day a third of the 3,000 trucks are on their way to the border gate, Habur, to transport gasoline, diesel, and the fluid gas, LPG. Almost half of them have Golek's logo on them. Uygur picks up his calculator. "One truck load conveys an average of twenty tons, so that means that Iraq gets about three quarters of its civil gasoline requirement from Turkey." The representative of RAOT on location with his broad Texan accent is full of praise for his Turkish partner: "They are absolutely reliable, and

I do not know anyone who does this job better." This job is not for every-one. First the truck drivers have to spend days in Mersin until their trucks have been loaded. Then it takes two days to drive to the border, where they wait for three days to be processed. Beyond that, most of them only drive to Zakho, the first city in Iraqi Kurdistan.

It is not only Mersin that is booming, the section along the historical Silk Road, along the border to Syria is, too. The trucks cross the provinc-es Gaziantep, Şanlıurfa, Mardin and Şırnak. "From these four provinces more than 55,000 trucks drive into Iraq," the transport entrepreneur Sül-eyman Akdağ says. He is from Kızıltepe near Mardin, a city that lives most-ly from trade. This is where the US Army had wanted to erect their cen-tral storage warehouse before the Iraq War. But that did not come about because Turkey refused to get involved. Now the approximately 250,000 people of this dusty and hot city have a different source of income: Iraq. "On average there are thirty to forty trucks for each large family consist-ing of 30 to 40 family members," says the Kurd Akdağ, who looks and laughs like Charlie Chaplin.

Without exception, all of the truck drivers from Kızıltepe earn their money in Iraq, and they feed their families well. "Where there is work there is no terror," Akdağ preaches in front of a portrait of the entrepre-neur Sakıp Sabancı who had recently died. He has put up a large model of a sail ship underneath the portrait. "We don't have an ocean, so I want to look at a ship instead," he says gaily. He is doing well. He owns 75 trucks. They used to drive to Europe and Russia; today, without exception, they drive to Iraq.

Business between Mersin and Habur is booming, and it will contin-ue to boom. Onur Uçman, sales manager for trucks at the Mercedes rep-resentative Koluman in the prospering industrial city of Gaziantep, is intoxicated by his sales figures. "The transport companies have made a lot of money fast with their Iraq business," Uçman says between two con-versations with customers, while his cell phone rings incessantly, and he expects that the companies will invest their money in new trucks in order to be able to save on taxes.

One of Uçman's customers is İsmail Akan, a Kurd. His company Öza-kan İş Ticaret is small; it is not suitable for the large orders that the Amer-icans have. But he has also found a niche for himself. He uses his two trucks to transport food, detergents, and electronic devices into Iraq. He is buying a third Mercedes today. "There is no other company that I trust more," he says admiringly and pays cash out of a large plastic bag that he has brought along.

Small companies like Akan's have to go with the times, too. One-man companies established a flourishing border trade with their rusty trucks that have decorations which have been applied lovingly. Today they do not stand a chance as competitors. It used to be worthwhile to secretly transport cheap diesel in a plastic tank under the loading surface until the Turkish army stopped this kind of border trade because they assumed that it was the separatist PKK that was profiting. "The more money people made trading with Iraq the more probable it would become that terrorism would subside," Uçman said. "Today four or five of these formerly free chauffeurs get together, establish a company, and do well."

The two-lane highway passes along the border to Syria behind Kızıltepe. Kurds can see the Turkish villages of their relatives in the neighboring country across the flat land. High gates with barbed wire divide them from each other. There are watchtowers posted in regular intervals; they rise up from the hot, sunny, dry land. Shortly before the street meets up with the Tigris valley the land becomes hilly and sparse. The heat here glitters as brightly. Downhill you see the Kurdish city of Cizre.

Mahmut, a Kurd from Adana, is using a welding apparatus to work on car wrecks on a hill over the river and the city. Right before the Iraq War started, Turkey had closed the border to Iraq. The people who had previously made their living smuggling and illegally transporting cheap diesel into Iraq were suddenly out of work. But they had to continue paying taxes. Many were unable to, and so they scrapped their trucks in junkyards like the one Mahmut owns. Life in Cizre came to a standstill at the time. Since that time Mahmut has been taking apart old trucks and sending the parts to an ironworks in Hatay's industrial district of Iskenderun.

Down in Cizre district the offices are all located along a dusty highway. The flat buildings are generally only one story high, are secured with iron bars, and reach far back to where Hacı Onuk is sitting in his modern office. There is an air-conditioner on the wall. "In Batman, the next province in the North, there is a refinery, and there are jobs all around it," says the entrepreneur. Things are quite different in Cizre. There is no industry whatsoever, and agriculture came to a halt, cows no longer graze in the fields, and the little town of Cizre has swollen to 120,000 inhabitants in just a couple of years.

And so 95% of the people in Cizre make their living by trading with Iraq. 13,000 trucks drive to Iraq from the province of Şırnak, which Cizre is also a part of—most of them tank trucks. Of those, 27 belong to Hacı Onuk. He complains that work has become more difficult due to the situation in Iraq and the tougher competition. His neighbor has been missing a driver for the last 23 days who last reported from Bagdad. "In early 2007 a truck could do three trips from Mersin to Zahkho or Mosul in 30 days, now it would require almost 50 days for two trips," Onuk calculates. In Mosul the trucks have to wait longer for an Iraqi semi-truck to take over their load. So Hacı Onuk has temporarily postponed new acquisitions.

There are junk yards along the street that leads out of Cizre, too. These huge junkyards continue along the highway towards the border, and 10 kilometers before the border, the three-lane queue starts. The right lane is for transporters of fluid gas who don't have to get in line but who can drive through for security reasons. The others are processed after 5 pm so that the customs officials are rewarded with overtime for working at night.

At the height of the boom nearly 5,000 trucks arrived in Habur on a daily basis. Now that number has dropped to 3,000. They transport gasoline, diesel, and LPG, but also vegetables and potatoes, sugar and noodles, refrigerators and ovens, even cement and steel, because Turkey manufactures a lot of the goods that are needed in Iraq. Recently, Turkish construction companies have been crowding into the Kurdish part of Iraq.

Verimli, a little village town right before the border, is one of the few towns that survived the armed conflict. Very untypically the town lives from wheat and lentils. Only the mayor of the town, Mehmet Tatar, makes his money with transport, but not during the bad times when the border was closed. But Tatar had enough money, not to have to junk his trucks. The family has something to say in politics too because his uncle was elected to the Turkish Parliament for the second time after the elections in Silopi. He also won in November 2002 elections when he run as an independent candidate.

From his office, Madani Tatar, the brother of the mayor who is sitting on a sofa, can see how the line of trucks moves forward at a snail's pace. Above him is a picture of his deceased father Halil who has a huge mustache—the ideal image of a Kurd. Madani Tatar complains that the large transportation companies were increasingly outbidding the prices of the smaller companies. For each ton of gasoline they used to make 45 Euros, now they make 30 and that means 600 Euros for a normal truck. And that has to cover customs and various penalties that can accrue in Iraq claims Tatar, who says the Kurdish militias of the Peshmerge stop trucks, measure their fluid level, and for each liter they are under, the maximum the penalty is one dollar. But everyone knows that part of the gasoline evaporates when it is very hot. "The drivers are afraid, and the profit is smaller."

Then there is the fear that the domestic turbulence in Iraq will cause commerce to collapse again because more than 70% of all goods that are brought to Iraq past his office are for Arab areas beyond the safe Kurdish region. Tatar manages to relax by reassuring himself that the need for various goods beyond the border will not disappear in the future. "Because there are no longer functioning factories there, they really do need everything."

The truck drivers who are waiting are preoccupied thinking about something else. Almost no one drives past Mosul. The drive is only relatively safe up to Zakho which has become the place for the movement of goods into Iraq. There, only a few kilometers past the border, the truck trailers are attached to those of the Iraqi partners who bring the goods into the Arab part of the country. The empty trailers are brought back by the Turkish truck drivers to get new goods. The trucks roll on, and they symbolize hope for a better future for the Kurds between Mersin and Habur.

# Chapter III

---

## Mortgages and Wealth

# Mortgage I:
# Disadvantaged Groups

## Kurds in a Kemalist straightjacket

The Kurdish issue has become synonymous with many of the unsolved conflicts in Turkey because the axiom of uniformity of the Turkish nation and the illusion of a uniform social will do not provide much room for the individual citizens or groups that do not fit this state ideology. Therefore, official state ideology negates or disfavors the disadvantaged groups, primarily the Kurds, the Alevis and the non-Muslims. Among these, the Kurds are the ones who are hardest hit. A ban on using any other language than the "official" language, from 1984 to 1999, was specifically for Kurdish, and during the severe armed conflict with the PKK, which lasted from 1984 to 1999, the military evacuated more than 10,000 villages in the Southeast of the country. After the "deep state" had disabled those leading Kurdish figures who had been negotiators and intermediaries, it was confronted by the Kurdistan Workers' Party (PKK), which was the most radical Kurdish organization of all. As a result of the conflicts, more than three million people were forced to settle elsewhere. Until February, 1999, when Abdullah Öcalan, the leader of the PKK, was arrested, the years-long armed struggle resulted in more than 37,000 murders, committed mostly by the sanguinary PKK and the military, including especially the notorious Gendarmerie Intelligence and Anti-Terror Unit, which does not report to the Ministry of the Interior, but the military.

Long after the reforms of Turgut Özal, who had struggled hard and responded positively to the demands of all disadvantaged groups, especially the Kurds, in the eighties, the reforms introduced during the EU process granted the Kurds further cultural rights, even if they were limited and had large conditions attached—for example, using Kurdish in electronic media and in language schools. Turkish society is divided on many matters, but mainly regarding the Kurdish conflict. A survey conducted by the Open Society Institute, which was published in October, 2007, determined that 42% of those questioned demanded those who were not Turkish to take on Turkish citizenship. Only 29% accepted that these groups speak their own languages and maintain their own cultural heritage.

One side reduces the conflict to a terror problem that can only be solved militarily and is of the opinion that the economic development of underdeveloped Kurdish regions will only be of momentary help. This side is grouped around the military and Turkish nationalists. A political solution of the Kurdish question; in other words, granting them cultural autonomy and accepting Kurdish politicians in negotiations, would endanger the territorial integrity of the country, they believe. The traditional Kemalist circles fear that democratization will lead to greater self-determination of the Kurds. They point out that beyond the border, Iraq is in danger of falling apart, and an independent Kurdish state might be established in Northern Iraq. As a consequence, Turkey could fall apart, the defenders of this approach reason. So it would be only consistent that all official offices in the Kurdish Southeast have a picture of Atatürk, the founder of the Republic, wearing his uniform. In Western Turkey, he is generally pictured wearing civilian clothing.

In August 2007, the chairman of the Turkish History Association (TTK), Yusuf Halaçoğlu, who is internationally renowned as the intellectual leader of the denial of the "genocide" of the Armenians, represented this kind of thinking. He said that the Kurds who live in Turkey were of Turcoman origin. Those Kurds who profess to be Alevis, on the other hand, were "unfortunately of Armenian heritage." According to Halaçoğlu, by converting to Alevism, in 1915 and 1916, Armenians supposedly evaded being relocated, and therefore, the PKK was essentially not a Kurdish organization but an Armenian one. Then, he continued, in 1936 and 1937, the Turkish state had drawn up lists of people that it considered as converts, dating back to 1915 and 1916, and admitted that he himself had continued this list. Liberal newspapers then reminded readers that the Turkish state had always used those kinds of lists to judge the reliability of its personnel.

The Kemalist nationalists are faced with a liberal group that includes large parts of Erdoğan's government, most Kurdish politicians, and many civil groups. They are convinced that the territorial integrity will win, by granting more rights to the ethnic groups and by promoting the development of their regions. Furthermore, they call for a foreign policy that has good relations with all its neighboring countries, so that no neighbor can use the PKK to pressure Turkey.

The Republic of Turkey has assimilated many ethnic groups since its founding. They were more successful in doing so than the French Republic, which it had taken as its model in many things. For a certain period of time, assimilation seemed to work for the Kurds, too. They still represent one third of the delegates and a lot of ministers in the government; they are represented well in the private economy. But career and success can only take place for them if they present themselves as Turks. In the twenties and thirties, some Kurdish clans had rebelled against the Turkish central state for a while. Afterwards they kept a low profile for decades. During this time, they were officially referred to as "Mountain Turks."

In the seventies, the Kurds drew attention to themselves again. This time, a large number of them were represented in the Marxist-Leninist movement, and in 1978, they founded the PKK. A Kurdish nationalism arose from the leftist movements of the eighties. In 1984, the Marxist-Leninist PKK launched an armed struggle against "fascist colonial state Turkey," its ultimate goal being to found a new Kurdish state in Turkey using violence. Then, the PKK has never stopped at nothing to achieve that aim, however ruthless their acts may be, including launching attacks against the Kurdish civilians and the other significant Kurdish factions that do not support them. Since 1980, they had prepared for their battle in the Bekaa Valley, in Lebanon, where the armed struggle was reaching its fifth year. On August 15, 1984, the PKK launched its major armed conflict with attacks on two police stations and the officer housings in Eruh and Şemdinli and killed several officers. Two days later, the attacks were followed up by a raid on another police station in Siirt, which was followed this time by an ambush that killed eight officers in Çukurca, Hakkari.

The armed conflict came to a standstill every winter when there was a lot of snow in the mountains of the region. That spring, it was reignited on March 21, the Kurdish New Year, when they celebrate the victory of the blacksmith Kaway over the tyrant Dehak. He was the one who had called his people to resist and had lit a fire on the highest mountain after his victory. From 1984 to 1999, the New Year's Celebration was celebrated with the sign of fire and war.

Indeed, there had been many attempts to bring about a political solution. In 1988, the Prime Minister at the time, Turgut Özal, permitted people to speak Kurdish when visiting prisoners. In 1991, he ordered the acceptance of more than one hundred thousand Kurdish refugees from Iraq, stating that these Kurds had relatives in Turkey, thus admitting the existence of millions of Kurds in Turkey. In late 1991, the newly elected government of Prime Minister Süleyman Demirel, referred to the Southeast of Turkey as the, "land of Turks and Kurds," and in the late nineties, Prime Minister Mesut Yılmaz spoke of the fact that the path of Turkey into the EU leads through Diyarbakır—in other words, through the largest city in the Kurdish Southeast of Turkey.

Yet none of them were able to persist against the Kemalist naysayers of the Republic, who undermined all attempts towards a political solution. Resistance had already stirred against the attempts of Özal and Demirel. The Kemalist circles considered the recognition of Kurdish reality to be treason against the heritage of Atatürk. They felt justified on account of two developments. In August, 1991, a series of attacks were launched by the PKK and the Dev-Sol guerillas, whose assassins had been trained in the PKK camp in the Bekaa Valley. Then the PKK started enforcing their own laws in tribunals in those areas that they controlled. They had their own police and their own prisons, and checked IDs at controls. It launched many attacks against the civilians and education institutions in the region. In the 1993/1994 school year alone, the PKK burned down 300 schools and shot and killed more than 100 teachers. A lot of people, however, identified with the PKK during those years mainly due to the fact that the "deep state" had eliminated the spokespeople of the Kurds, and the massive human rights violations of the state and the gendarmerie benefitted the PKK.

The other opportunity they had for a new beginning was the parliamentary elections of October 20, 1991, during which six delegates of the social democratic SHP of Erdal İnönü, who considered themselves to be spokespersons of the Kurds, were elected. The first uproar came on November 6, 1991, during the swearing-in ceremony, when Leyla Zana wore a headband with the Kurdish colors—yellow, green, and red—and added the following sentence, in Kurdish, to her oath: "I will make sure that the

Kurdish people and the Turkish people live together in a democratic context."

On March 2, 1994, the immunity of Leyla Zana and five others was rescinded. They were arrested in the parliamentary building. The prosecutor demanded the death penalty; instead, the Court for State Security sentenced them to 15 years in prison on account of "treason and supporting a terrorist group." Those found guilty were Leyla Zana, Hatip Dicle, Selim Sadak, and Orhan Doğan. Ahmet Türk, however, spent only 22 months in prison. On June 9, 2004, the Cassation Court (Yargıtay) ordered that the four be released early, due to the fact that the legal situation had changed, based on the reforms carried out for the EU process. After a change in the constitution, international law ranked higher than national law, and the courts for state security that had sentenced the four were abolished.

And yet the spiral of violence accelerated again in July, 2004. A speaker of the PKK declared that the ceasefire that the organization had proclaimed when their leader, Öcalan, was arrested, in 1999, had expired. One of the triggers for their taking-up weapons again was that Öcalan was afraid that he could lose control over the Kurdish movement during the political process. Now, there were four alternatives to Öcalan's leadership: the four former Kurdish delegates who had been released again. In addition, the AK Party unexpectedly won the communal elections of April, 2004, in six Kurdish provinces. Moreover, a power struggle had commenced within the PKK: Osman Öcalan, the younger brother of the PKK's founder Abdullah Öcalan, took command, and he pleaded that the PKK be transformed into a political organization. But his counterpart, Murad Karayılan, won. He and his comrades-in-arms reasoned that during the years from 1999 to 2004, the military had carried out more than 700 operations against the PKK strongholds, despite the ceasefire that had been unilaterally declared.

Karayılan was in charge of approximately 5,000 comrades-in-arms in a rugged mountainous region between Iran and Iraq. The Qandil Mountains are situated in a 30-km-wide border strip that Saddam Hussein had depopulated and turned into a death zone. In the summer months of 2004, the first rebels returned to Turkey. From Iraq, where a civil war was raging, they brought dynamite, mainly C4, which they used for attacks on trains and on the Kuşadası and Çeşme resorts, where five vacationers were killed. The return to violence was instigated by the Freedom Falcons of Kurdistan, the most militant wing of the PKK.

Their return to violence meant that they were admitting they had failed. In early 2002, more than 300 delegates had decided to transform the PKK into a democratic movement and to rename the PKK, KADEK. Despite the new label, no one accepted them in negotiations—be it in Turkey, the United States, or the EU. They continued to remain on the list of terrorist organizations. The temporary moderation of the PKK was due to the fact that Turkey had fulfilled the key demands, from 1999 to 2002, and the support of the Kurdish people for the violent course of the PKK was disintegrating. The government suspended the state of emergency in the Kurdish provinces; the Parliament abolished the death penalty, so that Öcalan's sentence could be transformed into a lifelong sentence. There were initial attempts to use Kurdish in electronic media.

In August, 2005, there was an opportunity for a political solution to the Kurdish question when Erdoğan, whose advisors included Kurds such as Dengir Mir Mehmet Firat and Cüneyd Zapsu, debated the Kurdish question with Turkish and Kurdish intellectuals; during a rally, they promised to solve this issue, "with more democracy, more civil rights, and more wealth." They would have to make sure that every region in Turkey had a "different smell, a different color, and a different voice." Erdoğan admitted that the government had made mistakes. During the next meeting of the National Security Council (MGK), President Sezer and the generals challenged Erdoğan and demanded an explanation of his concept of the Kurdish problem. Erdoğan did not relent and said that the state must win its citizens. In April, 2006, his government rejected the demand of the "Committee to Combat Terrorism," made up of ministers and generals, to again proclaim a state of emergency in the Kurdish provinces.

This request came because the PKK had started increasing their level of violence and terror again. First, it proclaimed a Kurdish revolution, on February 15, 2006, the anniversary of the day Öcalan was arrested, then another insurrection on Kurdish New Year, March 21. Both times, nothing happened, because level-headed Kurdish politicians, such as Ahmet Türk, the head of the DTP, and Osman Baydemir, the first mayor of Diyarbakır, prevented it. Ahmet Türk is one of the most renowned Kurdish politicians in Turkey. His family is at the head of the Kurdish Kanco clan. When the Republic introduced family names, his family chose the surname "Türk."

But on March 28, 2006, a new wave of violence rocked the area. It was mostly Turkish soldiers that were killed. The violence was directed at the voices of Kurdish intellectuals, such as Abdülmelik Fırat, Ziya Ekinci, and Ümit Fırat, who were becoming louder, distancing themselves from the PKK, and demanding that Kurdish politics become non-violent. They questioned Öcalan's claim of being the sole representative of the Kurds. The Kurdish leaders in Iraq also turned against Öcalan. Neçirwan Barzani, Prime Minister of the autonomous Iraqi Kurdistan region, charged the PKK of damaging the Kurdish question more than any other movement. During an interview with *Newsweek*, in November, 2006, Karayılan offered Washington the services of the PKK as mercenaries in the fight against Islamist terror that originated in Iraq and Iran in order to expand his range of action and influence.

The traditional state elite backed up by the military continued to pour oil onto the fire in the Kurdish Southeast with their exclusively military approach and notorious human rights violations. The terror of the PKK also brought the process of democratization to a halt. A large number of people have a stake in terror in that area—the PKK as well as traditional elites that make more money from smuggling drugs when the shadow of a state of emergency hovers over the region. In a climate where weapons speak, political dialogue is not listened to. The right to free speech is limited, and so, too, is the option to demand more rights for the Kurds. Both sides need each other: the PKK can only flourish in a climate of violence, and the military justifies its dominant position by pointing to the PKK. The notorious "Gendarmerie Intelligence and Anti-Terror Unit" (JİTEM) operates in the underground. The Kurds and others consider this unit to be the incarnation of a dirty war and of an uncontrollable military apparatus that is probably responsible for most of the 2,000 murders that have occurred in the Southeast of Turkey.

Many of the soldiers who have been killed in the Southeast are draftees who have been dispatched to fight against the PKK terror after a completely insufficient training that only lasted a couple of months. And so they continue to get caught up in ambushes. Despite the claim that the PKK is the greatest threat to Turkey, the army sends these unprepared soldiers to the front instead of their elite units. Mothers and fathers report that their sons are being sent to slaughter. More than twenty cross-border operations of the Turkish army in Iraq have not gotten rid of the PKK.

On October 18, 2007, the Parliament authorized the government to give the authorization for the army to march into Northern Iraq, which provided this kind of an operation with a legal basis for the first time. The 24 cross-border operations that took place between 1983 and 1999 did not have that. 10,000 soldiers marched into Northern Iraq on February 22, 2008. They marched into the region, up to 25 km past the border. It happened because President Bush had confirmed that he would support Erdoğan in the fight against the PKK terror, on November 5, 2007. Washington provided their data on PKK positions in Northern Iraq, and the Turkish army started bombing these positions. The military operation happened in the middle of winter—earlier than expected. The ground offensive ended after only nine days, earlier than the nationalist parties CHP and MHP wanted. The military said that they had destroyed the positions of the PKK in the Zap Valley, which is considered to be an important pass beyond the border for the PKK's retreat. The army had wanted to use their winter offensive to surprise the PKK and show them that the army was capable of acting in winter, too. They also wanted to reestablish their credibility, which had suffered in the fight against the PKK. It is possible that the independence of Kosovo, which had just been proclaimed, also played a role. The army could use their ground offensive to signal to the Northern Iraqi Kurds not to imitate the Kosovars. Furthermore, the government and the army had agreed to improve political relations with the Iraqi Kurds after the ground offensive. A few days after the ground offensive was over, the long expected visit to Ankara of the Iraqi President, the Kurd Talabani, took place.

The military continued to insist on a military solution and the government elite continued to block a political solution to the conflict. And yet, during the July 22, 2007 elections, the AK Party received 55% of the vote in Kurdish regions, more than twice as much as the Kurdish DTP. The share of votes was higher than the 47% the AK Party had achieved all over the country. Since that time, the Kurds from the Southeast of Turkey have 80 of the 340 delegates within the AK Party. Without the Kurds, it would lose its absolute parliamentary majority. Since the army and other government institutions had managed to turn the Kurdish conflict into the most significant topic of Turkish politics for months, they subjected Erdoğan to a war of attrition and presented him with the alternative of either taking the position of Turkish nationalism or that of the Kurds. The government decided on the former, and thus largely lost the support of the Kurds. With the military insisting on a further ground offensive, it became active again, and the pending reforms as well as the debate on the design of a new constitution, disappeared into political oblivion.

By autumn 2007, the AK Party had gained the sympathy of the Kurdish people because they had invested in infrastructure—health care and schools—more than any other party. Obviously, when they went to vote, the Kurds saw the AK Party as a way out of the spiral of violence, as a way to have their Kurdish identity recognized, and a way to be granted more cultural rights, such as the broadcast of TV programs in their Kurdish mother tongue. On August 18, 2004, the supervisory board for electronic media (RTÜK) gave three private channels the license to broadcast in Kurdish. Initially, the government bureaucracy dictated that they cannot broadcast for longer than 45 minutes a day, that programs must be for adults, that they may not contain language lessons, and that they must have Turkish subtitles. However, there are now several Kurdish language TV stations in Turkey, including the state run TRT 6 and the private Dunya TV.

Since July 22, 2007, there are 20 delegates in the Parliament who were elected as independents for the Kurdish DTP. They had to go this path because the parties would have failed to pass the 10% election threshold—which is the minimum share of the vote a political party requires in order to obtain 20 seats in the Turkish Parliament, thus securing group representation as a party. For the first time since 1994, a Kurdish party that considers itself as the representative of the Kurdish identity has obtained group representation in the Parliament.

The competition in the parliamentary democracy has transformed the Islamist movement into a party that governed the country for long years with a liberal, yet culturally conservative, politics. Now, there is the opportunity that DTP's inclusion will make the Kurdish nationalism more moderate, so that it, too, becomes integrated with the political system in Turkey. The Turkish justice system will, however, make sure that they will not be tamed that quickly. Justice system continues to confront Kurdish politicians with various accusations. There are dozens of lawsuits on-going against Osman Baydemir, the mayor of Diyarbakır; against

Abdullah Demirbaş, the deposed mayor of the Sur district of Diyarbakır; and against all other DTP mayors. Baydemir and 55 other mayors, who are members of the DTP, must take responsibility for the fact that they asked the Danish Prime Minister, in a letter, not to ban the satellite channel Roj TV, which broadcasts Kurdish programs. That is what Turkey had demanded because they see Roj TV as being the mouthpiece of the PKK. Baydemir, however, referred to the broadcaster as a forum of the Kurdish public. They are now faced with prison terms of up to 15 years because of their "support of a terrorist organization." For the very reason that Baydemir took 8.50 Euro from the city treasury to pay for the corpse of a PKK member to be transported in a municipal hearse, he might be sentenced to one year in prison.

In addition, most of the accusations against Demirbaş are based on the fact that he offered the services of his city hall in Kurdish and other languages. Yet Kurdish was neither tolerated in a handicraft book, or in a software program; it might not be spoken in wedding speeches, or written on posters—not even those that are multi-lingual. A scientific study determined that 72% of the people who lived in his part of the Sur district spoke Kurdish, and only 24% Turkish. In June, 2007, the highest administrative court—the Council of State (Danıştay), deposed him and the city council of Sur. Demirbaş responded that he was unable to detect anything separatist in his statement, and that "Turkey has more than one identity, more than one culture, and more than one language." His case and the cases of other Kurdish mayors show that state law continues to be above the law of the legal state.

## The Alevis, Atatürk's disappointed followers

The concept of minorities is still not present in the minds of many Turks, mainly because of the centuries-long Ottoman practice. During the Ottoman Empire, a nation defined itself by its religion; there were thus no Muslim minorities in the Empire. According to the Ottoman *millet* system, all Muslims were accepted as one nation (*millet*); therefore, no difference was made between Turks and Kurds, Arabs and Circassians. Non-Muslims were accepted as different nations (*millets*), and the spiritual leaders of every religious community were regarded as their political leaders (ethnarch) during the long history of the Ottoman Empire. The new Republic also accepts minorities on the basis of religion. Accordingly, only those *millets* that were already around during the Ottoman Empire are accepted: the Greek-Orthodox and the Armenian-Apostolian Christians, the Jews as well as the Monophysite Syrian Orthodox Christians, from Tur Abdin, in the Southeast of the country.

Both the Sunni majority and the Alevi minority of Muslim Kurds rise up against the ideological foundation of the Republic because the ethnically-defined Turkish nationalism excludes them. The Alevis also started rising up gradually against the state doctrine of the secular Republic since Sunni Islam was becoming the unofficial state religion, and the state ideology has not recognized the Alevis as an independent denomination and a separate movement within Islam. The Alevis make up at least one-fourth of the Turkish population. The area where they settled historically is mainly those provinces in Eastern Central Anatolia. In the course of the rural migration that started after the Second World War, many of them settled along the coast of the Aegean and the Mediterranean, as well as in the greater Istanbul metropolitan area.

Indeed, the Alevis do not want to be seen as a minority, and not only because of their large numbers. They see themselves as the co-founders of the Republic. During the Ottoman Empire, they were persecuted as the "Rafidis" (literally, "deserters"), and could survive in remote areas. Therefore, they supported Atatürk's project of a secular republic from the beginning. On December 23, 1919, at the beginning of the War of Independence, Mustafa Kemal, who later became Atatürk, visited the spiritual center of the Alevis in Hacıbektaş, in Central Anatolia and secured their support. The Alevis fought in Atatürk's associations and he named the former head of the Alevis, Cemalettin Çelebi, as the vice president of the first provisional national assembly in Ankara.

The hopes of the Alevis to receive the same status as Sunni Muslims seemed to be fulfilled. Then, Atatürk's radical course of action against all of the institutions of Islam also hit them. The dervish lodges (*dergâhs*), and those of the Alevis and the Bektaşi, an order they sympathized with, were closed. They had been the most important meeting rooms of the Alevis. They were (and continue to be) hit even harder by the fact that the rigid laicism dissolved all Islamic institutions, and that the state religious authority promoted (and continues to promote) the Sunnification process for the sake of creating a unanimous nation. It was primarily after the Second World War that the religious authority built mosques in

Alevi villages, and sent Sunni Imams to the Alevis, who had assembled in buildings that were referred to as Cemevi. Two years after the 1980 military coup, the generals ordered Sunni religious classes for all pupils. Since 1990, at least Christians and Jews can apply for exemptions from such classes. A draft of the new constitution envisages freedom of choice for religion classes.

The distrust between Sunnis and Alevis has not disappeared much. It came about many centuries ago. Alevism dates back to the time when the nomadic Turcoman tribes arrived in Anatolia from Central Asia. It was mostly the wandering dervishes who converted these nomadic Turcoman tribes to Islam. The rural population was more receptive to their oral Sufi interpretation of Islam than to the orthodox legal Islam, with its strict devotion to scriptures. The Sufi dervishes were in the tradition of venerating Ali, the fourth caliph of Islam. In time, a religious interpretation came about in Anatolia that was composed of the oral tradition of the old Shamanist belief of the Turks from Central Asia, the newly-embraced Islam as well as the existing conviction-based practices. The believers of this heterodox religion, who lived in Anatolia, were the political subjects of the Ottoman Sultan. But they also honored the sheikhs of the Brotherhood of Safavids, in Ardabil, in present-day Iran.

When the Safavid Shah Ismail, who was of Turcoman origin, expanded his reign to include all of Persia, in 1501, and proclaimed the Shi'a as the new state religion in the Safavid Persia, the Turcoman Alevis were then considered to be the fifth column of the new opponent of the Ottomans, and were increasingly seen as heretics. Progressively, the Ottomans professed to be orthodox Sunni Muslims, to distinguish themselves from the Safavid Shiite zealots; some of the followers of the literalist orthodox religious orders called for the persecution of the Alevis. The Alevis could therefore only survive in remote areas. They mostly settled in Hacıbektaş, in Central Anatolia, the burial place of the Sufi mystic, Hajji Bektaş-ı Veli, the founder of the order of the Bektaşi.

Atatürk initially freed them from persecution and isolation. One can therefore find three pictures in many houses of the Alevis: Ali, the mystic Hajji Bektaş-ı Veli, who lived from 1209 to 1271 and in whose orders the Alevis have been meeting since the 16th century, and Atatürk. In the thirties, the persecution returned. In 1938, the army killed more than 70,000 people during the rebellion of Kurdish Alevis, in the province of

Dersim (present-day Tunceli); more than 100,000 people were forced to settle elsewhere. Approximately one-fifth of the Kurds are Alevis; the rebellion was preceded by a deportation of many Kurd Alevis to other parts of the country.

Later, there were renewed clashes between Sunni Muslims and Alevis. In 1977, Turkish right-wing nationalist Muslims attacked left-wing Alevis in Malatya; 100 people were killed in Kahramanmaraş, in 1978, during a pogrom directed at Alevis; 30 people were killed during another massacre, in Çorum, in 1980. Thirty-seven people were killed in Sivas, in 1993, when a Sunni mob set a hotel on fire, where a meeting between Alevi intellectuals and artists was taking place. The writer Aziz Nesin, who had previously translated Salman Rushdie's *Satanic Verses* into Turkish and who was not an Alevi, barely escaped. In 1995, the violent clashes in Istanbul's Gaziosmanpaşa district lasted for days after two people had died during shootings directed at coffeehouses frequented by Alevis.

During the summer of 1996, several hundred inmates in Turkish prisons participated in "death fasts," and twelve inmates died. The people who participated in these fasts were almost all Alevis who had been sentenced on account of their membership in extreme leftist groups. Erbakan's government was in office, which was troubling for most Alevis. Şevket Kazan, who had voluntarily taken on the defense of those accused in the Sivas incident, was now the Minister of Justice. The Alevis were therefore afraid of Erbakan's Welfare Party (RP).

The distrust between the Sunni majority and the Alevi minority is mainly because of their differing religious interpretations. It is increased by political polarization: many of the Sunnis are conservative and nationalistic; the Alevis generally represent Turkey's leftists. When the first wave of Alevis moved into the cities during the sixties, the youths interpreted the Alevi tradition of group solidarity and uprising against the government's suppression as the precursors of socialism. Alevis made up the core of the communist movement and extreme leftist movements in Turkey. During the eighties, the revolutionary furor began to subside in those who had been living in the cities for a while. But they remained leftists. The Alevis continued to represent the backbone of leftist extreme groups such as DHKP/C, TIKKO and TKP/ML.

A renaissance of Alevism commenced during the eighties, as Kurdish nationalism became stronger. For a long time, they tried to avoid attracting attention. In the course of the new civil society which was developing, they increasingly acknowledged their culture in public. Two perspectives of Alevism became apparent. The conservative wing sees the Alevis as the creators of "true" Turkish Islam that is in accordance with the special characteristics of the Turks, without the Arabic ingredients of orthodox Islam. The left wing, on the other hand, sees Alevism as a humanist ideology. For them, Alevism is less a religion, especially during times of progressive secularization, but more of a progressive lifestyle that fights for justice and against oppression.

The issue as to whether Alevism is a religion or a form of Islam is controversial among the Alevis. What is not controversial, however, is that most elements of Alevism have been taken from Islam with considerable modifications, such as Alevis not interpreting the Qur'an literally but in a mystical way and that they do not observe the five pillars of Islam, including the pilgrimage to Mecca or fasting during Ramadan. The women do not segregate from the men in Cemevis, where they meet in congregation; the Alevi women participate in the service alongside the men. They also have the same rights in everyday life.

However, Alevis bemoan the fact that there are 87,000 officially recognized mosques in Turkey, while there are only several hundred Cemevis. It is difficult to get building approvals for new Cemevis. They want fewer restrictions for building Cemevis, and they demand that the Sunni-focused religious culture course should no longer be an obligatory class for Alevi students. Some Alevis also want the Diyanet to hire Alevi spiritual leaders while some others wish for the word "Islam" to disappear from their passports. Some of these demands have been included in the EU Commission's Progress Report, since 2004. During the history of Turkey, the number of governors and the general directors of government institutions who were Alevis are significantly less than the Sunnis, and so Alevis also want to be able to have more opportunities in government service.

Traditionally, the majority of Alevis are affiliated with Atatürk's party of the CHP. This support, however, started diminishing to the extent that the former head of the CHP, Deniz Baykal, tried to get Sunni nationalist voters to vote for him by using anti-Alevi slogans.

During the elections of July 22, 2007, the majority of Alevis still gave the CHP their vote. The Alevis are the last great group in Turkey which the AK Party could not win over. Many Alevis still think of the AK Party as being Sunni Islam. Furthermore, Erdoğan had repeatedly deprived the Alevis of the status of a religious community. During the elections of July, 2007, three Alevi delegates were elected on the AK Party lists, led by the intellectual, Reha Çamuroğlu. The week before Election Day, Erdoğan and Gül visited an Alevi house of worship and spoke with the Alevi leaders there. They were trying to win the Alevis for themselves in the same way the AK Party had approached the Kurds.

## Christians, expulsion and exodus

When Muslims and Christians met in Anatolia, the two religions were different than we know them today. Islam of the Turkoman tribes differed from the orthodoxy of later centuries, while Christianity in Anatolia was also undergoing change. Anatolia was always a country in transit. Everyone brought along their own religious understanding, and it merged with what was already there. A lot could survive. There is a continuity that stretches from Kybele, the Anatolian earth mother, to Artemis, the virgin Hellenist God of Fertility, to Mary, the mother of Jesus. The most important sanctuary of Artemis was in Ephesus; its temple was one of the Seven Wonders of the World of Antiquity. Christianity reveres the place where Mary is to have died, in the wooded mountains over Ephesus.

Christianity cannot be imagined without Anatolia (a.k.a. Asia Minor). The first community with followers of Jesus outside of Palestine came about in Edessa, today's Şanlıurfa. In the cave churches of Antioch, present-day Antakya, those who believed in the resurrected Jesus referred to themselves as Christians for the first time. Paul, the people's apostle, travelled through Anatolia three times, on long missionary travels. The tent maker from the Turkish Tarsus was in Ephesus often; he wrote his Letter to the Galatians to the Celtic community of today's Ankara. He preached in Anatolia, and in Rome he became the victim of Nero's persecution of Christians.

The early Christian church was not monolithic at all. Many types of belief came about, caused by the controversies that pertained to Christology and the Doctrine of the Trinity, but also the various influences of Near Eastern, Greek, and Roman philosophy. Anatolia, and particularly Constantinople, the Second Rome, were the focus of these disputes. All seven ecumenical councils took place in larger Constantinople, from 325 to 788—three of them in the capital of the Empire. These theological disputes have had an impact on Christianity to modern times. Christians continue to recite the credo that the First Ecumenical Council of Nicaea agreed on in 325—the Nicene Creed.

In 301, the Armenian King Trdat III (280—330) declared Christianity as the state religion of his Armenian Empire, which he governed from his capital, Echmiadzin. He followed the advice of Gregor, a Parthic Prince who was born in Armenia in 240, grew up in Cappadocia, and became a Christian there. According to legend, he healed Trdat by the laying on of his hands on the king. Gregor became Krikor Lousavoritch the Enlightened, and founded the Armenian-Apostolic Church, succeeding the Apostles Thaddeus and Bartholomew.

Soon thereafter, in 312, Constantine I (d. 337) established himself as the sole ruler in Rome. According to legend, a vision of Christ led him to victory. From then on, he promoted Christianity, which Emperor Theodosius I declared to be the state religion in 380. Constantine I inaugurated his new capital in 330, which had been the old Byzantium. Constantinople was now named after the new Emperor Constantine. Unlike the first Rome, the second Rome had already been Christian. The Eastern Mediterranean region was superior to the West, both culturally and economically. The Council of Chalcedon (Kadıköy) bestowed the honorary title "Ecumenical Patriarch" to the Bishop of Chalcedonia, in 451. Then, Constantine's successor Justinian I (527–565) codified the five early Christian seats of the Patriarchs, which were led by Rome and Constantinople, followed by Jerusalem, Antioch, and Alexandria.

On May 29, 1453, Sultan Mehmet Fatih conquered Constantinople and shifted his capital to the Bosporus. The Byzantine Empire had ceased to exist, but not much changed for the Christians. The Ottoman Sultan turned the Byzantine churches into the Ottoman state institutions. In a *Firman,* an imperial edict, he assured the ecumenical Patriarch Gennadius II that the privileges his forebears had enjoyed would continue. In 1461, he created the Armenian patriarch, in Constantinople, for the Monophysite Christians. From 1840 on, the churches that were organized as *millets*, i.e. nations, had their own internal constitutions and became part of the Ottoman bureaucracy.

Towards the end of the Ottoman Empire, non-Muslims were still a majority in Istanbul, the capital of the Islamic World. Nationalism spread quickly in various parts of the Ottoman lands, in conjunction with the widespread appeal of nationalism on the entire European continent. During the First World War, only every fifth person in what would become the Republic was a Christian. Today, only about 100,000 of the 72 million Turks are Christians. It was not Islam that drove away the non-Muslims, but zealous Turkish nationalism.

The Armenians were its first victim. Known as "the Loyal Nation" (*Millet-i Sadıka*) for a long period of Ottoman history, Armenians had worked with the Turkish reformers as well—first with the Young Ottomans, then with the Young Turks. Except for the nationalist Hinchak Party, which was founded in the late 19th century with the aim of gaining independence from the Ottoman Empire, many Armenian reformers had not demanded autonomy from the Ottoman Empire. Rather, the moderate Hinchaks, the liberal wing of the Armenakans, and many of the Dashnaksutyuns were demanding economic and social reforms within the empire, while many of the socialist Dashnaksutyuns (also known as Armenian Revolutionary Federation) formed the *fedayi* armed groups and worked for the goal of creating an independent Armenia, similar to the Armenians of Van, who established the Armenakan Party to develop first the political principles behind Armenian nationalism, in secrecy, with the wider goal of winning to rule over themselves through revolution.

In 1902 and 1907, the moderate Armenian reformers appeared at the Conferences of Paris, together with the Turkish reformers. In 1914, during their party's caucus in Erzurum, the Party of the Dashnaksutyuns called for loyalty to the Ottoman Empire, and during the First World War, many Armenians were still holding intercession services for the victory of the Ottomans.

They were opposed by the Young Turks, a group of mostly European-educated young Turks (known in Turkish as "Jön Türkler," from the French "Les Jeunes Turcs"). They also included young Turkish army officers who generally came from poor backgrounds, but the newly established modern schools were providing them with career opportunities. After 1923, they made up the core of Atatürk's Republican People's Party (CHP); before that, they had organized themselves, in 1907, as the Committee for Unity and Progress. They got rid of the liberal reform wing, deposed Sultan Abdülhamid II, in 1907, and, in 1913, they seized power with a coup. The Armenians were a double obstacle for the Committee for Unity and Progress: because as the second largest revolutionary

group, they had not been eliminated yet, and because the Armenian people were like a wedge between the Turks in Anatolia and the Caucasus.

Several thousand people died during the first pogroms against the
Armenians, from 1894 to 1896, in Istanbul, and in 1909, in the Cilician
region. In early 1915, the Young Ottoman War Minister, Enver Pasha,
failed in an attempt to conquer the Caucasus. The winter was harsh, and
the Armenian units supported the Russian resistance. The infuriated Young
Turks had 235 Armenians arrested, in Istanbul, on April 24, 1915; the
majority was murdered. On May 27, 1915, the Young Turks triggered the
displacement of all Armenians in Anatolia, for which they used railway
cars, a crucial asset for the war. The law was the onset of the first ethnic
purge of the 20th century. Hundreds of thousands of exhausted women,
children, and elderly people died during the march into the Empire's Der
Zor Province (in present-day Syria). They became victims of diseases and
hunger, shootings and lootings.

The community of states did not codify the term until 1948. The
great historian of Turkey, Ahmet Refik, mentioned massacres as early as
the 1920s. But the perpetrators were not prosecuted, with few exceptions. The Peace Treaty of Lausanne agreed to an amnesty, in 1923. It
declared that all court procedures, from 1914 to 1923, were to be discontinued and that no new proceedings were to begin. To this day, official Turkey denies the ethnic cleansing—a majority of historians do not.
Though Turkey has estimated the number of victims as being 300,000 at
most, most historical writings claim that up to 1.5 million people were
killed. The denial of the ethnic purge became a constitutive part of Turkish ultra-nationalism and Kemalist state ideology. Yet there still has not
been much reconciliation, other than words of sympathy for the dead.
Recently, Turks and Turkish-Armenians gather and show their sorrow
in Istanbul's central squares of Taksim and Sultanahmet, on April 24, the
day Armenians commemorate the anniversary of the tragic events of 1915.
In addition, the Turkish government has recently repaired and restored
some of the historical Armenian churches, but out of about 2,500 churches and monasteries that were still in use in 1914, one hundred years later,
there are fewer than 200 in usable condition. On the other hand, Armenia turned down an offer from Erdoğan's government to open the archives
of the two countries and to form an international historical commission

in order for any reconciliation to be possible when the two sides search and depend more on the historical facts.

The non-Muslim minorities had lived alongside their fellow Turkish citizens for decades. In 1942, President İsmet İnönü and Prime Minister Şükrü Saraçoğlu issued the Asset Tax, (*Varlık Vergisi*) which was imposed on the fixed assets of all citizens, but those who suffered most were non-Muslim minorities. Indeed, Saraçoğlu admitted that the purpose of the tax was not to finance Turkey's defense expenses in case of an eventual entry into World War II, but to "Turkify" the economy. Of the 19,000 companies registered in Istanbul at the time, only 8,000 were Turkish Muslims. The tax, which was almost exclusively raised against Christian and Jewish independents, was so high that most of them could not pay it, even after selling their companies and their private assets. In the winter of 1942, they were interned in the Aşkale camp, in Eastern Anatolia. The 1999 Turkish drama film, "Salkım Hanımın Taneleri" (Mrs. Salkım's Pearls), which was based on the novel by the Turkish writer, Yılmaz Karakoyunlu, was the first time that Turkey learned about this part of its history.

The father of the prominent businessman İshak Alaton had also returned from Aşkale as a broken man. The young İshak Alaton immigrated to Sweden in the fifties to make a living as a guest worker. He had done a lot to support this controversial movie. He was already one of the leading building entrepreneurs and the driving force behind the Turkish reform movement. Together with other entrepreneurs, he founded TESEV that has remained the leading independent social economic research institute in Turkey.

On the Turkish St. Bartholomew's Night, on September 6, 1955, a massacre occurred. It was mainly directed against the Greek minority in Istanbul, and to a lesser extent against other non-Muslim minorities. In only nine hours, the rabble from many different provinces, equipped with tools of destruction, destroyed the property of Istanbul's Greek-Orthodox citizens and their 45 parishes. More than 100,000 were involved in the rampage that night. The vandals killed more than 30 people, ravaged 3,500 apartments, and more than 4,000 stores, offices, and doctors' practices. They set fire to 72 churches and 31 schools.

The Greek minority had, in part, recuperated from the Asset Tax. They had profited from the reforms of the Menderes' government, from 1950 on. Adnan Menderes had been encouraged by British diplomats to also stake out a claim on the island of Cyprus, to stop the growing pro-Greek movements on Cyprus. He staked the claim, and then he needed a scapegoat. For the first time, the Greek minority in Istanbul became the hostages of the enosis efforts of the Cypriot Greeks. After the Pogrom night, a lot of them left the city forever. The first mass exodus, on September 7, 1955, was followed by others, for which Cyprus always offered the cause. In 1955, the American Foreign Minister, Dulles, refused to criticize Turkey, by pointing out the strategic importance of Turkey during the Cold War.

A few years later, there followed the exodus of the Monophysite Syrian-Orthodox Christians, whose presence dates back to the early Christian communities in Antioch. During the sixties, 60,000 Syrian Orthodox Christians were still living in the 55 cities and villages of Tur Abdin. Today, there are less than 2,000. In Istanbul, 10,000 Syrian Orthodox Christians have settled. In Germany, there are more than 85,000, and in Sweden, 11,000. In only a few decades, the ratios of Christians in Midyat, a historical center of the ancient Near Eastern church, have been reversed. There, out of the 60,000 inhabitants, only 200 families profess to be Christians. In 1980, the 5,000 Syrian Orthodox families were merely faced with 20 Muslim-Kurdish families.

A number of factors have driven away the Syrian-Orthodox Christians from their historical settlements: the underdeveloped economy and the hope of a better life somewhere else; the infringements of Kurdish neighbors and landowners on their agricultural operations, as well as the armed conflicts, from 1984 to 1999, during which they had been exploited by both the PKK and the Turkish security forces. There was also the suppression by the state. On October 6, 1997, the governor of Mardin banned the two most important monasteries—Mor Gabriel, founded in 397, and the Bishop's Residence Deyrülzafaran—from taking in guests and teaching pupils religion in their native language.

The Syrian Orthodox church of Antioch has been affected by these things because it was not affected by the provisions in the Lausanne Treaty of 1923. Articles 37 to 43 of the treaty regulated the status of non-Muslim minorities in the new Republic. Accordingly, article 40 grants them the right to operate their own schools. Article 43 obligates the Turkish state to treat Muslim and non-Muslim foundations equally. The law protects the Greek-Orthodox and the Armenian-Apostolic Christians as well as the Jews. The Syrian Orthodox Patriarch, İlyas Şakir Alkan, however, had rejected being recognized as a minority, in 1923. He thought it would be better to keep a low profile in the new Republic, and after decades of tensions with the Kurdish neighbors, he did not want to expose his group as a minority.

But reference to the Treaty of Lausanne is not advantageous for the three officially recognized minorities. None of them has a legal status; they must be organized as "foundations." The Turkish state even denies the Ecumenical Patriarch his historical title. It invokes the fact that, by dissolving the caliphate, it dissolved all spiritual institutions with authority to issue directives beyond the borders of Turkey. In doing so, the spiritual leader of the 300 million orthodox Christians may only be named according to the municipal district they live in: Fener (Phanar). Furthermore, after the founding of the Republic, the street along which the Patriarch is situated was named after Sadrazam Ali Paşa, the grand vizier who had ordered the hanging of Patriarch Gregory V, and several Metropolitans, on April 10, 1821, an Easter Sunday, shortly before the onset of the Greek War of Independence.

Two decrees of the governor of Istanbul, from 1923 and 1970, also severely limit the election of a new patriarch by the Holy Synod. The first decree determined that only the Greeks who are Turkish citizens may be elected; the second one gave the mayor the pro curo to veto the election, and potentially to determine the patriarch himself. Since the traditional seminary that was founded in 1844 was closed on July 9, 1971, and the Greek-Orthodox Church can no longer train priests, and since the Turkish state does not give foreign priests residence permits, the existence of the bishop seat that dates back to Apostle Andrew, the older brother of Peter, is at stake.

The largest change came for non-Muslim minorities when the Republic got rid of the civil rights status for their communities. The state made them report to the "Directorate-General for Pious Foundations" and did not recognize most of their possessory titles from the time of the Ottoman Empire. Until 1912, most churches were entered in the land register with the name of the Saint to whom they had been dedicated. If the churches wanted the titles changed after 1923, then the land register officials demanded the approval of the Virgin Mary or Holy George. Therefore, many titles could not be altered, and therefore, they no longer had any legality.

The execution provisions, from 1935 and 1936, provided a further hurdle for the Foundation Law of 1926. They determined that both Muslim and non-Muslim foundations were not permitted to purchase real estate. But these were not applied until 1974, and, in fact, mostly against the non-Muslim minorities that lost a large part of the real estate that they had either inherited or they had received as gifts. In addition, some Muslim and non-Muslim places of worship were destroyed, and their lands were confiscated and became the property of the state.

Another hurdle was added in 1990. Since then, the office of the governor of Istanbul does not permit new elections of the executive bodies every two years, as was done in the past. The churches and monasteries became "abandoned" and "ownerless" as many executives who belonged to foundations, churches and monasteries die or move away. As a consequence, the General Directors of the Foundations, the *kayyum* (fiduciaries), named people who were to administer the real estate for the General Directors and collect the revenue. Then the General Directors fired the executives of foundations and replaced them with their fiduciary.

The list of real estate that was confiscated is long. But there is another one that is even longer: aside from the "abandoned" foundation, Turkish law also recognizes the term of "occupied" foundation (*mazbut*). This pertains to real estate that the communities purchased before 1936. In a large number of cases, the General Directors of Foundations did not recognize the purchase of real estate and confiscated it. The most well-known case was the orphanage on the Jesus Hill, of the Büyükada Prince Island. It is one of the largest wooden buildings in the world. The ecumenical patriarch may not use it. Another example is the monastery, Metamorphosis, on the Kınalı Prince Island.

Legal status for the Ecumenical Patriarchy is not in sight; it isn't for other churches, either. The seminary remains closed; the schools of the minorities are in danger. Since the mid-seventies, the number of pupils at schools operated by the Greek Orthodox minority of Istanbul dropped from 7,000 to 250. The school authority does not close the schools where the teaching has stopped. But they cannot be used for other purposes. There are not enough teachers; the clergymen are not allowed to enter minority schools and teach religion. At the schools in operation, it can take years until the authorities approve the purchase of books for the school's library.

The EU process has brought about some changes, but not an end to the discrimination. One example is the reformation of the Foundation Law, which the Turkish Parliament approved in 2001. For the first time, the law makes it possible for non-Muslim foundations to purchase real estate, but it does not deal with the reimbursement of property that has already been confiscated. The bureaucracy diluted all improvements. First, the execution provisions determined that the purchase of real estate must be approved by every member of the government. Then, a circular decree stated that an expert commission had to be installed in the municipal district of the purchasing foundation that would determine whether the foundation really needed the real estate.

On February 21, 2008, the Parliament agreed to a further reform of the Foundation Law. The Parliament passed the reform, in the sane form that former President Sezer had vetoed, against the votes of the CHP, MHP and DSP. After the law was passed, the opposition party CHP declared that they would lodge a complaint of unconstitutionality. The new law facilitates the daily operation of non-Muslim foundations, and for the first time makes it possible that foreign citizens can establish these kinds of foundations. Yet the law does not meet the expectations of minorities and the EU. It only makes it theoretically possible for minorities to have real estate, which had been lost due to dispossession, returned to them. The process itself is so complicated and expensive that no real estate would practically be returned.

Many hopes which Christians had placed in the EU process have not been fulfilled. Therefore, the annual progress reports of the EU Commission focus on the situation of non-Muslim minorities. The most significant improvement is that non-Muslim minorities now are entitled to build their own houses of worship again and may repair existing ones. Foreign chaplains, who temporarily care for foreigners who live in Turkey, now receive residence permits and are no longer only employees of the Consulate of their home country. Yet, despite these reforms, the multi-colored mosaic of Anatolia has yielded to a uni-colored Turkish-Muslim floor covering.

## The Jews: some remained but their language left

Water never separated the Jews of Istanbul; it always unified them. They used to live on both sides of the Golden Horn, facing each other, in Balat and Hasköy. Or, they lived in more elegant sections, such as Ortaköy and Kuzguncuk, facing each other on both sides of the Bosporus. These were home to the Sephardic Jews that Catholic Spain had chased away, in 1492. Ashkenazi Jews from Eastern Europe also found a home in the Ottoman capital. They settled around the Galata Tower, somewhat removed from the Levanter Christians which led their magnificent lives somewhat higher, along the Grande Rue du Pera (today's "Istiklal Street").

If you were a reputable Jew, and did not live in Galata, you had your business there—like Avram Kamondo, the legendary head of Istanbul's Jews. He was a close friend of the Ottoman reformer, Mustafa Reşit Paşa, and he financed the Sultan's Cremean War, from 1853 to 1856. Kamondo owned valuable real estate and a bank near the Galata Tower. A beautifully rounded stair case that carries his name leads downwards from there to the Bankalar Caddesi (Banks' Street). From 1863, Ottoman Bank, the private Central Bank of the Ottoman Empire, was situated there. A long time ago, the banks moved away to quarters that consist of glass and steel. But back then, the two parallel streets were the financial center of the great Ottoman Empire.

It was fashionable to live near the Galata Tower back then, and there were also seven synagogues to pray in. The banker Kamondo did just that; his family fled Spain in 1492. Initially, the family settled in Italy. Not until the late eighteenth century did the Kamondos and other Sephardic Jews arrive in Istanbul, and that is when they built the "Italian Synagogue," near the Galata Tower. It is still used today, even though many of the wealthy families moved to other parts of Istanbul a long time ago.

The Kamondos remained Austrian subjects until 1871, and Judeo-Spanish (a.k.a. Ladino) was the language of the Sephardic Jews, whom the Ottoman Sultan had brought to the Bosporus upon their expulsion from Spain in 1492. Yiddish, on the other hand, was the language of Ashkenazi synagogues, such as the Temple of Schneider (which means tailor in German). Quite a few Jews who arrived from Eastern Europe, in the 18th and 19th centuries, earned their money as tailors, such as the court tailor, Mayer Schönman, whom Sultan Abdülhamid II honored with the imperial certificate of decoration. He gave the Ashkenazi tailor the permission and the money to build a synagogue in the street that used to be named after Kamondo. So, in 1900, six years after the Schneider Temple was inaugurated, a second synagogue was built for the Jews from Eastern Europe. It was much more magnificent, and was situated right around the corner, near the steep rise "Yüksek Kaldırım" that leads to the Galata Bridge from the Galata Tower. The money was provided by the K.u.k. monarchy. Rich merchants and intellectuals met in this temple, while the Schneider Temple was where simple craftsmen congregated. But after a quarter of a century, two synagogues were too much for the Jewish population of the quarter, and the Schneider Temple was closed.

Since 1999, the building, on this narrow piece of land, is experiencing a renaissance. The classic façade is remarkable. There is a quote by the Prophet Isaiah in Hebrew letters above the entrance: "My house is called a house of prayer for all." The term synagogue is Greek and derived from synágein, which means "to bring together." The simple interior of the synagogue is no longer for Jews who want to pray, but for people who are interested in art. Robert Schild, who organizes events, grew up right along the Galata Tower. His father's grandfather immigrated from Czernowitz, in Bukovina, and the son became one of the leading tailors of vests in Istanbul. The mother's grandfather was from Odessa. The language of their ancestors was Yiddish, and despite the Shoah (literally "calamity," meaning the Holocaust), Schild's mother tongue is German. He passed the German language and culture on to his children, too.

Schild wants to familiarize non-Jews with Jewish culture and embed that life in Istanbul's cultural fabric, using the Schneider Temple as an example, together with the caricaturist, Izel Rozental, and Mario Frayman, the former president of the Ashkenazi community in Istanbul. They've organized programs in hopes of achieving this goal, including the Mahler Quartet, Mozart and Brahms, and also Max Bruch's Cello Variations called "Kol Nidre," which is about a prayer that is spoken at the beginning of Yom Kippur. They also organized a performance of Israeli artists singing Sephardic songs in the Ashkenazi Synagogue, and also the group Aufwind from Berlin in cooperation with Istanbul's Goethe Institute. They were going to play Klezmer, the music performed in the streets of Eastern Europe. Every year, an exhibition is dedicated to the Holocaust, displaying things like pictures of Auschwitz or documentation of the life of

Anne Frank. The other exhibitions showed caricatures about Jewish life in Vienna.

It was not only the Schneider Temple that brought together the businessman Schild and the caricaturist Rozental. They also work together on the weekly newspaper, *Şalom* (the Turkish spelling of the Hebrew word, "Shalom"). It's printed with a circulation of 5,000 and is the most important organ of the Jewish community in Istanbul. It became renowned because it is the last publication to publish a page in Judeo-Spanish. Very few Istanbulian Jews still have a command of this language, which has its roots in Medieval Spanish. And very few understand Yiddish, which goes back to Middle High German. Robert Schild cannot speak it either. He has therefore made it one of his tasks to pass on the culture of his ancestors to future generations.

Around the turn of the 20th century, Judeo-Spanish and Yiddish had reached their zenith. Every fifth person who lived in Istanbul at the time was Jewish, and every tenth person of these hundred thousand Istanbul Jews was Ashkenazi. Today, 20,000 Jews live in Istanbul, and only 500 of them are considered to be Ashkenazi. Over the decades, the interest in Judeo-Spanish and Yiddish continuously decreased because it wasn't taught along with high literature in schools. At any rate, the richer circles preferred French, which was the language of private schools, including the "Alliance Israélite Universelle," which was built in Istanbul with the help of the Kamondo family.

A few years ago, however, Judeo-Spanish started experiencing a new heyday. Since the Turks have also discovered travelling, they realize that they can get along in Spain with the help of this ancient language. In Istanbul, the Spanish Cervantes Institute offers classes in Judeo-Spanish. Groups, such as Los Pasaros Sefaradis, Erensiya Sefaradi, Janet ve Jak Esim, and—for church music—Maftirim use repertoires that comprise all Sephardic music.

Yet if you look for traces of another group of Istanbulian Jews, you will be disappointed. Only a few last names, such as Galimidi, Istroti, Papo and Politi are reminiscent of the Romaniotes, who settled in Asia Minor and Byzantium Constantinople after the destruction of the Temple. Their ancestors spoke Greek and had translated the Torah into Greek. Their large synagogue was closed, in 1660, and they have now been subsumed by the Sephardic Community, which took up most of the Jews who were forced to flee from Spain and Portugal. More than 100,000 Jews had left Sefarad, which is what the Medieval Jews called Spain at the time, and they brought their culture with them to the Ottoman Empire. Doctors, traders, scientists, and literary people came. Yasef Nasi became one of the most influential advisors at court; Samuel bin Nahmiyas founded the first printing press in Istanbul, in 1493. And the Ottoman Sultan Bayczid II (1481–1512) shook his head about King Ferdinand, who had driven away the Jews: "He lets his country become impoverished, and he enriches my empire."

When the Sephardic Jews arrived in Istanbul, the Ashkenazi Jews had already been settled there for a long time. Isaak Zarfati, a Frankfurt Rabbi from Edirne, wrote to his fellow believers at home, who were beset that everyone in Edirne could live in peace under their fig trees. The Ottoman Empire repeatedly saved Eastern European Jews, who managed to escape pogroms. During the 16th century, more Jews lived in Constantinople than in any other city in Europe. While they were not on equal terms as Muslims, they did not have to fear for their lives. They never questioned their loyalty to the Ottoman Empire, and they never rebelled against the state. Once, Theodor Herzl negotiated about Palestine with Sultan Abdülhamid II (1876–1909), who rejected it; Herzl did not pursue it.

Many families that immigrated over the centuries emigrated again in the 20th century. There was latent anti-semitism, which the Turkish historian Rifat Bali proved recently, but there were no specific anti-semitic riots, except for the one in East Thrakia, in 1934. The Asset Tax of 1942, for instance, was directed at all minorities, not to the Jewish in particular. If someone spoke Judeo-Spanish, they frequently found a new home in South America; Zionists went to Israel, in 1948. The Turkish Jewish settlements are near Tel Aviv—for example, Bat Yam. They became the most important ambassador for Turkey in Israel.

Many Jews who fled to the Bosporus left traces there. There was only one group that did not: the German Jews who were persecuted by the Nazi dictatorship, and were the major players in a modern university system, including really great names: the legal expert, Ernst Hirsch and the economist Gerhard Kessler; the specialist in Romance languages, Erich Auerbach, and the expert in ancient orientalism, Benno Landsberger; the doctors Philipp Schwartz and Alfred Kantorowicz; the botanist, Alfred Heilbronn and geologist, Wilhelm Salomon Calvi; the musicologist, Carl Ebert, and the architect, Bruno Taut.

None of them were integrated into the Ashkenazi community. Only Hirsch mentions his friendship with Sami Günsberg, the dentist of Atatürk and İnönü, in his memoirs. None of them lived in Galata near the Tower. They came and they left. They had a great impact on the Turkish university system, but not on the Ashkenazi community in Istanbul. Nowadays, one does not live near the Tower as an Istanbulian Jew, so Yiddish is not heard there, except in the Schneider Temple.

# Mortgage II:
# Violence in Society

## Paramilitary gangs: the "deep state"

I t is only a short distance from Gladio to the Grey Wolves. At the beginning of the Cold War, a lot of cells were founded in many NATO states that could have executed guerilla operations during an attack by the Warsaw Pact. One secret organization that existed, at least until 1990, was called Gladio. They had munition warehouses, and their members lived in various different countries, supposedly carrying out terrorist acts, including in Turkey, where the beginning of the Cold War and the beginning of democracy had coincided. The enemy was, therefore, not only at the border of the Caucasus; the enemy was also living right in the Republic. Anyone who rebelled against the illusion of a homogeneous Turkish nation could be an enemy. The aim was not only to protect NATO, but also the Turkish state.

In other countries reference is made to a "parallel world"—one that eludes security organizations and their democratically legitimized institutions. In Turkey, these structures are called the "deep state." The violence directed against dissidents emanates from the inside of the state. Abdullah Çatlı, the "Executioner Gladios" and the godfather of the Turkish underworld, was a right-wing extremist and leader of the Grey Wolves, which is also the name for members of the Party of the Nationalist Movement (MHP). The Gladio's Turkish cell supposedly included Çatlı and Mehmet Ali Ağca. Çatlı organized violence against leftist students during the seventies; Ağca murdered the prominent Turkish journalist, Abdi İpekçi, and then tried to kill Pope John Paul II, in 1981. It was Çatlı who freed Ağca from prison and equipped him with international travel documents to be able to do this.

At the time, Bülent Ecevit already had a premonition of the deep state. His eternal rival, Süleyman Demirel, who had been ousted twice by the military, was of the opinion that the deep state was run by military officers.

Tayyip Erdoğan said that these structures were not very new in the Republic, because they had probably already been in existence during the Ottoman Empire. And Erdoğan was right. In 1891, Sultan Abdülhamid II used illegal means to establish the paramilitary, "Hamidiye Alayları" (Hamidiye Regiment), to protect the Ottoman Empire against enemies from without and within. He provided Kurdish tribes with weapons to fight against Armenians and Russians in Eastern Anatolia, and against the Alevites and the Yezides.

The Young Turks did not want to do without the useful presence of this underground militia, but in 1910, they renamed it "Aşiret Süvari Alayları" (Tribal Cavalry Regiments). They played an important role during the systematic mass murder of Armenians, in 1915 and 1916, and during the suppression of later rebellions.

In Europe, the excitement surrounding Gladio had almost been forgotten when it really started in Turkey. The code word for it was Susurluk, named after the place where a black Mercedes 500 raced under a truck, and three of the passengers in the Mercedes were killed on the night of November 3, 1996: Abdullah Çatlı; the boss of the Police Academy in Istanbul, Hüseyin Kocadağ; and the beauty queen, Gonca Us. The owner of the car, Sedat Bucak, a delegate of the party that was in power at the time, the True Path Party (DYP), survived. They found weapons of Turkish security forces in the trunk of the car and several passports on Çatlı, including a firearms license which Mehmet Ağar, the Minister of the Interior, had provided, in 1994.

It was no coincidence that this quartet got together. From 1993 to 1995, Mehmet Ağar was the Chief of Police in Turkey, and until the day he resigned, on November 8, 1996, he was Minister of the Interior. He provided 1,500 weapons to the Kurdish Bucak tribe, whose members were to use them in the battle against the PKK. Because Ağar did not trust his colleague Bucak, he assigned Çatlı to observe him. During his career with the police, Ağar had worked well with Çatlı when the former wanted to remove "enemies of the state."

Çatlı, the godfather of the underworld, was not the only one who had a diplomatic passport. His colleague, Alaattin Çakıcı, had one, too, which he had obtained from Yavuz Ataç, a high-ranking officer of the Turkish Intelligence Service (MIT). Ataç had been best man, in 1991, at Çakıcı's sister's wedding; at the time, he was in charge of fighting the Armenian terror, and he allegedly used Çakıcı's services. After the accident of Susurluk, Ataç was deposed and sent to the Turkish embassy in Beijing. There, his friend Çakıcı visited him, and Ataç was supposedly involved in the rebellions of the Turkic Uyghur minority. Dündar Kılıç, himself a drug dealer and VIP of the underworld, said that his son-in-law, Çakıcı, had been covering for Mehmet Eymür, one of the leading Secret Service people in Turkey. However, on August 17, 1998, the French police handed over Çakıcı, who had been arrested, to Turkey. The role of the mafia boss, Süleyman Çakır, in the controversial TV series, *Kurtlar Vadisi* (Valley of the Wolves), was modeled after him. Right at the beginning of the series, the series' hero, Alemdar Polat, saves his life.

The secret service agent, Eymür, was the head of the counter-terrorism department of the National Intelligence Service (MIT) until he was liquidated in 1997. During his exile in Washington, he repeatedly provided details of what happened and admits that he even once used the contract killer, Mahmut Yıldırım, whose alias was, "Yeşil" (Green). Eymür described how the special units (Özel Tim) used against the Kurds in the Southeast of Turkey were created within the state and presumably also outside of the "Gladio" structures. There has been no proof yet, but there is a strong suspicion: they were presumably responsible for a large number of unsolved murders of Kurdish intellectuals and activists.

Susurluk was continued on November 9, 2005, in the small Kurdish town of Şemdinli. Previously, there had been a dozen, unsolved assassinations in the province Hakkari, where Şemdinli is situated. On that fated November 9, Veysel Ateş threw a hand grenade into the bookstore of the Kurd Seferi Yılmaz, who had spent time in a Turkish prison, from 1985 to 2000, for being a PKK activist. Ateş missed his target and killed Zahir Korkmaz, who was walking nearby, instead. Ateş wanted to escape in a white Renault, which was parked nearby. But the bookstore owner and his neighbors seized him—and discovered something that became the continuation of the Susurluk incident: two members of the gendarmerie were waiting for Ateş in the car. He had deserted the Turkish army in 1991, and was trained in a camp in Northern Iraq, until the Iraqi Kurds handed him over to Turkey, where he immediately landed in prison. He made use of the "Penitence Law," was released one year later, but was made to work for the Turkish state.

His senior officer, Ali Kaya, who had served his country for decades in the Southeast of Turkey, was waiting for him in the car. He had the reputation of being able to make Kurdish prisoners talk quickly, and not only because he has a good command of Kurdish. Kaya was a member of the infamous "Gendarmerie Intelligence and Anti-Terror Unit" (JITEM, Jandarma İstihbarat ve Terörle Mücadele). There were lists that contained references to the loyalty of Kurdish tribes, a list with the names of 105 Kurds, and drawings of their houses and stores, including one bookstore that had been just attacked as well as Kalashnikovs and hand grenades.

Civil justice took up the case and put Ateş and his two senior officers in prison, but not for long. In Ankara, the Cassation Court (Yargıtay) ordered that civil justice was not responsible for members of the Gendarmerie, and sent them to a military court. Furthermore, it cancelled the individual prison terms, of 39 years each, for the members of the Gendarmerie who had been involved, Ali Kaya and Özcan İldeniz, which the Criminal Court of the city of Van had imposed on them. The Prosecutor, Ferhat Sarıkaya, who managed the case, received a dishonorable discharge from serving the state, because he had initiated inquiries against General Yaşar Büyükanıt, who at the time was the chief of the army, and in August, 2006, became the Chief of the General Staff. The reason for this was Büyükanıt's remark that he had known Kaya from the time when he himself was a general in the Southeast. He claimed he had worked with him at the time, and that Kaya was a "great chap." On December 14, 2007, a military court in Van acquitted the three accused.

The assumption that there really is a "deep state" is based on the obvious events, such as Susurluk and Şemdinli. According to this belief, notorious groups form within state institutions, and influential people protect them. The structures are not visible. An organization can be recognized that controls and organizes. But the network reaches deep into the state. What its members have in common is that they think Turkey is threatened, and they want to defend it with all means that they have at their disposal: with those of the state, but also with those of the underworld and the mafia.

Ideologically, they are assembled in the Kızılelma (Red Apple) coalition. That is how Ziya Gökalp, the founder of Turkish nationalism, had referred to the ideal Turkish country, which reaches from Anatolia to Central Asia. Both the extreme right wing and the extreme left wing are part of the coalition. In other words, they are all those who think that Turkey is threatened from the outside: by the EU, the United States, imperialism, and Zionism. They fight the Kurds as the lackeys of the Americans and the Armenians. Aside from the hand grenade, Paragraph 301 of the Penal Code, which penalizes the vilification of Turkishness with long prison terms, is one of their weapons. It was usually Kemal Kerinçsiz who lodged the complaints, including against the Nobel Prize Winner Orhan Pamuk, and later against the Turkish-Armenian intellectual Hrant Dink, the writer Elif Şafak, the civil rights activist Murat Belge, and many more.

The famous members of the Kızılelma world were in court on most days: Kerinçsiz, the retired Two Star General Veli Küçük, the retired Major Muzaffer Tekin, and the retired non-commissioned officer, Oktay Yıldırım. They joined the violent protests in front of Istanbul's Bilgi University during a conference on the Tehcir Incident of 1915. The most important representative of the group is Veli Küçük. The political scientist, Toktamış Ateş, proved that Küçük is the ideologist of Kızılelma nationalism. A lot more has come to light about this former officer of the Gendarmerie. He was involved in drug smuggling, and he had threatened to kill Dink several times while on the phone with him during the months before the murder. Hrant Dink said that he got nervous when he saw Küçük in court.

Years before, on November 3, 1996—the day of Susurluk, Küçük had supposedly been the last person to talk to Çatlı on his mobile. He was never questioned in a civil court. A military court acquitted the founder of the "Gendarmerie Intelligence and Anti-Terror Unit" (JİTEM). The Turkish media reported that he had a hand-drawn map in his office that added parts of Northern Iraq, Syria, and the Southern Balkans to Turkey. It was not only the intelligence service agent Mehmet Eymür, but also Küçük, who had used the professional killer Mahmut Yıldırım (a.k.a. "the Green"). There were telephone calls between Küçük and Yıldırım during those years, in which Küçük was active in the provinces Giresun and Kocaeli. There were an unusually high number of murders of Kurdish freelancers that were never solved during those years, in both provinces. In an interview with the *Sabah* newspaper, Küçük said that he did not work with amateurs. Quote: "Whenever my state said 'do this,' I answered 'Yes, sir!' and then I did it."

Küçük is friends with the lawyer, Kerinçsiz. There is a picture that shows Muzaffer Tekin, another key figure of the deep state, kissing his hand, and another picture documents a confidential relationship between Küçük and Alparslan Arslan, who killed the judge, Mustafa Yücel Özbilgin, in the Danıştay building on May 17, 2006, in Ankara. Initially, radical Islamists were thought to be responsible for this attack, but later, things were found on Alparslan Arslan that showed he had communicated with Taner Ünal, the head of the ultranationalist paramilitary group, "Power Union of Patriotic Forces" (VKGB). During a raid, Ünal and eleven members of his group were arrested and accused of staging a coup and spreading child pornography. Those who were arrested were the retired soldiers, such as General Hasan Kundakçı, the commander in the Southeast of Turkey and Cyprus during his later years, as well as judges, lawyers, and the arms dealer, Halit Bozdağ Güngör. Arslan was also a member of this army, and he was also good friends with the attorney of the underground godfather, Sedat Peker.

Oktay Yıldırım was a member of another ultranationalist paramilitary group—"the National Forces" (Kuvayi Milliye). For a long time, he was a soldier in Hakkari; then he became the head of the National Forces, in Istanbul. It had been founded by the retired Colonel Mehmet Fikri Karadağ. He gave his group the name of the irregular associations with which Atatürk had used to free Anatolia of the western occupiers after 1919. The National Forces became famous in February, 2007, when the acceptance of a new member was filmed secretly and handed to the Turkish media. The new members swore an oath on the Qur'an, the Turkish flag, and a pistol as follows:

"I swear on the Holy Qur'an, our flag, and our weapons. I was born as a child of a Turkish mother and father; I am Turkish with no apostates among my ancestors. As a member of the National Forces, I am aware of my historical responsibility. I swear that I will work for the eternal existence of my state and the fatherland, the Republic, and the flag and will give my blood with joy. How lucky is the person who can say that he is a Turk." According to information provided by the National Forces, they have a list of 13,500 "fatherland traitors." On their website, they praise the special units of the military as guerilla units that are necessary to protect the country against occupiers and civil war.

On June 12, 2007, the police cleared a weapons warehouse, full of hand grenades and explosives, in Istanbul's Ümraniye district. It had been created by the Istanbul chairman of Kuvai Milliye, Oktay Yıldırım. These were supposedly the stocks from which the weapons came that were used against the judge, Özbilgin, and the newspaper, *Cumhuriyet*. The same evening, a weapons depot was cleared in Eskişehir that belonged to the retired Major, Fikret Emek.

Muzaffer Tekin is friends with the owners of the weapons' depots. When Tekin was arrested, on June 16, 2007, the Turkish press quoted Yıldırım as saying: "But he only awakened the principles of Atatürk and his ideology to a new life. What is happening is a conspiracy against the Turkish military and the patriots." Tekin, on the other hand, admired Yıldırım as being one of the best soldiers that he knew. Only a few hours later, Yıldırım was arrested as a member of a terrorist group. Even the lawyer, Kerinçsiz, was not able to stop the arrest of his friend, Tekin. When Yıldırım was led away, his followers shouted from the crowd: "My commander!"

What had happened? The police found documents that the retired Colonel Tekin was not supposed to have. For example, the National Security Council's strictly confidential "Red Book," which is considered to be the bible for all security issues from within and without. Very few people have access to it. Furthermore, they found the minutes of meetings of the National Security Council (MGK), as well as suggestions on the future design of the state with a coded name, all of which was just as confidential. On Yıldırım's computer, they found a document with the title, "Ergenekon," the plains surrounded by mountains in the legend of Turkey's origins. Ergenekon stands for the myth of Turkey's origin. The document is a draft of a design for a fascist state that Yıldırım envisaged. The Turkish press referred to Ergenekon as the Turkish version of Gladio.

Another plan for the future Turkish state had been drafted by Semih Gülaltay, the head founder of the extreme right National Unity Party (UBP), and it was even more concrete. During a bugged phone call, he said that he was going to be the President and that would not happen without blood being spilled. He was arrested on June 27, 2007. Gülaltay was friends with Muzaffer Tekin, and together with Alparslan Arslan, they discussed the final plans for the assassination of the judge Mustafa Yücel Özbilgin, in mid-May, 2006. On May 17, 2006, Arslan killed him. Gülaltay was also responsible for another assassination. On May 12, 1998, he had severely injured the prominent human rights activist, Akın Birdal. He prepared the assassination attempt as the leading member of the "Turkish Revenge Brigades" (TİT). He went to prison for more than four years. Gülaltay's paramilitary Revenge Brigades had been founded with the help of Mehmet Kulaksızoğlu, the godfather of the underworld who, like Çakıcı, had also covered for the secret agent.

This is only the tip of the iceberg. Ultra-nationalistic and paramilitary gangs and their weapons depots have been excavated repeatedly. Their members are always retired soldiers and policemen. Sometimes, they are called the Sauna Gang, according to where they are discovered; sometimes they are called the Atabeyler Gang. The Atabeyler Gang had plans to murder Prime Minister Erdoğan and his advisor, Cüneyd Zapsu, and stage a coup. Nine members of the gang were arrested, among them a retired major and an active Captain.

In January, 2007, the Police and the Justice system, affiliated with Aykut Cengiz Engin, clamped down on this. After conducting surveillance of the retired General Veli Küçük for one year, they arrested Muzaffer Tekin, the attorney Kemal Kerinçsiz, and more than 30 other members of the clandestine Ergenekon circle. They all wanted to protect Turkey from the "damaging" influences from abroad. The documents that were secured suggest that the gang wanted to throw the country into chaos with assassinations and an intensification of the Turkish-Kurdish conflict. They wanted to take over power with a military coup. The gang's death list included Nobel Prize winner, Orhan Pamuk. They had already appointed his murderer, who was also arrested, in January, 2008. On March 21, 2008, the police arrested three well-known leftist Kemalists on account of their affiliation with Ergenekon: İlhan Selçuk, the editor of *Cumhuriyet*; Kemal Alemdaroğlu, a leading rector of the University of Istanbul; and Doğu Perinçek, the leader of the left wing Workers' Party (İP). The police found plans for the murder of the chief prosecutor, Yalçınkaya, who had initiated the ban of the AK Party; the planned assassination was to be part of the destabilization of Turkey.

It came as a surprise that İlhan Selçuk had connections to Ergenekon. But it was not surprising, if you look at his past. During the sixties, he had belonged to a circle of extreme leftist nationalists, affiliated with Doğan Avcıoğlu, the editor of the magazine, *Devrim* (Revolution), and Deniz

Gezmiş, the founder of the People's Liberation Army (Türkiye Halk Kurtuluş Ordusu). Cemal Madanoğlu, a retired Lieutenant General, was the leading military official of the National Democratic Revolutionaries (Millî Demokratik Devrimciler) who had emerged from the Workers' Party (IP), which was founded by Perinçek. They all rejected democracy as being dangerous to Kemalism, and they wanted to cut all relations with the West in order for Turkey not to be victimized by Western imperialism. Thus, they planned a coup for March 9, 1971, and wanted to use the military junta. The plan was stopped by less radical officers staging a coup on March 12, 1971, and deposing Süleyman Demirel. Decades later, İlhan Selçuk had not changed, which is why the prosecutor in charge referred to him as the intellectual head of Ergenekon. The group affiliated with the retired general Küçük had already staged several assassination attempts before they were arrested. Yet the trail of blood continued until Hrant Dink.

## Political murder: Hrant Dink not the only one

Political assassinations are nothing new in Turkey. The assassinations stretch back to July 11, 1978, when Bedrettin Cömert, the president of the association of all academics, was murdered. This was followed by the murder of the journalist Abdi İpekçi in February 1, 1979, by Mehmet Ali Ağca who later tried to assassinate the Pope. On March 7, 1990, Çetin Emeç, who worked for the newspaper *Hürriyet*, was killed; on October 6 of the same year, the reform theologist, Bahriye Üçok became another victim. The well-known columnist, Uğur Mumcu, who worked for *Cumhuriyet*, was ripped apart on January 24, 1993, by a car bomb while he was working on drug and weapon smuggling; and on October 21, 1999, the leftist journalist, Ahmet Taner Kışlalı, became the victim of another assassination.

The political assassinations did not stop. On November 9, 2005, members of the Gendarmerie again tried to ignite the hate between the state authority and the Kurds in Şemdinli. On February 5, 2006, the Italian priest, Andrea Santoro, was killed by young nationalists in Trabzon. The assassination of the judge Özbilgin followed, on May 17, 2006. On January 19, 2007, a 17 year old nationalist killed the Armenian-Turkish intellectual, Hrant Dink, by shooting him twice, and on April 18, 2007, five young men murdered two Turkish men and a German missionary in Malatya, with a bestiality that was reminiscent of a ritual murder.

It was the murder of Dink that caused the largest uproar. He died because fanatical nationalists did not want to accept that a person who is not an ethnic Turk can be a Turkish citizen. By the time he was killed, Hrant Dink had been imprisoned twice because of "Derogation of Turkishness." In 2002, he had been charged because he said the following during a television program: "I am not a Turk, but a Turkish citizen and Armenian." He was accused of disparaging Turkishness. Yet the judge refused to open the proceedings. This changed when Dink proved that Sabiha Gökçen, born in 1913, one of Atatürk's adopted daughters, and the first female pilot in Turkey, was an Armenian who had lost her family during the Tehcir incident, in 1915.

The number of murder threats that Dink received increased during the years before he was killed, yet he refused to leave Turkey. He wrote the following in the last edition of his weekly newspaper *Agos*: "It is my true wish to live in Turkey." And, he continued, he was indebted to thousands of friends who wanted to fight for a democratic Turkey with him. If he would have to leave Turkey one day, then he would leave with his feet, like the exiled Armenians in 1915, but not with his heart. The reason for his prosecution was an interview that Reuters had conducted with him which he reprinted in *Agos*, on July 21, 2005. Of course he would talk about the purge of the Armenians, he said, because there was almost nothing left of that people, who had lived there for 4,000 years. The term "genocide" is not what was important to him. He knew that the Turks would only be able to be guided to the truth step-by-step. One day, he wanted to hear the Turks say "Sorry" about the suffering of the Armenians.

In Turkey, he reached all social classes with his charm and his humor. He embodied the civil courage of the new Turkey. Cem Özdemir, a member of the German Green Party, therefore referred to him as a "provocation for nationalists." Dink was fighting for a modern Turkey that was to be open and tolerant, democratic and secular, and that would offer room for all its minorities. That is why the dark hands of the deep state had him exterminated. A few steps from the building where the headquarters of his newspaper was situated, along the Halâskârgazi Street, in Istanbul's Şişli district, he was shot by Ogün Samast, who was unemployed and only 17 years old. Istanbul's Police Chief said the same day that it had been the deed of an individual person, not a clandestine group. It was not. Despite this, very little light was shed about the background of the crime.

More than 100,000 people accompanied Dink's casket along the eight kilometers from his office to the Armenian Patriarch Church. It was the largest demonstration that Istanbul had ever seen. The banners said "We are all Hrant Dink" and "We are all Armenians." They were demonstrating for a democratic Turkey and against the deep state. With their slogan, "we are all Armenians," they did away with the axes of the Republic, which is based on the majority of a dominant Turkish nation. The majority had empathy with the minority. Empathy replaced ostracizing the other.

The day after the murder, Ogün Samast took the bus to head home to Trabzon. Half way there, in Samsun, he was identified and arrested. But some policemen celebrated with him; they had pictures taken together with him and the Turkish flag. When the pictures were published in the Turkish media, there were huge protests. The policemen were immediately suspended.

Initially, there was a version of the crime according to which Samast said that he had received the order to kill Dink from Yasin Hayal, who in turn stated that he had received the order, and the weapon and money, from Erhan Tuncel. Samast, Hayal, and Tuncel are all from the poor part of the Pelitli town of Trabzon, along the Black Sea. Tuncel is also said to have killed the priest Santoro, in 2006, in Trabzon. When he was first questioned in court, on July 2, 2007, the matter was no longer clear. Then, Hayal was saying that Erhan Tuncel coordinated the plot, but they had been led by a group of policemen operating in the background. "The state used us," Hayal said, and they did the job for the state.

Nine suspects were to be put on trial for the murder of Dink. Most of them were young, unemployed men from Pelitli; some of them were members of the rightist nationalist BBP. Hayal and Tuncel had been members of a discussion group of the nationalist party in Trabzon. Members of the police and the Gendarmerie, however, were not accused, yet they could have prevented the murder. During the court proceedings, policemen blamed their superiors. According to Yasin Hayal, they had informed their bosses, in August, 2006, of the plans to murder Dink. But nothing had been done about it.

Yasin Hayal had been released from prison once before, in early 2005. He had been serving a prison sentence of 11 months for attacking a subsidiary of McDonald's. He was a hero among the unemployed youth of Trabzon. First he beat up a priest so badly that the priest had to spend time in hospital—Hayal was never accused—then he became aware of the discussions surrounding Hrant Dink while spending time in internet cafés. During this time, his friend, Erhan Tuncel, became an official informant of the police. Hayal decided to kill Dink.

At least that is what Hayal's brother-in-law told the police in Trabzon. They also had telephone conversations of Hayal's that had been recorded. The Trabzon police informed Istanbul's police in writing and by telephone. The police knew what Hayal's plans were, where he was in Istanbul, and how he wanted to proceeded. Hayal really did spend time there to lead the young contract killer. When he was led to the judge on January 23, he also threatened Orhan Pamuk. When Hayal was arrested, the police chief in Trabzon was said to have calmed Hayal's father by saying that he should not be afraid. The reports would be changed in such a way that no one would suspect his son. But the police are still under suspicion. Of all people, it was the chief of the police news department in Trabzon that was let go. He had been the one to inform the police in Istanbul of the plan to murder Dink. On the other hand, the police refused to hand over the recordings of telephone conversations between Hayal and Tuncel, which had been tapped since 2006, over to the prosecutor. Furthermore, the recordings, made by a security camera in the hours before the murder, have disappeared. There are no minutes of the first police interrogation of Tuncel, in Trabzon. Similarly, the SIM card of Ogün Samast's mobile phone, with which the perpetrator called him during the bus ride to Samsun, has also disappeared. On the other hand, in September, a telephone recording of a call between Erhan Tuncel and Muhittin Zenit, a policeman in Trabzon, appeared. It took place only a few minutes after the murder and sounded confidential. Zenit was calling his ex-informant, who asked him, "Is he dead?" and Zenit answered, "Of course." The justice department launched investigations against the media which published the recording, but it did not launch them against Zenit.

October 1, 2007, was to be the second day of the proceedings. Ogün Samast was driven to court in an armored wagon that carried the slogan of the radical Turkish nationalists emblazoned on it: Love Turkey or leave it. Samast said that Hayal had forced him to do the deed. The day the crime took place, he had taken the drug ecstasy. If he had known that Dink had a family, he would not have killed him, he claimed. After the Dink's murder, his son continued the *Agos* weekly paper. But he has not being spared by the Turkish justice system either. On October 11, 2007, a court sentenced him in his father's place for an article that had been published on July 21, 2006 because of "denigration of Turkishness." He was then on one year probation for the prison term.

Only three months had passed after the murder of Hrant Dink when five nationalist youths killed three Christians in Malatya, the place where Dink was born. They not only killed them; they tortured them to death by stabbing them hundreds of times. Necati Aydın had become a Christian in 1997; he was the head of a small community of converts in Malatya, and worked at the publishing house, Zirve, which sells Christian literature. Uğur Yüksel also worked there. The German, Tilman Geske, had been with them. Geske was a translator and missionary, and he lived in Malatya with his family. Five youths, aged 19 to 20, murdered these men in an extremely cruel way. They were arrested right after the crime and confessed. The motive they gave was the missionary work of the men. The indictment, on which the proceedings against the five perpetrators were based, used 16 of its 31 chapters describing the deeds of the missionaries. These take up more space than the crime itself. The indictment arrived at the conclusion that the leader of the gang saw the missionaries as helpers of a conspiracy being conducted by the United States and Israel, which had the objective of weakening the Turkish nation and Islam. Thus, the five men had been provoked. In December, 2007, the Minister of the Interior, Beşir Atalay, sent two special investigators to Malatya. They were to pursue claims that the perpetrators had been in close contact with the local police and with military officers.

One of the 80 communities of converts is located in Malatya, where more than 5,000 Christians, who converted from Islam to Christianity, meet. They are the ones the campaign of Turkish nationalists is directed against. The editor-in-chief of *Hürriyet*, Ertuğrul Özkök, asked his readers, after the murder, what state Turkey was in if the country could not even tolerate churches and a few missionaries. But it is the distrust of the nationalists that is aimed at the missionaries. Most of the missionaries are from the United States and Korea, and they are seen as political agents. They are not a religious challenge, but a political provocation for nationalists.

The campaign against the missionaries had started in the spring of 2001, when the couple, Bülent and Rahşan Ecevit, wanted to identify foreigners who could pose a danger to the territorial integrity—aside from buyers of real estate and missionaries. In April, 2001, even the National Security Council approved a document that warned of missionary dangers. The Ecevits bemoaned the selling out of Turkey under Prime Minister Ecevit, and the heads of the nationalist parties of Bahçeli's MHP and Yazıcıoğlu's BBP spoke of an alarming wave of missionary activity. In 2004, the Chamber of Commerce, in Ankara, a bastion of nationalism, said that the West was using missionaries as political agents with the goal of undermining the Turkish state.

The killers of the three Christians in Malatya used knives, but it is just as easy to get a hold of guns. Every ninth Turk owns a pocketknife or gun. "Turkey is a violent society," said Yalçın Doğan, a columnist who writes for *Hürriyet*, in a resigned way, when asked about the murder of Hrant Dink. The parliamentary commission on crimes committed by youths determined that one out of ten youths has a knife and every twentieth one has a gun. One in 12 teenagers belongs to a gang. Ömer Özyılmaz, delegate of the AK Party from Erzurum and a member of the commission, said that a generation of teenagers is coming of age that applies violence to reach its goals.

Psychotherapist Murat Paker, who is a professor at Istanbul's Bilgi University, stated that violence has increased and said there are two reasons: on the one hand, the economic consequences for society as a result of rural migration, and the liberal economic policies that entailed unemployment and pessimism. And so crime has increased due to the resolution of traditional structures. The losers of the change that society is undergoing use weapons as their last resort, and they see that illegal means and belonging to mafia organizations pays.

Secondly, Paker said that the violence is based on the philosophical background of the Republic: on the political culture of a "statist nationalist mentality," and that violence was always used to achieve political goals. That is how it was when the generals staged their coup in 1980 and during the sixties when one million people were interred. He added that this was being repeated with the Kurdish issue, the "solution" of which was to drive away three million people from their villages and hometowns.

The military won the conflict, but had to settle for defeat because the state was pursuing a military solution, not a peaceful one. Violence became violence of the state, is what Paker said. The state has still not processed the Ottoman Empire's trauma of losing about 90% of its territory. Susurluk taught the Turks that the state used violence illegally. The TV series, "Kurtlar Vadisi" (Valley of the Wolves), acquitted the deep state and honors those who murder in the name of the state as heroes. This kind of atmosphere makes it possible to declare a newspaper columnist a "traitor" and to make him the target of violence.

During her eulogy at the funeral, Hrant Dink's widow, Rakel Dink, demanded that Turkey investigate how Samast could have grown up to become a murderer. Haluk Şahin, of the liberal newspaper *Radikal*, said that TV series, such as the Valley of the Wolves, were not the only reason, but part of the reason. Şahin is a professor of communications and is not alone in his opinion. Never before had the supervisory committee for electronic media (RTÜK) received as many telephone calls about a TV series as for the Valley of the Wolves, which is why they put the series in hiatus in February, 2007.

The times for the hero, Alemdar Polat, to descend into the Valley of the Wolves in the name of the state and to save the honor of the Turkish nation and settle accounts with the enemies of the Turkish nation were over. On average, the protagonist killed 32 people every evening. A movie of the same name was shot later. In a key scene of the film, the Turkish Rambo has the highest ranking American officer of the region come to see him, and lets him insult him only to reply proudly: "I am not a politician, and I am not a diplomat. I am a Turk." And as such, he was rebelling against tyranny.

## Patriarchal society: "honor killings"

Violence in the name of the "deep state" has increased, but violence has also increased within families. When the state's power started to wane, it applied violence. And in order to stop the erosion of his power within the family, men have been using their fists. Pychiatrist Murat Paker surmised that, structurally, violence within the state is no different from violence of men in their families. "Men beat their wives and the state beats its citizens." The feminist, Jülide Aral, says that 90% of all women become the victim of violence within their family at least once during their lifetime. For women, this means being beaten up, economically pressured, or even raped. But Paker observed that the willingness of women to accept being beaten up by their husbands as being "legitimate" has diminished.

Nebahat Akkoç decided to defend these women. Four years passed since her husband was murdered under mysterious circumstances and three years later, as the head of the Teachers' Union in Diyarbakır, she was arrested and thrown in prison for reporting on the frequent murders of teachers. So in 1997, she founded the "Women's Center" (Kadın Merkezi, KAMER for short) with other women. KAMER has instituted more than 20 subsidiaries and has become one of the most important women's organizations in Turkey. The center offers women a place to hide; the centers give them psychological support and advise them in legal questions. The women in the center have created a task force that reacts quickly, in cooperation with the administrative authorities in the provinces and the religious authority Diyanet. Its job is to help women to be saved from violence, including those who have been threatened to be killed in an honor killing. In order to pre-empt honor killings, they have begun a campaign during which they hang placards at the entrances of mosques in order to raise the awareness of the congregation towards this problem.

The family council passes a decision and, generally, a minor is used to reinstate the "tainted" honor of the family. The minor is not given a long sentence. Murderers who were "saving" the family's honor generally received a lighter sentence, until the Penal Code was amended in 2004. The reasoning of the judges was that an honor killing was based on a prior provocation. "Provocations" included women losing their virginity during a rape in the family or the woman speaking with a man the family did not know outside of the house.

Honor killings are men's answer to women overstepping boundaries that they were given by pre-modern society and a world dominated by men. Honor killings were spread all over the Eastern Mediterranean region. They are a relic of the pre-Islamic patriarchal society and from a time that did not recognize individuals, but instead only members of large families. Within that kind of a society, no one could refuse to carry out an "honor killing," because it was the way that "honor" (*namus*) was handled that decided how someone was ranked within a male-dominated society. Furthermore, the untouched honor of women is still a chattel in some places. In Southeast Turkey, two out of three men pay a price for their bride. That is what they base their demand on: that the bride is a virgin and their control over the woman's sexuality.

More than 5,000 women in Turkey lost their lives on account of their "honor" between 2002 and 2006—either they were killed by their husbands, or they were driven to commit suicide when their sentences were increased, Nurselen Toygar, Professor of Medicine at the University in Izmir, said. She has also determined that violence is an everyday obstacle for 64% of the women in Turkey who are not educated, and even for 9% of the women who are educated. On the other hand, women make up 34% of doctors, 44% of teachers and 27% of judges in Turkey. Yet, on March 8, 2007, International Women's Day, the press reported that of the 3,225 mayors in Turkey, only 18 were women.

The myth that the reforms accomplished under Atatürk and his successors emancipated and liberated Turkish women remained for a long time. It was not until the seventies that sociologists, such as Deniz Kandiyoti and Şirin Tekeli, documented that the reforms never reached beyond the urban elite—in other words, that they never reached the large majority of women. The Kemalist women's movement ossified and became the official state feminism. It provided career opportunities to the women of the urban elite, but apart from that, it reduced its activism to the question of what clothing is compatible with modernity and what clothing is not.

Kemalist state feminism was unable to achieve equal rights for men and women in the Civil Code and the Penal Code. As a consequence, during the eighties, a feminist movement branched off that was more compatible with that of the West and that has increasingly questioned the Kemalist ideology. During the eighties, there was also such a thing as Islamist feminism. It gave conservative and religious women more public space for their activities, and so the Welfare Party (RP) had more female members and activities than any other party in the nineties.

According to a study prepared by the European Stability Initiative, there were two phases during which women's rights progressed a lot: right after the founding of the Republic and after 2002, under the government of the AK Party and its Prime Minister, Recep Tayyip Erdoğan. The Kemalist nationalist women's rights activists are proud of the achievements of Atatürk's Cultural Revolution, from 1924 to 1934. Polygamy was abolished and the right to vote was introduced. Atatürk opened schools and universities, public space, and the working world for women. In 1926, the first female doctor took up her work; in 1927, the first attorney; in 1930, the first judge; and in 1932, the first pilot.

But little changed outside of the cities. Not even the legal texts secured equal rights for women and men. The penal code was oriented along the family's "honor" and not the right of women as individuals. Even more than 75 years after the founding of the Republic, the rights of women did not compare well with other countries. In a 2006 index which the World Economic Forum presented on the inequality between men and women, among 115 countries, Turkey only ranked 105th.

Not until the last few years did a chain of reforms place the rights of women on a firmer foundation: in 2001, the Parliament passed the new Civil Code; in 2003, there was the reform of the Work Law; the same year family courts were installed; and in 2004, after having consulted with women's groups, the majority of the AK Party approved the new and completely revised Penal Code. Erdoğan's wife, Emine, launched a campaign that informed women of their rights in the Kurdish Southeast, where she is from.

Men and women are equal partners with the same rights after a divorce in the new Civil Code, and they have the same rights concerning their children and property. People who later became members of the AK Party had also voted for these reforms in 2001. In 2004, a new Penal Code was long overdue. The old law had protected "honor" killers, and instead of referring to "rape" (*tecavüz*), it referred to the "penetration of honor" (*ırza geçmek*). According to the spirit of the law, women were the property of men; crimes against women were crimes against the honor of the family.

Nothing of that is left in the new Penal Code. The parliamentary commission that worked out the amendments turned to the leading women's rights groups and took account of their wishes. All 35 paragraphs that had to do with the rights of women were amended. Sexual transgressions against women are no longer seen as a transgression against the family, but as a transgression against the rights of women. Thus, according to the authors of the study of the European Stability Initiative, Turkey has entered the post-patriarchal era. With energetic women's rights groups such as KAMER, the situation of women who lived far away from the large cities began to change.

# Escape into death: the women of Batman

Saliha Demir was 18 years old when she committed suicide by hanging herself with an electric cable. Her parents wanted her to marry a 60-year-old man. She was to become his third wife. Her name was entered into the list of young women who put an end to their own lives in the East Anatolian city of Batman; Saliha Demir was the fifteenth one to do so in 2006. Most of them were driven to commit suicide by the men in their families, because they had supposedly transgressed against the "honor" of the families.

Nurten Üzümcü, the young deputy of the mayor, was upset that the whole world was talking about the suicides in Batman. She said that even more people committed suicide in the West Anatolian Province of Muğla. But in Batman, it was young women who do not see any other escape than death. That was why a movement started to help women to decide on life.

The two women working for the Women's Center were in their early twenties and full of idealism. İnci Erdoğan did not wear a veil, but instead tight pants and bright pink sneakers. She got her high school degree at a distance learning school, while Seher Süer covered her hair with a colorful scarf and wore a long, wide skirt. They are the first people the women who need help talk to, the women who do not want to return to their families because they are afraid of the men.

The Women's Center of Batman was founded in 2003 and modeled after the center in Diyarbakır. KAMER's network is now represented in thirteen cities in Kurdish Southeast Anatolia. In Batman, İnci Erdoğan and Seher Süer offer the first round of help, then they include a psychologist and legal expert, who work for them pro bono. Thirteen groups get together on a regular basis. The women talk to professionals about topics such as violence in the family and how to raise children. "We meet as women, not as teachers and students," İnci Erdoğan said.

There is a kindergarten on the ground floor of the plain Women's Center, on the Aydın Arslan Street. It is financed by contributions. The women put into practice there what they have learned in theoretical courses. "We believe that sons and daughters are equal and that the sons should also help at home," said İnci Erdoğan. There had been no threats. Sometimes, men would come and tell them to do what the police would do: send the women home to solve their problems there.

"These men really do believe that feminism means animosity against men," Erdoğan laughed. And so they reply that feminism as a way to defend women's rights is part of human rights. Two decades ago, not a single woman had been reported to have committed suicide in Batman, though the inhumane custom of honor-killings had long been in place. Indeed, two developments have increased the deaths which changed the city. "Thirty years of conflicts traumatized the women," the deputy mayor, Nurten Üzümcü, said. During the armed conflict, women had lost their husbands and sons. "And they landed in the cities with psychological problems that had not been worked through."

The main streets in Batman are modern. There are glass and steel buildings, and teenagers stroll past the cinema that is named after Yılmaz Güney, the legendary leftist film maker and actor of Kurdish descent whose movies were banned in Turkey for a long time. The first impression is not right. In ten years, the number of people who live in Batman has doubled to half a million, and the quarters behind the elegant main streets are archaic, as are many of the people who live there. The people who live downtown kept up with the modernization, İnci Erdoğan observed, which has not been the case in poorer sections of the suburbs, where Kurds settled, as well as in the quarters where radical Islamists, the Hizbullahis, live and who insist on women wearing veils.

Many women who live in the quarters of the religious fanatics and the newcomers are illiterate. The first time the municipal authorities put up an information tent there was in March, 2005, Nurten Üzümcü remembered. The men had denied that the activities of the women were to be taken seriously. But the women were adamant in continuing to confront the women who lived in these quarters, with the help of town administrators.

The men continue to meet in coffeehouses and the women now meet in the three newly-opened "people's houses." There is a new radio station that broadcasts to women at home, the ones that are not allowed to leave the house. The radio's purpose is also to correct the effect that television has. "They see beautiful life being lived on TV, but in reality, their life is the complete opposite," the feminist Seher Süer said. The young men can flee to the beautiful life of Istanbul and the other cosmopolitan cities, whereas the women have no way to flee.

İnci Erdoğan pointed out that women have no rights: "When there are inheritances, they get nothing; frequently, they are the victims of incest. Their fathers refuse to send them to school because they could learn how to write, and thus would know how to write love letters." The violence often emanates from the fathers, but frequently, it is the sons who apply it. Recently, a girl described how her brothers had threatened her because she was wearing jeans, İnci Erdoğan reported. "Namus" is the code word, the honor of the family that may not be tainted. "But *namus* means that the daughters are put in a closed box," she complained. A large number of the suicides that were reported were therefore murders disguised as "suicide" to protect family members from the prison sentence for honor killing. This was confirmed by the autopsies, which were usually not included in an investigative report.

"The men and their sons think much more traditionally than the women," said Seher Süer, who wears a scarf. They often continue to insist on marriages between cousins without taking into account the birth of handicapped children. If a daughter wants to marry, all cousins are considered first. "If one of them agrees, then she can forget about marrying the other man." Everyone agreed that education and work could break open the archaic social structures. Selis, the city municipality's women's center, offers literacy courses for women of all ages, and also psychological help, according to its manager, Gülistan Taşkın. And KAMER has recently been giving women small credits for them to start their own businesses.

The women of Batman will no longer accept the suicides. When Saliha Demir was buried, nine girls who lived in her quarter, Camlıca, got together. They gathered with signs that said "No More Salihas," and that the suicides would have to stop. They walked through the streets of Batman with these signs. Even the press in far-away Istanbul said that their march set a positive example for all women in Batman.

# Wealth I:
## Germany and Turkey

### Brothers-in-arms and economic partners

Germany and Turkey are very closely affiliated. The singing of Prussia's Gloria could be heard to right up to the Ottoman Sublime Porte. Atatürk's Republic took up persecuted German scientists when the Nazis were in power, and after 1964, millions of Turks from Anatolia moved to Germany to find jobs.

Initially, it was the elites of the two countries that met, and mainly the military. The first—albeit short—contact came about in 1190, long before there were Germans and Turks, when Friedrich Barbarossa was faced by the Seljuk Turks during the Third Crusade, in Konya. He admired their weapons and took a number of Turkish craftsmen back with him. It was only hundreds of years later that the real brotherhood of arms came about. In 1761, the Prussia, of Frederick the Great, and the Ottoman Empire, of Sultan Mustafa III, entered into a friendship agreement. Frederick wanted an alliance against the Habsburgians, and Sultan Mustafa wanted to modernize his state and his army. The Sultan preferred recruiting officers in Berlin, rather than in Paris and London, to re-organize his army. Two years later, the two countries exchanged diplomats for the first time, and in 1789, Prussia sent their first military advisors to the Bosporus.

Helmuth Graf von Moltke (1800–1891) was the one to lay the cornerstone for a close German-Turkish friendship. In 1835, during the reign of Sultan Mahmud II, King Friedrich Wilhelm III sent Moltke, who was later to become Field Marshall, to the Bosporus to help modernize the Turkish army. During the following years, Moltke travelled all over Anatolia for his edification. An upswing commenced for the Ottoman Army. In June, 1839, it conquered the Egyptian troops of Ibrahim Pasha. Moltke's diary, "Under the Crescent: Letters on Conditions and Events in Turkey from 1835 to 1839," contains some of the most beautiful writings about Turkey ever written in German.

Decades later, the young Colmar Freiherr von der Goltz (1843–1916) noticed Moltke, now the Chief of the General Staff. In 1883, von der Goltz recommended that Moltke, a war theoretician and teacher at the Military Academy, be sent to the Bosporus to modernize the military education system. In 1895, von der Goltz returned to Berlin. Without the foundation that von Moltke and von der Goltz laid, the Turkish Army would not be what it is today. Like his great benefactor, Moltke's final years with the military also culminated in a military victory. After the First World War had started, Kaiser Wilhelm II sent his field marshall back to Turkey, where Moltke took over the job of the deputy General Chief of Staff leading the Ottoman Army to its final victory. In April, 1916, his division defeated the British Army near Kut al-Amara, in Mesopotamia. Von der Goltz died in Baghdad, of a fever, on April 18, 1916. It was his last will to be wrapped in a Turkish flag and buried in the German Soldier Cemetery in Tarabya, with a view of the Black Sea.

The Young Turkish triumvirate affiliated with Enver Pasha had already deposed the Sultan and a pro-British government on January 13, 1913. At the outbreak of the First World War, the young nationalists feared that if the Entente Powers were victorious, they would divide up the Ottoman Empire. That is why they joined the Germans. Enver Pasha, the strong man of the triumvirate, was the military attaché, from 1909 to 1911 in Berlin; he spoke German and loved Prussia. From then on, Germany and the German officers in Constantinople—still one of the official names of Istanbul then—supported Enver Pasha, and in 1914 he was promoted and became War Minister against the protestations of pro-England circles. He negotiated a secret federal pact with the German Reich. On October 20, 1914, he ordered to attack the Russian fleet without having declared war. Turkey had sided with Germany in the war.

That would not have been possible without the presence of German military missions in Constantinople. From 1909 on, this presence had been expanded, more and more. For a long time, the pro-German Grand Vezier and General Mahmud Şevket Pasha cooperated with von der Goltz. Shortly before he was murdered, in June, 1913, he explained to the German Ambassador Freiherr von Wangenheim that the German Reich would have to take on a special role when the Ottoman Empire was redesigned and that a German general must completely reform the Ottoman army with an almost dictatorial guidance. German officers also attested that the Ottoman Empire was in a desolate condition due to the fact that the suspicious Sultan Abdülhamid II had undermined the attempts to modernize the army.

The renewed modernization was the consequence of the Ottoman defeat in the Balkan Wars of 1912/13. The emperor transferred it to his lieutenant general, Otto Liman von Sanders (1855–1929). He appointed Sanders as the leader of the new military mission of Constantinople, on June 30, 1913. Russia and Great Britain had failed to prevent Sanders naming Liman as the Commander of the Straits. They had good reason to. Von Sanders was unpopular because he was over-bearing, but in April, 1915 he led the Fifth Ottoman Army to an unexpected victory on the Dardanelles by fighting off the landing attempts of the Entente and by defending the Straits. During the First World War, the German Reich increased its military presence to 800 officers and 25,000 soldiers. In 1917, Kaiser Wilhelm II travelled to Turkey for the third time, following visits in 1889 and 1898. During his second trip, Adolf Freiherr Marschall von Bieberstein was the German Ambassador, and during the many years he spent at the Bosporus from 1897 to 1912, he was considered to be the most influential foreign advisor of Sultan Abdülhamid II.

Liman von Sanders appointed Turkish officers as members of his general staff on the Dardanelles, among them Mustafa Kemal Pasha, who later became Atatürk. At the end of the war, Sanders gave the industrious young officer his supreme command. Unlike the War Minister, Enver Pasha, who liked the Germans, Mustafa Kemal had always opposed them, and was against giving German officers the responsibility for the lives of Turkish soldiers during the war. Increasingly, he was more concerned about protecting his soldiers. He also wanted to prevent Turkey from becoming a colony of the German Empire—Deutsches Reich.

When Kaiser Wilhelm II visited Constantinople and his confederation partner, Sultan Abdülhamid II, the first time in 1889, he promoted buying huge amounts of arms from German companies. During that decade, Bulgaria, Serbia, and Montenegro rearmed. Arms orders were part of the reorganization of the Ottoman Army, and German officers procured large orders of weapons. 500 cannons, manufactured by Krupp, fortified the Dardanelles, and Krupp soon had an arms monopoly in the Ottoman

Empire. It remained one of the Kaiser's most important goals to secure the outstanding position of Krupp in Turkey. Mauser, a weapons factory in Oberndorf, also supplied the Ottoman Army with guns.

Von der Goltz had propagated building the Baghdad railway when he was head of the German Asian Society. It was to secure the German and the Ottoman Empire's influence towards the East. Initially, the German banker, Baron Maurice de Hirsch (1831–1896), obtained the concession to connect Constantinople to Europe's railway systems. He financed the construction of the Orient Express, which connected Constantinople and Paris. At the time, the Baron was already the largest German investor in the Ottoman Empire. Hirsch was edged out of this position by the Deutsche Bank, founded in 1870. In 1888, Sultan Abdülhamid gave the concession for the first section of the railway, which was to go to Baghdad and Basra, to a consortium under their leadership. Only two years later, Hirsch sold his shares in Turkey to the Deutsche Bank.

 Deutsche Bank had thus risen to become the largest railway company in the Balkans and the Middle East. The bank prospered mainly due to its projects in the Ottoman Empire, despite the German economic downturn from 1883 to 1895. It exported capital; Krupp exported the rails. The bank became so strong throughout the Ottoman Empire that England had to fear for its leadership in India, and France saw its capital interests disappear in the empire. At the end of the First World War, the stretch of railroad to Nusaybin, at the Turkish-Syrian border was completed; it did not lead to Baghdad until 1940.

The Prussian military wanted to secure the Reich; the German economy wanted new markets and sources for cheap raw materials. In 1898, the German Oriental Trade Association had been founded. From that year on, the magazine *Orient* provided recommendations on what to export. In 1906, the Oriental Bank was founded, and it was interwoven with the German Dresdner Bank, which quickly opened subsidiaries in the Ottoman Empire. The foundations for close and permanent cooperation had been laid. Even during the Third Reich, Germany remained Turkey's most important trade partner.

It was German officers who had the idea to build the Baghdad railway. They were also the first to suggest a bridge over the Bosporus. In 513 BC, the Persian King Darius I had ships linked with one another to walk across to reach Europe from Asia. This time, the officers who were stationed in Constantinople wanted to have the Orient Express connected with the Baghdad railway for the soldiers to reach the Eastern front faster. But then, Martin Wagner, a municipal planner from Berlin who fled Germany and the Nazis to Turkey in 1937, forecasted that the number of people who lived in Istanbul would remain constant at 750,000, and that therefore a bridge over the Bosporus would not be necessary.

Right after the 27 year-long one party rule of CHP ended with the first free elections in 1950, there was a rapid economic upswing and urbanization in Turkey, especially in Istanbul, and so the plans were tackled again in 1951. Krupp and Paul Bonatz, an architect from Stuttgart, suggested a bridge from Ortaköy to Beylerbeyi at the most narrow place of the Bosporus, and construction began there in 1970. This time, the architects were British, and the engineering firm was Freeman, Fox & Partners. However, it was constructed by Hochtief AG, in Essen. On October 29, 1973, the fiftieth anniversary of the founding of the Republic, President Fehmi Korutürk, whose son later became the ambassador to Germany, inaugurated the bridge. The bridge is as elegant as a silver line stretching across the strait; it is 64 meters high and 1560 meters long, which made it the longest bridge in Europe at the time.

In 1991, the newly established German-Turkish Chamber of Commerce moved to Ortaköy, right below the bridge. The number of German companies investing in Turkey rose steeply. For a long time, only large companies with their own capital had invested: Mercedes, MAN, Bosch, Bayer, and of course, Hoechst and Siemens. By 2007, there were already more than 2,700 German companies invested in Turkey, more than in any other country. All industries and sizes of companies were represented. Half of all German subsidiaries were founded between 2004 and 2007.

Rolf Königs was someone who recognized the future of Turkey early on. When he built the first factory for automobile textiles in Turkey, in 1989, his Aunde Group, from Mönchengladbach, was one of the first 300 German investors on the Bosporus. He built his factory in Bursa, an industrial city which was quickly growing to become the center of Turkish automobile production, making Turkey the seventh largest producer in Europe. Königs was in Turkey at the right time. He profited from the growth and from the opening up of the Turkish economy. Today, he has 10 factories in Turkey. They manufacture seats for buses and seat covers, have full order books, and have three subsidiaries in Eastern Europe that also produce seat covers. Königs is successful because he did not invest in Turkey because of cost savings, which would only have been temporary anyway. Rather, he believed in the country because he sensed that there would be a long-lasting upswing.

Parallel trade with Germany multiplied, too. In 2001, there were less than 1,000 German subsidiaries along the Bosporus, and Germany exported goods worth 6 billion Euros to Turkey. In 2006, the value of the exports had increased to 14.5 billion Euros, while the growth rates were in the double digits. Turkey is thus a larger sales market than the EU states Greece, Ireland, and Portugal, and is even larger than the oil monarchies of the Gulf.

Every year, Turkish exports to Germany grow by more than 10%. In 2006, they reached a record value of 9.1 billion Euros. Textiles and clothing are the leaders, followed by automobiles and car parts, as well as electronic products, particularly television sets. 40% of the televisions that are sold in Germany were made in Turkey. The products of Vestel, Beko, and Profilo are technologically advanced with LCD and plasma screens.

The automobile industry is just one example for how closely the two economies are interwoven. Mercedes and MAN produce modern buses in their production plants in Turkey that are sold all over the world. Every third Mercedes bus driven in Germany was made in the plant in Hoşdere, near Istanbul. Three out of four German car manufacturers get their original car parts from Turkish companies, or they have subsidiaries in Turkey themselves. In total, 70% of Turkish-made car parts are for export, just like 70% of all cars and commercial vehicles that are produced in Turkey. Turkey continues to be the main supplier of textiles and clothing for Germany. Most international companies have their clothes sewn in Turkey. Hugo Boss invested four million Euros in its own product plant in Izmir. And the leading Turkish textile manufacturers supply the big international fashion houses with high-quality cloth.

The times when Turkey exported agricultural products and cheap textiles are long gone. With its diversified economy, the country ranks as the 20th largest supplier for Germany. If the dynamics of the recent years continue, Turkey could become one of the most important trade partners for Germany. Large Turkish companies are investing abroad. The Koç Group bought Grundig, the symbol of the German economic miracle after the Second World War. In 2006, the Eczacıbaşı Group purchased

Villeroy & Boch, the renowned German producer of china and ceramics, and the Sabancı Group which is one of the largest producers of synthetic fibers worldwide, now produces in Germany.

The brothers-in-arms and the arms suppliers of the German Reich triggered this. Nowadays, they hardly play a role at all. Now, capital and trade is what makes the two economies so interconnected. A friendship that was initiated by the aristocracy and the military has gained in breadth and depth.

## Architects and archeologists

The founding of the Republic of Turkey ended the influence that the German military had on Turkey. But Atatürk did not want to forego German expertise either. Initially, he consulted architects and city planners, and not military strategists. He had a certain concept of Berlin as a city and his new capital Ankara was to become a model for the Republic. It was to cast off the Oriental ballast of the old capital city of Istanbul. Ankara was to embody the modernization of the Republic. It was going to be modern and the architecture of the buildings was also to represent a break with the past.

Carl Christoph Lörcher, from Stuttgart, was the first to present a building plan for Ankara, in 1925. His concept still characterizes the new capital. Lörcher turned the Ulus Square into the center of the city. It is where the first parliament of the Republic met and where the equestrian statue of Atatürk stands. From there, he laid the great axis of Ankara towards the hills of Çankaya, where Atatürk later built his presidential palace. It is called the Atatürk Boulevard, and it is lined with ministries and embassies.

Lörcher's work was continued by the Berliner, Hermann Jansen, the winner of an international competition in 1928. The French architect, Léon Jaussely, who had also won competitions in Paris and Barcelona, submitted a draft that maintained the Oriental characteristics of Ankara. But that is just what his clients did not want. Jansen understood what Atatürk envisioned, and so he oriented himself more towards Berlin than Baghdad. Jansen referred to himself as a city architect; he did not want to be a city planner. He did not want to plan Ankara, he wanted to redesign it. What became reality in Ankara later happened in Brasilia and Canberra. Jansen redesigned Lörcher's plans and redesigned the tangent from Ulus to Çankaya so that it still continues to reflect the individual phases of the history of the Republic. He designed garden cities. The Turks referred to these green city quarters as Bahçelievler (literally, "Houses with gardens," or Garden City).

Jansen had planned a monument for one of the new urban centers along the great axis—the Kızılay (Red Crescent) Square. Atatürk inaugurated it on October 29, 1934. It shows the police aiding the people. There is a quote of Atatürk's in bronze letters on the red sand stones: "O Turk! Be proud, work hard, and trust." The Austrian sculptors, Anton Hanak and Josef Thorak, created the sculpture, and it was designed by Clemens Holzmeister, an architect who significantly influenced Ankara. From 1927 to 1932, he designed more than a dozen representative state buildings. Shortly before he died, Atatürk had given him the job of designing the new parliamentary building.

Clemens Holzmeister, Paul Bonatz, and Ernst Egli, all from Vienna, brought a new style to Ankara. The monumentality of their neoclassicist international style was a break with the modesty of the first national style, during which Turkish architects had decorated their buildings with Oriental elements. The cubus replaced the cupola; large uni-colored stones replaced colorful small tiles. With its municipal architecture and its buildings, the new capital of the young Republic had arrived in Europe.

German architects designed the new city of Turkey, and German archeologists dug out the old cities of Anatolia. In 1929, the German Archeological Society (DAI) founded its third foreign institute in Istanbul. Only the ones in Athens and Rome are older. Those two were to research the Hellenist-Roman world. The institute in Istanbul, on the other hand, was supposed to occupy itself with all epochs of the history of Anatolia, from the Neolithic age to the Ottoman Empire. Turkey is a treasure trove for archeologists: no other country has such a range of archeological sites.

Anatolia never constituted a uniform cultural space. Whenever the borders were shifted, there were new centers for human civilization: like Göbekli Tepe, which documents the Neolithic transformation to a new kind of living in settlements; like Hattusha, the capital of the Hittite Empire that compared itself to the pharaohs; like the myth of Troy, with which Schliemann's name is linked; like Pergamon, which the Hohenzollern Emperors had great sympathy with because they rose from modest beginnings to become a supreme power. German archeologists still dig at these sites to this day. In 1991, three years before he died, the Turkish archeologist Ekrem Akurgal wrote that the most important cultural treasures in Turkey can be attributed to the work of German archeologists.

For example, Carl Humann (1839–1869) interrupted his studies at the Prussian Bauakademie and arrived in Anatolia at the age of 22 to heal the tuberculosis he had come down with. He built streets for the Sultan. In 1869, he moved his building yard to Bergama. When he was still at the academy, he had drawn antique building parts and sculptures at Berlin museums, and so he realized that the people who lived in the upwardly mobile town of Bergama were using valuable things to heat their homes. They burned marble down to lime to extract mortar. The marble was from the hills of the antique city of Pergamon. Humann sent fragments to Berlin, and the archeologist Alexander Conze saw how valuable they were and travelled to Bergama immediately. Together, they uncovered the altar of Zeus; in 1886, they concluded their work. They saved the most beautiful object that German archeology has ever excavated: nowhere in the world is the pathos of the battle of the Gods and Giants depicted as beautifully as by the sculptured figures of the frieze of the Pergamon Altar.

From 1972 to 2005, Wolfgang Radt was the sixth German archeologist who excavated along the castle hill of Pergamon. When he arrived in Pergamon, the great representative monuments had already been excavated. He therefore rebuilt the Temple of the Roman Emperor Trajan (98–117) on the spectacular supportive arches. It crowns the castle hill with its white and shiny marble, and can be seen from afar. Radt mainly researched the domiciles along the hills, excavated the alleys, discovered a "heroon" and a marble hall for a rich citizen, and then worked on what was referred to as Building Z. That is how Wilhelm Dörpfeld (1853–1940) disrespectfully referred to the Peristyle house, which dated back to the Hellenist era. But Radt had excavated breathtakingly beautiful mosaics in it: with satyrs and raging maenads, with gamecocks, tigers and panthers.

Troy is the most famous excavation. Heinrich Schliemann (1822–1890) was a very rich entrepreneur, and then he learned Latin and Greek at the Sorbonne in Paris. From 1866 on, he studied the Antiquities, and in 1870, he started to excavate at the entrance of the Dardanelles, near the Hills of Hisarlık. In 1873, he discovered the treasure of Priamos; from 1876, on he continued his excavations in Mycenae, in Greece.

More than a hundred years after Schliemann, the archeologist Manfred Korfmann (1942–2005) continued the German excavations in Troy. Korfmann agreed with Schliemann that Homer was not a storyteller and that the events described had actually happened in Troy. He thought Troy was a city oriented towards Anatolia, which had had connections to the Hittites and entertained trade relations with the Caucasus and even Central Asia.

Hattusha, the capital of the Hittites, which is 200 km east of Ankara, was discovered by the French archeologist, Charles Texier, in 1834. From 1906 on, German archeologists, including Kurt Bittel, Peter Neve, and Jürgen Seeher, excavated Hattusha. They uncovered one of the largest cities of Antiquity. Jürgen Seeher used wheat silos and drinking water networks to explain how cities fed their people more than 3,000 years ago. The partially reconstructed city wall gives the observer an idea of the power that used to emanate from this place.

The excavations of Harald Hauptmann and Klaus Schmidt produced even earlier evidence. Before the Atatürk Dam flooded parts of the Euphrates valley, Hauptmann had made a sensational discovery in the early Neolithic settlement of Nevali Çori: in 1979, he found a ritual settlement whose columns were decorated with reliefs such as snake heads and depictions of humans. Three years after the Atatürk Dam flooded Nevali Çori, Hauptmann—who was from Heidelberg and was the head of the German Archeological Institute in Istanbul at the time—and another German archeologist, Schmidt, found the first stone cult settlements on the hills of Göbekli Tepe, close to the border with Syria. They dated back to the tenth century BC, which makes them several thousand years older than the megaliths of Stonehenge.

These cult settlements were built when people became sedentary. Down in the valley of Mesopotamia and the fertile Half Moon, they had still been hunters and gatherers. They watched gazelles, oxen, and wild horses there. Up in the mountains, they worshipped their gods. They worshipped them in stone cult buildings which were later turned into temples. The cult buildings had a diameter of 20 meters, and their columns were up to five meters high. They contained depictions of animals that were important for their survival: ducks and foxes, aurochs and cranes, snakes, rams, and lions. It was the first time the artists of Göbekli Tepe created plaster reliefs and large-form sculptures.

Hauptmann and Schmidt thus documented one of humanity's first revolutions, the transition to settlements in the Neolithic era. It took place where the fertile Mesopotamia merges with the Anatolian mountains, and where the great cultures and empires of the East and the West kept clashing. This exchange has produced more archeological sites in Anataolia than in any other region. The fact that many of them are excavations is also thanks to German scholarship.

## Professors and pedagogues

German scholarship left other traces in Turkey, too. The military set the pace once again. Ottoman Sultan Abdülhamid II had asked the German Imperial Chancellor, Otto von Bismarck (1815–1898), to modernize his army. Prussia acted quickly, and in 1878, sent a delegation headed by General Otto Kähler to Istanbul. Conversely, Turkish officers also came to Germany. In Istanbul, it became obvious that Kähler's military delegation lacked an expert for the modernization of the military education system.

It was Colmar Freiherr von der Goltz who was chosen. He moved to the Bosporus in 1883, and revolutionized the cadet schools and military academies during the 12 years he lived there. The cadets were no longer beaten, new teaching material was purchased, and more than 4,000 pages of new textbooks, new teaching methods, and new sciences were written. The first Young Turk officers, who held the reins from 1913 on, were produced in these schools, and later, Atatürk and the officers of the War of Independence went there. When von der Goltz returned to Berlin in 1895, the Ottoman Army had first-rate training and first-rate weapons. In 1896/97, it finally won a war again, the one against Greece.

When von der Goltz died in 1916, the first stage of the German-Turkish education cooperation had been completed. From 1915 to 1918, two dozen German professors taught at Istanbul University, then known as Darülfunun—the House of Sciences, which was reorganized in 1900. Among them were the German chemist Fritz Arndt (1885–1969), who wrote four textbooks in Turkish at the time, and the German Semitist Gotthelf Bergsträsser (1886–1933). They had to sign a work contract which stated that they had to wear a fez to work. They were also obligated to learn Turkish, because Turkish was the language in which the classes were held.

244 | Where Is Turkey Headed?

On July 31, 1933, Atatürk dissolved Darülfunun. Its professors had not subjugated themselves to the new state ideology and refused to be their spokespeople. They rebelled against the "Sun Language Theory" dogma that claimed that Turkish was the original language of mankind. Professors who criticized the theory were fired immediately. It was the first mass firing at a Turkish university. On August 1, 1933, the University of Istanbul was founded. It remained the only university in Turkey until 1944. The pedagogue Albert Malche, from Geneva, had produced a draft plan. Now, Atatürk was looking for foreign scientists that were to generate a spurt of innovation. After this spurt was triggered, Turkish universitics continued their development without foreign help.

The same year, several thousand scientists were driven away from universities in Germany following the "Law of the Reestablishment of Professional Civil Servants" (in 1933). By 1941, every fifth professor employed by a German university in 1933 had left Germany to escape the Third Reich. A lot of them turned to the "Emergency Association of German Scientists Abroad" (Notgemeinschaft deutscher Wissenschaftler im Ausland) that Philipp Schwartz, an MD from Frankfurt, had established in Zurich, Switzerland, in 1933, and that was the contact that enabled many German professors to flee to Istanbul. The Republic of Turkey offered them refuge and asylum.

More than 200 German professors and teachers found a new home in Turkey. The biggest group consisted of doctors (86), followed by scientists (54). Among the ones who went to Turkey were Fritz Neumark, an economist, and Fritz Baade, Alexander Rüstow, and Wilhelm Röpke; the legal expert Ernst Hirsch and Leo Spitzer, an expert in Romanist languages; the musicians Paul Hindemith and Carl Ebert; the doctor Rudolf Nissen; the biologist Curt Kosswig and, of course, Ernst Reuter, the professor for Urban Sciences.

Their task was to establish modern universities, write textbooks, and teach students who would one day take over their positions. Quite a few of them also participated in building the New Republic. Ernst Hirsch participated in the writing of the Commercial Law and Copyright Law in Turkey; Fritz Neumark advised a large number of governments as an expert; Ernst Reuter led politicians and civil servants into communal politics with a practical orientation. After the end of the Second World War, they returned home to Germany to assist in reconstructing their German homeland. Neumark and Hirsch became the rectors of the universities in Frankfurt and Berlin, Reuter became the Governor of Berlin; Rüstow and Röpke were among the circle around Ludwig Erhard, who created Germany's social market economy.

Ernst Reuter referred to Turkey as "my country" and was proud when someone called him the "great Turk." He died in 1953. Four years later, Turkey and Germany signed a cultural agreement. It levelled the way for the Association Agreement between the EEC and Turkey to be signed in 1963 and was the beginning of political integration of Turkey into Europe. From 1958 on, German teachers started teaching again at the prestigious Istanbul Lisesi (Istanbul High school), where 22 teachers from Germany had worked during the First World War. The Agreement was also the framework, in 1986, to send German teachers to the Anadolu Liseleri (Anatolian High schools)—the selective public schools with a foreign language intensive education, mainly English—to introduce German as well.

The first time the Agreement of 1957 was expanded to universities was in 1991. The German "Deutsche Akademische Austauschdienst" (DAAD) gave its approval to finance its largest project at Istanbul's Marmara University. There were two German departments for German scientists to conduct research and teach: one department for Economic Computer Sciences and one for Business Administration. They are among the best that Turkish universities have to offer in these areas. Forty years after the cultural agreement was signed, Chancellor Kohl and Prime Minister Yılmaz agreed to erect a German-speaking university.

The German-Turkish education cooperation thus contributes to internationalize the educational authorization in Turkey, while the Turkish government is pursuing its ambitious goal of pushing their economy forward from rank 17 to top 10 largest economies of the world. This will only succeed if young people are better prepared for the requirements of the working world and if they learn foreign languages and acquire scientific expertise. Moreover, since 2005, foreign cultural policies in Germany have a high priority again. Their funds are no longer being slashed; the expenditures for schools abroad and other areas of foreign cultural policies are increasing faster than other budget items. Presently, there are 117 German foreign schools; one of them is Alman Lisesi (German School) in Istanbul. German teachers teach there and at several other Anatolian High schools that teach in various foreign languages.

Germany is also contributing education on a European level. The EU implements the Erasmus program to promote universities' cooperation. It facilitates and supports the exchange of students and teachers between the EU states and states wishing to join the EU. Turkish students are also included. 30% of them that study abroad choose a German university in the course of the Erasmus program.

The Ernst-Reuter Initiative wants to bring the hearts and minds of young Germans and Turks closer together on a bilateral level. The foreign ministers in Germany and Turkey presented the initiative on September 7, 2006. Aside from economics, media, and civil society, they list education and science. School partnerships were launched. Berlin's Humboldt University and the Middle East Technical University in Ankara entered into a university partnership. Since the winter semester of 2007/2008, they have offered a Masters in a social studies program at both universities as a dual degree diploma. Then there is Marmara University and the University of Lüneburg, which has taken on sponsoring the two German departments that are funded by the DAAD. This small university in Lüneburg has taken on a leading role in the Bologna Process, whose goal is to create comparable university degrees in Europe and to remove mobility obstacles between universities. Turkey is getting access to this program via German universities.

Presently, Germany and Turkey are working on three fields of education policies. German schools are opening in several cities in Turkey, other than Istanbul and Ankara. Unlike earlier Turkish governments, the present Turkish government has an open attitude towards foreign schools and sees them as an expansion. One example is the Istanbul Lisesi, where teachers from Germany teach Turkish pupils in German. The school has an international orientation, participates in foreign exchange programs, and their pupils tend to win competitions in Europe. The ÖSS, the central Turkish University Entrance Exam, opposes the expansion of the education cooperation. All over the world, the German Baccalaureate (Abitur) is sufficient to be accepted at a university, but not in Turkey. There, the Abitur only qualifies students to take part in the entrance exam, ÖSS. Thus, Turkish pupils' interest in obtaining the Abitur is slight. Instead, they study for the ÖSS's multiple choice questions.

The second focus is the creation of a German-speaking university in Istanbul. This goal is at the center of the Ernst-Reuter Initiative. The bilateral contract was signed by Kohl and Yılmaz in 1997. Now, it is finally to be realized, with up to 5,000 students and at least four faculties: engineering, law, the humanities, and social studies. They are aiming high. It will compete with the best universities in Turkey, the elite universities Boğaziçi, ODTÜ and Bilkent. All three of them teach in English.

Thirdly, the German-Turkish education program also provides impulses for professional training. There is a German Turkish task force that is defining projects for professional training that the German Federal Institute for Professional Training will formulate. Various projects will prepare Turkish pupils for tourism, metal processing, and nursing. Turkey introduced dual education in 1985. Yet while the state is against transferring all competence to the private economy, the companies bemoan the fact that the schools do not train their pupils well and have two alternative models they use. They train their own personnel, which means that some German companies offer a professional training that is also accepted in Germany. On the other hand, they have established professional academies which train specialized personnel.

The world has changed since the Cultural Agreement of 1957. The agreement is so general that it provides a good foundation for closer cooperation in all important areas that have to do with education. The arch of the German-Turkish education cooperation that started with Colmar von der Goltz's arrival in Turkey in 1883 at the Bosporus was continued by the cultural agreement in 1957, and will therefore undoubtedly reach far into the future.

# Wealth II:
# Culture with a European
# Orientation

## End of the monopoly

C rises and conflicts have accompanied Turkey's coming of age. They are responsible for the fact that violence and discrimination continues. Ideological claims in terms of the exclusive control of the Kemalist state elites are tossed overboard; the state no longer dominates society. Now NGOs speak for them. The CHP has turned into an opposition party; with its huge growth spurt, Anatolia is catching up to the big cities. Culture reflects what goes on in politics, society, and the economy. It is becoming more diverse and moving away from the cultural monopoly of the Kemalist state. Culture is growing beyond the space that the state elite delineated for it.

The discussion surrounding the destruction of Atatürk Kültür Merkezi (the Atatürk Cultural Center) has symbolic value. It has been the dominant feature of the central Taksim Square since 1969, and thus the heart of modern Istanbul. While Atatürk was still alive, the founders of the Republic wanted to build a modern opera and theater building here that would underline their claim that Turkey was turning towards modern Western culture. First the Second World War delayed the project, then it was pushed back by the chronic financial straits of Istanbul's municipal administration. In 1953, the 500th anniversary of the city's being conquered by the Ottomans, the municipal administration had the architects Paul Bonatz and Clemens Holzmeister present designs. The Turkish architect Hayati Tabanlıoğlu worked on the project, from 1956 on. An opera house with cutting edge modern equipment opened with Verdi's

Aida, on April 12, 1969. In 1970, part of the building burned down. The German architect Willi Ehle was engaged for the renovation work.

The strict cubic building emanates a kind of functional coldness. It provided access to the operas of Europe to little more than one generation of Turks, but the state did not provide enough means. The salaries for the musicians were low, as was the budget for the upkeep for the plain, yet functional building. When it rained, water dripped through holes in the roof, and during some performances cats chased mice on the stage. Therefore, people were in favor of it being torn down. It was debated whether that should take place before 2010—---- the year of Istanbul's being the Culture Capital of Europe—or afterwards. At the time this book was being written, there was a network of modern and non-governmental art surrounding the building. Culture is no longer connected with Atatürk's name; it has become more than just the casting of busts of Atatürk and organizing folkloristic evenings with Mevlana Dervishes.

Turkey has changed since the middle of the eighties. First, Özal's economic reforms opened the country and integrated it into the world economy, and then the EU reforms under Erdoğan liberalized politics. The state has retreated. Like the economy, culture has been privatized, and artists have increasingly retreated from the Kemalist state doctrine. Culture and art are no longer oriented along ideological guidelines, but environment and everyday life. The national state of the Republic and the creation of a modern Turkey are no longer the reference points, but art instead focuses on the diversity of Turkish reality, the creative chaos of the cities, and the rapid transformation of society in Turkey. The cultural institutions of the state lost their influence. For almost a century, the state had tailored high culture to westernize it in a way it envisaged for Turkey. It has lost this monopoly. The artists and creative people in Turkey have become free and independent.

For a long time, they had only been instruments of the state. What was wanted were copies of what Europe had already created. The first deviation started during the seventies, when the Turkish left found a new cultural language, which was, however, strongly influenced by the West. During the eighties, the culture rebelled against the repressive climate the generals had created after the 1980 coup. When globalization of the nineties offered the opportunity to connect with international culture, even more artists retreated from the control of the state. Conversely, the culture of the West found intriguing new ground in Turkey.

The quality of art and culture was changing. The state and its institutions continued to pursue conservative and nationalist cultural politics. Their understanding of culture remained conventional. They continued to send dancing Dervishes and colorful Kütahya tiles to Europe as advertising campaigns. Modern culture was evolving from below and was incomprehensible to them. Conversely, the artists no longer wanted to be instruments of the state. Their topic was no longer the illusion of a society that acts homogeneously. Rather, they were occupied with a world of minorities: with non-Muslims, Kurds and other ethnicities, homosexuals and other fringe groups. Culture thus became a part of Turkey that wanted to be democratic.

Beral Madra, curator and leading Turkish art critic, says the two factors that were responsible for improving the quality in the nineties included the work of the foreign cultural institutes and the Biennial that, since 1987, brings together Turkish and international artists every two years in Istanbul. Cultural institutes from the countries of the European Union showed cultural trends from their countries, and the Biennial gave Turkish artists the opportunity for an exchange with international artists and to exhibit together with them. The fact that modern philosophers, such as Michel Foucault and Gilles Deleuze, were being translated into Turkish and read in Turkey for the first time brought with it another surge.

The impact that Istanbul's Biennial has on the development of modern art in Turkey cannot be underestimated. Marcus Graf sees more parallels to Kassel's Documenta than to the Biennial in Venice. The Biennial is familiarizing Turkey with modern art the way the Documenta did in Germany after 1955. It has become a modernization process for Turkey. Graf criticized the first two Biennials, in 1987 and 1989, as being too provincial and including too many Turkish artists. From 1995 on, this changed drastically with the fourth Biennial. Under its curator, René Block, it became a large international platform for modern art. The motto that was chosen was called "Orientation," in other words the relationship between East and West. 118 artists from 52 countries were no longer exhibited in the large historical buildings of Istanbul, but in a warehouse of the old port, in Antrepo No 1.

Not everyone liked this opening, including the art critic, Sezer Tansuğ (1930–1998), who criticized a "degeneration" of the Biennial after 1989, saying that it contributed to Turkish art being overtaken by a dominating foreign art scene which would only create an inferiority complex. Graf, however, says that Istanbul's Biennial has become the most important one of its kind in only 20 years—that it has developed from a provincial exhibition to a Biennial with international class and that it sped up the development of art in Turkey and has become a symbol of freedom for the arts—and even society. Therefore, the prosecutor—as instructed by the army—initiated inquiries against the 9th Biennial. The military felt denigrated and insulted by a depiction of soldiers. The prosecutor's office also confiscated all catalogues of the exhibition.

Increasingly, young artists retreated from the axioms of state ideology. Taboos were no longer feared, and they fell. Halil Altındere is one of the interesting young artists. In 1971, he was born in a village near Mardin that the military evacuated 20 years later during the armed struggle against the PKK. In 1997, he had Atatürk holding his hands in front of his face on a Turkish Lira note out of shame for the many inflations; in 1998, he dedicated a stamp series to a political activist who had gone missing, and the same year he designed a huge mural showing the nationalists' motto on the wall in red: On the left side, he wrote "ya sev" (love it), and on the right side, "ya terket" (or leave it), and in between the words was the red background of the Turkish flag with the white crescent and the star. On the left, a participant is leaving the picture, his eyes to the ground; on the right, the artist is leaving the picture, looking ahead.

The artist Osman Bozkurt, who was born in Istanbul in 1970, spoofed the reduction of Turkish democracy to formal procedures with 20 photos of a purple index finger. Every Turkish voter had to dip his index finger into purple ink after voting to avoid second votes. The group, Hafriyat (which literally means "excavations"), and Mustafa Pancar, who was born in 1964, is shaking people up. Their name says it all. They want to "excavate"—to get to the bottom of things. At the tenth Biennial, from September to November, 2007, they wrote variations of Atatürk's motto: "Ne mutlu Türküm diyene" "How happy is the person who can say he is a Turk," underneath 18 different portraits. But only one of the eighteen portraits had this sentence on its poster. The seventeen others were variations where they said they were a Kurd or they were an Alevi; under the picture of Hrant Dink, professing to be Armenian. Under the one of the patriarch, Artholomaios, professing to be Orthodox Christian. Others said of themselves that they were homosexual or simply that they grow their hair long. A woman who was wearing a veil complained that she could not live her religion, and on another there was a head that was wrapped with bandages that stated that the man was living in Malatya as a missionary. The artists of Hafriyat changed the famous sentence and left a gap: The adjective was missing. "How ____ is the person who can say he is a Kurd?" The artists wanted to indicate that none of these 17 "other Turks" were happy ("mutlu" in Turkish), and so they demanded of the observers to take a red pen and think of another word for *mutlu*. There were not many installations that visitors of the Biennial stood in front of as pensively as the portrait gallery of the eighteen Turks who were so different.

In the fall of 2007, Hafriyat presented the exhibition, "Allah Korkusu" (the Fear of God), in which they addressed the tense relationship that Turkey lives in between Kemalism and Islam. "Fear not," the poster says of pictures of a young woman with a red veil who is wearing a white blouse or either a red T-shirt with the image of Atatürk or of Che Guevara or a logo of Playboy magazine. The poster closes with the message: "Wherever fashion is, we are there." Another poster shows a white key on a computer keyboard that says "tövbe" (remorse); another one is of the profile of Atatürk, but without his face.

## Diversity and an opening towards Anatolia

The nineties provided the basis for a new Turkish art scene and during the new century, it started to bloom. During one of the worst recessions in the history of Turkey, the conventional art scene also ceased to exist. Everybody had to start at zero. Ideas had become more important as a market value, and modern art was also present for the new beginning. Private art museums, such as the Istanbul Modern and Project 4L, opened during that phase. They were going to demonstrate that Turkey was striving towards Europe and the EU after its liberation from the state's guardianship. The EU candidate status and the inclusion into negotiations freed the means that the Turkish art scene needed so desperately.

In June 2005, the EU Commission launched the program for a "civil society dialogue EU-Turkey," with the intention of discussing sensitive topics beyond state institutions. The program was to sharpen understanding for Europe in Turkey, and lead the country closer to the EU. The subprogram, "cultural bridges," became a central part of the dialogue, in July, 2007. It provided 6 million Euros to those cultural institutions of the EU states, mainly those institutes that are active in Turkey. The culture institutes and their Turkish partners are to conduct projects that must fulfill three requirements: they are to increase visibility of European culture in Turkey, convey respect for cultural diversity, and give a comprehensive insight into the cultural events in Turkey. Projects in the areas of music and literature, art, and cultural management are applicable. The first projects started during the first quarter of 2008.

These projects aroused expectations and stimulated the Turkish cultural scene. "A cultural scene unfolds for which there has never been government support or support from private institutions, such as Istanbul's Cultural Foundation (İKSV)," observes Claudia Hahn-Raabe, director of the Goethe Institute since 2005. Now talents could unfold that had remained unobserved previously. A lot of smaller institutions mobilized and organized to participate together when Istanbul attracted a lot of attention as cultural capital.

Cihangir, which extends from Taksim Square to Fındıklı along the Bosporus, is the part of Istanbul that has produced the greatest density of artists and scientists. The writer Orhan Pamuk lives here, as does the musician Mehmet Güreli, the film director Çağan Irmak, the designer Sadık Karamustafa, as well as many actors, photographers, and journalists. They meet in cafés, bars, and galleries. They live scattered apart and frequently don't know anything about each other—which is something the project "Cihangirlink" is to do away with. The EU is supporting an electronic data base of this artists' quarter which—particularly in view of 2010—is to give an overview and facilitate cooperation. Cihangirlink will be the platform for an exchange between this quarter and the artist community in Berlin.

Various small groups flourished in this young and lively artist community in Istanbul. They gave themselves names such as Apartman Projesi (Apartment Project), Oda Projesi (Room Project), Galata Perform, or ÇGSG. The artists' cooperative, Çağdaş Gösteri Sanatları Girişimi (ÇGSG, Contemporary Performing Arts Initiative), would never have had the opportunity of being promoted by the state or a large private sponsor. In fact, independent theater and dance groups never received support before, due to the fact that traditional sponsors were not open-minded towards innovations of these small theater and dance groups that liked to experiment and confront social reality. The groups were called "Bilsak" and "Semaver Kumpanya," (Samovar Roadshow) or named after streets, "5 Sokak Tiyatro" (Road 5 Theater) and "Tiyatro TEM" (Theater TEM Highway). Then there is DOT Tiyatro, which not only performs, but also conducts readings of European works that have been translated into Turkish.

Several small groups got together and founded ÇGSG, and they use it to connect Turkey to modern theater. Their groups perform in small rooms, and they also offer dance and acting courses in a house that is situated in Beyoğlu. The first time they presented their productions was in 2007, in Kadıköy, a part of the city on the Asian side of Istanbul. They are called "Sahne Sanatları Buluşması 01," the First Meeting for Stage Art. Before every one of the 13 performances, renowned newspaper critics would familiarize the audience with what they were about to see. One dance group called their piece, "Fear of Thinking"—contrasting the limitations of the body with flexibility of thought. During the piece "Glass People," two dancers dance on ten glasses—their dance symbolizing the fragility of life. The choreography, "Mehmet loves Peace" is a sharp criticism of the militarization of Turkish society. Then there was a variation on Shakespeare's Richard III for five actors and a doll.

The EU supports initiatives such as the ÇGSG, and thanks to cooperation with Bilgi University and Osman Kavala's Anadolu Kültür Vakfı (Anatolian Culture Foundation), they have found a larger audience. Both have brought a breath of fresh air to the scene. Bilgi University has opened a center for contemporary art in Istanbul's Kağıthane, the "Santralistanbul." Its first exhibition was of the development of Turkish art from 1950 to the present. The intention was to show the connection between art and politics during this era. The goal of Kavala's foundation is to promote culture outside of the large cities, and thus fulfill one of the EU's accession criteria, to reduce the imbalance between the developed Turkey in the West and the underdeveloped East.

Thanks to its diversity, Istanbul has become a center for the European art scene. This was to the detriment of Ankara. Istanbul attracted artists and energies. The government bureaucracy did nothing to hold artists in the capital. Istanbul, on the other hand, promises better opportunities to grow thanks to its inclusion in globalization. That is why the artists in Ankara either went to Istanbul or abroad in the nineties. Symptomatic of this was that the project for a museum for contemporary art in Ankara just petered out.

Despite the undisputed dominance of Istanbul, the contrast between the center and the periphery has been disintegrating. There are exhibitions in Istanbul from Anatolia, and foundations like Osman Kavala's promote cultural development outside the large cities. The turning point came with the exhibition Plajın Altında Kaldırım Taşları (Cobblestones under the Beach), that Vasıf Kortun and Halil Altındere organized in late 2002, in the Proje4L museum. They invited 22 young Turkish artists from Istanbul, New York, Germany, and Anatolian cities. The topics included urbanity and homelessness. Fikret Atay presented the sadness of old oil pumps in his east Anatolian home town of Batman; Erkan Özgen showed the Kurdish video, "Welat," with Turkish subtitles, in which he described the Kurdish trauma. The art critic, Şener Özmen, referred to this exhibition as being the "first attack of the East" on Istanbul due to the presence of Kurdish artists, but he did not mean this in a negative way.

Six months later, Halil Altındere selected only artists from eastern Anatolia for the exhibition, "I am too sad to kill you," among them the internationally renowned Fikret Atay. In return, Osman Kavala's foundation, Anadolu Kültür, in Diyarbakır, installed the culture center, Diyarbakır Kültür Merkezi, which became the most important platform for the city's artists. Overnight, the Kurds had presented themselves to the Turkish art community. Diyarbakır's Art Academy, which only teaches academic painting, struggled with these newcomers. Özmen remembers that the teachers thought that these young artists were, "more dangerous than terrorism." The Kurdish artists also had a breakthrough in Istanbul. They obtained access to Istanbul's Biennial, and since 2002, the cultural foundations, such as Borusan, have been increasingly accepting Kurdish artists with the support of Anadolu Kültür.

Osman Kavala's foundation, Anadolu Kültür, promotes the expansion of culture all over Turkey. Frequently, the European "Festival on Wheels" shows European films in the cultural centers of its foundation, Anadolu Kültür. The foundation is also financed by the EU program Cultural Bridges, a project of the Goethe Institute, in which German writers whose texts have been translated into Turkish present their works in 24 cities and the three major cities. The goal of the project is to familiarize the population with Western works. Sweden and the Netherlands have also shown interest in these kinds of projects, as have the new EU member states Rumania, Slovenia, and Hungary.

Even before this project, the Goethe Institute had the courage to move further into Eastern Anatolia. The institute had gone on tour with two exhibitions of the works of Ernst Barlach and "Haymatloz" that were dedicated to German immigrants who were permitted to live in Turkey during the Third Reich. The cultural foundation, "Kulturstiftung der deutsch-türkischen Wirtschaft," that is financed by leading German corporations in Turkey, financed the Ernst Barlach Exhibition, while the Goethe Institute conducted workshops on cultural management in Eastern Anataolia. "The Anatolians long for culture and are more than willing to participate," Claudia Hahn-Raabe, who has traveled Anatolia widely, says enthusiastically.

## The state and private sponsors

Turkey's EU process and private initiatives, such as those of Osman Kavala, have opened new doors for the Turkish cultural scene. Before that, artists depended on two sponsors: the state and its culture ministry, and the great private sponsors in Istanbul under the roof of the Istanbul Foundation for Art and Culture (İKSV). The number of institutions that promote culture increased at the beginning of the new century. In the future, the state institutions will support official culture, operas and concerts, theaters and ballet. In cities like Izmir, they remain the center of cultural life, although their spectrum is narrow due to limited funding and ideological restrictions.

The industrial family, Eczacıbaşı, founded the Istanbul Art and Culture Foundation (İKSV), in 1973, the 50th anniversary of the Republic, and it remained the most important sponsor for years. Their logo consisted of a long-leafed tulip, the flower of the Ottoman Court. With the help of private Turkish companies, the foundation sponsored five festivals and the Festival of Classical Music, during which the performances in Istanbul of its leading orchestras and soloists from Europe have been the main attraction. Then there was a film festival (1982), the Biennial (1987), the Theater Festival (1989), and the Jazz Festival (1994). The festivals for music, theater, and film give Turkish artists a platform, but they are not supported in their productions. Their main objective is to bring international art to Istanbul. From 2004 on, İKSV started introducing Turkish culture in international festivals abroad. The goal was to promote cultural dialogue during the EU process. It started in 2004, with the Festival "Şimdi" (*şimdi* is the Turkish word for "now"); in 2005, "Şimdi Stuttgart" followed. More than 70% of the budget of İKSV is mostly financed by sponsors, so they do not require government funds.

From the nineties on, various large Turkish banks instituted cultural foundations and occupied the most important niches in doing so. They primarily settled on İstiklal Caddesi in Beyoğlu, the heart of the Turkish cultural scene. Aksanat, the cultural foundation of Akbank, supports an orchestra and a gallery. The gallery, "Garanti Platform," of the Garanti Bank, became a center of contemporary art. The İşbank integrated a concert hall in its headquarters and performs a remarkable concert series of classical and popular music there. The Yapı Kredi Bank opened a publishing house of its own that publishes sophisticated books, literature, and art publications. The gallery of the bank exhibited international and Turkish artists at its center on İstiklal Caddesi. The most spectacular exhibition featured 145 Joseph Beuys drawings that attracted 10,000 visitors and that the gallery organized in cooperation with the Goethe Institute, which is only a few steps away. The façade of the gallery had been decorated with a huge depiction of a serious looking Joseph Beuys for weeks.

Museums that meet the specifications of art insurers have only been in operation for a few years in Istanbul. Until that time, they did not meet international criteria and only small exhibitions were brought to Istanbul. Now, three museums meet the prerequisite criteria for insurances to insure valuable exhibits. Each museum belongs to one of the three large industrial families in Turkey. In 2004, the Ezcacıbaşı family opened the "Istanbul Modern," a museum for contemporary art, in a warehouse off the port in Karaköy. In cooperation with the Goethe Institute, they presented works of a German photographer in 2007. In 2005, the Koç family transformed a large residential building, originally built in 1893, into the Pera Museum.

But the Sabancı family was the first. The villa of the "Sakıp Sabancı Museum" had been the summer residence of the Sabancı family on the Bosporus for more than half a century. In 2002, it became the first museum to open in Turkey to meet modern standards. The curators of all three museums organize at least two exhibitions a year that the international community takes note of. The concept of the exhibition of Nazan

Ölçer, the curator of the "Sakıp Sabancı Museum," featured Picasso and Rodin exhibitions, and a retrospective of the leftist Turkish painter, Abidin Dino (1913–1993). Dino was one of the first critics of the Kemalist order, and he had also been friends with the poet Nazim Hikmet, who died while in exile.

Originally, the museum started with a collection of Ottoman calligraphies owned by one of the richest entrepreneurs in Turkey and stored in his private residence. The collection went on a world tour in 1998, and when the calligraphies returned, in the summer of 2002, the owner transformed his villa into a museum. Sakıp Sabancı (1933–2004) had lived in the villa on the Bosporus since 1966, the year his father died. Before that, the villa had been the residence of Princess İffet, a granddaughter of the Egyptian Khedive İsmail. Hacı Ömer Sabancı (1906–1966) acquired it in 1951 as an Istanbulian summer residence for his family. At the time, he was still living in Adana as a cotton carrier, where he had then risen to become one of the most successful Turkish entrepreneurs.

During those years, his compatriots were still collecting rugs and gold. Hacı Ömer Sabancı, however, was one of the first Turks who became interested in international art: ceramics and sculptures and European furniture of the 18th and 19th century.

Today, the collection is exhibited on the ground floor of the white villa on the Bosporus. When his oldest son, Sakıp Sabancı, became the director of the family holding, he also turned into a passionate collector. He likes to tell the story about how his business partners "were at fault" because they preferred talking about their art collections to talking about business. Sakıp Sabancı was fascinated by Turkish art, and for him, initially, Turkish art meant calligraphy. The second permanent exhibition of the new museum therefore presents four hundred Ottoman calligraphies. The collection is one of the most important ones of its kind. It has been shown in New York, Paris, Berlin, and Frankfurt. Sakıp Sabancı also collected Turkish 19th and 20th century paintings. 318 of them are exhibited in the modern gallery that is beneath the surface of the very large property. Shortly before he died, Sabancı purchased 123 paintings that completed his collection.

About sixty private collectors inform the Istanbul Museum for Islamic Art about the size of their collections. Sakıp Sabancı was one of them. Then, he was the first one to make his collection accessible to the public at a point in time at which he had been active as a philanthropist for two decades. He financed thirty schools, libraries, and theaters, as well as more than a dozen cultural centers. Finally, he founded the Sabancı University, which is connected to the Museum on the Bosporus. When he founded the museum, he decided to break with a negative Turkish tradition in that the property is divided among the children which would have meant that the collection would then no longer be a collection. But the white villa on the Bosporus is not a family museum, but a lively place for meetings, including a restoration center for calligraphies and paintings. The new exhibits attract even more visitors than the permanent exhibitions. The hope of the first artistic director of the museum, Emin Balcıoğlu, was that the museum would inspire other wealthy Turks and private collectors to imitate Sakıp Sabancı by spending a part of their advertising budget on promoting art and new museums.

Private patrons and art lovers are filling a gap that the state created with its insufficient means and ideological guidelines. Erdoğan's government promoted the opening of new private museums, such as Istanbul Modern and Santralistanbul. In the last few years, the government's culture policy developed, mainly since Culture Minister Ertuğrul Günay took up office. Günay had been the mastermind of Turkish social democracy. From 1993, until his resignation in 1995, he was the General Secretary of the CHP; before the elections in 2007, he became a member of the AK Party. As a Culture Minister, he places great value in familiarizing people with the cultural wealth of Anatolia. He promotes films and the translations of Turkish literature into other languages, mainly into German. In late 2007, three films were shown in Turkey that all had to do with "honor murders"; the most well known one was "Saklı Yüzler" (Lost Faces). They became well known only because they were shown during film festivals promoted by the Ministry of Culture. "Beynelmilel" (International) was also shown during one of these festivals. It is a critical film about the coup of 1980. The Ministry supported the production of the movie, "Takva" (Piety) that describes how the devout Muslim Muharrem is confronted with the modern world and with brokers of religion who use him for their purposes, which is why he ultimately breaks down.

The Turkish cinema scene is centered around Istanbul's Beyoğlu and its pedestrian zone, İstiklal Caddesi, which is also where most of the small private theaters in Istanbul are located, and also cafés and bars. During the Ottoman Empire, the street had been named Grande Rue de Pera. Back then, the upper echelons of society promenaded along this long and narrow street. It extends from the Taksim Square in the north to the Tünel, the first subway of the city, which was built in 1875. At the time, the women wore white lace gloves and the men the modern and stiff suits from Europe. They strolled by the magnificent embassies, sat in elegant cafés, such as the Markiz, and purchased objects that were fashionable in Europe in stores that belonged to Greeks, Armenians, and Jews.

After the founding of the Republic it was renamed and is now called İstiklal Caddesi, the Street of Independence. The loss of the dignity of being the capital degraded the embassies to consulates. Pera, the old Greek name of the city, became the Turkish Beyoğlu. What has remained is that the street and the maze of its alleys continue to attract people, mainly young people. On weekdays and weekends, the throngs move up and down the streets before the historical backdrop of art nouveau buildings. People buy books and music, disappear in cinemas and cafés—and into art galleries, because there is no entrance fee. Most of them would like to enter the elegant galleries of the noble district of Nişantaşı, but Istanbul's youth is at home in Beyoğlu, and with it, the lively Turkish cultural scene.

## Orhan Pamuk, the unpopular Nobel Prize winner

The photo could have been taken in Europe. Şeküre Pamuk, dressed in a "fifties" suit and with permed hair, is holding her son, Orhan. The young boy is looking over the balcony into a sunny spring day. In the background, the flowers are in bloom on the trees, there is a high-rise, and another one is being constructed behind scaffolding. The photo was made on the balcony of the residence of the Pamuk family, in Istanbul's Nişantaşı. More than half a century later, Orhan received the Nobel Prize for Literature, in Oslo, and the same year, the memories of his childhood and youth appeared in the German translation of his book, *Istanbul*. That is where he describes the balcony of the Pamuk Apartment, which is where, he says "my mother picked me up and showed me the world."

Istanbul is the world of the young Orhan Pamuk and also of the mature writer. When he was a child, he lived in Switzerland for a short time, and he spent important years, from 1985 to 1988, at New York's Columbia University. But Orhan Pamuk conquered the world in Istanbul.

When he was a writer, he moved from Şişli into the artists' quarter Cihangir, and there his view of the world expanded—to a panorama that is unequalled. With a silhouette in which the fishing cutters and black passenger steam ships on the water mingle with the semi-round cupolas and thin minarets on land. The further away the contours are, the more they become nebulous. Here, the Hagia Sophia, the most magnificent building of Christendom; there the mosque of Suleyman the Magnificent on another hill, the answer of the Muslims to Justinian's building. On the one side is Europe, and on the other Asia.

Istanbul is the world that his mother, Şeküre, showed him for the first time, and Istanbul became a synonym for Pamuk's search for his soul and the soul of Turkey. While others darkly conjured up the clash of civilizations, Pamuk provided a literary condensation of the two parties. Pamuk's long and convoluted sentences may seem old-fashioned, but his great literary achievement lies less with the language he uses, but the fact that he has dedicated his whole life to one endless variation of one topic: how the Occident manages to deal with the Modernity of the West. Always, they captivate with imagination and the art of narration as a result of the mixture of the narrative art of the mystical Sufis with those of Western crime novels.

In *The White Fortress* (1985), he has a Venetian caught by the Turks after a battle at sea who becomes the slave of an Islamic theologian. The more the two have to do with each other, the more the world of the Venetian, who believes in science, and the world of the Hodja, who remains caught in his conservative world, become blurred. The contours between subject and object increasingly become indistinct. The foreign world and the "I" mingle; the two protagonists become interchangeable. Pamuk continues this thought in *The Black Book* (1990). He turns Istanbul of the sixties into a labyrinth in which Galip goes looking for his wife, Rüya (Dream). He thinks she is with his half-brother, Celal, a famous columnist. He looks through Celal's columns for an indication where they could be. Galip becomes Celal more and more, and finally pretends he is Celal, while he continues to search for his identity in the other.

In his novel, *My Name is Red* (1998), Pamuk introduces the reader to the winter of 1591 and the scene of the miniaturists at court in Istanbul. Pamuk did a lot of research for this novel until he had familiarized himself with the details of miniature painting. Again, the question of identity, and again he does not find an unequivocal answer. One of the sultan's miniaturists wants to include elements of western Frankonian painting and is murdered by traditionalists for doing it. Ultimately, Pamuk rejects the bullheadedness of those who want to cling to tradition as much as he rejects taking lightly what comes from the West.

"White, black, red," could be Pamuk's color trilogy. In 1999, he added a collection of essays to the three novels, the title of which was *The Other Colors.* Three years later, his political novel *Snow* was published. He promised that it will remain his only political novel. *Snow* is the novel that is read most outside of Turkey, and probably the novel that is misunderstood most. Pamuk has the city Kars, in Eastern Anatolia, covered with snow ("kar") during the winter, and Ka, a Turkish-German man from Frankfurt, becomes a victim of the rigidity of the village's people. This is not a warning that the Islamists are going to take over, which is some readers' interpretation. Rather, he paints a fresco of the microcosm of all those powers that block each other and Turkey. In the end Ka, the hero, perishes on account of the bigotry of everyone involved, mainly the Kemalists who suggest that they would bring the West to Turkey, and the Islamists who believe that they will find their salvation in the letters of the Qur'an.

Pamuk did not know any women who wore scarves in the quarter where he grew up because his parents and his family were proud followers of Atatürk and his westernized attitude. His grandfather was an engineer who made a lot of money in railway building. The only women who wore scarves at the time were the wives of the janitors of the elegant residential buildings in his quarter; religion was a matter of the servants. And still, Pamuk became alienated by the authoritarian dogma that cast a spell on his formative years. He was a leftist at the university where he studied architecture for a few years; maybe he was even a Marxist. Reading Virginia Woolf, William Faulkner, Thomas Mann, and Marcel Proust kept him from becoming narrow minded like other students, he said later. When he was young, he wanted to become a painter, but then he recognized that, "writing was the only way to raise your voice with words while painting symbolizes muteness."

Pamuk was the first intellectual of the Islamic world who condemned Khomeinis' fatwa against Salman Rushdie. Immediately following the terrorist attacks of September 11, 2011, Pamuk wrote in Germany's *Süddeutsche Zeitung*: "The West unfortunately does not have an inkling of the feeling of degradedness that a large majority of the world's population is living through." Because he also did not want to be silent about the shortcomings of his own country, he was accused twice. Once, he had told the magazine section of the Swiss *Zürcher Tagesanzeiger*, on February 5, 2005: "More than 30,000 Kurds were killed here and one million Armenians. And no one has the courage to mention it. So I do and they hate me for it."

Those who hate him insult him and send him death threats. Educated Kemalists would say that Orhan Pamuk is a terrible writer and that they hate him and would never read a book of his. One of *Hürriyet*'s columnists wrote: "This person is so incapable that it is not even worth seeing him as an enemy." On December 16, 2005, the court case began; it was stopped on January 22, 2006, because there was another court proceeding already on-going against him. On October 20, he had told the German newspaper, *Die Welt*, that the Turkish army posed a greater threat to Turkish democracy than the AK Party. The nationalist lawyer, Kemal Kerinçsiz, was the one who had initiated the proceedings against other intellectuals, such as Hrant Dink and Elif Şafak. And it had already been a few years since he had rejected an award to be given by the Turkish Parliament, which wanted to make him a life-long poet-scholar of the Turkish people.

This rejection had already irked quite a few people, and Turkey's reaction to Pamuk's being awarded the Nobel Peace Prize on October 12, 2006, was petty. Turkey was unable to celebrate its great writer. Turks associated the prize with Pamuk's statement on the Armenians. The editor-in-chief of the newspaper *Hürriyet* asked: "Was the Nobel Prize awarded to a Turk or the statement about the country of this Turk?" The nationalist lyricist, Fazil Hüsnü Dağlarca, even went further: "A person who does not praise the Armenians is not awarded; that is the fashion of the day," and said that Nobel prizes were not awarded because of literary accomplishments. The lyricist, Özdemir İnce, was even more spiteful, commenting that it was not Turkish literature that was being awarded the Nobel Prize, but Pamuk who, with his assertion of the Armenian "genocide," was putting Turkey "up for sale" and that "he would very probably also sell Turkish history." The leftist liberal intellectual, Ali Bayramoğlu, reprimanded İnce in the newspaper, *Yeni Şafak*, by saying that his kind of thinking was demented because Pamuk was opening the doors of the world to Turkey and that Pamuk was as much above politicians as Dostoyevski was above Lenin. Tuğrul Eryılmaz, the editor of the magazine *Radikal*, which has cult status among Turkish intellectuals, protected the Nobel Prize, stating that Pamuk loves the city in which he lives, that he loves his country, and that he is a writer with a universal aura.

In an essay for the *Frankfurter Allgemeine Zeitung*, Pamuk once posed the question why he was unable to leave Istanbul and answered because he could not imagine a life anywhere else other than Istanbul and that his writer's imagination demanded that he remain in the same city, in the same street, in the same house with the same view, adding, "Istanbul's fate is my fate." Even in decades in which there was very little glamour of the past, he was always in search of Istanbul's spirit. In his memoires of *Istanbul*, he writes about an observation Flaubert once made while he was walking through Istanbul, 102 years before Pamuk was born on June 7, 1952. According to Pamuk, Flaubert had come to the conclusion that Constantinople was going to be the capital of the world in 100 years. As a result of the downfall of the Ottoman Empire, the opposite happened, Pamuk says. "When I was born, Istanbul was in such a bad state, weakened and isolated like never before in its 2,000-year-old history." He was always busy trying to combat the melancholia to then finally submit himself to it, like all Istanbulians.

Pamuk had looked for the world in Istanbul and had found it in his father Gündüz's library. In his acceptance speech after receiving the Peace Prize of the German Book Trade (Friedenspreis des deutschen Buchhandels), on October 23, 2005, in the Pauls Church in Frankfurt, he said: "My father had a vast library and told me about great writers such as Thomas Mann, Kafka, Dostoevsky or Tolstoy the way other fathers talked about generals or saints. Even when I was a child, all of these novels and authors were one with Europe." He continued by saying that novels were one of the most important art forms that Europe ever produced: "Together with orchestra music and renaissance art, the novel is the foundation of the European character and culture." In the novels that he had read during his youth, Europe was not defined by Christendom, but rather by individualism and the battle of the protagonists for liberty. He is fascinated by novels because they make it possible to tell one's history by telling someone else's history, adding that he uses novels to try and feel like what it is to be someone else and to change and liberate himself with this power of imagination.

Pamuk himself became a master of the art form of the European bourgeoisie. His mother showed him the world on the balcony of his Istanbul house. As a teenager, he conquered the world in his father's library. He read. Much later, he was awarded the Nobel Prize for his writing, in which he brings together the two sources of civilization that Turkey feeds on. His soul, like the soul of Turkey, is torn. He observes reality through the eyes of a European through the art form of the novel.

# Appendices

# Middle East's struggle for democracy: Going beyond headlines[1]

T he ongoing struggle in the Middle East is not between the so-called Islamists and secularists. It's not pro-Morsi vs. pro-military in Egypt, or even Assad vs. opposition in Syria. The real struggle is between those committed to the core values of democracy and human rights and those who want to maintain a status quo of authoritarianism and domination.

Western observers often place Middle East actors and their motives into well-intentioned but partially inaccurate or sometimes misleading categories. For example, the three major groups in Iraq are labeled as Shiites, Sunnis and Kurds. The first two are religious categories, while the third is ethnic. The majority of Kurds are Sunni, and the majority of Iraqi Shiites are ethnically Arabs. So the right, albeit inconvenient, categories would be Sunni-Kurds, Sunni-Arabs and Shiite-Arabs.

These categories would be trivial details if it weren't for the fact that Middle Eastern realities of these labels do not always overlap with established western understanding. For instance, those in the Middle East who call themselves "secularists" would be perceived in the west as the "good guys" who believe in democracy and separation of church and state.

But Turkey's historic self-proclaimed "secularists" in practice were anything but secular or democratic. As Edhem Eldem, Professor of History at Istanbul's prestigious Bogazici University observed, Turkish "secularism" often "marginalized and oppressed those who openly displayed their beliefs; head-scarf-wearing women were banned from universities, and few protections were given to religious minorities." The government ran every single mosque and prescribed the preachers' sermons. Turkey's self-proclaimed secularists were also aggressive nationalists, who

[1]   This article by Alp Aslandoğan, President of the Alliance for Shared Values, first appeared in TheHuffingtonPost.com on December 13, 2013.

denied millions of Kurdish citizens their cultural rights, including the right to speak their mother tongue. Those who did not embrace the official government ideology were sometimes beaten and jailed.

Counter-intuitive to a western audience, on the other side were participants of the Hizmet social movement, originated by Turkey's most influential preacher and social advocate, Fethullah Gülen, who advocated for democracy, equal opportunity and social justice, and defended religious rights of all faiths in Turkey, including Orthodox Christians and Jews. Gülen's sympathizers started free tutoring centers in Turkey's Southeast, serving tens of thousands of children from low-income families, often of Kurdish descent, helping protect them from recruitment by terrorist organizations operating around Turkey's borders.

In 2008, when the Turkish judiciary prosecuted military officials charged with planning or perpetrating military coups, western media called it a struggle between Islamists and Seculars. In reality, as correctly observed by Dr. John Esposito of Georgetown University, it was a struggle between pro-democracy groups and those military officers who were found guilty of some of the worst crimes against their fellow citizens. Kurdish citizens, many of who saw their loved ones disappear under military-dominated periods, celebrated this development alongside journalists who were intimidated or fired from their jobs during the same periods.

Last month, when Hizmet representatives criticized the government-proposed legislation that calls for banning exam prep schools, Turkish and Western journalists labeled this opposition as a feud between Prime Minister Erdoğan and Mr. Gülen because roughly 15-25 percent of these prep schools were founded by Hizmet participants according to various estimates.

But that is an oversimplification because this underlying struggle is between democracy and free enterprise on the one hand against government overreach and authoritarianism on the other. If enacted, this legislation would make Turkey the only country in the world to ban a whole category of legitimate private enterprise—one that provides math, science and language arts training to children of low-income families who cannot afford private tutoring.

It is ironic that the ruling AK Party that fought against authoritarian government overreach during its first term, from 2003-2007, has since taken steps that completely contradict its earlier record. From recent discourse on regulating student homes and government's heavy-handed reaction to Gezi Park protests, to restrictions on freedom of the press, Turkey is rekindling its historic struggle between those committed to democracy and those who benefit from authoritarianism and dominance.

Turkey is often cited as an example for struggling Middle East countries such as Egypt and Tunisia; after all, Turkey experienced a similar transition 60 years ago. But as the Turkish experience shows, democracy is a messy process with a steep learning curve. It sometimes can seem like too much to ask of both governments and the governed to have patience to learn the difference between legitimate democratic opposition and rebellion; enforcement and oppression. Nevertheless, abandoning the path to democracy is not an option.

What was termed an Arab spring is actually a beginning of the fall of authoritarian regimes that will hopefully lead to a spring of democracy. But let's be prepared that spring will come only after a harsh winter of authoritarian establishments resisting democratizing reforms. What is clear is that people in the Middle East yearn for their freedoms, and we hope that their struggle leads them toward democracy and away from the yoke of domination. For outside observers, understanding this struggle requires going beyond the convenient labels of the news headlines.

# Erdoğan game plans have faltered[2]

T he real challenge to the legacy of Prime Minister Recep Tayyip Erdoğan in the Turkish political landscape now comes from Erdoğan himself as he has been rapidly moving from a progressive stand through which he was able to appeal to a broad-based electorate to an authoritarian conservative platform with a strong dominance of political Islam.

A growing disillusionment among Turks, something the weak opposition parties have failed to capitalize on, is now being fed by the leader of ruling Justice and Development Party (AK Party) himself, albeit unconsciously and inadvertently. As Erdoğan tries to unload what he considers excess baggage en route to an ultimate consolidation of his power, he has started making a series of mistakes that may prove to be difficult to recover from.

For one, he lost his reformist and progressive appeal when he introduced an Islamist agenda on both domestic and foreign policy choices. At home, he has strengthened the anti-Erdoğan opposition camp by alienating more groups including liberals and moderate conservatives. Turks are no longer buying into sugarcoated legislative reforms embedded in an actually regressive and hidden policy agenda. Rigging the fourth judicial reform package, which was supposed to align Turkish legislation with the judgments of the European Court of Human Rights (ECtHR), with a last-minute amendment before summer that actually reduced sentences for those who squandered taxpayers' money in public contracts, was a recent example in order to save political cronies. Now Erdoğan offers harsher penalties for those who exercise the right to freedom of assembly in ostensibly a democratization package the government forwarded to Parliament last week. I suppose the proverbial saying of "Fool me once, shame on you; fool me twice, shame on me" is in order in the eyes of voters.

---

[2]    This article by Abdullah Bozkurt first appeared in *Today's Zaman* on December 9, 2013.

Abroad, foreign policy choices along ideological lines have contributed to the near-isolation of Turkey both in the Middle East and North Africa region and beyond. Although Foreign Minister Ahmet Davutoğlu dismisses criticism flat out by highlighting the frequent flyer miles he has clocked, the meetings he has held and the number of Turkish embassies around the globe, the bitter fact is that Turkey has been sidelined in many issues in its own region, to say nothing of in world affairs. Erdoğan vows that the world will eventually agree with the Turkish view on Syria and Egypt, two countries with which Ankara cut off ties. The efforts to pick up the broken pieces on the foreign policy front by trying to repair relations with Iraq and finally agreeing to the EU's position on the readmission agreement after dragging its feet are testament to a failed foreign policy. That is why Erdoğan scrambled Davutoğlu and his diplomats to fix the picture on the eve of the election period in Turkey.

Erdoğan's democratic credentials at home were dealt severe blows just in four weeks alone when he attempted to shut down privately funded popular prep schools that train and educate schoolchildren by offering supplementary courses for highly competitive state-administered exams. The move, seen by many as an assault on the right to free enterprise and the right to education, to forcefully close some 4,000 prep schools sparked outrage among millions of parents. It turned out the government did not even calculate the economic costs let alone legal and social challenges emanating from such a closure. It was Erdoğan himself who pushed the agenda with a small cadre of his advisors and now the plan has blown up in his face when even Cabinet members and AK Party deputies have started to question the wisdom of such a drastic ban. Erdoğan had to take a step back and has shelved the idea for the time being. He ended up with his reputation greatly damaged.

Then came the massive profiling revelations when the liberal daily Taraf published confidential National Security Council (MGK) documents dated 2004 when Erdoğan and his minister signed on to a plan to crack down on faith-based groups in the country including the powerful Hizmet movement inspired by Islamic scholar Fethullah Gülen. The daily continued publishing more documents indicating that the profiling and blacklisting of people and diverse groups from Alevis to Christian missionaries went on even in 2013. The government admitted the authenticity of documents but denied it ever acted upon them. That turned out be false when the daily published articles detailing how people profiled by the government were denied public service or shifted to low-key positions. As a last resort, Erdoğan turned to intimidation tactics, just as meddlesome generals in this country once used to do, by launching criminal and civil lawsuits against the paper and its investigative reporters who uncovered the government's dirty laundry. That followed with financial threats as auditors from the revenue administration started to show up at businesses.

That was the second biggest mistake Erdoğan committed in a month. He could have easily come out clean by offering a simple apology to the public for the profiling programs that victimized people and violated their constitutional right to privacy. Instead of cutting his losses and allowing an independent judiciary to investigate the culprits behind the profiling, Erdoğan decided to fight back using and perhaps abusing state powers. Perhaps his administration was up to its neck in profiling dirt. As Erdoğan got angrier in his public speeches, he crossed the fine line of separation of powers between the executive and judiciary. He called on the judiciary to intervene and punish those who publish scandalous government documents. He even said if the judiciary remains idle and does nothing, it would violate the constitution. Taraf fired back at Erdoğan, accusing him of violating constitutionally protected rights such as the right to privacy and the right to free speech.

Where do we go from here? I think Erdoğan is fighting a losing public battle. Turks historically and traditionally feel great sympathy towards victimized groups and very much despise condescending, uncompromising and overbearing leadership. That was the key point once-powerful generals overlooked for years before realizing that it was too late to make changes. Second, this is not a fight for sharing power between Erdoğan and Gülen as government people tried to portray it. It is much more than that. Erdoğan, the strongman of Turkey, wants to railroad any and every opposition that comes in his way so that he can create a new Turkey of his own image. That may be generals yesterday, liberals and conservative groups including Gülen today and President Abdullah Gül loyalists tomorrow. As Erdoğan tries to impose values of his own orthodox version of political Islam on Turkish society, he will keep clashing with many diverse groups that may disagree with his vision of Turkey.

Is this sustainable, though? Hardly. In a very vibrant and dynamic Turkish society boasting a young population, Erdoğan's push will trigger stronger push-backs, eventually trapping him in his own corner. The polarization in Turkish society may become unbearable, and Erdoğan is risking a big backlash from the public by forcing his own agenda. The business community is not comfortable with the foreign policy choices of the Erdoğan government because they are losing market share and opportunities. Considering that the economic outlook does not look so gloomy during election periods, the AK Party may not be able to ride out the stormy impact of global economic changes as easily as it once thought. That is why Erdoğan kept slamming what he describes as the interest lobby because roll-over debts on credit cards have snowballed to the point that people feel squeezed as they are trying to make ends meet under the burden of consumer debts including car loans and mortgages.

What card is left for Erdoğan to play? As he has proven himself to no longer be so keen on building coalitions, I believe the Turkish prime minister decided to fight back with the way he knows best: Creating a villain dressed up with all kinds of crazy conspiracy theories. Erdoğan will attack his opponents by floating ideas such as that the world Jewish lobby and imperialist powers are after him and his government. He did so during the May-June Gezi park incidents by claiming that an interest lobby was behind the anti-government protests, perhaps an implicit reference to the Jewish lobby. When he was pressured on Egypt, where his government has burned all bridges with the interim government backed by the military after Mohammed Morsi's ouster by a coup, Erdoğan said Israel was behind it and had evidence to back that claim up. It turned out he was referring to a YouTube video where French intellectual Bernard-Henri Lévy, who is Jewish, made some comments two years ago in a panel discussion at Tel Aviv University. Similar attacks against the Hizmet movement and Mr. Gülen by hired guns in pro-government media lately are also part of the same pattern.

I suppose we will see an aggressive campaign period in Turkey where conspiracy theories sell easily and serve as a convenient tool for politicians to distract the public from real and substantive issues. As the elections get nearer, Erdoğan will turn up the volume on Chavez-style rhetoric.

# Turkey's graft investigation and PM Erdoğan's response[3]

## Q&A on the corruption cases and investigation

### Have Erdoğan or the AK Party offered any proof of their conspiracy allegations?

- Prime Minister Recep Tayyip Erdoğan and the ruling Justice and Development Party (AK Party) have not produced any form of evidence to justify their conspiracy allegations. Instead they have put forth a number of arguments:

*Argument 1: The investigating police did not inform their superiors of their investigation*

- The government argued very strongly that the fact that the investigating police units did not inform their superiors within the police force for the past 14/15 months of the ongoing investigations was proof that these investigations were not genuine but part of an international plot to topple the government.

- However, according to Section 164(2) of the 2004 code on Criminal Procedure (CMK) and the relevant bylaw of 2005, police officers and police units are only answerable to the public prosecution service when investigating on their behalf. A police officer or unit cannot inform its superior within the police force of an ongoing investigation it is undertaking on behalf of the public prosecution service. The police cannot divulge any information whatsoever—even of the very existence of the investigation. Only the investigating prosecutor (not even the chief prosecutor) can decide who should be informed, when and how. Contravening this would be unlawful and could lead to prosecution.

---

[3]  This article by Kerim Balcı, Editor-in-Chief, *Turkish Review*, first appeared in *Turkish Review* on January 2, 2014.

- This law was passed by the AK Party government to bring it into line with EU laws and to prevent sensitive investigations from being compromised through leaks.
- Despite its rhetoric to the contrary, the government has tacitly acknowledged that there was no wrongdoing on the part of the police as it reassigned (not dismissed) officers and speedily amended the relevant bylaw of 2005. By doing so, it indirectly acknowledged that police officers could not lawfully inform their superiors within the force while the law remained as it did at the time.
- The amendment meant that any investigation will now be shared by the investigating police unit with its superiors, which in turn will eventually be shared with the Interior Ministry.
- However, the Supreme Court of Appeal (*Danıştay*) has since revoked this amendment on the grounds that it is unlawful and contravenes the secrecy and independence of judicial enquiry and due process.

*Argument 2: Three separate investigations were launched at the same time to undermine the government*

- On Dec. 17 the police took in several people for questioning and carried out searches at a number of premises. As far as can be seen, these actions were related to three separate investigations. The government claims that the fact that the detentions and search warrants were carried out on the same day is proof that the investigations are not genuine but were executed in this manner to maximize impact.
- It is impossible to know the exact reasoning of the prosecutors for deciding to carry out these detentions and exercise these search warrants on the same day, as they are barred from commenting to the press while carrying out an investigation. However, many commentators have suggested that the prosecutors acted in this way fearing that if they launched one investigation first, the government might react and try to suppress the other investigations before vital evidence could be collected and the relevant suspects questioned.
- Steps taken by the government since Dec. 17 would appear to support this reasoning. Note that on Dec. 25 a second phase in the graft investigation run by Prosecutor Muammer Akkaş was blocked. Despite a court order, 41 new suspects are yet to be detained for questioning and search orders are yet to be carried out at seven premises. The

police are yet to execute these orders. Instead, on Dec. 26, Akkaş was removed from the investigation.

*Argument 3: The timing of the detentions and search warrants (three months prior to local elections) proves that these investigations are not genuine but seek to damage the AK Party at the polls*

- On March 30 Turkey will go to local elections. If no change is made to their dates the presidential election will take place on the last day of August 2014, and general elections on June 14, 2015.

- Based on leaked evidence, it is alleged that the prosecutors decided to launch the detentions and search warrants at the time that they did because they had heard the suspects had got wind of the investigations and had started to destroy vital evidence.

### What are Gülen's views on the ongoing graft investigation in Turkey?

- Fethullah Gülen has stated that such investigations can take place in any country and that the government should cooperate with the judiciary to assist the judicial process.

- Gülen and the Journalists and Writers Foundation (GYV), of which he is the honorary chairperson, denied any involvement with the ongoing investigations. Furthermore, they invited state authorities to prove those allegations, and take legal action if any evidence is found substantiating them through due process—not by undermining the institutions and processes charged with investigating such claims and allegations as they claim the government is doing. Gülen's lawyer condemned and rejected the allegations as an attempt to divert public attention away from a massive bribery scandal and defame his client.

- A number of commentators close to the movement have pointed out that the investigations date back at least 14/15 months and therefore cannot have any bearing on the government's recent decision to close down university prep schools (a decision the movement strongly opposes).

- Gülen states that the premier's attempts at pinning the investigation on an international conspiracy, of which the movement is allegedly the domestic partner, and the reassigning of hundreds of innocent people to different posts, is an attempt to misdirect the public's attention away from the real issue and constitutes interference with an ongoing investigation.

- While denying that he has anything to do with these investigations, Gülen has also pointed out that these police officers and police chiefs have been changed and reassigned many times over already. Gülen also invoked "God's curse" on himself and those rightly or wrongly associated with him if they have acted in contravention of Islam, modern law and democracy. In addition, if some people are trying to cover up their corruption by blaming innocent people, then God's curse be upon them. This form of prayer is called *mulaana* or *mubahala* in Islam. It is based on the Qur'an and Sunnah and is undertaken when two parties make diametrically opposing claims and reach a deadlock in resolving an issue. It is a two-way conditional prayer.

### Gülen and the Hizmet movement were supportive of Erdoğan and his government. What happened?

- Gülen is on record as expressing his support for democracy, the non-instrumentalization of religion in politics, the rule of law, human rights, freedom of religion and belief, the rule of law, equality and celebration of diversity, consultative and inclusive decision-making, meritocracy and accountability, a strong vibrant resilient and compassionate civil society.
- The GYV has issued various press releases reiterating the movement's position on democracy, the rule of law, press freedom, politics and supporting a particular party or political candidate.
- Gülen and the movement associated with him (a faith-inspired community known as Hizmet) gave full support to the demilitarization of Turkish politics. In particular the Ergenekon and Sledgehammer (Balyoz) cases received support from Hizmet-related media. Both cases ended in the punishment of ex-army personnel and civilians linked to coup plots against the AK Party government. The decisions of the Turkish courts were applauded by the EU as positive steps toward democratization and prevention of military intervention into politics.
- Prosecutor Zekeriya Öz, the prosecutor who launched the first corruption case on Dec. 17,was presiding over the Ergenekon case and was also lauded by AK Party supporters at the time of the coup case.
- Gülen and the Hizmet movement supported those policies of Erdoğan and the government that furthered democracy, the rule of law, human rights, equality, EU accession, respect and freedom for diversity and

pluralism. Policies that strengthened civil society, removed non-democratic tutelage, provided greater freedom to religious minorities and sought to resolve Turkey's long-lasting internal and external problems. The reason Gülen and the movement no longer support Erdoğan and his policies is because they no longer seek to achieve the above.

- Erdoğan has adopted an increasingly authoritarian style of governance in recent years. Rather than reforming constitutional bodies and structures that are deeply undemocratic and possess far too much power over any elected government, he has sought to maintain and govern through them. He has strengthened state power at the expense of civil society and is more inclined towards the Shanghai Cooperation than the EU. What is more, he is increasingly showing signs of readopting the "political Islam" he had rejected when founding the AK Party.

- The following are some examples between 2010 and today demonstrating this change of direction: slowing down of EU negotiations, the Uludere incident (a military airstrike in which dozens of civilians were killed), the rhetoric developed during the Gezi Park protests and the attempt to ban prep schools.

- The final rift came when Prime Minister Erdoğan started claiming that Hizmet has infiltrated the state apparatus and formed a "parallel state" plotting the recent corruption cases against his party, and that Hizmet was working as a domestic arm of foreign powers who did not want Turkey to become a global player.

### Has the Hizmet movement infiltrated Turkey's police and judiciary? Is the Hizmet movement a "parallel state"?

- These allegations have been made about Gülen and Hizmet before. Gülen was tried and acquitted by Turkey's staunchly secular courts in the 1980s and 1990s—that is prior to the birth of the AK Party. Most recently, in 2006, Gülen was acquitted of such allegations after a six-year trial. The prosecutors appealed this decision but the Court of Appeal upheld Gülen's acquittal in 2008.

- Furthermore, from the 1990s onward the movement has been active outside of Turkey. Today the movement is active in over 150 different countries in a range of fields, primarily education and interfaith dialogue.

- Gülen encourages Muslims to take part in every part of society and not to be confined to conventional roles and jobs. He encourages practicing Muslims to work in all sectors and industries, including the civil service, police, judiciary, media, military and academia—in the past these were sectors knowingly avoided by and closed to observant Muslims in Turkey. A learned estimate suggests that 8 percent of the Turkish population regard themselves as Hizmet affiliated. With such a huge support base, it is inevitable that more and more observant Muslims should be taking up such positions.

- Gülen's teachings have helped remove the cultural and religious dogma that previously prevented pious Muslims from being proactively engaged in society and working in the public sector. As a consequence many practicing Turkish Muslims now work in the police force and other public services. The question is not be whether there are practicing Muslims inspired by Gülen working in the police force, but why such people were discouraged from such jobs and positions—be it in the police force or other public sectors—in the past.

- If the assertion is that members of the police force who are inspired by Gülen are somehow engaged in improper activities (i.e. that they act in the best interest of Gülen and/or Hizmet as opposed to the rule of law and proper procedure) then this is not only illegal it is also contrary to Gülen's teachings. If there is any wrongdoing of this or any other type such people should be tried according to due process. This cannot be achieved by undermining the judicial institutions and processes required to investigate such claims.

- Gülen is on record stating that anyone acting contrary to the law should be investigated and tried; he has stated many times before that if there are any groups within the police force or any other public body acting contrary to the law and even the code of conduct, that these people should be investigated and if found guilty, punished according to the letter of the law.

# Oligarchic clique's devious plans[4]

As I have previously written in my newspaper column, when former Interior Minister Idris Naim Şahin resigned from his party, he said in his resignation letter, "When it comes to governing, it is understood that [the party] prefers the guidance of a small oligarchic clique comprising politicians and bureaucrats whose intentions are uncertain."

Şahin, a longtime friend and political partner of Prime Minister Recep Tayyip Erdoğan, insisted that "the government is run by a small oligarchy of elites in a way that excludes broad segments of the party constituency and the Turkish people." This narrow oligarchic group is composed of a number of bureaucrats and young advisers. News portal rotahaber.com's chief editor, Unal Tanık, has written that Erdoğan gave up on getting regular feedback from his party's parliamentarians years ago, and that since 2013 even his ministers have begun to lament to their close associates that they don't have access to Erdoğan. Tanık wrote that Erdoğan seems to be talking to only one of his ministers, his intelligence chief, and a few other bureaucrats and advisers.

It seems that this elite clique headed by Erdoğan is waging psychological warfare against the Hizmet movement, trying to present it as a terrorist organization. Erdoğan keeps referring to the movement as a terrorist organization that, acting on the orders of foreign powers, is trying to stage a coup against him. He even likened Hizmet volunteers to hashish-consuming assassins, the Hashashins (the so-called assassins of 12th century Persia and Syria).

I am seriously concerned about four major—and devious—developments that may follow. First, Erdoğan and his oligarchic clique may arrange for a prosecutor to prepare a lawsuit against Hizmet on terrorism charges. The Yeni Şafak daily's Cem Küçük, who seems to be very close to the National Intelligence Organization (MİT), keeps writing that some aca-

---

4    This article by Dr. İhsan Yılmaz, teaching at Fatih University, first appeared in *Today's Zaman* on February 1, 2014.

demics, journalists, prosecutors and police officers who are allegedly affiliated with the Hizmet movement could be charged with both terrorism and spying charges. According to Küçük and some other pro-Erdoğan journalists, some prominent figures of the *Zaman* daily, *Today's Zaman*, the *Bugün* daily, Samanyolu TV and the Journalists and Writers Foundation (GYV), together with some academics (myself possibly included), may face charges of terrorism and spying. Küçük says that this "spy organization" steals national security information and gives it to foreign countries at GYV meetings.

Second, as Emre Uslu, the columnist for *Today's Zaman* has said, a fake assassination attempt on Erdoğan may be staged so the finger can be pointed at Hizmet. They can never prove these stupid allegations, but with fabricated evidence, etc., they can confuse the public and throw a smokescreen over the corruption investigations. In 1930, an assassination attempt on Mustafa Kemal Ataturk was staged, and he used this opportunity purge all his critics and potential rivals. Some of my readers will recall my mention of how a Justice and Development Party (AKP) deputy told me just after the Gezi incidents that seeing Erdoğan so easily bend the truth about consuming alcohol and doing illicit things in a mosque, he was worried about such a terrible plan.

Third, as the same AKP deputy told me, there may be a fake coup attempt against the Erdoğan government that would make him a victim and a hero just before the elections and give him the opportunity to send all his critics to jail. Remember that Boris Yeltsin became a hero after this kind of coup attempt.

Fourth, there are rumors that this oligarchic clique is trying to turn the Hrant Dink assassination case upside down and accuse the Hizmet movement of plotting the deed. Until now, everyone, including the AKP, firmly believed that Ergenekon was working to convince international observers that the so-called Islamist alliance between the AKP and the Hizmet movement was putting pressure on non-Muslims in Turkey. According to the rumors, this clique will first peg the Dink assassination on some police officers and then try to link them to the movement.

The evidence revealed so far shows that the corruption cases are so strong and the amount of money involved so unbelievably large that Erdoğan and his clique may do everything they can to stop the investigations.

# On Hizmet exceptionalism[5]

Although military service is compulsory in Turkey, it has sometimes been possible to serve a greatly reduced time in the army by paying a fee. Those who benefited from this privilege would tease those spending months or years in the barracks: "We had to bear the entire year's burden, with all its weight, condensed into a few weeks!" We have had a similar feeling in Turkey since the beginning of the graft probe: The relativity of time has never been so acute.

Turkey is fertile soil for the news media, and catching up with the pace of unfolding events is always difficult. Even by these standards time in Turkey feels like it's been compressed. Days and weeks have been so contracted that the life expectancy of each news piece has been the shortest ever; each article outdated even before the columnist clicks "send."

Recent years in Turkey have witnessed some truly historic moments, ones that will be remembered in the future as perhaps no less significant than and perhaps even as definitive as a Turkish version of the French Revolution or the Emancipation Proclamation.

Hizmet—the movement affiliated with Muslim preacher Fethullah Gülen and the largest faith-inspired social movement in Turkey—had a significant share in these developments thanks to its exceptional nature. The term "Hizmet exceptionalism" was recently used by Jessica Rehman in the context of violence generated by group identity: "[U]sually defense of identity manifests violently. This is not always the case. Hizmet is an exception to this policy, because it fosters empathy."[6]

This author's take on Hizmet exceptionalism shares a similar premise of identity, but with a stronger emphasis on its ontologically nuanced,

---

5    This article by Hakan Yeşilova, Editor-in-Chief, *The Fountain*, first appeared in *Turkish Review* on January 2, 2014.

6    From Jessica Rehman's presentation, titled "The Violence of Identity Formation and the Case of Hizmet Exceptionalism," in the International Symposium "The Hizmet Movement and Peacebuilding: Global Cases," October 24-26, 2013, Washington DC.

independently civil nature; it is free from political abuse and intervention, yet does not compromise on its faith-inspired principles. This exceptionalism is also the main factor behind the prime minister's recent attempts to crack down on Hizmet.

This essay tries to explain why some authorities paint Hizmet as a "parallel state" or "criminal gang," and why some have even gone so far as to liken Hizmet's members to the first terrorist group in the history of mankind: the assassins of Hassan Sabbah. There have even been serious attempts to portray Hizmet as if it falls outside the Sunni school of thought because it does not join the bloc of other religious communities that openly support the government.

## (D)evolution of events

It was a very thrilling eight years between 2002 and 2010, marked by serious steps taken toward EU accession and sincere efforts devoted to real democracy. Turkey was finally able to settle accounts with a long-standing tutelary regime and move on to establish a truly civilian government. The path was not an easy one. Turkey survived a failed presidential election in May 2007; the Justice and Development Patty (AK Party) managed to stand firm, announcing early elections in July 2007 from which they came back stronger (thanks to a landslide win of 47 percent). Abdullah Gül, whose wife wears a headscarf, was elected president later that year.

The following year saw a closure case filed against the AK Party accusing it of being a focal point for activities against secularism—ultimately the Constitutional Court rejected the prosecutor's case.

The historic Ergenekon and Balyoz trials started in 2008 and 2010, respectively, and unraveled some very complex, dirty relations between a group of retired military officers, journalists, politicians and others. For the first time in Turkish history, a coup was considered a serious crime, and those convicted received lengthy sentences. All these achievements and a remarkably well-performing economy were crowned with a jaw-dropping win in the 2011 elections for the AK Party, beginning what Prime Minister Recep Tayyip Erdoğan has called his "master period."

Things started to turn bad in 2013, when accession to the EU was almost removed from the to-do list, attempts for a new constitution failed, and international diplomacy on all fronts (but especially in Syria and Egypt) helped do nothing but isolate Turkey. Then came the Gezi Park protests, which were handled terribly. And, finally, a series of investigations based on grave corruption charges were made against a number of ministers as 2013 drew to a close, triggering what is shaping up to be the gravest of all political and social crises of the last decade.

The current Turkish crisis relates to a so-called conflict between "former allies" the AK Party and Hizmet. For no sensible reason in November 2013 the government attempted to close down private schools training students for the university entrance exam; an estimated quarter of these prep schools were run by Hizmet-inspired organizations. It was also discovered, again in 2013, that confidential profiling of citizens, based on religious affiliations, had been made since 2004, apparently to identify Hizmet-related staff in the bureaucracy and to keep them away from higher positions. When the corruption charges were made against the government in December 2013, the government responded by removing the police chiefs and prosecutors behind the case.

This "split" with Hizmet surprised many. Since 2002, when the AK Party came to office for the first time, Gülen and the movement named after him were frequently claimed to have very close ties with the government. An early hint that this assumption was false came when Gülen said he did not agree with the Mavi Marmara initiative to break through the blockade placed on Gaza that had been loudly supported by the government. In fact the assumption had always been misguided, because Hizmet has always maintained a certain distance (or proximity) between itself and all political parties.

## Strength in independence

This is not a fight between the government and Hizmet. This is a unilateral war waged by a once-progressive government now turned even more authoritarian than the old status quo. It is a reincarnation of Nero burning Rome to rebuild it as he sees fit; a monopoly instead of a separation of powers. Almost more disappointing than this change in the AK Party is its subjugation of a great majority of religious groups through the generous funding they receive from the government.

Hizmet, meanwhile, supports any government or political party that serves the country through democratic and social reforms. Opening schools, dialogue centers and organizing relief work in over 150 countries, Hizmet is active and in direct contact with all sorts of cultures, religions and, of course, political regimes.

What makes Hizmet successful is not only its highly motivated positive activism, but more importantly, its immaterial, abstract nature and lack of a centralized headquarters. Hizmet is diffused in society with no imposed structure, set of rituals, political or ideological affiliations, or economic interests. It is freely embraced by volunteers. Its porous borders allow a two-way traffic of free entry and exit based on willing, conscientious commitment. This is perceived as a threat by power-hungry authorities seeking unconditional obedience. Whenever these authorities endure a blow and cannot locate its source, or harbor delusions of an imagined power struggle, they have a subject to accuse: Hizmet. This is the ghost of a "parallel state" they keep referring to. As for the political reasons, partisanship, by its very nature, means taking sides—thus being naturally opposed to the voters of other parties. Hizmet's being unaffiliated with any political party allows it to adopt a supra-political discourse and reach out to everyone, without bias. For Hizmet, politics is a slippery domain—one can easily be tempted by a passion for greater recognition, power, and fame. Hizmet vows to keep clear of such mistakes by remaining independent.

When studying the economic reasons for Hizmet's independence, it is important to define its difference from other religious communities, many of which are sponsored by the government. Hizmet initiatives usually begin with a start-up investment by philanthropists. In time, these start-ups are expected to self-subsist through their own business operations, competing in their field by providing high-quality services. Economic independence saves Hizmet from being subjugated to the rule of the lender, whereas other, government-funded, religious communities feel obliged to support the government, for their survival depends on its funding.

As for personal reasons, it is important to acknowledge Turkey's reputation for blacklisting its own citizens. Recently leaked documents (*Taraf*, Dec. 2, 2013) suggest that the AK Party has inherited this state tradition and profiled civil servants according to their ideology, faith tradition and religious practice. Another confidential national security document, dated Aug. 25, 2004, shows government endorsement of a plan by the National Security Council (MGK) to crack down on the Hizmet movement. Faced with such Orwellian surveillance over citizens' personal lives, Hizmet's porous, structure-free and all-embracing nature allows its volunteers to easily adapt to circumstances as independent individuals, free from self-excluding risks of identity formation; it allows them to act as law-abiding servants, and pursue their careers into state bureaucracies and private businesses, while also continuing their voluntary Hizmet activities.

## Understanding Hizmet

Because Hizmet has such a wide support base, those who share its goals have ended up in diverse disciplines all over Turkey—including in government. But to claim that their work within the government has been under the guise of "establishing a parallel state" is simply false, and misreads Hizmet's purpose. Thousands of police officers and prosecutors have been reassigned in the witch-hunt after the graft probe. Some of these officers are perhaps related to Hizmet or another group; no one knows.

Hizmet volunteers and sympathetic individuals—who are from all walks of life, with differing worldviews, and different levels of commitment—have been trying to survive in their positions. They are working, so to speak, not to be defanged in the face of accusations of "establishing a parallel state" or "not being transparent enough." Such accusations—when no crime or unlawful act has been committed—are a time-worn propaganda cliché, and violate the basic human rights expected in a free and democratic society.

There are some who suggest that Hizmet should institutionalize, with a name and central address, giving examples of groups in other Muslim countries. Those who make these suggestions reveal their ignorance about the nature of Hizmet and about the concept of civil society, both in its modern sense and in the sense of *ulama* (scholars) tradition, which in the past stood for the autonomous non-governmental institution of Islamic civilization. The extremely political and confrontational nature of other groups in some Muslim countries has not benefitted their society or their group's interests. They have often perpetuated violence, and widened the rifts within their nations.

Hizmet, on the other hand, works hard to create a culture of understanding and coexistence in an increasingly globalized world, and tries to build bridges among different cultures. No signpost can carry the weight of the spiritual representative personality of Hizmet. For fair governance—at least in the socio-political culture inherited from ancient times—religious scholars and communities should never compromise their autonomous natures and must stand against what is not right.

The identity of the AK Party seems not to have completely detached from its political Islamist roots, which are scarred by traumatic memories from the Kemalist regime. In a struggle to reverse the tide, it seeks empowerment to subdue a recurring sense of having been victims in the past, and it does so using the same instruments of violent rhetoric, defamation, and cracking down on the constitutive "other," a hypothetical enemy: Hizmet. What they fail to understand is that Hizmet is not a building you can shut down by locking its doors, or a phenomenon you can get rid of when you fire civil servants. It is a worldview, a lifestyle that inevitably continues without physical form or identity.

What is perhaps saddest about this witch-hunt is that Hizmet is a priceless resource for any government. It serves without any burden on public funds and efforts. It is a rich source of reliable manpower devoted to selfless service and ready to raise the banner of Turkey, on peaceful terms, alongside the flags of all other nations around the world. Instead of being propelled by this free energy, and benefitting from its resources, the Turkish government acts in jealousy, and tries to destroy it.

In the past, Hizmet mobilized its significant resources to work with the AK Party to make Turkey a more democratic state governed by the rule of law. It continues to work toward that goal, and will do so with any party, or government, that moves in the same direction.

# The limits of political Islam:
# the new AK Party[7]

Over the past decade international consensus began to emerge that Turkey was moving rapidly toward full political democracy. The AK Party and the Gülen movement were credited with bringing, consolidating and expanding the democratic space within the country. Suddenly, in 2013, the "Muslim democracy" AK Party rule had come to be identified with lost momentum and started showing signs of political fatigue.

All the recent moves and responses from the government—the mishandling of the Gezi protests; the decision to close down, or as the government termed it, "transform," private university exam preparatory schools (*dershane*s); the threatening of a *Taraf* journalist who uncovered details of an alleged 2004 "political deal" between the AK Party government and the military to monitor members of faith movements, the movement associated with Fethullah Gülen in particular; the terming of corruption investigations a "conspiracy to destabilize the government" and dismissal of several police chiefs and officers involved—are signs of a cocktail of political nervousness, fear and arrogance. This has gripped the government and led it to act in desperation, exercising coercive power and displaying apparent disregard for the rule of law.

The unfortunate recent measures and political positioning of the government has jolted Turkey's democratic credentials and image, strengthened and legitimized the reluctance of the European Union to offer membership to Turkey, and reinforced the widespread misconception that Muslim nations are incapable of institutionalizing democratic rule in general.

---

7   This article by Prof. Anwar Alam, teaching at Zirve University, first appeared in *Turkish Review* on January 2, 2014.

One has to understand that this is the same party that rode to political success with a comfortable majority for three consecutive terms since 2002, and that it did so on an agenda of political democratization, civil liberties and economic development. Furthermore, in the past the AK Party demonstrated its political will to achieve these goals by undertaking incremental measures such as de-militarization of the political arena; exposure of the complex face of Turkey's "deep state" through cases like Ergenekon; provision of increased rights to the Kurdish minority community; and improvement of religious freedoms by ending the headscarf ban in the public sector (excluding the judiciary and military). Added to this was the AK Party's unparalleled economic track record. How then has it come to pass that this party now seems to be displaying arbitrary exercises of power, a personality-driven authoritarian mode of decision making and a culture of threat and intimidation—all when there is no credible opposition to the party and its rule?

The popular explanation in both the foreign and domestic media relates to a falling out between the Gülen movement and the AK Party. This narrative had them linked in an informal alliance cooperating on the marginalization of army: With this goal achieved both were left with no choice but to compete in the game of power-politics. In this regard, according to media pundits, Prime Minister Recep Tayyip Erdoğan's decision to shut down the prep schools amounted to an "existential threat" to the Gülen movement, leading to retaliation in the form of the current corruption investigations. Such narratives, even if not politically motivated, reflect at best a modern state of mind accustomed to seeing any conflict in terms of power dynamics.

This same modern mind is quick to pick up certain terms such as "parallel state" and "state-within- a-state" and use them liberally to label any organization—such as the Gülen movement—without understanding the semantics, context and history of such words. These terms are normally applied to organizations that develop and maintain a secret apparatus with the ultimate objective of capturing state power. How strange then, that media pundits and critics never used these terms in reference to Christian missionary organizations running vast networks of schools and hospitals both within and outside Western countries. Perhaps this is because such missionary movements did not question the secular foundation of the nation-state and certainly did not aim to acquire state power. Such is certainly the case with the Gülen movement, in whose Islamic imagination the state is essentially a secular entity. However, the "Islamic identity" of the movement is sufficient proof for the same modern mind to associate it with plans for state takeover. Such actions only serve to delegitimize the organization in the public eye, and lend support to illegal and illegitimate actions by the state. However, these sorts of narratives do not hold water for long and quickly expose multiple contradictions:

First, Gülen himself has been accused of supporting the military coup of 1980; if that is true then Gülen personally does not see military as an obstacle to his Islamic vision. This would negate the need for collaboration with the AK Party vis-à-vis marginalization of the military. Second, any serious observer of the Gülen movement would discover that the movement's focus is the ethical and moral transformation of individual, and has nothing to do with either state/government or state politics. Third, if there is an informal alliance between the two, why then did the AK Party government apparently enter into secret deals with the military back in 2004 to supervise, profile and eventually liquidate the movement at both the individual and organizational level? Fourth, what are the advantages accrued to the Gülen movement due to the supposed informal alliance with the government? Probably none. The movement has never asked for favors from the government, as confirmed by Erdoğan himself: "Why don't they [the Gülen movement] ask for anything?"

Fifth, the Turkish volunteers of the Gülen movement have voted for the AK Party—and would perhaps continue do so, given the current political choices in Turkey. This political preference for the AK Party does not imply a programmatic alliance between the Gülen movement and the AK Party unless the latter is a product of the former, which is certainly not the case. The AK Party is an offshoot of Necmettin Erbakan's Welfare Party (RP) and hails from the Islamic political tradition of "Milli Görüş" (National View)—albeit distantly. Moreover, the Gülen movement is a strictly non-political, faith-inspired movement. Finally, if the military power in Turkey has been tamed, curtailed or marginalized, why should this be seen as a consequence of an "informal alliance" between the Gülen movement and the AK Party government rather than that of a gradual democratization process of the Turkish society and state, in sync with a larger global trend?

The democratic deficit currently being witnessed in Turkey is deeply related to the crisis of morality with which the AK Party, its political functionaries and its leadership has been afflicted. What needs to be understood here is that despite coming from the Islamic tradition, the AK Party has never conceived itself as a "moral actor," rather it sees itself as a "political actor" dedicated to the goal of acquiring state power. As a result, despite an overwhelming public mandate, it still apparently resorted to striking a deal with the (unelected) military in 2004. The panicked response of the government to the publication of these allegations in *Taraf* is also interesting. Prime Minister Erdoğan himself threatened to punish the journalist in question for making a state secret document public. Legislation like official secrets acts are relics of colonial rule, designed to protect officials from their misdeeds while governing the subject population. The invocation of such legislation by an incumbent Turkish premier, for a nation that had never been colonized, suggests an anti-democratic and authoritarian mindset. One can understand, if not approve of, secret pacts/deals concluded between two sovereign nations, but secret deals between two state organs vis-à-vis that state's own people certainly contradict the democratic principle of governance that demands transparency in the functioning of all public bodies, particularly the state and government.

The same anti-democratic and authoritarian mindset was reflected in the decision to close the prep schools. No reasonable explanation was provided by the government for this decision. If the government cannot ensure uniformity and standardization of education throughout the country, it has no moral right to put an end to initiatives aimed to promote "equalizing" measures. By providing a high-quality educational service, the Gülen movement is helping many struggling students—rich or poor—to be able to compete in the workforce. If the underlying purpose of the government was to finish off the Gülen movement, which according to various estimates owns 25 percent of all prep schools in Turkey, then it would anyway not succeed. The movement has already outgrown this sort of organizational form.

In this display of an authoritarian mindset, the AK Party and its leader Prime Minister Erdoğan are also supported by both the political tradition of political Islam and the political tradition of Turkey. Political Islam, ranging from public recognition of Islam to the creation of an

Islamic state and Shariah rule, is all about acquiring state power. Beyond a crude instrumentalization of Islam, the religion's ethical and moral perspectives cease to be a factor in the country's governance. It is the preservation of state, not the normative value of Islam, which becomes the end. The AK Party is no exception to this trend. The regime takes preventive measures to ensure its unfettered rule by crushing any opposition—imaginary or real—emanating from within the state or civil society.

Turkey's historical political tradition, in which the state is looked upon as a benevolent father or guardian, personified in a strong individual, also lends its support to and legitimizes the state's authoritarian tendencies. A nation addicted to hero worship or cult of personality found in Erdoğan just such a leader. As Erdoğan reaches the height of his political career and the state power structure, he is gradually transforming himself into the role of Amir al-Mu'minin (leader of the faithful), becoming AK Party, state, government and nation in one. It is at this stage that what appears to the outside world as authoritarianism becomes a normal, routine exercise of power for him, leading to errors of which he is unaware. One such political blunder is his actions against the Gülen movement—a movement that in a short span of time has added tremendous soft power to Turkey, facilitated Turkish business globally and spread the Turkish language to many nations. A "political" Erdoğan may triumph temporarily, but a "moral" Gülen will live forever.

# References

## General Reference Material

Bora, Tanıl (ed.): *Modern Türkiye'de Siyasi Düşünce*. (Political Thought in Modern Turkey. Vols 1–7. Vol. 1: Tanzimat and the accumulation of constitutionalism; Vol. 2: Kemalism; Vol. 3: Modernization and Westernization; Vol. 4: Nationalism; Vol. 5: Conservatism; Vol. 6: Islamism; Vol. 7: Liberalism). İletişim Yayınları: Istanbul, 2004 and 2005.

Dismorr, Ann: Turkey Decoded. Saqi: London, 2008.

Kinzer, Stephen: *Crescent and Star: Turkey between Two Worlds*. Farrar, Straus and Giroux: New York, 2002.

Kramer, Heinz: *A Changing Turkey: the Challenge to Europe and the United States*. Brookings: Washington, 2000.

Kreiser, Klaus: *Kleines Türkei-Lexikon. Wissenswertes über Land und Leute* [Short Turkish Dictionary: Things worth knowing about the country and the people]. C.H. Beck: Munich, 1991.

Kreiser, Klaus and Neumann, Christoph K.: *Kleine Geschichte der Türkei* [A Short History of Turkey]. Reclam: Stuttgart, 2003.

Mango, Andrew: *The Turks Today*. Overlook TP: New York, 2006.

Pope, Nicole und Hugh: *Turkey Unveiled. Atatürk and After*. John Murray: London, 1997.

Steinbach, Udo: *Die Türkei im 20. Jahrhundert. Schwieriger Partner Europas* [Turkey in the 20th Century: Europe's Difficult Partner]. Bergisch Gladbach: Lübbe, 1996.

Zürcher, Erik J.: *Turkey: A Modern History*. I.B. Tauris: London and New York, 1993.

## The Basic Order of the Turkish Republic

Jung, Dietrich and Wolfgango Piccoli: *Turkey at the Crossroads: Ottoman Legacies and a Greater Middle East*. Zed Books: London, 2001.

Kadioglu, Ayşe: "The Paradox of Turkish Nationalism and the Construction of Official Identity," in *Middle Eastern Studies*, Vol. 32, Issue 2, April 1996.

Mardin, Şerif: "Center-Periphery Relations: A Key to Turkish Politics," in *Daedalus*, Winter 1973.

_____. *Religion, Society and Modernity in Turkey*. Syracuse University Press: Syracuse, NY, 2006.

## The State and Its Elite

Jenkins, Gareth: *Context and Circumstance: the Turkish Military and Politics*. The International Institute for Strategic Studies, Adelphi Paper 337, Oxford University Press: NY, 2001.

## The Dogma of the Elite

Ceylan, Deniz and Irzik, Gürol (ed.): *Human Rights Issues in Textbooks; The Turkish Case*. Tarih Vakfı: Istanbul, 2004.

Karakaş, Cemal: *Turkey: Islam and Laicism between the Interests of State, Politics, and Society*. Peace Research Institute Frankfurt: Frankfurt, 2007.

Toprak, Binnaz and Çarkoğlu, Ali: *Türkiye'de Din, Toplum ve Siyaset*. (Religion, Society, and Politics in Turkey). TESEV: Istanbul, 2000.

## From Outsiders to Counter-Elite

Bozdoğan, Sibel and Kasaba, Reşat (eds.): *Rethinking Modernity and National Identity in Turkey*. University of Washington Press: Seattle and London, 1997.

Çakır, Ruşen: *Ne Şeriat Ne Demokrasi: Refah Partisini Anlamak*. (Neither Shariah nor Democracy. Understanding the Welfare Party) Metis: Istanbul, 1994.

European Stability Initiative (2005). "Islamic Calvinists: Change and Conservatism in Central Anatolia," Berlin, Istanbul, September 2005. www.esiweb.org

Kandiyoti, Deniz and Saktanber, Ayşe (ed.): *Fragments of Culture: the Everyday of Modern Turkey*. I.B.Tauris: London and New York, 2002.

Öniş, Ziya: "The Political Economy of Islam and Democracy in Turkey: From the Welfare Party to the AKP," in *Democracy and Development: New Political Strategies for the Middle East*. Dietrich Jung (ed.) Palgrave: New York, 2006.

Seufert, Günter: *Café Istanbul. Alltag, Religion und Politik in der modernen Türkei* (Everyday Life, Religion and Politics in Modern Turkey). C.H.Beck: Munich, 1997.

Tarih Vakfı: *Anadolu'da Modernleşme Sürecinde Konut ve Yerleşme* (Housing and Settlement in Anatolia in the Process of Modernization.) Tarih Vakfı: Istanbul, 1996.

White, Jenny B.: *Islamist Mobilization in Turkey: a Study in Vernacular Politics*. University of Washington Press: Seattle, 2002.

Yavuz, Hakan: *Islamic Political Identity in Turkey*. Oxford University Press: NY, 2003.

_____. *Modernleşen Müslümanlar: Nurcular, Nakşiler, Milli Görüş ve AK Parti.* (Muslims on the way to becoming modern: Nurcus, Naqhshibandis, the Milli Görüş and the AK Party) Kitap Yayınevi: Istanbul, 2005.

Yavuz, Hakan and Esposito John L. (eds.): *Turkish Islam and the Secular State: the Gulen Movement.* Syracuse University Press: Syracuse, NY, 2003.

## Conquering Government Power

Ammann, Ludwig and Göle, Nilüfer (eds.): *Islam in Sicht. Der Auftritt von Muslimen im öffentlichen Raum.* (Islam in Sight: Muslims in the Public Space) Transcript Verlag: Bielefeld, 2004.

Atasoy, Yıldız: *Turkey, Islamists and Democracy: Transition and Globalization in a Muslim State.* I.B. Tauris: London and New York, 2005.

Aydın, Senem and Çakır, Ruşen: "Political Islam in Turkey," CEPS Working Documents, No. 265, April 2007.

Çakır, Ruşen and Çalmuk, Fehmi: *Recep Tayyip Erdoğan: Bir dönüşüm öyküsü* (Recep Tayyip Erdoğan: the story of a transformation). Metis: Istanbul, 2001.

Hermann, Rainer: "Die drei Versionen des politischen Islam in der Türkei," (The Three Versions of Political Islam in Turkey) in *Orient*, Year 37, No. 1, March 1996.

_____. "Political Islam in Secular Turkey," in: *Islam and Christian Muslim Relations*, Vol. 14, No. 3, July 2003.

## The Dispute between the Old and New Elite

Bozan, İrfan: *Demokratikleşme Devlet ile Toplum Arasında. Bir okul: İmam Hatip Liseleri, Bir Kurum: Diyanet İşleri Başkanlığı* (The democratization between the state and society, a school: İmam Hatip high schools, an institution: the Directorate of Religious Affairs). TESEV: Istanbul, March 2007.

Göle, Nilüfer: *Republik und Schleier. Die muslimische Frau in der modernen Türkei* (Muslim Women in Modern Turkey). Babel Verlag: Berlin, 1995.

## The New Elite and Islam

Agai, Bekim: "Zwischen Netzwerk und Diskurs. Das Bildungsnetzwerk um Fethullah Gülen," (Between Network and Discourse: the Education Network around Fethullah Gülen). *Die flexible Umsetzung modernen islamischen Gedankenguts*, Band 2 (The Flexible Implementation of Modern Islamic Philosophy). Vol. 2, EB-Verlag: Bonner Islamstudien, Hamburg, 2004.

Amirpur, Katajun and Amman, Ludwig (ed.): *Der Islam am Wendepunkt. Liberale und konservative Reformer einer Weltreligion* (Islam at a Turning Point: Liberal and Conservative Reformers of a World Religion) Herder: Freiburg, 2006.

Bozan, İrfan: *Demokratikleşme Devlet ile Toplum Arasında. Bir okul: İmam Hatip Liseleri, Bir Kurum: Diyanet İşleri Başkanlığı* (The democratization between the state and society, a school: İmam Hatip high schools, an institution: the Directorate of Religious Affairs). TESEV: Istanbul, March 2007.

Hermann, Rainer: "Fethullah Gülen – eine muslimische Alternative zur Refah-Partei?" (Fethullah Gülen—A Muslim Alternative to the Refah Party?) in *Orient*, Year 37, No. 4, December 1996.

Körner, Felix: *Revisionist Koran Hermeneutics in Contemporary Turkish University Theology*. Ergon-Verlag Gmbh: Würzburg, 2005.

_____. *Alter Text – Neuer Kontext. Koranhermeneutik in der Türkei heute. Ausgewählte Texte, übersetzt und kommentiert von Felix Körner SJ* (Old Text, New Context: Qur'an Hermeneutics in Turkey Today. Selected texts, Translated and commented by Felix Körner). Herder, Basel, Wien: SJ Freiburg, 2006.

## The Politics of the New Elite

Barysch, Katynka and Hermann, Rainer: "EU Business and Turkish Accession," CER Essays: London, 2007.

Haarmann, Ulrich: "Ideology and History, Identity and Alterity: the Arab Image of the Turk from the 'Abbasids to the Modern Egypt," in *International Journal for Middle Eastern Studies*, vol. 20, 1988.

Öniş, Ziya: "Conservative Globalists versus Defensive Nationalists: Political Parties and Paradoxes of Europeanization in Turkey," in *Journal of Southern Europe and the Balkans*, Issue 9, 2007.

Oran, Baskın (ed.): *Türk Dış Politikası* (Turkish Foreign Policy). Vol. 1: 1919 to 1980, Vol. 2: 1980 to 2001. İletişim Yayınları: Istanbul, 2006

Taşpınar, Ömer: "An Uneven Fit? The Turkish Model and the Arab World," in *Brookings Institution, US Policy towards the Islamic World*, Analysis Paper No. 5.

## Mortgage I: Disadvantaged Groups

Dalrymple, William: *From the Holy Mountain: a Journey in the Shadow of Byzantium*. Flamingo: London, 1998.

Durak, Attila (Photos) and Altınay, Ayşe Gül (ed.): *Ebru: Reflections on the Cultural Diversity in Turkey*. Metis: Istanbul, 2007.

Hermann, Rainer: "Zur Situation der syrisch-orthodoxen Minderheit," in Ursula Spuler-Stegemann (ed.): *Feindbild Christentum im Islam. Eine Bestandsaufnahme* ("On the situation of the Syrian-Orthodox minority," in: *Concept of the Enemy of Christianity in Islam: An appraisal*). Freiburg i.Br: Herder, 2004, pp. 87–101.

Macar, Elçin and Gökaçtı, Mehmet Ali: *Discussions and Recommendations on the Future of the Halki Seminary*. TESEV: Istanbul, 2006.

Oran, Baskın: *Türkiye'de Azınlıklar. Kavramlar, Teori, Lozan, İç Mevzuat, İçtihat, Uygulama* (Minorities in Turkey: Terms, Theory, Treaty of Lausanne, Laws, Interpretation, application). İletişim Yayınları: Istanbul, 2007.

White, Paul: *Primitive Rebels or Revolutionary Modernizers? The Kurdish National Movement in Turkey*. Zed Books: London, 2006.

## Mortgage II: Violence in Society

Cemal, Hasan: *Kimse kızmasın, kendimi yazdim.* (No one is to become enraged, I wrote it for myself: Memoires of the Sixties and the Military Coup of 1971). Doğan Kitap: Istanbul, 1999.

Esim, Simel and Cindoğlu, Dikel: "Women's Organizations in 1990's Turkey: Predicaments and Prospects," in *Middle Eastern Studies*, Issue 35, January 1999.

European Stability Initiative: *Sex and Power in Turkey: Feminism, Islam and the Maturing of Turkish Democracy*. Berlin, Istanbul. July 2007. www.esiweb.org

Paker, Murat: *Psiko-politik Yüzleşmeler* (Psycho-political confrontations) Birikim Yayınları: Istanbul, 2007.

Sağlar, Fikri and Özgönül, Emin: *Kod Adı Susurluk* (Code name Susurluk). Boyut Kitapları: Istanbul, 1998.

Yalçın, Soner and Yurdakul, Doğan: *Reis: Gladio'nun Türk Tetikçisi* (The Leader. The Turkish executor of Gladio: Abdullah Çatlı). Öteki Yayınevi: Istanbul, 1997.

## Wealth I: Germany and Turkey

Deutsches Archäologisches Institut in der Türkei (German archeological institute in Turkey): *Searching for Lost Times*. Yapı Kredi Kültür: Istanbul, 1999.

Haymatloz: *Exile in Turkey 1933 to 1945*. Catalogue for exhibition. Verein Aktives Museum: Berlin, 2000.

Şen, Faruk and Halim, Dirk (eds.): *Exil unter Halbmond und Stern. Herbert Scurlas Bericht über die Tätigkeit deutscher Hochschullehrer in der Türkei während der Zeit des Nationalsozialismus.* (Exile under Crescent and Star: Herbert Scurlas' Report on the Activities of German Professors in Turkey during the Nazi Era). Klartext: Essen, 2007.

## Wealth II: Culture with a European Orientation

Altındere, Halil and Evren, Süreyya: *Kullanma Kilavuzu: Türkiye'de Güncel Sanat* (User's Manual: Contemporary Art in Turkey. 1986–2006). Frankfurt a.M., Revolver, Archiv für aktuelle Kunst (Revolver, Archive for Contemporary Art), 2007.

## Turkish Newspapers Used

*Cumhuriyet* (leftist Kemalist, nationalistic)
*Hürriyet* (mass circulation paper
*Milliyet* (mass circulation paper, center-leftist)
*Radikal* (quality newspaper, leftist liberal)
*Today's Zaman* (quality newspaper, English, affiliated with the Hizmet movement)
*Yeni Şafak* (affiliated with the AK Parti)
*Zaman* (quality newspaper, affiliated with the Hizmet movement)

# Index of People

## A

Abdülhamid II, Sultan, 66, 199, 206, 209, 212, 235, 243

Agai, Bekim, 157, 297

Ağar, Mehmet, 212

Ağca, Mehmet Ali, 211, 219

Ahmadinejad, Mahmud, 167

Akan, İsmail, 177-178

Akdağ, Süleyman, 177

Akdoğan, Yalçın, 68

Akkoç, Nebahat, 226

Aksu, Abdülkadir, 125

Akurgal, Ekrem, 241

Alaton, İshak, ix, 201

Alemdaroğlu, Kemal, 135, 218

Alexander the Great, King, 161

Ali, Sabahattin, 73

Alkan, İlyas Şakir, 203

Alkış, İsmail, 104

Alpogan, Mehmet Yiğit, 37, 44

Altan, Mehmet, 78, 84

Altınay, Ahmet Refik, 298

Altındere, Halil, 252, 256, 300

Aral, Jülide, 225

Arınç, Bülent, 125

Arndt, Fritz, 243

Arslan, Alparslan, 216, 217

Arslan, Osman, 69

Arslan, Saffet, 89, 90

Aslan, Süleyman, xxiv

Aşkın, Yücel, 24, 25, 44

Ataç, Yavuz, 213

Atalay, Beşir, 223

Atatürk, Mustafa Kemal, 1-2, 4, 6, 8, 15-22, 25, 27-29, 31, 33-34, 37, 40-41, 43, 49, 52-54, 56, 58, 61, 63-64, 66, 70, 74-77, 86, 88, 92, 99-100, 124, 130-131, 143-144, 157, 166, 168, 171, 184, 186, 192-194, 196, 199, 210, 216-217, 220, 227, 233, 235, 239-240, 242-244, 249-250, 252-253, 263, 295

Atay, Fikret, 256

Atay, Hüseyin, 148

Ateş, Altan, 78

Ateş, Toktamış, 215

Ateş, Veysel, 37, 213

Atsız, Nihal, 73

Auerbach, Erich, 209

Avcıoğlu, Doğan, 218

Aydın, Koray, 115

Aydın, Mehmet, 144

Aydın, Necati, 19, 223

## B

Baade, Fritz, 244

Babacan, Ali, 125

Bağış, Egemen, xxiv, 126

Bahçeli, Devlet, 74, 105, 115, 162, 224

Balcıoğlu, Emin, 260

Balduk, Mehmet, 105, 107

Bali, Rifat, 209

Balkaner, Avni, 113

Bardakoğlu, Ali, 143, 145-147

Barlach, Ernst, 257

Bartholomaios I., Patriarch, 154

Barzani, Neçirwan, 189

# Subject Index

## A

Adana, 107, 178, 259

*Agos*, weekly journal, 51, 73, 220, 223

AK Party; aggressive campaigns of, xiv, xvii, xxiii, 269, 275; aggressive rhetoric of, xiv; and hate speech, xix, xxi; ; authoritarianism of, xxv, 269-271, 294; and bribery, xv-xvi, xxiv, 278, 282; and corruption, xiv-xvi, xviii, xix-xxiv, 276, 279-280, 282-283, 286, 290-291; and corruption scandal, xiv, xviii, xix, 278, 282, 283; democratic initiatives of, xiv-xv; discriminatory language of, xix; intervening in judiciary, xx; lynching campaigns of, xvii, xxiii; "mastership period" of the government of , xiv; passing Internet censorship law, xxiv; "othering" and demonizing certain people and important segments of society, xiv; obstructing justice, 111; and perception management, xxii; purging and removing the civil servants, xvii; reforms of, 4, 163; rigging state tenders, xviii-xix

alcohol; 86, 93, 121, 130; bans, xvi

Alevis, 8, 124, 145, 183-184, 192-197; distrust of, 194-195

Alexandria, 198

Alman Lisesi, 245

Anatolia, 2-3, 5-6, 8-9, 11-12, 15-18, 23-24, 32, 36, 55, 69, 71-72, 79-82, 84-85, 87, 89-90, 92-93, 96-97, 104- 106, 121, 132, 153, 157, 166, 170-171, 193-194, 197, 200-201, 205, 212, 215-216, 229, 233, 240-242, 249, 253, 256-257, 260, 263, 296

Anatolian Culture Foundation, the, 255

Anatolian high schools (Anadolu liseleri), 245

Anatolian; music, 11; periphery, xxv, 7, 22-27, 52, 55, 62, 96, 118, 256, 296; periphery vs. the center, 24-25; tiger(s), 90

Ankara, 6, 8, 15-16, 25, 27, 32, 38, 44, 46, 49, 52-53, 56-57, 62, 79, 81, 87-88, 90, 93-94, 99, 105, 107, 121, 137, 143, 146-152, 165, 168, 190, 193, 197, 214, 216, 224, 239-240, 242, 246, 255-256

Antakya (Antioch), 197, 198, 202

Arabs, 9, 17, 70, 154, 166-170, 192

al-Arabiyya, news channel, 168

*Arayış*, magazine, 57

architecture, 239-240, 263

Ardabil, 194

Armenian(s), 7-9, 11, 16-20, 30, 50-51, 53, 55, 73-74, 88, 184, 193, 198-200, 202, 212-213, 215, 219-221, 253, 262, 264; Apostolian Church, 20; displacement of, 18, 200; purge, 18, 200, 220

Army; Turkish, 7, 26, 28, 30-42, 51, 57, 69, 90, 97, 159, 163, 165, 177-178, 189-190, 194, 199, 213-214, 216, 219, 233-236, 243, 252, 264, 279, 284, 291, 301; as the guarantor of

### N

### O

### P